*Learn Docker in a Month of Lunches*

## Get the eBooks FREE!

(PDF, ePub, Kindle, and liveBook all included)

We believe that once you buy a book from us, you should be able to read it in any format we have available. To get electronic versions of this book at no additional cost to you, purchase and then register this book at the Manning website.

Go to https://www.manning.com/freebook and follow the instructions to complete your pBook registration.

## That's it!
## Thanks from Manning!

# Learn Docker in a Month of Lunches

ELTON STONEMAN

MANNING

SHELTER ISLAND

Manning Publications Co.
20 Baldwin Road
PO Box 761
Shelter Island, NY 11964

| | |
|---|---|
| Acquisitions editor: | Michael Stephens |
| Development editor: | Becky Whitney |
| Technical development editor: | Mike Shepard |
| Review editor: | Aleksandar Dragosavljević |
| Production editors: | Anthony Calcara and Lori Weidert |
| Copy editor: | Andy Carroll |
| Proofreader: | Keri Hales |
| Technical proofreader: | Yan Guo |
| Typesetter: | Dennis Dalinnik |
| Cover designer: | Leslie Haimes |

ISBN: 9781617297052
Printed in the United States of America

*I wrote this book in a barn in Gloucestershire, England. During many late nights, my fantastic wife, Nikki, kept the family running, so this book is for her— and for our fabulous children, Jackson and Eris.*

# brief contents

# contents

# *preface*

By 2019 I'd been working with Docker and containers for five years—speaking at conferences, running workshops, training people, and consulting—and in that time I never had a go-to book that I felt I could recommend to every audience. There are some very good Docker books out there, but they assume a certain background or a certain technology stack, and I felt there was a real gap for a book that took a more inclusive approach: welcoming both developers and ops people, and both Linux and Windows users. *Learn Docker in a Month of Lunches* is the result of me trying to write that book.

Docker is a great technology to learn. It starts with one simple concept: packaging an application together with all its dependencies, so you can run that app in the same way anywhere. That concept makes your applications portable between laptops, data-centers, and clouds, and it breaks down barriers between development and operations teams. It's the enabler for the major types of IT project organizations are investing in, as you'll learn in chapter 1, but it's also a straightforward technology you can learn in your own time.

Manning's *Month of Lunches* series is the perfect vehicle to help you, as you'll get much more from the experience of running exercises and trying labs than you will from reading the theory of how operating systems isolate container processes. This is very much a "real-world" book, and you'll find that each chapter has a clear focus on one useful topic, and that the topics build on each other to give you a thorough understanding of how you'll use Docker in practice.

# acknowledgments

Writing for Manning is a real pleasure. They take great care to help you make your book as good as it can be, and I'd like to thank the reviewers and publishing team whose feedback led to countless improvements. I'd also like to thank everyone who signed up for the early access program, read the drafts, tried out the exercises, and provided comments—I really appreciate all the time you put in. Thank you.

I would also like to thank all the reviewers, whose suggestions helped make this a better book: Andres Sacco, David Madouros, Derek Hampton, Federico Bertolucci, George Onofrei, John Kasiewicz, Keith Kim, Kevin Orr, Marcus Brown, Mark Elston, Max Hemingway, Mike Jensen, Patrick Regan, Philip Taffet, Rob Loranger, Romain Boisselle, Srihari Sridharan, Stephen Byrne, Sylvain Coulonbel, Tobias Kaatz, Trent Whiteley, and Vincent Zaballa.

# *about this book*

My goal for this book is quite clear: I want you to be confident about running your own applications in Docker when you've finished; you should be able to run a proof-of-concept project to move your apps to containers, and you should know what you need to do after that to take them to production. Every chapter is focused on real-world tasks and incrementally builds up your experience with Docker, distributed applications, orchestration, and the container ecosystem.

This book is aimed at new and improving Docker users. Docker is a core technology that touches lots of areas of IT, and I've tried hard to assume a minimum amount of background knowledge. Docker crosses the boundaries of architecture, development, and operations, and I've tried to do the same. This book should work for you, whatever your background in IT.

There are a lot of exercises and labs in the book, and to get the most out of your learning, you should plan to work through the samples as you're reading the chapter. Docker supports lots of different types of computers, and you can follow along with this book using any of the main systems—Windows, Mac, or Linux, or even a Raspberry Pi is fine.

GitHub is the source of truth for all the samples I use in the book. You'll download the materials when you set up your lab in chapter 1, and you should be sure to star the repository and watch for notifications.

## How to use this book

This book follows the Month-of-Lunches principles: you should be able to work through each chapter in an hour, and work through the whole book in a month. "Work" is the key word here, because the daily 60 minutes should be enough time to read the chapter, work through the try-it-now exercises, and have a go at the hands-on lab. It's working with containers that will really cement the knowledge you gain in each chapter.

### Your learning journey

Docker is a great technology to teach because you can easily build a clear learning path that starts simple and gradually adds more and more until you get to production. This book follows a proven path I've used in dozens of workshops, webinars, and training sessions.

Chapter 1 will tell you how this book works, and go over the importance of containers, before walking you through installing Docker and downloading the resource files for the exercises in the book.

Chapters 2 through 6 cover the basics. Here you'll learn how to run containers, how to package applications for Docker and share them on Docker Hub and other servers. You'll also learn about storage in containers and how you can work with stateful applications (like databases) in Docker.

Chapters 7 through 11 move on to running distributed applications, where each component runs in a container connected to a virtual Docker network. It's where you'll learn about Docker Compose and patterns for making your containerized application production-ready—including healthchecks and monitoring. This section also covers moving apps between environments and building a CI process with Docker.

Chapters 12 through 16 are about running distributed applications using a container orchestrator, which is a cluster of machines all running Docker. You'll learn about joining servers together and extend your knowledge of Docker Compose to deploy applications on the cluster. You'll also learn how to build Docker containers which are cross-platform so they run on Windows, Linux, Intel, and Arm. That portability is a key feature of Docker, which will become increasingly important as more clouds support cheaper, more efficient Arm processors.

Chapters 17 through 21 cover more advanced topics. There's production readiness in there, with hints for optimizing your Docker containers, and patterns for integrating your application's logging and configuration with the Docker platform. This part of the book also covers approaches for breaking down monolithic applications into multiple containers using powerful communication patterns: reverse proxies and message queues.

The final chapter (chapter 22) offers guidance on moving on with Docker—how to run a proof-of-concept to move your own applications to Docker, how to get stakeholders on board in your organization, and planning your path to production. By the end of the book you should be confident in bringing Docker into your daily work.

### Try-it-nows

Every chapter of the book has guided exercises for you to complete. The source code for the book is all on GitHub at https://github.com/sixeyed/diamol—you'll clone that when you set up your lab environment, and you'll use it for all the sample commands, which will have you building and running apps in containers.

Many chapters build on work from earlier in the book, but you do not need to follow all the chapters in order. In the exercises you'll package applications to run in Docker, but I've already packaged them all and made them publicly available on Docker Hub. That means you can follow the samples at any stage using my packaged apps.

If you can find time to work through the samples, though, you'll get more out of this book than if you just skim the chapters and run the final sample application.

### Hands-on labs

Each chapter also ends with a hands-on lab that invites you to go further than the try-it-now exercises. These aren't guided—you'll get some instructions and some hints, and then it will be down to you to complete the lab. There are sample answers for all the labs in the sixeyed/diamol GitHub repo, so you can check what you've done—or see how I've done it if you don't have time for one of the labs.

### Additional resources

The main resource for looking further into the topics I'll cover in this book is Docker's own documentation at https://docs.docker.com, which covers everything from setting up the Docker engine, through syntax for Dockerfiles and Docker Compose, to Docker Swarm and Docker's Enterprise product range.

Docker is a popular topic on social media too. Docker posts daily on Twitter and Facebook, and you'll find a lot of my content out there too. You can follow me on Twitter at @EltonStoneman, my blog is https://blog.sixeyed.com, and I post YouTube videos at https://youtube.com/eltonstoneman.

## About the code

This book contains many examples of Dockerfiles and application manifests, both in numbered listings and in line with normal text. In both cases, source code is formatted in a `fixed-width font like this` to separate it from ordinary text.

The code for the examples in this book is available for download from the Manning website at https://www.manning.com/books/learn-docker-in-a-month-of-lunches and from GitHub at https://github.com/sixeyed/diamol.

## liveBook discussion forum

Purchase of *Learn Docker in a Month of Lunches* includes free access to a private web forum run by Manning Publications where you can make comments about the book, ask technical questions, and receive help from the author and from other users. To access the forum, go to https://livebook.manning.com/#!/book/learn-docker-in-a-month-of-lunches/discussion. You can also learn more about Manning's forums and the rules of conduct at https://livebook.manning.com/#!/discussion.

Manning's commitment to our readers is to provide a venue where a meaningful dialogue between individual readers and between readers and the author can take place. It is not a commitment to any specific amount of participation on the part of the author, whose contribution to the forum remains voluntary (and unpaid). We suggest you try asking the author some challenging questions lest his interest stray! The forum and the archives of previous discussions will be accessible from the publisher's website as long as the book is in print.

# about the author

Elton Stoneman is a Docker Captain, a multi-year Microsoft MVP, and the author of over 20 online training courses with Pluralsight. He spent most of his career as a consultant in the .NET space, designing and delivering large enterprise systems. Then he fell for containers and joined Docker, where he worked for three furiously busy and hugely fun years. Now he works as a freelance consultant and trainer, helping organizations at all stages of their container journey. Elton writes about Docker and Kubernetes at https://blog.sixeyed.com and on Twitter @EltonStoneman.

# Part 1

# Understanding Docker containers and images

Welcome to *Learn Docker in a Month of Lunches*. This first part will get you up to speed quickly on the core Docker concepts: containers, images, and registries. You'll learn how to run applications in containers, package your own applications in containers, and share those applications for other people to use. You'll also learn about storing data in Docker volumes and how you can run stateful apps in containers. By the end of these first chapters, you'll be comfortable with all the fundamentals of Docker, and you'll be learning with best practices baked in from the start.

# Before you begin

Docker is a platform for running applications in lightweight units called *containers*. Containers have taken hold in software everywhere, from serverless functions in the cloud to strategic planning in the enterprise. Docker is becoming a core competency for operators and developers across the industry—in the 2019 Stack Overflow survey, Docker polled as people's number one "most wanted" technology (http://mng.bz/04lW).

And Docker is a simple technology to learn. You can pick up this book as a complete beginner, and you'll be running containers in chapter 2 and packaging applications to run in Docker in chapter 3. Each chapter focuses on practical tasks, with examples and labs that work on any machine that runs Docker—Windows, Mac, and Linux users are all welcome here.

The journey you'll follow in this book has been honed over the many years I've been teaching Docker. Every chapter is hands-on—except this one. Before you start learning Docker, it's important to understand just how containers are being used in the real world and the type of problems they solve—that's what I'll cover here. This chapter also describes how I'll be teaching Docker, so you can figure out if this is the right book for you.

Now let's look at what people are doing with containers—I'll cover the five main scenarios where organizations are seeing huge success with Docker. You'll see the wide range of problems you can solve with containers, some of which will certainly map to scenarios in your own work. By the end of this chapter you'll understand why Docker is a technology you need to know, and you'll see how this book will get you there.

## 1.1    *Why containers will take over the world*

My own Docker journey started in 2014 when I was working on a project delivering APIs for Android devices. We started using Docker for development tools—source code and build servers. Then we gained confidence and started running the APIs in containers for test environments. By the end of the project, every environment was powered by Docker, including production, where we had strict requirements for availability and scale.

When I moved off the project, the handover to the new team was a single README file in a GitHub repo. The only requirement for building, deploying, and managing the app—in any environment—was Docker. New developers just grabbed the source code and ran a single command to build and run everything locally. Administrators used the exact same tools to deploy and manage containers in the production cluster.

Normally on a project of that size, handovers take two weeks. New developers need to install specific versions of half a dozen tools, and administrators need to install half a dozen completely different tools. Docker centralizes the toolchain and makes everything so much easier for everybody that I thought one day every project would have to use containers.

I joined Docker in 2016, and I've spent the last few years watching that vision becoming reality. Docker is approaching ubiquity, partly because it makes delivery so much easier, and partly because it's so flexible—you can bring it into all your projects, old and new, Windows and Linux. Let's look at where containers fit in those projects.

### 1.1.1    *Migrating apps to the cloud*

Moving apps to the cloud is top of mind for many organizations. It's an attractive option—let Microsoft or Amazon or Google worry about servers, disks, networks, and power. Host your apps across global datacenters with practically limitless potential to scale. Deploy to new environments within minutes, and get billed only for the resources you're using. But how do you get your apps to the cloud?

There used to be two options for migrating an app to the cloud: infrastructure as a service (IaaS) and platform as a service (PaaS). Neither option was great. Your choice was basically a compromise—choose PaaS and run a project to migrate all the pieces of your application to the relevant managed service from the cloud. That's a difficult project and it locks you in to a single cloud, but it does get you lower running costs. The alternative is IaaS, where you spin up a virtual machine for each component of your application. You get portability across clouds but much higher running costs. Figure 1.1 shows how a typical distributed application looks with a cloud migration using IaaS and PaaS.

Docker offers a third option without the compromises. You migrate each part of your application to a container, and then you can run the whole application in containers using Azure Kubernetes Service or Amazon's Elastic Container Service, or on your own Docker cluster in the datacenter. You'll learn in chapter 7 how to package

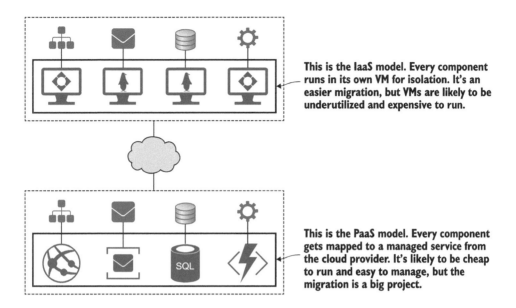

This is the IaaS model. Every component runs in its own VM for isolation. It's an easier migration, but VMs are likely to be underutilized and expensive to run.

This is the PaaS model. Every component gets mapped to a managed service from the cloud provider. It's likely to be cheap to run and easy to manage, but the migration is a big project.

Figure 1.1 The original options for migrating to the cloud—use IaaS and run lots of inefficient VMs with high monthly costs, or use PaaS and get lower running costs but spend more time on the migration.

and run a distributed application like this in containers, and in chapters 13 and 14 you'll see how to run at scale in production. Figure 1.2 shows the Docker option, which gets you a portable application you can run at low cost in any cloud—or in the datacenter, or on your laptop.

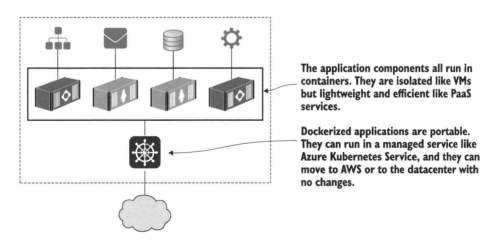

The application components all run in containers. They are isolated like VMs but lightweight and efficient like PaaS services.

Dockerized applications are portable. They can run in a managed service like Azure Kubernetes Service, and they can move to AWS or to the datacenter with no changes.

Figure 1.2 The same app migrated to Docker before moving to the cloud. This application has the cost benefits of PaaS with the portability benefits of IaaS and the ease of use you only get with Docker.

It does take some investment to migrate to containers: you'll need to build your existing installation steps into scripts called Dockerfiles and your deployment documents into descriptive application manifests using the Docker Compose or Kubernetes format. You don't need to change code, and the end result runs in the same way using the same technology stack on every environment, from your laptop to the cloud.

### 1.1.2  *Modernizing legacy apps*

You can run pretty much any app in the cloud in a container, but you won't get the full value of Docker or the cloud platform if it uses an older, monolithic design. Monoliths work just fine in containers, but they limit your agility. You can do an automated staged rollout of a new feature to production in 30 seconds with containers. But if the feature is part of a monolith built from two million lines of code, you've probably had to sit through a two-week regression test cycle before you get to the release.

Moving your app to Docker is a great first step to modernizing the architecture, adopting new patterns without needing a full rewrite of the app. The approach is simple—you start by moving your app to a single container with the Dockerfile and Docker Compose syntax you'll learn in this book. Now you have a monolith in a container.

Containers run in their own virtual network, so they can communicate with each other without being exposed to the outside world. That means you can start breaking your application up, moving features into their own containers, so gradually your monolith can evolve into a distributed application with the whole feature set being provided by multiple containers. Figure 1.3 shows how that looks with a sample application architecture.

This gives you a lot of the benefits of a microservice architecture. Your key features are in small, isolated units that you can manage independently. That means you can test changes quickly, because you're not changing the monolith, only the containers that run your feature. You can scale features up and down, and you can use different technologies to suit requirements.

Modernizing older application architectures is easy with Docker—you'll do it yourself with practical examples in chapters 20 and 21. You can deliver a more agile, scalable, and resilient app, and you get to do it in stages, rather than stopping for an 18-month rewrite.

### 1.1.3  *Building new cloud-native apps*

Docker helps you get your existing apps to the cloud, whether they're distributed apps or monoliths. If you have monoliths, Docker helps you break them up into modern architectures, whether you're running in the cloud or in the datacenter. And brand-new projects built on cloud-native principles are greatly accelerated with Docker.

The Cloud Native Computing Foundation (CNCF) characterizes these new architectures as using "an open source software stack to deploy applications as microservices,

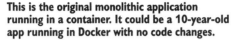

**This is the original monolithic application running in a container. It could be a 10-year-old app running in Docker with no code changes.**

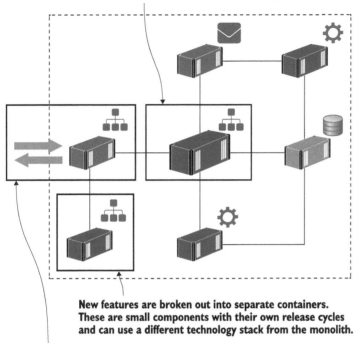

**New features are broken out into separate containers. These are small components with their own release cycles and can use a different technology stack from the monolith.**

**All external requests are sent to a single component, which routes them to the monolith or to a new container based on the requested route. The monolith can be broken down without a full rewrite.**

Figure 1.3  Decomposing a monolith into a distributed application without rewriting the whole project. All the components run in Docker containers, and a routing component decides whether requests are fulfilled by the monolith or a new microservice.

packaging each part into its own container, and dynamically orchestrating those containers to optimize resource utilization."

Figure 1.4 shows a typical architecture for a new microservices application—this is a demo application from the community, which you can find on GitHub at https://github.com/microservices-demo.

It's a great sample application if you want to see how microservices are actually implemented. Each component owns its own data and exposes it through an API. The frontend is a web application that consumes all the API services. The demo application uses various programming languages and different database technologies, but every component has a Dockerfile to package it, and the whole application is defined in a Docker Compose file.

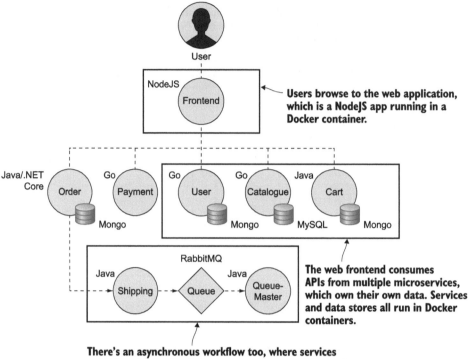

Figure 1.4   Cloud-native applications are built with microservice architectures where every component runs in a container.

You'll learn in chapter 4 how you can use Docker to compile code, as part of packaging your app. That means you don't need any development tools installed to build and run like this. Developers can just install Docker, clone the source code, and build and run the whole application with a single command.

Docker also makes it easy to bring third-party software into your application, adding features without writing your own code. Docker Hub is a public service where teams share software that runs in containers. The CNCF publishes a map of open source projects you can use for everything from monitoring to message queues, and they're all available for free from Docker Hub.

### 1.1.4   *Technical innovation: Serverless and more*

One of the key drivers for modern IT is consistency: teams want to use the same tools, processes, and runtime for all their projects. You can do that with Docker, using containers for everything from old .NET monoliths running on Windows to new Go applications running on Linux. You can build a Docker cluster to run all those apps, so you build, deploy, and manage your entire application landscape in the same way.

Technical innovation shouldn't be separate from business-as-usual apps. Docker is at the heart of some of the biggest innovations, so you can continue to use the same tools and techniques as you explore new areas. One of the most exciting innovations (after containers, of course) is serverless functions. Figure 1.5 shows how you can run all your applications—legacy monoliths, new cloud-native apps, and serverless functions—on a single Docker cluster, which could be running in the cloud or the datacenter.

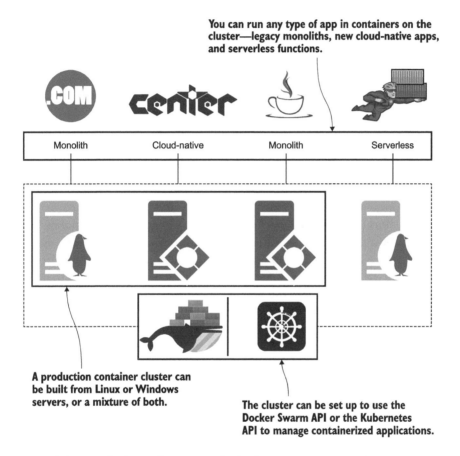

Figure 1.5  A single cluster of servers running Docker can run every type of application, and you build, deploy, and manage them all in the same way no matter what architecture or technology stack they use.

Serverless is all about containers. The goal of serverless is for developers to write function code, push it to a service, and that service builds and packages the code. When consumers use the function, the service starts an instance of the function to process the request. There are no build servers, pipelines, or production servers to manage; it's all taken care of by the platform.

Under the hood, all the cloud serverless options use Docker to package the code and containers to run functions. But functions in the cloud aren't portable—you can't take your AWS Lambda function and run it in Azure, because there isn't an open standard for serverless. If you want serverless without cloud lock-in, or if you're running in the datacenter, you can host your own platform in Docker using Nuclio, OpenFaaS, or Fn Project, which are all popular open source serverless frameworks.

Other major innovations like machine learning, blockchain, and IoT benefit from the consistent packaging and deployment model of Docker. You'll find the main projects all deploy to Docker Hub—TensorFlow and Hyperledger are good examples. And IoT is particularly interesting, as Docker has partnered with Arm to make containers the default runtime for Edge and IoT devices.

### 1.1.5  *Digital transformation with DevOps*

All these scenarios involve technology, but the biggest problem facing many organizations is operational—particularly so for larger and older enterprises. Teams have been siloed into "developers" and "operators," responsible for different parts of the project life cycle. Problems at release time become a blame cycle, and quality gates are put in to prevent future failures. Eventually you have so many quality gates you can only manage two or three releases a year, and they are risky and labor-intensive.

DevOps aims to bring agility to software deployment and maintenance by having a single team own the whole application life cycle, combining "dev" and "ops" into one deliverable. DevOps is mainly about cultural change, and it can take organizations from huge quarterly releases to small daily deployments. But it's hard to do that without changing the technologies the team uses.

Operators may have a background in tools like Bash, Nagios, PowerShell, and System Center. Developers work in Make, Maven, NuGet, and MSBuild. It's difficult to bring a team together when they don't use common technologies, which is where Docker really helps. You can underpin your DevOps transformation with the move to containers, and suddenly the whole team is working with Dockerfiles and Docker Compose files, speaking the same languages and working with the same tools.

It goes further too. There's a powerful framework for implementing DevOps called CALMS—Culture, Automation, Lean, Metrics, and Sharing. Docker works on all those initiatives: automation is central to running containers, distributed apps are built on lean principles, metrics from production apps and from the deployment process can be easily published, and Docker Hub is all about sharing and not duplicating effort.

## 1.2  Is this book for you?

The five scenarios I outlined in the previous section cover pretty much all the activity that's happening in the IT industry right now, and I hope it's clear that Docker is the key to it all. This is the book for you if you want to put Docker to work on this kind of real-world problem. It takes you from zero knowledge through to running apps in containers on a production-grade cluster.

The goal of this book is to teach you how to use Docker, so I don't go into much detail on how Docker itself works under the hood. I won't talk in detail about `containerd` or lower-level details like Linux `cgroups` and `namespaces` or the Windows Host Compute Service. If you want the internals, Manning's *Docker in Action,* second edition, by Jeff Nickoloff and Stephen Kuenzli is a great choice.

The samples in this book are all cross-platform, so you can work along using Windows, Mac, or Linux—including Arm processors, so you can use a Raspberry Pi too. I use several programming languages, but only those that are cross-platform, so among others I use .NET Core instead of .NET Framework (which only runs on Windows). If you want to learn Windows containers in depth, my blog is a good source for that (https://blog.sixeyed.com).

Lastly, this book is specifically on Docker, so when it comes to production deployment I'll be using Docker Swarm, the clustering technology built into Docker. In chapter 12 I'll talk about Kubernetes and how to choose between Swarm and Kubernetes, but I won't go into detail on Kubernetes. Kubernetes needs a month of lunches itself, but Kubernetes is just a different way of running Docker containers, so everything you learn in this book applies.

## 1.3 Creating your lab environment

Now let's get started. All you need to follow along with this book is Docker and the source code for the samples.

### 1.3.1 Installing Docker

The free Docker Community Edition is fine for development and even production use. If you're running a recent version of Windows 10 or macOS, the best option is Docker Desktop; older versions can use Docker Toolbox. Docker also supplies installation packages for all the major Linux distributions. Start by installing Docker using the most appropriate option for you—you'll need to create a Docker Hub account for the downloads, which is free and lets you share applications you've built for Docker.

#### INSTALLING DOCKER DESKTOP ON WINDOWS 10

You'll need Windows 10 Professional or Enterprise to use Docker Desktop, and you'll want to make sure that you have all the Windows updates installed—you should be on release `1809` as a minimum (run `winver` from the command line to check your version). Browse to www.docker.com/products/docker-desktop and choose to install the stable version. Download the installer and run it, accepting all the defaults. When Docker Desktop is running you'll see Docker's whale icon in the taskbar near the Windows clock.

#### INSTALLING DOCKER DESKTOP ON MACOS

You'll need macOS Sierra 10.12 or above to use Docker Desktop for Mac—click the Apple icon in the top left of the menu bar and select About this Mac to see your version. Browse to www.docker.com/products/docker-desktop and choose to install the stable version. Download the installer and run it, accepting all the defaults. When Docker Desktop is running, you'll see Docker's whale icon in the Mac menu bar near the clock.

#### INSTALLING DOCKER TOOLBOX

If you're using an older version of Windows or OS X, you can use Docker Toolbox. The end experience with Docker is the same, but there are a few more pieces behind the scenes. Browse to https://docs.docker.com/toolbox and follow the instructions—you'll need to set up virtual machine software first, like VirtualBox (Docker Desktop is a better option if you can use it, because you don't need a separate VM manager).

#### INSTALLING DOCKER COMMUNITY EDITION AND DOCKER COMPOSE

If you're running Linux, your distribution probably comes with a version of Docker you can install, but you don't want to use that. It will likely be a very old version of Docker, because the Docker team now provides their own installation packages. You can use a script that Docker updates with each new release to install Docker in a non-production environment—browse to https://get.docker.com and follow the instructions to run the script, and then to https://docs.docker.com/compose/install to install Docker Compose.

#### INSTALLING DOCKER ON WINDOWS SERVER OR LINUX SERVER DISTRIBUTIONS

Production deployments of Docker can use the Community Edition, but if you want a supported container runtime, you can use the commercial version provided by Docker, called Docker Enterprise. Docker Enterprise is built on top of the Community Edition, so everything you learn in this book works just as well with Docker Enterprise. There are versions for all the major Linux distributions and for Windows Server 2016 and 2019. You can find all the Docker Enterprise editions together with installation instructions on Docker Hub at http://mng.bz/K29E.

### 1.3.2   *Verifying your Docker setup*

There are several components that make up the Docker platform, but for this book you just need to verify that Docker is running and that Docker Compose is installed.

First check Docker itself with the `docker version` command:

```
PS> docker version
Client: Docker Engine - Community
 Version:           19.03.5
 API version:       1.40
 Go version:        go1.12.12
 Git commit:        633a0ea
 Built:             Wed Nov 13 07:22:37 2019
 OS/Arch:           windows/amd64
 Experimental:      false

Server: Docker Engine - Community
 Engine:
  Version:          19.03.5
  API version:      1.40 (minimum version 1.24)
```

```
Go version:        go1.12.12
Git commit:        633a0ea
Built:             Wed Nov 13 07:36:50 2019
OS/Arch:           windows/amd64
Experimental:      false
```

Your output will be different from mine, because the versions will have changed and you might be using a different operating system, but as long as you can see a version number for the Client and the Server, Docker is working fine. Don't worry about what the client and server are just yet—you'll learn about the architecture of Docker in the next chapter.

Next you need to test Docker Compose, which is a separate command line that also interacts with Docker. Run `docker-compose version` to check:

```
PS> docker-compose version
docker-compose version 1.25.4, build 8d51620a
docker-py version: 4.1.0
CPython version: 3.7.4
OpenSSL version: OpenSSL 1.1.1c  28 May 2019
```

Again, your exact output will be different from mine, but as long as you get a list of versions with no errors, you are good to go.

### 1.3.3 Downloading the source code for the book

The source code for this book is in a public Git repository on GitHub. If you have a Git client installed, just run this command:

```
git clone https://github.com/sixeyed/diamol.git
```

If you don't have a Git client, browse to https://github.com/sixeyed/diamol and click the Clone or Download button to download a zip file of the source code to your local machine, and expand the archive.

### 1.3.4 Remembering the cleanup commands

Docker doesn't automatically clean up containers or application packages for you. When you quit Docker Desktop (or stop the Docker service), all your containers stop and they don't use any CPU or memory, but if you want to, you can clean up at the end of every chapter by running this command:

```
docker container rm -f $(docker container ls -aq)
```

And if you want to reclaim disk space after following the exercises, you can run this command:

```
docker image rm -f $(docker image ls -f reference='diamol/*' -q)
```

Docker is smart about downloading what it needs, so you can safely run these commands at any time. The next time you run containers, if Docker doesn't find what it needs on your machine, it will download it for you.

## 1.4    *Being immediately effective*

"Immediately effective" is another principle of the Month of Lunches series. In all the chapters that follow, the focus is on learning skills and putting them into practice.

Every chapter starts with a short introduction to the topic, followed by try-it-now exercises where you put the ideas into practice using Docker. Then there's a recap with some more detail that fills in some of the questions you may have from diving in. Lastly there's a hands-on lab for you to go the next stage.

All the topics center around tasks that are genuinely useful in the real world. You'll learn how to be immediately effective with the topic during the chapter, and you'll finish by understanding how to apply the new skill. Let's start running some containers!

# Understanding Docker
# and running Hello World

It's time to get hands-on with Docker. In this chapter you'll get lots of experience with the core feature of Docker: running applications in containers. I'll also cover some background that will help you understand exactly what a container is, and why containers are such a lightweight way to run apps. Mostly you'll be following try-it-now exercises, running simple commands to get a feel for this new way of working with applications.

## 2.1 Running Hello World in a container

Let's get started with Docker the same way we would with any new computing concept: running Hello World. You have Docker up and running from chapter 1, so open your favorite terminal—that could be Terminal on the Mac or a Bash shell on Linux, and I recommend PowerShell in Windows.

You're going to send a command to Docker, telling it to run a container that prints out some simple "Hello, World" text.

**TRY IT NOW** Enter this command, which will run the Hello World container:

```
docker container run diamol/ch02-hello-diamol
```

When we're done with this chapter, you'll understand exactly what's happening here. For now, just take a look at the output. It will be something like figure 2.1.

There's a lot in that output. I'll trim future code listings to keep them short, but this is the very first one, and I wanted to show it in full so we can dissect it.

First of all, what's actually happened? The docker container run command tells Docker to run an application in a container. This application has already been

15

**This** `run` **command starts a container from an application package called** `diamol/ch02-hello-diamol`.

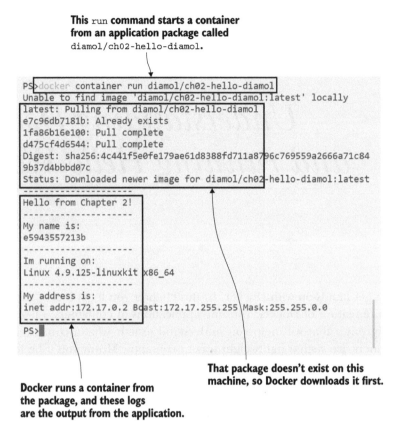

**That package doesn't exist on this machine, so Docker downloads it first.**

**Docker runs a container from the package, and these logs are the output from the application.**

**Figure 2.1   The output from running the Hello World container. You can see Docker downloading the application package (called an "image"), running the app in a container, and showing the output.**

packaged to run in Docker and has been published on a public site that anyone can access. The container package (which Docker calls an "image") is named `diamol/ch02-hello-diamol` (I use the acronym *diamol* throughout this book—it stands for *Docker In A Month Of Lunches*). The command you've just entered tells Docker to run a container from that image.

Docker needs to have a copy of the image locally before it can run a container using the image. The very first time you run this command, you won't have a copy of the image, and you can see that in the first output line: `unable to find image locally`. Then Docker downloads the image (which Docker calls "pulling"), and you can see that the image has been downloaded.

Now Docker starts a container using that image. The image contains all the content for the application, along with instructions telling Docker how to start the application. The application in this image is just a simple script, and you see the output which starts `Hello from Chapter 2!` It writes out some details about the computer it's running on:

- The machine name, in this example `e5943557213b`
- The operating system, in this example `Linux 4.9.125-linuxkit x86_64`
- The network address, in this example `172.17.0.2`

I said your output will be "something like this"—it won't be exactly the same, because some of the information the container fetches depends on your computer. I ran this on a machine with a Linux operating system and a 64-bit Intel processor. If you run it using Windows containers, the `I'm running on` line will show this instead:

```
---------------------
I'm running on:
Microsoft Windows [Version 10.0.17763.557]
---------------------
```

If you're running on a Raspberry Pi, the output will show that it's using a different processor (`armv71` is the codename for ARM's 32-bit processing chip, and `x86_64` is the code for Intel's 64-bit chip):

```
---------------------
I'm running on:
Linux 4.19.42-v7+ armv71
---------------------
```

This is a very simple example application, but it shows the core Docker workflow. Someone packages their application to run in a container (I did it for this app, but you will do it yourself in the next chapter), and then publishes it so it's available to other users. Then anyone with access can run the app in a container. Docker calls this *build, share, run.*

It's a hugely powerful concept, because the workflow is the same no matter how complicated the application is. In this case it was a simple script, but it could be a Java application with several components, configuration files, and libraries. The workflow would be exactly the same. And Docker images can be packaged to run on any computer that supports Docker, which makes the app completely portable—portability is one of Docker's key benefits.

What happens if you run another container using the same command?

**TRY IT NOW** Repeat the exact same Docker command:

```
docker container run diamol/ch02-hello-diamol
```

You'll see similar output to the first run, but there will be differences. Docker already has a copy of the image locally so it doesn't need to download the image first; it gets straight to running the container. The container output shows the same operating system details, because you're using the same computer, but the computer name and the IP address of the container will be different:

```
---------------------
Hello from Chapter 2!
---------------------
My name is:
858a26ee2741
---------------------
Im running on:
Linux 4.9.125-linuxkit x86_64
---------------------
My address is:
inet addr:172.17.0.5 Bcast:172.17.255.255 Mask:255.255.0.0
---------------------
```

Now my app is running on a machine with the name `858a26ee2741` and the IP address `172.17.0.5`. The machine name will change every time, and the IP address will often change, but every container is running on the same computer, so where do these different machine names and network addresses come from? We'll dig into a little theory next to explain that, and then it's back to the exercises.

## 2.2    So what is a container?

A Docker container is the same idea as a physical container—think of it like a box with an application in it. Inside the box, the application seems to have a computer all to itself: it has its own machine name and IP address, and it also has its own disk drive (Windows containers have their own Windows Registry too). Figure 2.2 shows how the app is boxed by the container.

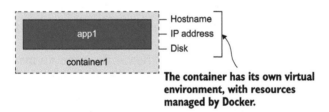

The container has its own virtual environment, with resources managed by Docker.

Figure 2.2   An app inside the container environment

Those things are all virtual resources—the hostname, IP address, and filesystem are created by Docker. They're logical objects that are managed by Docker, and they're all joined together to create an environment where an application can run. That's the "box" of the container.

The application inside the box can't see anything outside the box, but the box is running on a computer, and that computer can also be running lots of other boxes. The applications in those boxes have their own separate environments (managed by Docker), but they all share the CPU and memory of the computer, and they all share the computer's operating system. You can see in figure 2.3 how containers on the same computer are isolated.

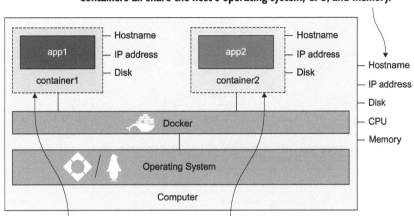

Figure 2.3  Multiple containers on one computer share the same OS, CPU, and memory.

Why is this so important? It fixes two conflicting problems in computing: isolation and density. Density means running as many applications on your computers as possible, to utilize all the processor and memory that you have. But apps may not work nicely with other apps—they might use different versions of Java or .NET, they may use incompatible versions of tools or libraries, or one might have a heavy workload and starve the others of processing power. Applications really need to be isolated from each other, and that stops you running lots of them on a single computer, so you don't get density.

The original attempt to fix that problem was to use virtual machines (VMs). Virtual machines are similar in concept to containers, in that they give you a box to run your application in, but the box for a VM needs to contain its own operating system—it doesn't share the OS of the computer where the VM is running. Compare figure 2.3, which shows multiple containers, with figure 2.4, which shows multiple VMs on one computer.

That may look like a small difference in the diagrams, but it has huge implications. Every VM needs its own operating system, and that OS can use gigabytes of memory and lots of CPU time—soaking up compute power that should be available for your applications. There are other concerns too, like licensing costs for the OS and the maintenance burden of installing OS updates. VMs provide isolation at the cost of density.

Containers give you both. Each container shares the operating system of the computer running the container, and that makes them extremely lightweight. Containers start quickly and run lean, so you can run many more containers than VMs on the same

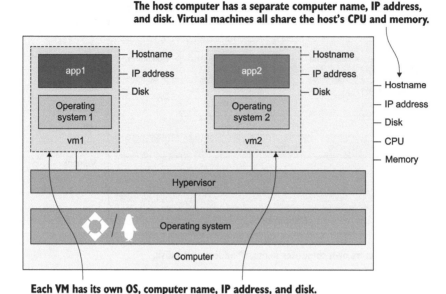

**The host computer has a separate computer name, IP address, and disk. Virtual machines all share the host's CPU and memory.**

**Each VM has its own OS, computer name, IP address, and disk.**

**Figure 2.4   Multiple VMs on one computer each have their own OS.**

hardware—typically five to ten times as many. You get density, but each app is in its own container, so you get isolation too. That's another key feature of Docker: efficiency.

Now you know how Docker does its magic. In the next exercise we'll work more closely with containers.

## 2.3    Connecting to a container like a remote computer

The first container we ran just did one thing—the application printed out some text and then it ended. There are plenty of situations where one thing is all you want to do. Maybe you have a whole set of scripts that automate some process. Those scripts need a specific set of tools to run, so you can't just share the scripts with a colleague; you also need to share a document that describes setting up all the tools, and your colleague needs to spend hours installing them. Instead, you could package the tools and the scripts in a Docker image, share the image, and then your colleague can run your scripts in a container with no extra setup work.

You can work with containers in other ways too. Next you'll see how you can run a container and connect to a terminal inside the container, just as if you were connecting to a remote machine. You use the same `docker container run` command, but you pass some additional flags to run an interactive container with a connected terminal session.

**TRY IT NOW**   Run the following command in your terminal session:

```
docker container run --interactive --tty diamol/base
```

The `--interactive` flag tells Docker you want to set up a connection to the container, and the `--tty` flag means you want to connect to a terminal session inside the container. The output will show Docker pulling the image, and then you'll be left with a command prompt. That command prompt is for a terminal session inside the container, as you can see in figure 2.5.

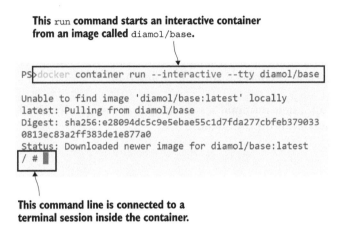

**This `run` command starts an interactive container from an image called** `diamol/base`.

```
PS>docker container run --interactive --tty diamol/base

Unable to find image 'diamol/base:latest' locally
latest: Pulling from diamol/base
Digest: sha256:e28094dc5c9e5ebae55c1d7fda277cbfeb379033
0813ec83a2ff383de1e877a0
Status: Downloaded newer image for diamol/base:latest
/ #
```

**This command line is connected to a terminal session inside the container.**

Figure 2.5   Running an interactive container and connecting to the container's terminal.

The exact same Docker command works in the same way on Windows, but you'll drop into a Windows command-line session instead:

```
Microsoft Windows [Version 10.0.17763.557]
(c) 2018 Microsoft Corporation. All rights reserved.

C:\>
```

Either way, you're now inside the container and you can run any commands that you can normally run in the command line for the operating system.

**TRY IT NOW**   Run the commands `hostname` and `date` and you'll see details of the container's environment:

```
/ # hostname
f1695de1f2ec
/ # date
Thu Jun 20 12:18:26 UTC 2019
```

You'll need some familiarity with your command line if you want to explore further, but what you have here is a local terminal session connected to a remote machine—the machine just happens to be a container that is running on your computer. For instance, if you use Secure Shell (SSH) to connect to a remote Linux machine, or

Remote Desktop Protocol (RDP) to connect to a remote Windows Server Core machine, you'll get exactly the same experience as you have here with Docker.

Remember that the container is sharing your computer's operating system, which is why you see a Linux shell if you're running Linux and a Windows command line if you're using Windows. Some commands are the same for both (try ping google.com), but others have different syntax (you use ls to list directory contents in Linux, and dir in Windows).

Docker itself has the same behavior regardless of which operating system or processor you're using. It's the application inside the container that sees it's running on an Intel-based Windows machine or an Arm-based Linux one. You manage containers with Docker in the same way, whatever is running inside them.

> **TRY IT NOW**   Open up a new terminal session, and you can get details of all the running containers with this command:

```
docker container ls
```

The output shows you information about each container, including the image it's using, the container ID, and the command Docker ran inside the container when it started—this is some abbreviated output:

```
CONTAINER ID  IMAGE         COMMAND     CREATED         STATUS
f1695de1f2ec  diamol/base   "/bin/sh"   16 minutes ago  Up 16 minutes
```

If you have a keen eye, you'll notice that the container ID is the same as the hostname inside the container. Docker assigns a random ID to each container it creates, and part of that ID is used for the hostname. There are lots of docker container commands that you can use to interact with a specific container, which you can identify using the first few characters of the container ID you want.

> **TRY IT NOW**   docker container top lists the processes running in the container. I'm using f1 as a short form of the container ID f1695de1f2ec:

```
> docker container top f1
PID                     USER            TIME            COMMAND
69622                   root            0:00            /bin/sh
```

If you have multiple processes running in the container, Docker will show them all. That will be the case for Windows containers, which always have several background processes running in addition to the container application.

> **TRY IT NOW**   docker container logs displays any log entries the container has collected:

```
> docker container logs f1
/ # hostname
f1695de1f2ec
```

Docker collects log entries using the output from the application in the container. In the case of this terminal session, I see the commands I ran and their results, but for a real application you would see your code's log entries. For example, a web application may write a log entry for every HTTP request processed, and these will show in the container logs.

> **TRY IT NOW**  `docker container inspect` shows you all the details of a container:

```
> docker container inspect f1
[
    {
        "Id":
      "f1695de1f2ecd493d17849a709ffb78f5647a0bcd9d10f0d97ada0fcb7b05e98",
        "Created": "2019-06-20T12:13:52.8360567Z"
```

The full output shows lots of low-level information, including the paths of the container's virtual filesystem, the command running inside the container, and the virtual Docker network the container is connected to—this can all be useful if you're tracking down a problem with your application. It comes as a large chunk of JSON, which is great for automating with scripts, but not so good for a code listing in a book, so I've just shown the first few lines.

These are the commands you'll use all the time when you're working with containers, when you need to troubleshoot application problems, when you want to check if processes are using lots of CPU, or if you want to see the networking Docker has set up for the container.

There's another point to these exercises, which is to help you realize that as far as Docker is concerned, containers all look the same. Docker adds a consistent management layer on top of every application. You could have a 10-year-old Java app running in a Linux container, a 15-year-old .NET app running in a Windows container, and a brand-new Go application running on a Raspberry Pi. You'll use the exact same commands to manage them—run to start the app, `logs` to read out the logs, `top` to see the processes, and `inspect` to get the details.

You've now seen a bit more of what you can do with Docker; we'll finish with some exercises for a more useful application. You can close the second terminal window you opened (where you ran `docker container logs`), go back to the first terminal, which is still connected to the container, and run `exit` to close the terminal session.

## 2.4  *Hosting a website in a container*

So far we've run a few containers. The first couple ran a task that printed some text and then exited. The next used interactive flags and connected us to a terminal session in the container, which stayed running until we exited the session. `docker container ls` will show that you have no containers, because the command only shows running containers.

**TRY IT NOW**    Run docker container ls --all, which shows all containers in any status:

```
> docker container ls --all
CONTAINER ID   IMAGE                    COMMAND
CREATED            STATUS
f1695de1f2ec   diamol/base              "/bin/sh"
About an hour ago  Exited (0)
858a26ee2741   diamol/ch02-hello-diamol "/bin/sh -c ./cmd.sh"  3 hours
ago         Exited (0)
2cff9e95ce83   diamol/ch02-hello-diamol "/bin/sh -c ./cmd.sh"  4 hours
ago         Exited (0)
```

The containers have the status Exited. There are a couple of key things to understand here.

First, containers are running only while the application inside the container is running. As soon as the application process ends, the container goes into the exited state. Exited containers don't use any CPU time or memory. The "Hello World" container exited automatically as soon as the script completed. The interactive container we were connected to exited as soon as we exited the terminal application.

Second, containers don't disappear when they exit. Containers in the exited state still exist, which means you can start them again, check the logs, and copy files to and from the container's filesystem. You only see running containers with docker container ls, but Docker doesn't remove exited containers unless you explicitly tell it to do so. Exited containers still take up space on disk because their filesystem is kept on the computer's disk.

So what about starting containers that stay in the background and just keep running? That's actually the main use case for Docker: running server applications like websites, batch processes, and databases.

**TRY IT NOW**    Here's a simple example, running a website in a container:

```
docker container run --detach --publish 8088:80 diamol/ch02-hello-
    diamol-web
```

This time the only output you'll see is a long container ID, and you get returned to your command line. The container is still running in the background.

**TRY IT NOW**    Run docker container ls and you'll see that the new container has the status Up:

```
> docker container ls
CONTAINER ID     IMAGE
COMMAND                    CREATED            STATUS
PORTS                      NAMES
e53085ff0cc4     diamol/ch02-hello-diamol-web
"bin\\httpd.exe -DFOR…"   52 seconds ago     Up 50 seconds
443/tcp, 0.0.0.0:8088->80/tcp   reverent_dubinsky
```

The image you've just used is `diamol/ch02-hello-diamol-web`. That image includes the Apache web server and a simple HTML page. When you run this container, you have a full web server running, hosting a custom website. Containers that sit in the background and listen for network traffic (HTTP requests in this case) need a couple of extra flags in the `container run` command:

- `--detach`—Starts the container in the background and shows the container ID
- `--publish`—Publishes a port from the container to the computer

Running a detached container just puts the container in the background so it starts up and stays hidden, like a Linux daemon or a Windows service. Publishing ports needs a little more explanation. When you install Docker, it injects itself into your computer's networking layer. Traffic coming into your computer can be intercepted by Docker, and then Docker can send that traffic into a container.

Containers aren't exposed to the outside world by default. Each has its own IP address, but that's an IP address that Docker creates for a network that Docker manages—the container is not attached to the physical network of the computer. Publishing a container port means Docker listens for network traffic on the computer port, and then sends it into the container. In the preceding example, traffic sent to the computer on port 8088 will get sent into the container on port 80—you can see the traffic flow in figure 2.6.

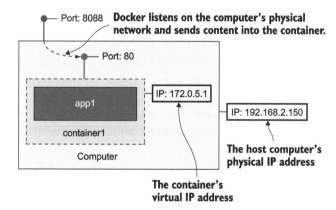

**Figure 2.6 The physical and virtual networks for computers and containers**

In this example my computer is the machine running Docker, and it has the IP address `192.168.2.150`. That's the IP address for my physical network, and it was assigned by the router when my computer connected. Docker is running a single container on that computer, and the container has the IP address `172.0.5.1`. That address is assigned by Docker for a virtual network managed by Docker. No other computers in my network can connect to the container's IP address, because it only exists in Docker, but they can send traffic into the container, because the port has been published.

> **TRY IT NOW**   Browse to http://localhost:8088 on a browser. That's an HTTP request to the local computer, but the response (see figure 2.7) comes from the container. (One thing you definitely won't learn from this book is effective website design.)

**Browsing to the published port on the host computer; the content comes from the container.**

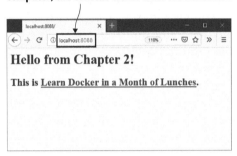

**Figure 2.7   The web application served from a container on the local machine**

This is a very simple website, but even so, this app still benefits from the portability and efficiency that Docker brings. The web content is packaged with the web server, so the Docker image has everything it needs. A web developer can run a single container on their laptop, and the whole application—from the HTML to the web server stack—will be exactly the same as if an operator ran the app on 100 containers across a server cluster in production.

The application in this container keeps running indefinitely, so the container will keep running too. You can use the docker container commands we've already used to manage it.

> **TRY IT NOW**   docker container stats is another useful one: it shows a live view of how much CPU, memory, network, and disk the container is using. The output is slightly different for Linux and Windows containers:

```
> docker container stats e53
CONTAINER ID   NAME                 CPU %   PRIV WORKING SET   NET I/O
BLOCK I/O
e53085ff0cc4   reverent_dubinsky   0.36%   16.88MiB           250kB / 53.2kB
19.4MB / 6.21MB
```

When you're done working with a container, you can remove it with docker container rm and the container ID, using the --force flag to force removal if the container is still running.

We'll end this exercise with one last command that you'll get used to running regularly.

**TRY IT NOW**    Run this command to remove all your containers:

```
docker container rm --force $(docker container ls --all --quiet)
```

The `$()` syntax sends the output from one command into another command—it works just as well on Linux and Mac terminals, and on Windows PowerShell. Combining these commands gets a list of all the container IDs on your computer, and removes them all. This is a good way to tidy up your containers, but use it with caution, because it won't ask for confirmation.

## 2.5    *Understanding how Docker runs containers*

We've done a lot of try-it-now exercises in this chapter, and you should be happy now with the basics of working with containers.

In the first try-it-now for this chapter, I talked about the *build, share, run* workflow that is at the core of Docker. That workflow makes it very easy to distribute software—I've built all the sample container images and shared them, knowing you can run them in Docker and they will work the same for you as they do for me. A huge number of projects now use Docker as the preferred way to release software. You can try a new piece of software—say, Elasticsearch, or the latest version of SQL Server, or the Ghost blogging engine—with the same type of `docker container run` commands you've been using here.

We're going to end with a little more background, so you have a solid understanding of what's actually happening when you run applications with Docker. Installing Docker and running containers is deceptively simple—there are actually a few different components involved, which you can see in figure 2.8.

- The *Docker Engine* is the management component of Docker. It looks after the local image cache, downloading images when you need them, and reusing

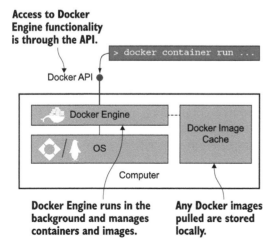

**Access to Docker Engine functionality is through the API.**

**Docker Engine runs in the background and manages containers and images.**

**Any Docker images pulled are stored locally.**

Figure 2.8    The components of Docker

them if they're already downloaded. It also works with the operating system to create containers, virtual networks, and all the other Docker resources. The Engine is a background process that is always running (like a Linux daemon or a Windows service).

- The Docker Engine makes all the features available through the *Docker API*, which is just a standard HTTP-based REST API. You can configure the Engine to make the API accessible only from the local computer (which is the default), or make it available to other computers on your network.
- The *Docker command-line interface* (CLI) is a client of the Docker API. When you run Docker commands, the CLI actually sends them to the Docker API, and the Docker Engine does the work.

It's good to understand the architecture of Docker. The only way to interact with the Docker Engine is through the API, and there are different options for giving access to the API and securing it. The CLI works by sending requests to the API.

So far we've used the CLI to manage containers on the same computer where Docker is running, but you can point your CLI to the API on a remote computer running Docker and control containers on that machine—that's what you'll do to manage containers in different environments, like your build servers, test, and production. The Docker API is the same on every operating system, so you can use the CLI on your Windows laptop to manage containers on your Raspberry Pi, or on a Linux server in the cloud.

The Docker API has a published specification, and the Docker CLI is not the only client. There are several graphical user interfaces that connect to the Docker API and give you a visual way to interact with your containers. The API exposes all the details about containers, images, and the other resources Docker manages so it can power rich dashboards like the one in figure 2.9.

This is Universal Control Plane (UCP), a commercial product from the company behind Docker (https://docs.docker.com/ee/ucp/). Portainer is another option, which is an open source project. Both UCP and Portainer run as containers themselves, so they're easy to deploy and manage.

We won't be diving any deeper into the Docker architecture than this. The Docker Engine uses a component called containerd to actually manage containers, and containerd in turn makes use of operating system features to create the virtual environment that is the container.

You don't need to understand the low-level details of containers, but it is good to know this: containerd is an open source component overseen by the Cloud Native Computing Foundation, and the specification for running containers is open and public; it's called the Open Container Initiative (OCI).

Docker is by far the most popular and easy to use container platform, but it's not the only one. You can confidently invest in containers without being concerned that you're getting locked in to one vendor's platform.

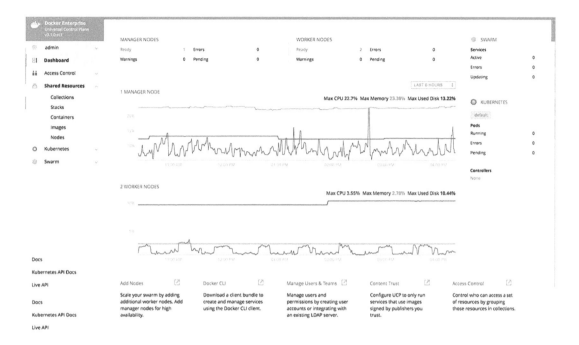

**Figure 2.9   Docker Universal Control Plane, a graphical user interface for containers**

## 2.6   *Lab: Exploring the container filesystem*

This is the first lab in the book, so here's what it's all about. The lab sets you a task to achieve by yourself, which will really help you cement what you've learned in the chapter. There will be some guidance and a few hints, but mostly this is about you going further than the prescriptive try-it-now exercises and finding your own way to solve the problem.

Every lab has a sample solution on the book's GitHub repository. It's worth spending some time trying it out yourself, but if you want to check my solution you can find it here: https://github.com/sixeyed/diamol/tree/master/ch02/lab.

Here we go: your task is to run the website container from this chapter, but replace the index.html file so when you browse to the container you see a different homepage (you can use any content you like). Remember that the container has its own filesystem, and in this application, the website is serving files that are on the container's filesystem.

Here are some hints to get you going:

- You can run docker container to get a list of all the actions you can perform on a container.

- Add `--help` to any `docker` command, and you'll see more detailed help text.
- In the `diamol/ch02-hello-diamol-web` Docker image, the content from the website is served from the directory `/usr/local/apache2/htdocs` (that's `C:\usr\local\apache2\htdocs` on Windows).

Good luck :)

# 3

# *Building your own Docker images*

You ran some containers in the last chapter and used Docker to manage them. Containers provide a consistent experience across applications, no matter what technology stack the app uses. Up till now you've used Docker images that I've built and shared; in this chapter you'll see how to build your own images. This is where you'll learn about the Dockerfile syntax, and some of the key patterns you will always use when you containerize your own apps.

## 3.1 Using a container image from Docker Hub

We'll start with the finished version of the image you'll build in this chapter, so you can see how it's been designed to work well with Docker. The try-it-now exercises all use a simple application called web-ping, which checks if a website is up. The app will run in a container and make HTTP requests to the URL for my blog every three seconds until the container is stopped.

You know from chapter 2 that docker container run will download the container image locally if it isn't already on your machine. That's because software distribution is built into the Docker platform. You can leave Docker to manage this for you, so it pulls images when they're needed, or you can explicitly pull images using the Docker CLI.

**TRY IT NOW** Pull the container image for the web-ping application:

```
docker image pull diamol/ch03-web-ping
```

You'll see output similar to mine in figure 3.1.

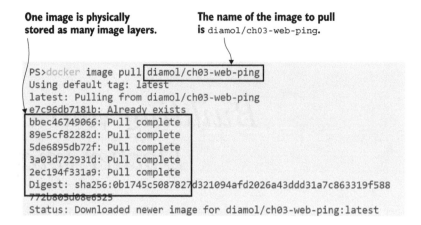

One image is physically
stored as many image layers.

The name of the image to pull
is `diamol/ch03-web-ping`.

```
PS>docker image pull diamol/ch03-web-ping
Using default tag: latest
latest: Pulling from diamol/ch03-web-ping
e7c96db7181b: Already exists
bbec46749066: Pull complete
89e5cf82282d: Pull complete
5de6895db72f: Pull complete
3a03d722931d: Pull complete
2ec194f331a9: Pull complete
Digest: sha256:0b1745c5087827d321094afd2026a43ddd31a7c863319f588
772b805d08e6525
Status: Downloaded newer image for diamol/ch03-web-ping:latest
```

Figure 3.1   Pulling an image from Docker Hub

The image name is `diamol/ch03-web-ping`, and it's stored on Docker Hub, which is the default location where Docker looks for images. Image servers are called *registries*, and Docker Hub is a public registry you can use for free. Docker Hub also has a web interface, and you'll find details about this image at https://hub.docker.com/r/diamol/ch03-web-ping.

There's some interesting output from the `docker image pull` command, which shows you how images are stored. A Docker image is logically one thing—you can think of it as a big zip file that contains the whole application stack. This image has the Node.js runtime together with my application code.

During the pull you don't see one single file downloaded; you see lots of downloads in progress. Those are called image layers. A Docker image is physically stored as lots of small files, and Docker assembles them together to create the container's filesystem. When all the layers have been pulled, the full image is available to use.

**TRY IT NOW**   Let's run a container from the image and see what the app does:

```
docker container run -d --name web-ping diamol/ch03-web-ping
```

The `-d` flag is a short form of `--detach`, so this container will run in the background. The application runs like a batch job with no user interface. Unlike the website container we ran detached in chapter 2, this one doesn't accept incoming traffic, so you don't need to publish any ports.

There's one new flag in this command, which is `--name`. You know that you can work with containers using the ID that Docker generates, but you can also give them a friendly name. This container is called `web-ping`, and you can use that name to refer to the container instead of using the random ID.

My blog is getting pinged by the app running in your container now. The app runs in an endless loop, and you can see what it's doing using the same `docker container` commands you're familiar with from chapter 2.

**TRY IT NOW**    Have a look at the logs from the application, which are being collected by Docker:

```
docker container logs web-ping
```

You'll see output like that in figure 3.2, showing the app making HTTP requests to blog.sixeyed.com.

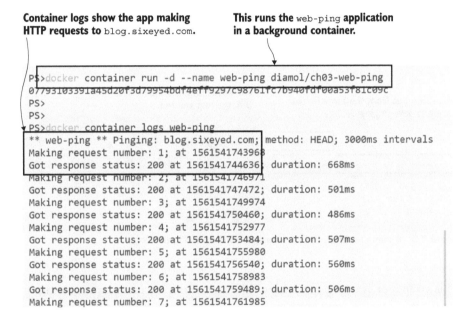

**Figure 3.2   The web-ping container in action, sending constant traffic to my blog**

An app that makes web requests and logs how long the response took is fairly useful—you could use it as the basis for monitoring the uptime of a website. But this application looks like it's hardcoded to use my blog, so it's pretty useless to anyone but me.

Except that it isn't. The application can actually be configured to use a different URL, a different interval between requests, and even a different type of HTTP call. This app reads the configuration values it should use from the system's environment variables.

*Environment variables* are just key/value pairs that the operating system provides. They work in the same way on Windows and Linux, and they're a very simple way to store small pieces of data. Docker containers also have environment variables, but instead of coming from the computer's operating system, they're set up by Docker in the same way that Docker creates a hostname and IP address for the container.

The web-ping image has some default values set for environment variables. When you run a container, those environment variables are populated by Docker, and that's what the app uses to configure the website's URL. You can specify different values for environment variables when you create the container, and that will change the behavior of the app.

**TRY IT NOW**   Remove the existing container, and run a new one with a value specified for the TARGET environment variable:

```
docker rm -f web-ping
docker container run --env TARGET=google.com diamol/ch03-web-ping
```

Your output this time will look like mine in figure 3.3.

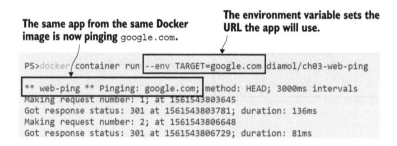

Figure 3.3   **A container from the same image, sending traffic to Google**

This container is doing something different. First, it's running interactively because you didn't use the --detach flag, so the output from the app is shown on your console. The container will keep running until you end the app by pressing Ctrl-C. Second, it's pinging google.com now instead of blog.sixeyed.com.

This is going to be one of your major takeaways from this chapter—Docker images may be packaged with a default set of configuration values for the application, but you should be able to provide different configuration settings when you run a container.

Environment variables are a very simple way to achieve that. The web-ping application code looks for an environment variable with the key TARGET. That key is set with a value of blog.sixeyed.com in the image, but you can provide a different value with the docker container run command by using the --env flag. Figure 3.4 shows how containers have their own settings, different from each other and from the image.

The host computer has its own set of environment variables too, but they're separate from the containers. Each container only has the environment variables that Docker populates. The important thing in figure 3.4 is that the web-ping applications

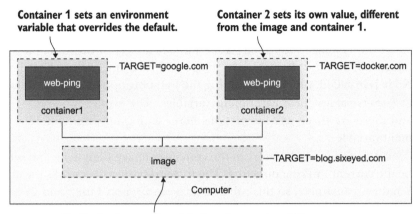

**Figure 3.4  Environment variables in Docker images and containers**

are the same in each container—they use the same image, so the app is running the exact same set of binaries, but the behavior is different because of the configuration.

It's down to the author of the Docker image to provide that flexibility, and you're going to see how to do that now, as you build your first Docker image from a Dockerfile.

## 3.2  *Writing your first Dockerfile*

The Dockerfile is a simple script you write to package up an application—it's a set of instructions, and a Docker image is the output. Dockerfile syntax is simple to learn, and you can package up any kind of app using a Dockerfile. As scripting languages go, it is very flexible. Common tasks have their own commands, and for anything custom you need to do, you can use standard shell commands (Bash on Linux or PowerShell on Windows). Listing 3.1 shows the full Dockerfile to package up the web-ping application.

**Listing 3.1  The web-ping Dockerfile**

```
FROM diamol/node

ENV TARGET="blog.sixeyed.com"
ENV METHOD="HEAD"
ENV INTERVAL="3000"

WORKDIR /web-ping
COPY app.js .

CMD ["node", "/web-ping/app.js"]
```

Even if this is the first Dockerfile you've ever seen, you can probably take a good guess about what's happening here. The Dockerfile instructions are FROM, ENV, WORKDIR,

COPY, and CMD; they're in capitals, but that's a convention, not a requirement. Here's the breakdown for each instruction:

- FROM—Every image has to start from another image. In this case, the web-ping image will use the diamol/node image as its starting point. That image has Node.js installed, which is everything the web-ping application needs to run.
- ENV—Sets values for environment variables. The syntax is [key]="[value]", and there are three ENV instructions here, setting up three different environment variables.
- WORKDIR—Creates a directory in the container image filesystem, and sets that to be the current working directory. The forward-slash syntax works for Linux and Windows containers, so this will create /web-ping on Linux and C:\web-ping on Windows.
- COPY—Copies files or directories from the local filesystem into the container image. The syntax is [source path] [target path]—in this case, I'm copying app.js from my local machine into the working directory in the image.
- CMD—Specifies the command to run when Docker starts a container from the image. This runs Node.js, starting the application code in app.js.

That's it. Those instructions are pretty much all you need to package your own applications in Docker, and in those five lines there are already some good practices.

**TRY IT NOW**    You don't need to copy and paste this Dockerfile; it's all there in the book's source code, which you cloned or downloaded in chapter 1. Navigate to where you downloaded it, and check that you have all the files to build this image:

```
cd ch03/exercises/web-ping
ls
```

You should see that you have three files:

- Dockerfile (no file extension), which has the same content as listing 3.1
- app.js, which has the Node.js code for the web-ping application
- README.md, which is just documentation for using the image

You can see these in figure 3.5.

You don't need any understanding of Node.js or JavaScript to package this app and run it in Docker. If you do look at the code in app.js, you'll see that it's pretty basic, and it uses standard Node.js libraries to make the HTTP calls and to get configuration values from environment variables.

In this directory you have everything you need to build your own image for the web-ping application.

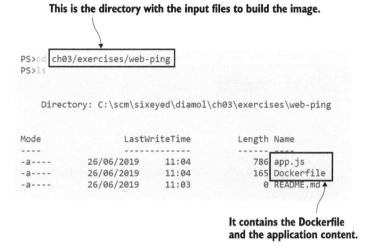

**This is the directory with the input files to build the image.**

```
PS>cd ch03/exercises/web-ping
PS>ls

    Directory: C:\scm\sixeyed\diamol\ch03\exercises\web-ping

Mode                 LastWriteTime         Length Name
----                 -------------         ------ ----
-a----        26/06/2019     11:04            786 app.js
-a----        26/06/2019     11:04            165 Dockerfile
-a----        26/06/2019     11:03              0 README.md
```

**It contains the Dockerfile
and the application content.**

Figure 3.5   The content you need to build the Docker image

## 3.3   *Building your own container image*

Docker needs to know a few things before it can build an image from a Dockerfile. It needs a name for the image, and it needs to know the location for all the files that it's going to package into the image. You already have a terminal open in the right directory, so you're ready to go.

> **TRY IT NOW**   Turn this Dockerfile into a Docker image by running `docker image build`:

```
docker image build --tag web-ping .
```

The `--tag` argument is the name for the image, and the final argument is the directory where the Dockerfile and related files are. Docker calls this directory the "context," and the period means "use the current directory." You'll see output from the `build` command, executing all the instructions in the Dockerfile. My build is shown in figure 3.6.

If you get any errors from the `build` command, you'll first need to check that the Docker Engine is started. You need the Docker Desktop app to be running on Windows or Mac (check for the whale icon in your taskbar). Then check that you're in the right directory. You should be in the `ch03-web-ping` directory where the Dockerfile and the app.js files are. Lastly, check that you've entered the `build` command correctly—the period at the end of the command is required to tell Docker that the build context is the current directory.

If you get a warning during the build about file permissions, that's because you're using the Docker command line on Windows to build Linux containers, thanks to Docker Desktop's Linux container mode. Windows doesn't record file permissions in

**The "tag" is the name of the image to build.**

**This is the directory where Docker will find the content—"." means use the current directory.**

```
PS>docker image build --tag web-ping .
Sending build context to Docker daemon   4.096kB
Step 1/7 : FROM diamol/node
 ---> 9dfa73010b19
Step 2/7 : ENV TARGET="blog.sixeyed.com"
 ---> Running in 271fd8fafdca
Removing intermediate container 271fd8fafdca
 ---> 184364920df8
Step 3/7 : ENV METHOD="HEAD"
 ---> Running in 519bc1b02aad
Removing intermediate container 519bc1b02aad
 ---> aeac2009c2d8
Step 4/7 : ENV INTERVAL="3000"
 ---> Running in 0f356eae6f42
Removing intermediate container 0f356eae6f42
 ---> f255921aee9b
Step 5/7 : WORKDIR /web-ping
 ---> Running in 3c1e496ac175
Removing intermediate container 3c1e496ac175
 ---> 2f119d903989
Step 6/7 : COPY app.js .
 ---> 0f7036862799
Step 7/7 : CMD ["node", "/web-ping/app.js"]
 ---> Running in aaaabba6eecc
Removing intermediate container aaaabba6eecc
 ---> 76f3436762e9
Successfully built 76f3436762e9
Successfully tagged web-ping:latest
```

**Figure 3.6   Output from building the web-ping Docker image**

the same way that Linux does, so the warning is telling you that all the files copied from your Windows machine are set with full read and write permissions in the Linux Docker image.

When you see the "successfully built" and "successfully tagged" messages in the output, your image is built. It's stored locally in your image cache, and you can see it with the Docker command to list images.

**TRY IT NOW**   List all the images where the tag name starts with "w":

```
docker image ls 'w*'
```

You'll see your web-ping image listed:

```
> docker image ls w*
REPOSITORY    TAG       IMAGE ID       CREATED         SIZE
web-ping      latest    f2a5c430ab2a   14 minutes ago  75.3MB
```

You can use this image in exactly the same way as the one you downloaded from Docker Hub. The contents of the app are the same, and the configuration settings can be applied with environment variables.

> **TRY IT NOW**   Run a container from your own image to ping Docker's website every five seconds:

```
docker container run -e TARGET=docker.com -e INTERVAL=5000 web-ping
```

Your output will be like mine in figure 3.7, with the first log line confirming that the target web URL is docker.com and the ping interval is 5000 milliseconds.

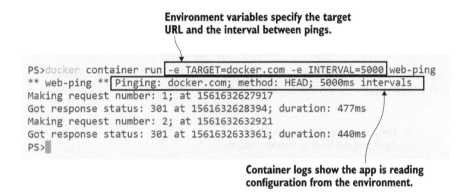

**Environment variables specify the target URL and the interval between pings.**

```
PS>docker container run -e TARGET=docker.com -e INTERVAL=5000 web-ping
** web-ping ** Pinging: docker.com; method: HEAD; 5000ms intervals
Making request number: 1; at 1561632627917
Got response status: 301 at 1561632628394; duration: 477ms
Making request number: 2; at 1561632632921
Got response status: 301 at 1561632633361; duration: 440ms
PS>
```

**Container logs show the app is reading configuration from the environment.**

**Figure 3.7   Running the web-ping container from your own image**

That container is running in the foreground, so you'll need to stop it with Ctrl-C. That ends the application, and the container will go into the exited state.

You've packaged a simple application to run in Docker, and the process is exactly the same for more complicated apps. You write the Dockerfile with all the steps to package your app, collect the resources that need to go into the Docker image, and decide how you want users of your image to configure the behavior of the app.

## 3.4   *Understanding Docker images and image layers*

You'll be building plenty more images as you work through this book. For this chapter we'll stick with this simple one and use it to get a better understanding of how images work, and the relationship between images and containers.

The Docker image contains all the files you packaged, which become the container's filesystem, and it also contains a lot of metadata about the image itself. That includes a brief history of how the image was built. You can use that to see each layer of the image and the command that built the layer.

> **TRY IT NOW**   Check the history for your web-ping image:

```
docker image history web-ping
```

You'll see an output line for each image layer; these are the first few (abbreviated) lines from my image:

```
> docker image history web-ping
IMAGE          CREATED        CREATED BY
47eeeb7cd600   30 hours ago   /bin/sh -c #(nop)  CMD ["node" "/web-ping/ap…
<missing>      30 hours ago   /bin/sh -c #(nop)  COPY file:a7cae366c9996502…
<missing>      30 hours ago   /bin/sh -c #(nop)  WORKDIR /web-ping
```

The CREATED BY commands are the Dockerfile instructions—there's a one-to-one relationship, so each line in the Dockerfile creates an image layer. We're going to dip into a little more theory here, because understanding image layers is your key to making the most efficient use of Docker.

A Docker image is a logical collection of image layers. Layers are the files that are physically stored in the Docker Engine's cache. Here's why that's important: image layers can be shared between different images and different containers. If you have lots of containers all running Node.js apps, they will all share the same set of image layers that contain the Node.js runtime. Figure 3.8 shows how that works.

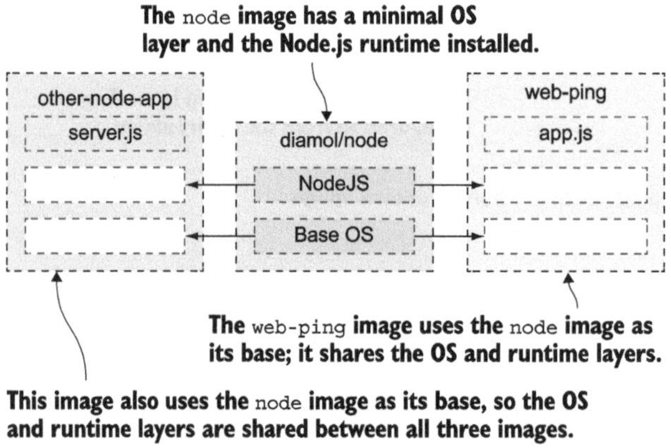

The node **image has a minimal OS layer and the Node.js runtime installed.**

The web-ping **image uses the** node **image as its base; it shares the OS and runtime layers.**

This image also uses the node **image as its base, so the OS and runtime layers are shared between all three images.**

Figure 3.8  How image layers are logically built into Docker images

The diamol/node image has a slim operating system layer, and then the Node.js runtime. The Linux image takes up about 75 MB of disk (the base OS layer for Windows containers is larger, so the Windows version of the image uses closer to 300 MB). Your web-ping image is based on diamol/node, so it starts with all the layers from that image—that's what the FROM instruction in the Dockerfile gives you. The app.js file you package on top of the base image is only a few kilobytes in size, so how big is the web-ping image in total?

**TRY IT NOW**  You can list images with docker image ls, which also shows the size of the image. If you don't include a filter in the command, you'll see all images:

```
docker image ls
```

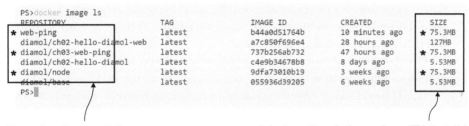

**These three images all share the same Node.js base layers.**

**It looks as though they each use 75 MB of disk space, but this is the logical size of the image, without accounting for shared layers.**

Figure 3.9    Listing images to see their sizes

Your output will be like mine in figure 3.9.

It looks like all the Node.js images take up the same amount of space—75 MB each on Linux. There are three of those: `diamol/node`, the original sample app you pulled from Docker Hub in `diamol/ch03-web-ping`, and the version you built yourself in `web-ping`. They should be sharing the base image layers, but the output from `docker image ls` suggests they're each 75 MB in size, so that's 75 * 3 = 225 MB in total.

But not exactly. The size column you see is the logical size of the image—that's how much disk space the image would use if you didn't have any other images on your system. If you do have other images that share layers, the disk space Docker uses is much smaller. You can't see that from the image list, but there are Docker system commands that tell you more.

**TRY IT NOW**    My image list shows a total of 363.96 MB of images, but that's the total logical size. The `system df` command shows exactly how much disk space Docker is using:

```
docker system df
```

You can see in figure 3.10 that my image cache is actually using 202.2 MB, meaning 163 MB of image layers are being shared between images, a 45% saving on disk space. The amount of disk space you save through reuse is typically much larger when you

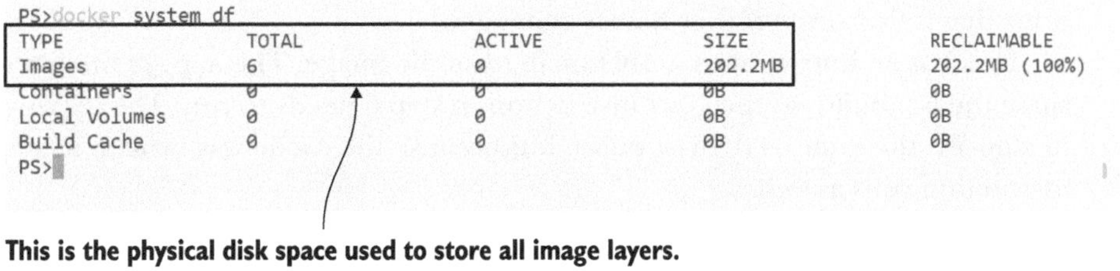

```
PS>docker system df
TYPE              TOTAL        ACTIVE       SIZE          RECLAIMABLE
Images            6            0            202.2MB       202.2MB (100%)
Containers        0            0            0B            0B
Local Volumes     0            0            0B            0B
Build Cache       0            0            0B            0B
PS>
```

**This is the physical disk space used to store all image layers.**

Figure 3.10    Checking Docker's disk space usage

have a large number of application images all sharing the same base layers for the runtime. Those base layers might have Java, .NET Core, PHP—whatever technology stack you use, Docker's behavior is the same.

One last piece of theory. If image layers are shared around, they can't be edited—otherwise a change in one image would cascade to all the other images that share the changed layer. Docker enforces that by making image layers read-only. Once you create a layer by building an image, that layer can be shared by other images, but it can't be changed. You can take advantage of that to make your Docker images smaller and your builds faster by optimizing your Dockerfiles.

## 3.5    Optimizing Dockerfiles to use the image layer cache

There's a layer of your `web-ping` image that contains the application's JavaScript file. If you make a change to that file and rebuild your image, you'll get a new image layer. Docker assumes the layers in a Docker image follow a defined sequence, so if you change a layer in the middle of that sequence, Docker doesn't assume it can reuse the later layers in the sequence.

> **TRY IT NOW**   Make a change to the `app.js` file in the `ch03-web-ping` directory. It doesn't have to be a code change; just adding a new empty line at the end of the file will do. Then build a new version of your Docker image:

```
docker image build -t web-ping:v2 .
```

You'll see the same output as mine in figure 3.11. Steps 2 through 5 of the build use layers from the cache, and steps 6 and 7 generate new layers.

Every Dockerfile instruction results in an image layer, but if the instruction doesn't change between builds, and the content going into the instruction is the same, Docker knows it can use the previous layer in the cache. That saves executing the Dockerfile instruction again and generating a duplicate layer. The input is the same, so the output will be the same, so Docker can use what's already there in the cache.

Docker calculates whether the input has a match in the cache by generating a hash, which is like a digital fingerprint representing the input. The hash is made from the Dockerfile instruction and the contents of any files being copied. If there's no match for the hash in the existing image layers, Docker executes the instruction, and that breaks the cache. As soon as the cache is broken, Docker executes all the instructions that follow, even if they haven't changed.

That has an impact even in this small example image. The `app.js` file has changed since the last build, so the `COPY` instruction in step 6 needs to run. The `CMD` instruction in step 7 is the same as the last build, but because the cache was broken at step 6, that instruction runs as well.

Any Dockerfile you write should be optimized so that the instructions are ordered by how frequently they change—with instructions that are unlikely to change at the start of the Dockerfile, and instructions most likely to change at the end. The goal is

**Steps 2 through 5 all come from the cache because the input is unchanged.**

```
PS>docker image build -t web-ping:v2 .
Sending build context to Docker daemon  4.096kB
Step 1/7 : FROM diamol/node
 ---> 9dfa73010b19
Step 2/7 : ENV TARGET="blog.sixeyed.com"
 ---> Using cache
 ---> 184364920df8
Step 3/7 : ENV METHOD="HEAD"
 ---> Using cache
 ---> aeac2009c2d8
Step 4/7 : ENV INTERVAL="3000"
 ---> Using cache
 ---> f255921aee9b
Step 5/7 : WORKDIR /web-ping
 ---> Using cache
 ---> 2f119d905989
Step 6/7 : COPY app.js .
 ---> 39d4c537d368
Step 7/7 : CMD ["node", "/web-ping/app.js"]
 ---> Running in 2d431f8776f9
Removing intermediate container 2d431f8776f9
 ---> f7f7ec332dd1
Successfully built f7f7ec332dd1
Successfully tagged web-ping:v2
```

**Step 7 executes even though the input hasn't changed, because the cache was broken in step 6.**

**Step 6 executes because the copied file contents have changed.**

Figure 3.11  Building an image where layers can be used from the cache

for most builds to only need to execute the last instruction, using the cache for everything else. That saves time, disk space, and network bandwidth when you start sharing your images.

There are only seven instructions in the web-ping Dockerfile, but it can still be optimized. The CMD instruction doesn't need to be at the end of the Dockerfile; it can be anywhere after the FROM instruction and still have the same result. It's unlikely to change, so you can move it nearer the top. And one ENV instruction can be used to set multiple environment variables, so the three separate ENV instructions can be combined. The optimized Dockerfile is shown in listing 3.2.

**Listing 3.2  The optimized web-ping Dockerfile**

```
FROM diamol/node

CMD ["node", "/web-ping/app.js"]

ENV TARGET="blog.sixeyed.com" \
    METHOD="HEAD" \
    INTERVAL="3000"

WORKDIR /web-ping
COPY app.js .
```

**TRY IT NOW**    The optimized Dockerfile is in the source code for this chapter too. Switch to the `web-ping-optimized` folder and build the image from the new Dockerfile:

```
cd ../web-ping-optimized
docker image build -t web-ping:v3 .
```

You won't notice too much difference from the previous build. There are now five steps instead of seven, but the end result is the same—you can run a container from this image, and it behaves just like the other versions. But now if you change the application code in `app.js` and rebuild, all the steps come from the cache except the final one, which is exactly what you want, because that's all you've changed.

That's all for building images in this chapter. You've seen the Dockerfile syntax and the key instructions you need to know, and you've learned how to build and work with images from the Docker CLI.

There are two more important things to take from this chapter, which will be of good service to you in every image you build: optimize your Dockerfiles, and make sure your image is portable so you use the same image when you deploy to different environments. That really just means you should take care how you structure your Dockerfile instructions, and make sure the application can read configuration values from the container. It means you can build images quickly, and when you deploy to production you're using the exact same image that was quality-approved in your test environments.

## 3.6   *Lab*

Okay, it's lab time. The goal here is to answer this question: how do you produce a Docker image without a Dockerfile? The Dockerfile is there to automate the deployment of your app, but you can't always automate everything. Sometimes you need to run the application and finish off some steps manually, and those steps can't be scripted.

This lab is a much simpler version of that. You're going to start with an image on Docker Hub: `diamol/ch03-lab`. That image has a file at the path `/diamol/ch03.txt`. You need to update that text file and add your name at the end. Then produce your own image with your changed file. You're not allowed to use a Dockerfile.

There's a sample solution on the book's GitHub repository if you need it. You'll find it here: https://github.com/sixeyed/diamol/tree/master/ch03/lab.

Here are some hints to get you going:

- Remember that the `-it` flags let you run to a container interactively.
- The filesystem for a container still exists when it is exited.
- There are lots of commands you haven't used yet. `docker container --help` will show you two that could help you solve the lab.

# Packaging applications from source code into Docker Images

Building Docker images is easy. In chapter 3 you learned that you just need a few instructions in a Dockerfile to package an application to run in a container. There's one other thing you need to know to package your own applications: you can also run commands inside Dockerfiles.

Commands execute during the build, and any filesystem changes from the command are saved in the image layer. That makes Dockerfiles about the most flexible packaging format there is; you can expand zip files, run Windows installers, and do pretty much anything else. In this chapter you'll use that flexibility to package applications from source code.

## 4.1 Who needs a build server when you have a Dockerfile?

Building software on your laptop is something you do for local development, but when you're working in a team there's a more rigorous delivery process. There's a shared source control system like GitHub where everyone pushes their code changes, and there's typically a separate server (or online service) that builds the software when changes get pushed.

That process exists to catch problems early. If a developer forgets to add a file when they push code, the build will fail on the build server and the team will be alerted. It keeps the project healthy, but the cost is having to maintain a build server. Most programming languages need a lot of tools to build projects—figure 4.1 shows some examples.

There's a big maintenance overhead here. A new starter on the team will spend the whole of their first day installing the tools. If a developer updates their local

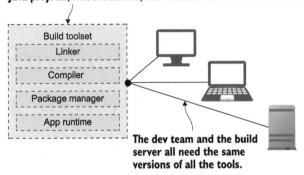

Tools needed to build software—could include Maven and the JDK for Java projects, NuGet MSBuild, and Visual Studio Build Tools for .NET.

**Build toolset**
Linker
Compiler
Package manager
App runtime

The dev team and the build server all need the same versions of all the tools.

Figure 4.1   Everyone needs the same set of tools to build a software project.

tools so the build server is running a different version, the build can fail. You have the same issues even if you're using a managed build service, and there you may have a limited set of tools you can install.

It would be much cleaner to package the build toolset once and share it, which is exactly what you can do with Docker. You can write a Dockerfile that scripts the deployment of all your tools, and build that into an image. Then you can use that image in your application Dockerfiles to compile the source code, and the final output is your packaged application.

Let's start with a very simple example, because there are a couple of new things to understand in this process. Listing 4.1 shows a Dockerfile with the basic workflow.

**Listing 4.1   A multi-stage Dockerfile**

```
FROM diamol/base AS build-stage
RUN echo 'Building...' > /build.txt

FROM diamol/base AS test-stage
COPY --from=build-stage /build.txt /build.txt
RUN echo 'Testing...' >> /build.txt

FROM diamol/base
COPY --from=test-stage /build.txt /build.txt
CMD cat /build.txt
```

This is called a multi-stage Dockerfile, because there are several stages to the build. Each stage starts with a `FROM` instruction, and you can optionally give stages a name with the `AS` parameter. Listing 4.1 has three stages: `build-stage`, `test-stage`, and the final unnamed stage. Although there are multiple stages, the output will be a single Docker image with the contents of the final stage.

Each stage runs independently, but you can copy files and directories from previous stages. I'm using the COPY instruction with the --from argument, which tells Docker to copy files from an earlier stage in the Dockerfile, rather than from the filesystem of the host computer. In this example I generate a file in the build stage, copy it into the test stage, and then copy the file from the test stage into the final stage.

There's one new instruction here, RUN, which I'm using to write files. The RUN instruction executes a command inside a container during the build, and any output from that command is saved in the image layer. You can execute anything in a RUN instruction, but the commands you want to run need to exist in the Docker image you're using in the FROM instruction. In this example I used diamol/base as the base image, and it contains the echo command, so I knew my RUN instruction would work.

Figure 4.2 shows what's going to happen when we build this Dockerfile—Docker will run the stages sequentially.

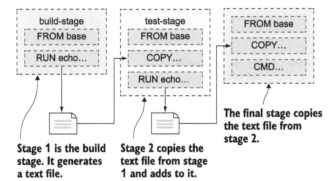

**Stage 1 is the build stage. It generates a text file.**

**Stage 2 copies the text file from stage 1 and adds to it.**

**The final stage copies the text file from stage 2.**

Figure 4.2  Executing a multi-stage Dockerfile

It's important to understand that the individual stages are isolated. You can use different base images with different sets of tools installed and run whatever commands you like. The output in the final stage will only contain what you explicitly copy from earlier stages. If a command fails in any stage, the whole build fails.

**TRY IT NOW**  Open a terminal session to the folder where you stored the book's source code, and build this multi-stage Dockerfile:

```
cd ch04/exercises/multi-stage
docker image build -t multi-stage .
```

You'll see that the build executes the steps in the order of the Dockerfile, which gives the sequential build through the stages you can see in figure 4.3.

This is a simple example, but the pattern is the same for building apps of any complexity with a single Dockerfile. Figure 4.4 shows what the workflow looks like for a Java application.

**Steps 1 and 2 are the** build-stage;
**this generates a file called** build.txt.

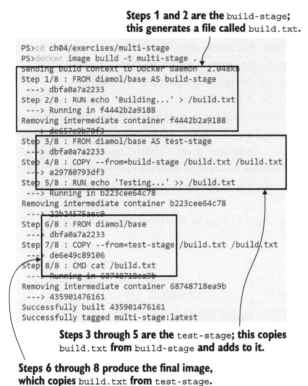

```
PS>cd ch04/exercises/multi-stage
PS>docker image build -t multi-stage .
Sending build context to Docker daemon  2.048kB
Step 1/8 : FROM diamol/base AS build-stage
 ---> dbfa0a7a2233
Step 2/8 : RUN echo 'Building...' > /build.txt
 ---> Running in f4442b2a9188
Removing intermediate container f4442b2a9188
 ---> de657e9b70f3
Step 3/8 : FROM diamol/base AS test-stage
 ---> dbfa0a7a2233
Step 4/8 : COPY --from=build-stage /build.txt /build.txt
 ---> a29780793df3
Step 5/8 : RUN echo 'Testing...' >> /build.txt
 ---> Running in b223cee64c78
Removing intermediate container b223cee64c78
 ---> 22b24575aec9
Step 6/8 : FROM diamol/base
 ---> dbfa0a7a2233
Step 7/8 : COPY --from=test-stage /build.txt /build.txt
 ---> de6e49c89106
Step 8/8 : CMD cat /build.txt
 ---> Running in 68748718ea9b
Removing intermediate container 68748718ea9b
 ---> 435901476161
Successfully built 435901476161
Successfully tagged multi-stage:latest
```

**Steps 3 through 5 are the** test-stage; **this copies**
build.txt **from** build-stage **and adds to it.**

**Steps 6 through 8 produce the final image,**
**which copies** build.txt **from** test-stage.

**Figure 4.3   Building a multi-stage Dockerfile**

In the build stage you use a base image that has your application's build tools installed.
You copy in the source code from your host machine and run the build command.
You can add a test stage to run unit tests, which uses a base image with the test framework installed, copies the compiled binaries from the build stage, and runs the tests.
The final stage starts from a base image with just the application runtime installed,
and it copies the binaries from the build stage that have been successfully tested in the
test stage.

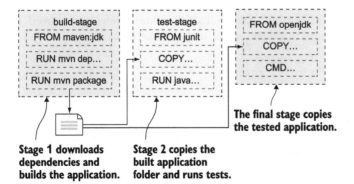

**Stage 1 downloads**
**dependencies and**
**builds the application.**

**Stage 2 copies the**
**built application**
**folder and runs tests.**

**The final stage copies**
**the tested application.**

**Figure 4.4   A multi-stage**
**build for a Java application**

This approach makes your application truly portable. You can run the app in a container anywhere, but you can also build the app anywhere—Docker is the only prerequisite. Your build server just needs Docker installed; new team members get set up in minutes, and the build tools are all centralized in Docker images, so there's no chance of getting out of sync.

All the major application frameworks already have public images on Docker Hub with the build tools installed, and there are separate images with the application runtime. You can use these images directly or wrap them in your own images. You'll get the benefit of using all the latest updates with images that are maintained by the project teams.

## 4.2 App walkthrough: Java source code

We'll move on to a real example now, with a simple Java Spring Boot application that we'll build and run using Docker. You don't need to be a Java developer or have any Java tools installed on your machine to use this app; everything you need will come in Docker images. If you don't work with Java, you should still read through this section—it describes a pattern that works for other compiled languages like .NET Core and Erlang.

The source code is in the repository for the book, at the folder path ch04/ exercises/image-of-the-day. The application uses a fairly standard set of tools for Java: Maven, which is used to define the build process and fetch dependencies, and OpenJDK, which is a freely distributable Java runtime and developer kit. Maven uses an XML format to describe the build, and the Maven command line is called `mvn`. That should be enough information to make sense of the application Dockerfile in listing 4.2.

> **Listing 4.2 Dockerfile for building a Java app with Maven**

```
FROM diamol/maven AS builder

WORKDIR /usr/src/iotd
COPY pom.xml .
RUN mvn -B dependency:go-offline

COPY . .
RUN mvn package

# app
FROM diamol/openjdk

WORKDIR /app
COPY --from=builder /usr/src/iotd/target/iotd-service-0.1.0.jar .

EXPOSE 80
ENTRYPOINT ["java", "-jar", "/app/iotd-service-0.1.0.jar"]
```

Almost all the Dockerfile instructions here are ones you've seen before, and the patterns are familiar from examples that you've built. It's a multi-stage Dockerfile, which you can tell because there's more than one FROM instruction, and the steps are laid out to get maximum benefit from Docker's image layer cache.

The first stage is called `builder`. Here's what happens in the builder stage:

- It uses the `diamol/maven` image as the base. That image has the OpenJDK Java development kit installed, as well as the Maven build tool.
- The builder stage starts by creating a working directory in the image and then copying in the `pom.xml` file, which is the Maven definition of the Java build.
- The first RUN statement executes a Maven command, fetching all the application dependencies. This is an expensive operation, so it has its own step to make use of Docker layer caching. If there are new dependencies, the XML file will change and the step will run. If the dependencies haven't changed, the layer cache is used.
- Next the rest of the source code is copied in—COPY . . means "copy all files and directories from the location where the Docker build is running, into the working directory in the image."
- The last step of the builder is to run `mvn package`, which compiles and packages the application. The input is a set of Java source code files, and the output is a Java application package called a JAR file.

When this stage completes, the compiled application will exist in the builder stage filesystem. If there are any problems with the Maven build—if the network is offline and fetching dependencies fails, or if there is a coding error in the source—the RUN instruction will fail, and the whole build fails.

If the builder stage completes successfully, Docker goes on to execute the final stage, which produces the application image:

- It starts from `diamol/openjdk`, which is packaged with the Java 11 runtime, but none of the Maven build tools.
- This stage creates a working directory and copies in the compiled JAR file from the builder stage. Maven packages the application and all its Java dependencies in this single JAR file, so this is all that's needed from the builder.
- The application is a web server that listens on port 80, so that port is explicitly listed in the EXPOSE instruction, which tells Docker that this port can be published.
- The ENTRYPOINT instruction is an alternative to the CMD instruction—it tells Docker what to do when a container is started from the image, in this case running Java with the path to the application JAR.

**TRY IT NOW**  Browse to the Java application source code and build the image:

```
cd ch04/exercises/image-of-the-day
docker image build -t image-of-the-day .
```

There's a lot of output from this build because you'll see all the logs from Maven, fetching dependencies, and running through the Java build. Figure 4.5 shows an abbreviated section of my build.

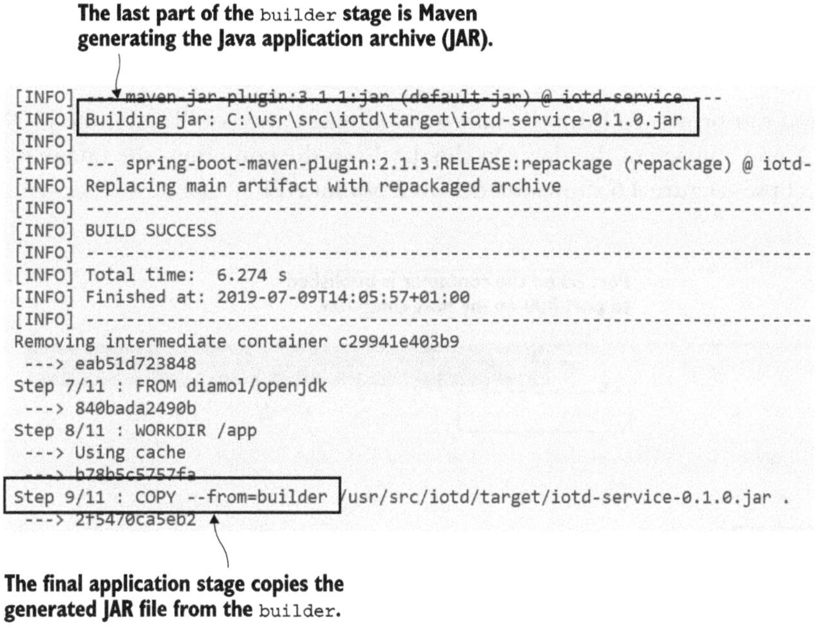

**The last part of the** `builder` **stage is Maven generating the Java application archive (JAR).**

```
[INFO] --- maven-jar-plugin:3.1.1:jar (default-jar) @ iotd-service ---
[INFO] Building jar: C:\usr\src\iotd\target\iotd-service-0.1.0.jar
[INFO]
[INFO] --- spring-boot-maven-plugin:2.1.3.RELEASE:repackage (repackage) @ iotd-
[INFO] Replacing main artifact with repackaged archive
[INFO] ------------------------------------------------------------------------
[INFO] BUILD SUCCESS
[INFO] ------------------------------------------------------------------------
[INFO] Total time:  6.274 s
[INFO] Finished at: 2019-07-09T14:05:57+01:00
[INFO] ------------------------------------------------------------------------
Removing intermediate container c29941e403b9
 ---> eab51d723848
Step 7/11 : FROM diamol/openjdk
 ---> 840bada2490b
Step 8/11 : WORKDIR /app
 ---> Using cache
 ---> b78b5c5757fa
Step 9/11 : COPY --from=builder /usr/src/iotd/target/iotd-service-0.1.0.jar .
 ---> 2f5470ca5eb2
```

**The final application stage copies the generated JAR file from the** `builder`**.**

**Figure 4.5   Output from running a Maven build in Docker**

So what have you just built? It's a simple REST API that wraps access to NASA's Astronomy Picture of the Day service (https://apod.nasa.gov). The Java app fetches the details of today's picture from NASA and caches it, so you can make repeated calls to this application without repeatedly hitting NASA's service.

The Java API is just one part of the full application you'll be running in this chapter—it will actually use multiple containers, and they need to communicate with each other. Containers access each other across a virtual network, using the virtual IP address that Docker allocates when it creates the container. You can create and manage virtual Docker networks through the command line.

**TRY IT NOW**   Create a Docker network for containers to communicate with each other:

```
docker network create nat
```

If you see an error from that command, it's because your setup already has a Docker network called nat, and you can ignore the message. Now when you run containers you can explicitly connect them to that Docker network using the --network flag, and any containers on that network can reach each other using the container names.

> **TRY IT NOW**   Run a container from the image, publishing port 80 to the host computer, and connecting to the nat network:

```
docker container run --name iotd -d -p 800:80 --network nat image-of-
    the-day
```

Now you can browse to http://localhost:800/image and you'll see some JSON details about NASA's image of the day. On the day I ran the container, the image was from a solar eclipse—figure 4.6 shows the details from my API.

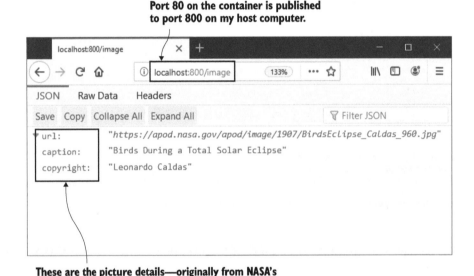

Figure 4.6   The cached details from NASA in my application container

The actual application in this container isn't important (but don't remove it yet—we'll be using it later in the chapter). What's important is that you can build this on any machine with Docker installed, just by having a copy of the source code with the Dockerfile. You don't need any build tools installed, you don't need a specific version of Java—you just clone the code repo, and you're a couple of Docker commands away from running the app.

One other thing to be really clear on here: the build tools are not part of the final application image. You can run an interactive container from your new image-of-the-day Docker image, and you'll find there's no mvn command in there. Only the contents of the final stage in the Dockerfile get made into the application image; anything you want from previous stages needs to be explicitly copied in that final stage.

## 4.3 *App walkthrough: Node.js source code*

We're going to go through another multi-stage Dockerfile, this time for a Node.js application. Organizations are increasingly using diverse technology stacks, so it's good to have an understanding of how different builds look in Docker. Node.js is a great option because of its popularity, and also because it's an example of a different type of build—this pattern also works with other scripted languages like Python, PHP, and Ruby. The source code for this app is at the folder path ch04/exercises/access-log.

Java applications are compiled, so the source code gets copied into the build stage, and that generates a JAR file. The JAR file is the compiled app, and it gets copied into the final application image, but the source code is not. It's the same with .NET Core, where the compiled artifacts are DLLs (Dynamic Link Libraries). Node.js is different—it uses JavaScript, which is an interpreted language, so there's no compilation step. Dockerized Node.js apps need the Node.js runtime and the source code in the application image.

There's still a need for a multi-stage Dockerfile though: it optimizes dependency loading. Node.js uses a tool called npm (the Node package manager) to manage dependencies. Listing 4.3 shows the full Dockerfile for this chapter's Node.js application.

> **Listing 4.3  Dockerfile for building a Node.js app with npm**

```
FROM diamol/node AS builder

WORKDIR /src
COPY src/package.json .

RUN npm install

# app
FROM diamol/node

EXPOSE 80
CMD ["node", "server.js"]

WORKDIR /app
COPY --from=builder /src/node_modules/ /app/node_modules/
COPY src/ .
```

The goal here is the same as for the Java application—to package and run the app with only Docker installed, without having to install any other tools. The base image for both stages is diamol/node, which has the Node.js runtime and npm installed. The builder stage in the Dockerfile copies in the package.json files, which describe all the application's dependencies. Then it runs npm install to download the dependencies. There's no compilation, so that's all it needs to do.

This application is another REST API. In the final application stage, the steps expose the HTTP port and specify the `node` command line as the startup command. The last thing is to create a working directory and copy in the application artifacts. The downloaded dependencies are copied from the builder stage, and the source code is copied from the host computer. The `src` folder contains the JavaScript files, including `server.js`, which is the entry point started by the Node.js process.

We have a different technology stack here, with a different pattern for packaging the application. The base images, tools, and commands for a Node.js app are all different from a Java app, but those differences are captured in the Dockerfile. The process for building and running the app is exactly the same.

**TRY IT NOW**   Browse to the Node.js application source code and build the image:

```
cd ch04/exercises/access-log
docker image build -t access-log .
```

You'll see a whole lot of output from npm (which may show some error and warning messages too, but you can ignore those). Figure 4.7 shows part of the output from my build. The packages that are downloaded get saved in the Docker image layer cache,

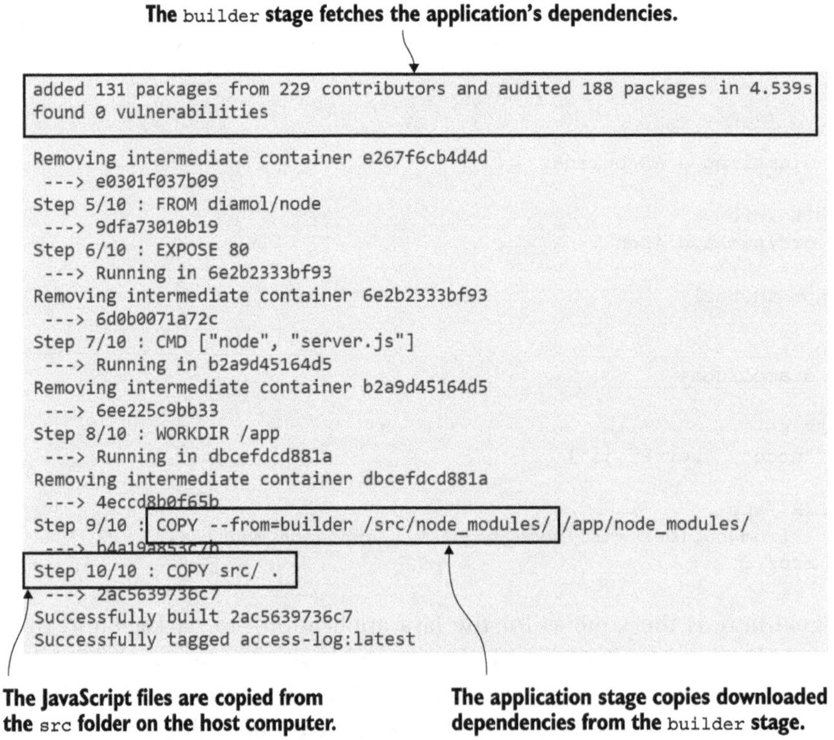

**The `builder` stage fetches the application's dependencies.**

```
added 131 packages from 229 contributors and audited 188 packages in 4.539s
found 0 vulnerabilities

Removing intermediate container e267f6cb4d4d
 ---> e0301f037b09
Step 5/10 : FROM diamol/node
 ---> 9dfa73010b19
Step 6/10 : EXPOSE 80
 ---> Running in 6e2b2333bf93
Removing intermediate container 6e2b2333bf93
 ---> 6d0b0071a72c
Step 7/10 : CMD ["node", "server.js"]
 ---> Running in b2a9d45164d5
Removing intermediate container b2a9d45164d5
 ---> 6ee225c9bb33
Step 8/10 : WORKDIR /app
 ---> Running in dbcefdcd881a
Removing intermediate container dbcefdcd881a
 ---> 4eccd8b0f65b
Step 9/10 : COPY --from=builder /src/node_modules/ /app/node_modules/
 ---> b4a19a853c7b
Step 10/10 : COPY src/ .
 ---> 2ac5639736c7
Successfully built 2ac5639736c7
Successfully tagged access-log:latest
```

**The JavaScript files are copied from the `src` folder on the host computer.**

**The application stage copies downloaded dependencies from the `builder` stage.**

**Figure 4.7   Building a multi-stage Dockerfile for a Node.js application**

so if you work on the app and just make code changes, the next build you run will be super fast.

The Node.js app you've just built is not at all interesting, but you should still run it to check that it's packaged correctly. It's a REST API that other services can call to write logs. There's an HTTP POST endpoint for recording a new log, and a GET endpoint that shows how many logs have been recorded.

**TRY IT NOW** Run a container from the log API image, publishing port 80 to host and connecting it to the same nat network:

```
docker container run --name accesslog -d -p 801:80 --network nat
    access-log
```

Now browse to http://localhost:801/stats and you'll see how many logs the service has recorded. Figure 4.8 shows I have zero logs so far—Firefox nicely formats the API response, but you may see the raw JSON in other browsers.

**Port 80 on the Node.js container is published to port 801 on my host computer.**

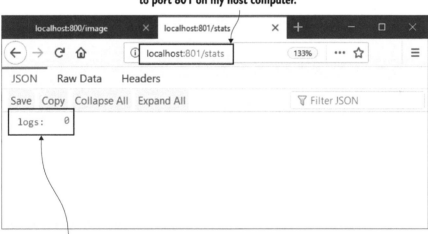

**No logs so far—this number will increase when other services use the log API.**

**Figure 4.8  Running the Node.js API in a container**

The log API is running in Node.js version 10.16, but just like with the Java example, you don't need any versions of Node.js or any other tools installed to build and run this app. The workflow in this Dockerfile downloads dependencies and then copies the script files into the final image. You can use the exact same approach with Python, using Pip for dependencies, or Ruby using Gems.

## 4.4 App walkthrough: Go source code

We've got one last example of a multi-stage Dockerfile—for a web application written in Go. Go is a modern, cross-platform language that compiles to native binaries. That means you can compile your apps to run on any platform (Windows, Linux, Intel, or Arm), and the compiled output is the complete application. You don't need a separate runtime installed like you do with Java, .NET Core, Node.js, or Python, and that makes for extremely small Docker images.

There are a few other languages that also compile to native binaries—Rust and Swift are popular—but Go has the widest platform support, and it's also a very popular language for cloud-native apps (Docker itself is written in Go). Building Go apps in Docker means using a multi-stage Dockerfile approach similar to the one you used for the Java app, but there are some important differences. Listing 4.4 shows the full Dockerfile.

> **Listing 4.4   Dockerfile for building a Go application from source**

```
FROM diamol/golang AS builder

COPY main.go .
RUN go build -o /server

# app
FROM diamol/base

ENV IMAGE_API_URL="http://iotd/image" \
    ACCESS_API_URL="http://accesslog/access-log"
CMD ["/web/server"]

WORKDIR web
COPY index.html .
COPY --from=builder /server .
RUN chmod +x server
```

Go compiles to native binaries, so each stage in the Dockerfile uses a different base image. The builder stage uses `diamol/golang`, which has all the Go tools installed. Go applications don't usually fetch dependencies, so this stage goes straight to building the application (which is just one code file, `main.go`). The final application stage uses a minimal image, which just has the smallest layer of operating system tools, called `diamol/base`.

The Dockerfile captures some configuration settings as environment variables and specifies the startup command as the compiled binary. The application stage ends by copying in the HTML file the application serves from the host and the web server binary from the builder stage. Binaries need to be explicitly marked as executable in Linux, which is what the final `chmod` command does (this has no effect on Windows).

> **TRY IT NOW**   Browse to the Go application source code and build the image:

```
cd ch04/exercises/image-gallery
docker image build -t image-gallery .
```

This time there won't be a lot of compiler output, because Go is quiet and only writes logs when there are failures. You can see my abbreviated output in figure 4.9.

**The app is compiled in the** `builder` **stage. Go doesn't write output logs when the build is successful.**

```
Step 3/10 : RUN go build -o /server
 ---> Running in 4c82369bdd7d
Removing intermediate container 4c82369bdd7d
 ---> 86dd4bcd457b
Step 4/10 : FROM diamol/base
 ---> 055936d39205
Step 5/10 : ENV IMAGE_API_URL="http://iotd/image"
 ---> Running in 71a2577def79
Removing intermediate container 71a2577def79
 ---> a876b44cbe31
Step 6/10 : CMD ["/web/server"]
 ---> Running in cdb6cbd72371
Removing intermediate container cdb6cbd72371
 ---> 9c32166ff4c9
Step 7/10 : WORKDIR web
 ---> Running in cfeff2048a98
Removing intermediate container cfeff2048a98
 ---> 69f36239586b
Step 8/10 : COPY index.html .
 ---> ac083fe04427
Step 9/10 : COPY --from=builder /server .
 ---> c03a4156eca6
```

**The web server binary is copied from the** `builder` **stage.**

**HTML assets are copied from the host computer into the final image.**

Figure 4.9   Building a Go application in a multi-stage Dockerfile

This Go application does do something useful, but before you run it, it's worth taking a look at the size of the images that go in and come out.

**TRY IT NOW**   Compare the Go application image size with the Go toolset image:

```
docker image ls -f reference=diamol/golang -f reference=image-gallery
```

Many Docker commands let you filter the output. This command lists all images and filters the output to only include images with a reference of `diamol/golang` or `image-gallery`—the reference is really just the image name. When you run this, you'll see how important it is to choose the right base images for your Dockerfile stages:

```
REPOSITORY       TAG      IMAGE ID      CREATED          SIZE
image-gallery    latest   b41869f5d153  20 minutes ago   25.3MB
diamol/golang    latest   ad57f5c226fc  2 hours ago      774MB
```

On Linux, the image with all the Go tools installed comes in at over 770 MB; the actual Go application image is only 25 MB. Remember, that's the virtual image size, so a lot of those layers can be shared between different images. The important saving isn't so much the disk space, but all the software that *isn't* in the final image. The application doesn't need any of the Go tools at runtime. By using a minimal base image for the application, we're saving nearly 750 MB of software, which is a huge reduction in the surface area for potential attacks.

Now you can run the app. This ties together your work in this chapter, because the Go application actually uses the APIs from the other applications you've built. You should make sure you have those containers running, with the correct names from the earlier try-it-now exercises. If you run `docker container ls`, you should see two containers from this chapter—the Node.js container called `accesslog` and the Java container called `iotd`. When you run the Go container, it will use the APIs from the other containers.

> **TRY IT NOW**   Run the Go application image, publishing the host port and con-
> necting to the nat network:

```
docker container run -d -p 802:80 --network nat image-gallery
```

You can browse to http://localhost:802 and you'll see NASA's Astronomy Picture of the Day. Figure 4.10 shows the image when I ran my containers.

**Port 802 on the host publishes port 80 from the
Go application container, which renders the web page.**

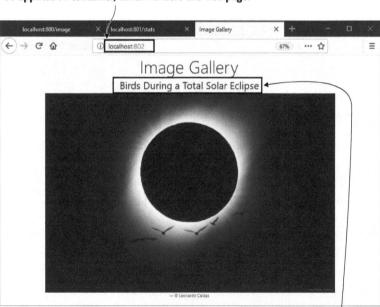

**The Go app fetches image details from the Java API,
running in a container on the same Docker network.**

Figure 4.10   The Go web application, showing data fetched from the Java API

Right now you're running a distributed application across three containers. The Go web application calls the Java API to get details of the image to show, and then it calls the Node.js API to log that the site has been accessed. You didn't need to install any tools for any of those languages to build and run all the apps; you just needed the source code and Docker.

Multi-stage Dockerfiles make your project entirely portable. You might use Jenkins to build your apps right now, but you could try AppVeyor's managed CI service or Azure DevOps without having to write any new pipeline code—they all support Docker, so your pipeline is just `docker image build`.

## 4.5 *Understanding multi-stage Dockerfiles*

We've covered a lot of ground in this chapter, and I'm going to end with some key points so you're really clear on how multi-stage Dockerfiles work, and why it's incredibly useful to build your apps inside containers.

The first point is about standardization. I know when you run the exercises for this chapter that your builds will succeed and your apps will work because you're using the exact same set of tools that I'm using. It doesn't matter what operating system you have or what's installed on your machine—all the builds run in Docker containers, and the container images have all the correct versions of the tools. In your real projects you'll find that this hugely simplifies on-boarding for new developers, eliminates the maintenance burden for build servers, and removes the potential for breakages where users have different versions of tools.

The second point is performance. Each stage in a multi-stage build has its own cache. Docker looks for a match in the image layer cache for each instruction; if it doesn't find one, the cache is broken and all the rest of the instructions are executed—but only for that stage. The next stage starts again from the cache. You'll be spending time structuring your Dockerfiles carefully, and when you get the optimization done, you'll find 90% of your build steps use the cache.

The final point is that multi-stage Dockerfiles let you fine-tune your build so the final application image is as lean as possible. This is not just for compilers—any tooling you need can be isolated in earlier stages, so the tool itself isn't present in the final image. A good example is curl—a popular command-line tool you can use for downloading content from the internet. You might need that to download files your app needs, but you can do that in an early stage in your Dockerfile so curl itself isn't installed in your application image. This keeps image size down, which means faster startup times, but it also means you have less software available in your application image, which means fewer potential exploits for attackers.

## 4.6 *Lab*

Lab time! You're going to put into practice what you've learned about multi-stage builds and optimizing Dockerfiles. In the source code for the book, you'll find a folder at ch04/lab which is your starting point. It's a simple Go web server application, which already has a Dockerfile, so you can build and run it in Docker. But the Docker-file is in dire need of optimizing, and that is your job.

There are specific goals for this lab:

- Start by building an image using the existing Dockerfile, and then optimize the Dockerfile to produce a new image.
- The current image is 800 MB on Linux and 5.2 GB on Windows. Your opti-mized image should be around 15 MB on Linux or 260 MB on Windows.
- If you change the HTML content with the current Dockerfile, the build exe-cutes seven steps.
- Your optimized Dockerfile should only execute a single step when you change the HTML.

As always, there's a sample solution on the book's GitHub repository. But this is one lab you should really try and find time to do, because optimizing Dockerfiles is a valu-able skill you'll use in every project. If you need it, though, my solution is here: https://github.com/sixeyed/diamol/blob/master/ch04/lab/Dockerfile.optimized.

No hints this time, although I would say this sample app looks very similar to one you've already built in this chapter.

# *Sharing images with Docker Hub and other registries*

You've spent the last few chapters getting a good understanding of the *build* and *run* parts of the Docker workflow—now it's time for *share*. Sharing is all about taking the images you've built on your local machine and making them available for other people to use. I really think this is the most important part of the Docker equation. Packaging your software along with all its dependencies means anyone can use it easily, on any machine—there are no gaps between environments, so there are no more days wasted setting up software or tracking down bugs that are actually deployment problems.

## 5.1 Working with registries, repositories, and image tags

Software distribution is built into the Docker platform. You've already seen that you can run a container from an image, and if you don't have that image locally, Docker will download it. The server that stores images centrally is called a Docker registry. Docker Hub is the most popular image registry, hosting hundreds of thousands of images, which are downloaded billions of times every month. It's also the default registry for the Docker Engine, which means it's the first place Docker looks for images that aren't available locally.

Docker images need a name, and that name contains enough information for Docker to find the exact image you're looking for. So far we've used very simple names with one or two parts, like `image-gallery` or `diamol/golang`. There are actually four parts to a full image name (which is properly called the *image reference*). Figure 5.1 shows all those parts in the full reference for `diamol/golang`:

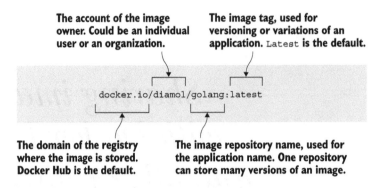

**Figure 5.1   Anatomy of a Docker image reference**

You'll be making use of all the parts of an image reference when you start managing your own application images. On your local machine you can name images anything you like, but when you want to share them on a registry, you'll need to add some more details, because the image reference is a unique identifier for one specific image on a registry.

Docker uses a couple of defaults if you don't provide values for parts of the image reference. The default registry is Docker Hub, and the default tag is latest. Docker Hub's domain is docker.io so my image, diamol/golang, is a short version of docker.io/diamol/golang:latest. You can use either of those references. The diamol account is an organization on Docker Hub, and golang is a repository within that organization. It's a public repository, so anyone can pull the image, but you need to be a member of the diamol organization to push images.

Large companies usually have their own Docker registry in their own cloud environment or their local network. You target your own registry by including the domain name in the first part of the reference, so Docker knows not to use Docker Hub. If I hosted my own registry at r.sixeyed.com, my image could be stored at r.sixeyed .com/diamol/golang. That's all pretty simple, but the most important part of the image reference is the tag.

You haven't used image tags so far because it's simpler to get started without them, but when you start building your own application images, you should always tag them. Tags are used to identify different versions of the same application. The official Docker OpenJDK image has hundreds of tags—openjdk:13 is the latest release, openjdk:8u212-jdk is a specific release of Java 8, and there are more for different Linux distributions and Windows versions. If you don't specify a tag when you create an image, Docker uses the default tag latest. That's a misleading name, because the image tagged "latest" might not actually be the most recent image version. When you push your own images, you should always tag them with explicit versions.

## 5.2   *Pushing your own images to Docker Hub*

We'll get started by pushing one of the images you built in chapter 4 up to Docker
Hub. You'll need a Docker Hub account for that—if you don't have one, browse to
https://hub.docker.com and follow the link to sign up for an account (it's free and it
won't get you a ton of spam in your inbox).

    You need to do two things to push an image to a registry. First you need to log in to
the registry with the Docker command line, so Docker can check that your user
account is authorized to push images. Then you need to give your image a reference
that includes the name of an account where you have permission to push.

    Every reader will have their own Docker Hub username, so to make it easier to fol-
low along with the exercises, let's start by capturing your own Docker ID in a variable
in your terminal session. After this, you'll be able to copy and paste the rest of this
chapter's commands.

> **TRY IT NOW**   Open a terminal session and save your Docker Hub ID in a vari-
> able. Your Docker ID is your username, not your email address. This is one
> command that is different on Windows and Linux, so you'll need to choose
> the right option:

```
# using PowerShell on Windows
$dockerId="<your-docker-id-goes-here>"

# using Bash on Linux or Mac
export dockerId="<your-docker-id-goes-here>"
```

I'm running Windows at the moment, and my Docker Hub username is sixeyed, so the
command I run is $dockerId="sixeyed"; on Linux I would run dockerId="sixeyed".
On any system, you can run echo $dockerId and you should see your username dis-
played. From now on, you can copy the commands in the exercises and they'll use
your Docker ID.

    Start by logging in to Docker Hub. It's actually the Docker Engine that pushes and
pulls images, but you authenticate using the Docker command line—when you run the
login command, it will ask for your password, which is your Docker Hub password.

> **TRY IT NOW**   Log in to Docker Hub. Hub is the default registry, so you don't
> need to specify a domain name:

```
docker login --username $dockerId
```

You'll see output like mine in figure 5.2—sensibly, Docker doesn't show the password
when you type it in.

    Now that you're logged in, you can push images to your own account or to any
organizations you have access to. I don't know you, but if I wanted your help looking
after the images for this book, I could add your account to the diamol organization,
and you would be able to push images that start with diamol/. If you're not a member
of any organizations, you can only push images to repositories in your own account.

**You log in to a registry using the Docker CLI. Docker Hub is the default registry, so you don't need to specify a domain.**

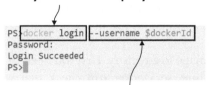

**The username is your registry username—your Docker Hub account in this case, which you've saved in a variable.**

Figure 5.2    Logging in to Docker Hub

You built a Docker image called `image-gallery` in chapter 4. That image reference doesn't have an account name, so you can't push it to any registries. You don't need to rebuild the image to give it a new reference though—images can have several references.

**TRY IT NOW**    Create a new reference for your existing image, tagging it as version 1:

```
docker image tag image-gallery $dockerId/image-gallery:v1
```

Now you have two references; one has an account and version number, but both references point to the same image. Images also have a unique ID, and you can see when you list them if a single image ID has multiple references.

**TRY IT NOW**    List the `image-gallery` image references:

```
docker image ls --filter reference=image-gallery --filter
    reference='*/image-gallery'
```

You'll see similar output to mine in figure 5.3, except your tagged image will show your Docker Hub username instead of `sixeyed`.

**They have the same image ID, which means it's one image with two references.**

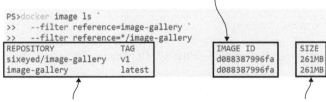

**There are two image references that match the filters 1 supplied— these could be two different images.**

**Both references have a virtual size of 261 MB, but physically they share the same image layers.**

Figure 5.3    One image with two references

You now have an image reference with your Docker ID in the account name, and you're logged in to Docker Hub, so you're ready to share your image! The `docker image push` command is the counterpart of the `pull` command; it uploads your local image layers to the registry.

**TRY IT NOW**    List the `image-gallery` image references:

```
docker image push $dockerId/image-gallery:v1
```

Docker registries work at the level of image layers in the same way as the local Docker Engine. You push an image, but Docker actually uploads the image layers. In the output you'll see a list of layer IDs and their upload progress. In my (abbreviated) output, you can see the layers being pushed:

```
The push refers to repository [docker.io/sixeyed/image-gallery]
c8c60e5dbe37: Pushed
2caab880bb11: Pushed
3fcd399f2c98: Pushed
...
v1: digest: sha256:127d0ed6f7a8d1... size: 2296
```

The fact that registries work with image layers is another reason why you need to spend time optimizing your Dockerfiles. Layers are only physically uploaded to the registry if there isn't an existing match for that layer's hash. It's like your local Docker Engine cache, but applied across all images on the registry. If you optimize to the point where 90% of layers come from the cache when you build, 90% of those layers will already be in the registry when you push. Optimized Dockerfiles reduce build time, disk space, and network bandwidth.

You can browse to Docker Hub now and check your image. The Docker Hub UI uses the same repository name format as image references, so you can work out the URL of your image from your account name.

**TRY IT NOW**    This little script writes the URL to your image's page on Docker Hub:

```
echo "https://hub.docker.com/r/$dockerId/image-gallery/tags"
```

When you browse to that URL, you'll see something like figure 5.4, showing the tags for your image and the last update time.

That's all there is to pushing images. Docker Hub creates a new repository for an image if it doesn't already exist, and by default that repository has public read rights. Now anyone can find, pull, and use your `image-gallery` application. They'd need to work out themselves how to use it, but you can put documentation on Docker Hub too.

Docker Hub is the easiest registry to get started with, and it gives you a huge amount of functionality for zero cost—although you can pay a monthly subscription for extra features, like private repositories. There are lots of alternative registries too.

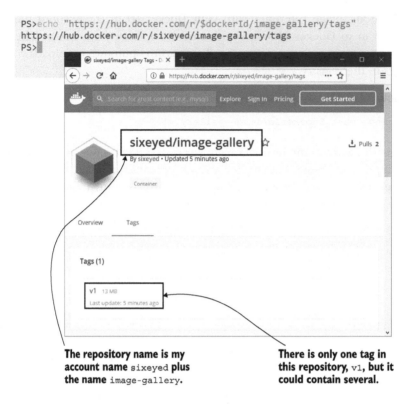

```
PS>echo "https://hub.docker.com/r/$dockerId/image-gallery/tags"
https://hub.docker.com/r/sixeyed/image-gallery/tags
PS>
```

**The repository name is my account name** sixeyed **plus the name** image-gallery.

**There is only one tag in this repository,** v1, **but it could contain several.**

Figure 5.4   Image listings on Docker Hub

The registry is an open API spec, and the core registry server is an open source product from Docker. All the clouds have their own registry services, and you can manage your own registry in the datacenter with commercial products like Docker Trusted Registry or you can run a simple registry in a container.

## 5.3   *Running and using your own Docker registry*

It's useful to run your own registry on your local network. It cuts down on bandwidth use and transfer times, and it lets you own the data in your environment. Even if you're not concerned about that, it's still good to know that you can spin up a local registry quickly, which you can use as a backup option if your main registry goes offline.

Docker maintains the core registry server on GitHub in the source code repository docker/distribution. It gives you the basic functionality to push and pull images, and it uses the same layer cache system as Docker Hub, but it doesn't give you the web UI you get with Hub. It's a super-lightweight server that I've packaged into a diamol image, so you can run it in a container.

**TRY IT NOW** Run the Docker registry in a container, using my image:

```
# run the registry with a restart flag so the container gets
# restarted whenever you restart Docker:
docker container run -d -p 5000:5000 --restart always diamol/registry
```

You now have a registry server on your local machine. The default port for the server is 5000, which this command publishes. You can tag images with the domain local-host:5000 and push them to this registry, but that's not really useful—you can only use the registry on your local machine. Instead, it's better to give your machine an alias so you can use a proper domain name for your registry.

This next command creates that alias. It will give your computer the name registry.local, in addition to any other network names it has. It does this by writing to the computer's hosts file, which is a simple text file that links network names to IP addresses.

**TRY IT NOW** Windows, Linux, and Mac machines all use the same hosts file format, but the file paths are different. The command is also different on Windows, so you'll need to choose the right one:

```
# using PowerShell on Windows
Add-Content -Value "127.0.0.1  registry.local" -Path
    /windows/system32/drivers/etc/hosts

# using Bash on Linux or Mac
echo $'\n127.0.0.1  registry.local' | sudo tee -a /etc/hosts
```

If you get a permissions error from that command, you'll need to be logged in with administrator privileges in an elevated PowerShell session on Windows, or use sudo on Linux or Mac. When you've run the command successfully, you should be able to run ping registry.local and see a response from your computer's home IP address, 127.0.0.1, as in figure 5.5.

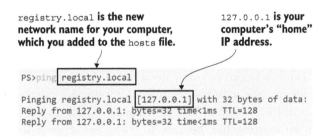

registry.local **is the new network name for your computer, which you added to the** hosts **file.**

127.0.0.1 **is your computer's "home" IP address.**

```
PS>ping registry.local

Pinging registry.local [127.0.0.1] with 32 bytes of data:
Reply from 127.0.0.1: bytes=32 time<1ms TTL=128
Reply from 127.0.0.1: bytes=32 time<1ms TTL=128
```

**Figure 5.5  Adding a new network alias for your computer**

Now you can use the domain name registry.local:5000 in your image references to use your registry. Adding the domain name to an image involves the same process of tagging that you've already done for Docker Hub. This time you just include the registry domain in the new image reference.

> **TRY IT NOW**   Tag your `image-gallery` image with your registry domain:

```
docker image tag image-gallery registry.local:5000/gallery/ui:v1
```

Your local registry doesn't have any authentication or authorization set up. That's obviously not production quality, but it might work for a small team, and it does let you use your own image-naming schemes. Three containers make up the NASA image-of-the-day app in chapter 4—you could tag all the images to group them together using `gallery` as the project name:

- `registry.local:5000/gallery/ui:v1`—The Go web UI
- `registry.local:5000/gallery/api:v1`—The Java API
- `registry.local:5000/gallery/logs:v1`—The Node.js API

There's one more thing you need to do before you can push this image to your local registry. The registry container is using plain-text HTTP rather than encrypted HTTPS to push and pull images. Docker won't communicate with an unencrypted registry by default, because it's not secure. You need to explicitly add your registry domain to a list of permitted insecure registries before Docker will let you use it.

This brings us to configuring Docker. The Docker Engine uses a JSON configuration file for all sorts of settings, including where Docker stores the image layers on disk, where the Docker API listens for connections, and which insecure registries are permitted. The file is called `daemon.json` and it usually lives in the folder `C:\ProgramData\docker\config` on Windows Server, and `/etc/docker` on Linux. You can edit that file directly, but if you're using Docker Desktop on Mac or Windows, you'll need use the UI, where you can change the main configuration settings.

> **TRY IT NOW**   Right-click the Docker whale icon in your taskbar, and select Settings (or Preferences on the Mac). Then open the Daemon tab and enter `registry.local:5000` in the insecure registries list—you can see my settings in figure 5.6.

The Docker Engine needs to be restarted to load any new configuration settings, and Docker Desktop does that for you when you apply changes.

If you're not running Docker Desktop, you'll need to do this manually. Start by opening the `daemon.json` file in a text editor—or create it if it doesn't exist—and add the insecure registry details in JSON format. The configuration settings will look like this—but if you're editing an existing file, be sure to leave the original settings in there too:

```
{
    "insecure-registries": [
        "registry.local:5000"
    ]
}
```

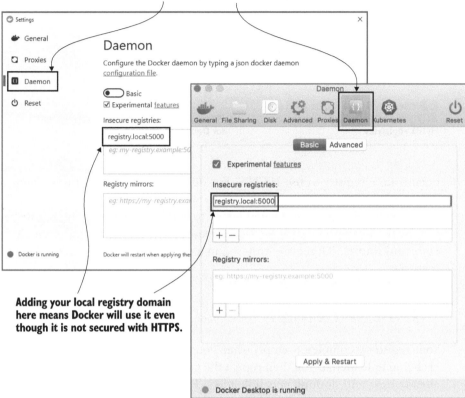

**Docker Desktop has different styling on Windows and Mac, but both allow you to configure the Docker Engine.**

**Adding your local registry domain here means Docker will use it even though it is not secured with HTTPS.**

Figure 5.6  Allowing an insecure registry to be used in Docker Desktop

Then restart Docker using `Restart-Service docker` on Windows Server, or `service docker restart` on Linux. You can check which insecure registries your Docker Engine allows, along with a stack of other information, using the `info` command.

**TRY IT NOW**  List the information about your Docker Engine and check your registry is in the insecure registries list:

```
docker info
```

At the end of the output, you'll see the registry configuration, which should include your insecure registry—you can see mine in figure 5.7.

You should be careful about adding insecure registries to your Docker configuration. Your connection could be compromised, and attackers could read layers when you push images. Or worse, they could inject their own data when you pull images. All the commercial registry servers run on HTTPS, and you can also configure Docker's

**The default registry is Docker Hub—you can't change this.**

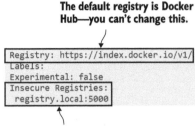

```
Registry: https://index.docker.io/v1/
Labels:
Experimental: false
Insecure Registries:
  registry.local:5000
```

**Registries listed here can be used over HTTP; otherwise Docker will only use HTTPS registries.**

Figure 5.7    Insecure registries allowed for Docker to use

open source registry to use HTTPS. For demonstrating with a local server, however, it's an acceptable risk.

You can now push your tagged image to your own registry. The registry domain is part of the image reference, so Docker knows to use something other than Docker Hub, and your HTTP registry running in a container is cleared in the list of insecure registries.

**TRY IT NOW**    Push your tagged image:

```
docker image push registry.local:5000/gallery/ui:v1
```

Your registry is completely empty when you run the first push, so you'll see all the layers being uploaded. If you then repeat the push command, you'll see that all the layers already exist and nothing gets uploaded. That's all you need to do to run your own Docker registry in a container. You could share it on your network using your machine's IP address or the real domain name.

## 5.4    *Using image tags effectively*

You can put any string into a Docker image tag, and as you've already seen, you can have multiple tags for the same image. You'll use that to version the software in your images and let users make informed choices about what they want to use—and to make your own informed choices when you use other people's images.

Many software projects use a numeric versioning scheme with decimal points to indicate how big a change there is between versions, and you can do that with your image tags. The basic idea is something like [major].[minor].[patch], which has some implicit guarantees. A release that only increments the patch number might have bug fixes, but it should have the same features as the last version; a release that increments the minor version might add features but shouldn't remove any; and a major release could have completely different features.

If you use the same approach with your image tags, you can let users choose whether to stick to a major version or a minor version, or just always have the latest release.

**TRY IT NOW** Create a few new tags for the Go application you have packaged in the image to indicate the major, minor, and patch release versions:

```
docker image tag image-gallery registry.local:5000/gallery/ui:latest
docker image tag image-gallery registry.local:5000/gallery/ui:2
docker image tag image-gallery registry.local:5000/gallery/ui:2.1
docker image tag image-gallery registry.local:5000/gallery/ui:2.1.106
```

Now imagine that an application has monthly releases, which increment the version numbers. Figure 5.8 shows how the image tags might evolve over releases from July to October.

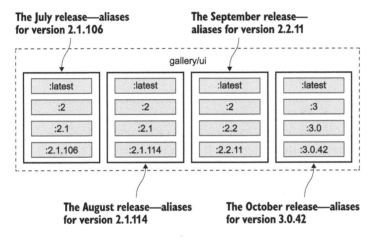

Figure 5.8 The evolution of image tags during software releases

You can see that some of these image tags are a moving target. `gallery/ui:2.1` is an alias for the 2.1.106 release in July, but in August the same 2.1 tag is an alias for the 2.1.114 release. `gallery/ui:2` is also an alias for 2.1.106 in July, but by September the 2 tag is an alias for the 2.2.11 release. The latest tag has the most movement—in July `gallery/ui` is an alias for 2.1.106, but in October it's an alias for 3.0.42.

This is a typical versioning scheme you'll see for Docker images. It's one you should adopt yourself, because it lets users of your image choose how current they want to be. They can pin to a specific patch version in their image pull commands, or in the FROM instruction in their Dockerfiles, and be sure that the image they use will always be the same. The 2.1.106 tag in this example is the same image from July through October. If they want to get patch updates, they can use the 2.1 tag, and if they want to get minor releases they can use the 2 tag.

Any of those choices is fine; it's just a case of balancing risk—using a specific patch version means the application will be the same whenever you use it, but you won't get security fixes. Using a major version means you'll get all the latest fixes, but there might be unexpected feature changes down the line.

It's especially important to use specific image tags for the base images in your own Dockerfiles. It's great to use the product team's build tools image to build your apps and their runtime image to package your apps, but if you don't specify versions in the tags, you're setting yourself up for trouble in the future. A new release of the build image could break your Docker build. Or worse, a new release of the runtime could break your application.

## 5.5 *Turning official images into golden images*

There's one last thing to understand when you're looking at Docker Hub and other registries: can you trust the images you find there? Anyone can push an image to Docker Hub and make it publicly available. For hackers, that's a nice way to distribute malware; you just need to give your image an innocent name and a fake description, and wait for people to start using it. Docker Hub solves that problem with verified publishers and official images.

*Verified publishers* are companies like Microsoft, Oracle, and IBM, who publish images on Docker Hub. Their images go through an approval process that includes security scanning for vulnerabilities; they may also be certified, which means they have the backing of Docker and the publisher. If you want to run off-the-shelf software in containers, certified images from verified publishers are the best bet.

*Official images* are something different—they're usually open source projects, maintained jointly by the project team and Docker. They're security scanned and regularly updated, and they conform to Dockerfile best practices. All the content for the official images is open source, so you can see the Dockerfiles on GitHub. Most people start using official images as the base for their own images but at some point find they need more control. Then they introduce their own preferred base images, called *golden images*—figure 5.9 shows you how it works.

Golden images use an official image as the base and then add in whatever custom setup they need, such as installing security certificates or configuring default environment settings. The golden image lives in the company's repositories on Docker Hub or in their own registry, and all application images are based on the golden image. This approach offers the benefits of the official image—with the best-practice setup by the project team—but with the extra config you need.

> **TRY IT NOW**   There are two Dockerfiles in the source code for this chapter that can be built as golden images for .NET Core apps. Browse to each folder and build the image:

```
cd ch05/exercises/dotnet-sdk
docker image build -t golden/dotnetcore-sdk:3.0 .

cd ../aspnet-runtime
docker image build -t golden/aspnet-core:3.0 .
```

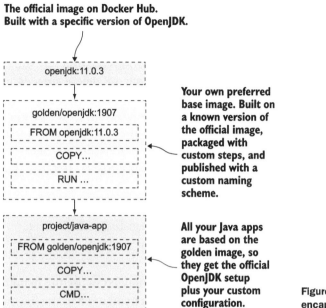

The official image on Docker Hub. Built with a specific version of OpenJDK.

Your own preferred base image. Built on a known version of the official image, packaged with custom steps, and published with a custom naming scheme.

All your Java apps are based on the golden image, so they get the official OpenJDK setup plus your custom configuration.

Figure 5.9 Using a golden image to encapsulate an official image

There's nothing special about golden images. They start with a Dockerfile, and that builds an image with your own reference and naming scheme. If you look at the Docker-files you've built, you'll see that they add some metadata to the image using the LABEL instruction, and they set up some common configuration. Now you can use those images in a multi-stage Dockerfile for a .NET Core application, which would look something like listing 5.1.

---

**Listing 5.1   A multi-stage Dockerfile using .NET Core golden images**

```
FROM golden/dotnetcore-sdk:3.0 AS builder
COPY . .
RUN dotnet publish -o /out/app app.csproj

FROM golden/aspnet-core:3.0
COPY --from=builder /out /app
CMD ["dotnet", "/app/app.dll"]
```

The application Dockerfile has the same format as any multi-stage build, but now you own the base images. The official images may have a new release every month, but you can choose to restrict your golden images to quarterly updates. And golden images open up one other possibility—you can enforce their use with tools in your continuous integration (CI) pipeline: Dockerfiles can be scanned, and if someone tries to build an app without using golden images, that build fails. It's a good way of locking down the source images teams can use.

## 5.6    *Lab*

This lab is going to take some detective work, but it will be worth it in the end. You're going to need to dig around the Docker Registry API v2 specification (https://docs .docker.com/registry/spec/api/), because the REST API is the only way you can interact with your local Docker registry—you can't search or delete images using the Docker CLI (yet).

The goal for this lab is to push all the tags for your gallery/ui image to your local registry, check that they're all there, and then delete them all and check that they're gone. We won't include the gallery/api or gallery/logs images because this lab focuses on images with multiple tags, and we have those for gallery/ui. Here are a few hints:

- You can use a single image push command to push all these tags.
- The URL for your local registry API is http://registry.local:5000/v2.
- Start by listing the image tags for the repository.
- Then you'll need to get the image manifest.
- You can delete images through the API, but you need to use the manifest.
- Read the docs—there's a specific request header you need to use in your HEAD request.

The solution is on the book's GitHub repository, and this is a rare case where it's OK to cheat a little. The first couple of steps should be straightforward for you to work out, but then it gets a little awkward, so don't feel too bad if you end up heading here: https://github.com/sixeyed/diamol/tree/master/ch05/lab.

Good luck. And remember to read the docs.

# Using Docker volumes
## for persistent storage

6

Containers are a perfect runtime for stateless applications. You can meet increased demand by running multiple containers on your cluster, knowing that every container will handle requests in the same way. You can release updates with an automated rolling upgrade, which keeps your app online the whole time.

But not all parts of your app will be stateless. There will be components that use disks to improve performance or for permanent data storage. And you can run those components in Docker containers too.

Storage does add complications, so you need to understand how to Dockerize stateful apps. This chapter takes you through Docker volumes and mounts, and shows you how the container filesystem works.

## 6.1 Why data in containers is not permanent

A Docker container has a filesystem with a single disk drive, and the contents of that drive are populated with the files from the image. You've seen that already: when you use the COPY instruction in a Dockerfile, the files and directories you copy into the image are there when you run a container from the image. And you know Docker images are stored as multiple layers, so the container's disk is actually a virtual filesystem that Docker builds up by merging all the image layers together.

Each container has its own filesystem, independent of other containers. You can run multiple containers from the same Docker image, and they will all start with the same disk contents. The application can alter files in one container, and that won't affect the files in other containers—or in the image. That's straightforward to see by running a couple of containers that write data, and then looking at their output.

**TRY IT NOW**    Open a terminal session and run two containers from the same image. The application in the image writes a random number to a file in the container:

```
docker container run --name rn1 diamol/ch06-random-number
```

```
docker container run --name rn2 diamol/ch06-random-number
```

That container runs a script when it starts, and the script writes some random data to a text file and then ends, so those containers are in the exited state. The two containers started from the same image, but they will have different file contents. You learned in chapter 2 that Docker doesn't delete the container's filesystem when it exits—it's retained so you can still access files and folders.

The Docker CLI has the `docker container cp` command to copy files between containers and the local machine. You specify the name of the container and the file path, and you can use that to copy the generated random number files from these containers onto your host computer, so you can read the contents.

**TRY IT NOW**    Use `docker container cp` to copy the random number file from each of the containers, and then check the contents:

```
docker container cp rn1:/random/number.txt number1.txt
```

```
docker container cp rn2:/random/number.txt number2.txt
```

```
cat number1.txt
```

```
cat number2.txt
```

Your output will be similar to mine in figure 6.1. Each container has written a file at the same path, `/random/number.txt`, but when the files are copied onto the local machine, you can see that the contents are different. This is a simple way of showing that every container has an independent filesystem. In this case it's a single file that's different, but these could be database containers that start with the same SQL engine running, but store completely different data.

The filesystem inside a container appears to be a single disk: `/dev/sda1` on Linux containers and `C:\` on Windows containers. But that disk is a virtual filesystem that Docker builds from several sources and presents to the container as a single unit. The basic sources for that filesystem are the image layers, which can be shared between containers, and the container's writeable layer, which is unique to each container.

Figure 6.2 shows how that looks for the random number image and the two containers. You should take away two important things from figure 6.2: image layers are shared so they have to be read-only, and there is one writeable layer per container, which has the same life cycle as the container. Image layers have their own life cycle—any images you pull will stay in your local cache until you remove them. But the container writeable layer is created by Docker when the container is started, and it's

**This runs two containers from the same image.** rn1 **and** rn2 **will start with the exact same filesystem contents from the image.**

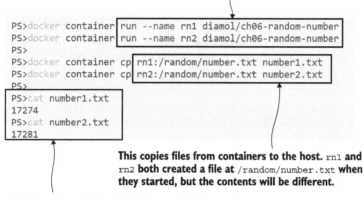

```
PS>docker container run --name rn1 diamol/ch06-random-number
PS>docker container run --name rn2 diamol/ch06-random-number
PS>
PS>docker container cp rn1:/random/number.txt number1.txt
PS>docker container cp rn2:/random/number.txt number2.txt
PS>
PS>cat number1.txt
17274
PS>cat number2.txt
17281
```

**This copies files from containers to the host.** rn1 **and** rn2 **both created a file at** /random/number.txt **when they started, but the contents will be different.**

**Reading the contents of the files copied from each container. The random numbers are different.**

**Figure 6.1   Running containers that write data, and checking the data**

**The writeable layer is unique to each container. This is how** /random/number.txt **exists with different contents in** rn1 **and** rn2.

```
   rn1                                              rn2

 writeable            diamol/ch06-                writeable
                      random-number

                        App layer

                        Base OS
```

**The image has two read-only layers.**

**Containers from the image use those layers and add a writeable layer of their own.**

**Figure 6.2   The container filesystem is built from image layers and a writeable layer.**

deleted by Docker when the container is removed. (Stopping a container doesn't automatically remove it, so a stopped container's filesystem does still exist.)

Of course, the writeable layer isn't just for creating new files. A container can edit existing files from the image layers. But image layers are read-only, so Docker does some special magic to make that happen. It uses a *copy-on-write* process to allow edits to files that come from read-only layers. When the container tries to edit a file in an image layer, Docker actually makes a copy of that file into the writable layer, and the edits happen there. It's all seamless for the container and the application, but it's the cornerstone of Docker's super-efficient use of storage.

Let's work through that with one more simple example, before we move on to running some more useful stateful containers. In this exercise you'll run a container that prints out the contents of a file from an image layer. Then you'll update the file contents and run the container again to see what's changed.

> **TRY IT NOW**   Run these commands to start a container that prints out its file contents, then change the file, and start the container again to print out the new file contents:

```
docker container run --name f1 diamol/ch06-file-display

echo "http://eltonstoneman.com" > url.txt

docker container cp url.txt f1:/input.txt

docker container start --attach f1
```

This time you're using Docker to copy a file from your host computer into the container, and the target path is the file that the container displays. When you start the container again, the same script runs, but now it prints out different contents—you can see my output in figure 6.3.

Modifying the file in the container affects how that container runs, but it doesn't affect the image or any other containers from that image. The changed file only lives

**This container prints out the contents of the** input.txt **file when it runs. This first run uses the** input.txt **contents from the image.**

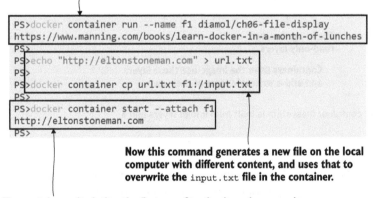

```
PS>docker container run --name f1 diamol/ch06-file-display
https://www.manning.com/books/learn-docker-in-a-month-of-lunches
PS>
PS>echo "http://eltonstoneman.com" > url.txt
PS>
PS>docker container cp url.txt f1:/input.txt
PS>
PS>docker container start --attach f1
http://eltonstoneman.com
PS>
```

**Now this command generates a new file on the local computer with different content, and uses that to overwrite the** input.txt **file in the container.**

**The container exited after the first run. Starting it again means it runs the same command, but now it's reading the new file contents.**

Figure 6.3   Modifying a container's state and running it again

in the writeable layer for that one container—a new container will use the original contents from the image, and when container f1 is removed, the updated file is gone.

> **TRY IT NOW** Start a new container to check that the file in the image is unchanged. Then remove the original container and confirm that the data is gone:

```
docker container run --name f2 diamol/ch06-file-display

docker container rm -f f1

docker container cp f1:/input.txt .
```

You'll see the same output as mine in figure 6.4. The new container uses the original file from the image, and when you remove the original container, its filesystem is removed and the changed file is gone forever.

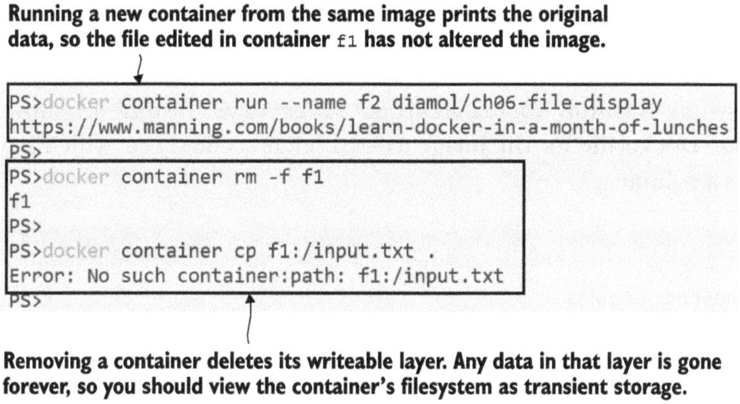

**Running a new container from the same image prints the original data, so the file edited in container f1 has not altered the image.**

```
PS>docker container run --name f2 diamol/ch06-file-display
https://www.manning.com/books/learn-docker-in-a-month-of-lunches
PS>
PS>docker container rm -f f1
f1
PS>
PS>docker container cp f1:/input.txt .
Error: No such container:path: f1:/input.txt
PS>
```

**Removing a container deletes its writeable layer. Any data in that layer is gone forever, so you should view the container's filesystem as transient storage.**

Figure 6.4   Modifying files in a container does not affect the image, and the container's data is transient.

The container filesystem has the same life cycle as the container, so when the container is removed, the writeable layer is removed, and any changed data in the container is lost. Removing containers is something you will do a lot. In production, you upgrade your app by building a new image, removing the old containers, and replacing them with new ones from the updated image. Any data that was written in your original app containers is lost, and the replacement containers start with the static data from the image.

There are some scenarios where that's fine, because your application only writes transient data—maybe to keep a local cache of data that is expensive to calculate or retrieve—and it's fine for replacement containers to start with an empty cache. In other cases, it would be a disaster. You can run a database in a container, but you wouldn't expect to lose all your data when you roll out an updated database version.

Docker has you covered for those scenarios too. The virtual filesystem for the container is always built from image layers and the writeable layer, but there can be additional sources as well. Those are *Docker volumes* and *mounts*. They have a separate life cycle from containers, so they can be used to store data that persists between container replacements.

## 6.2 *Running containers with Docker volumes*

A Docker volume is a unit of storage—you can think of it as a USB stick for containers. Volumes exist independently of containers and have their own life cycles, but they can be attached to containers. Volumes are how you manage storage for stateful applications when the data needs to be persistent. You create a volume and attach it to your application container; it appears as a directory in the container's filesystem. The container writes data to the directory, which is actually stored in the volume. When you update your app with a new version, you attach the same volume to the new container, and all the original data is available.

There are two ways to use volumes with containers: you can manually create volumes and attach them to a container, or you can use a VOLUME instruction in the Dockerfile. That builds an image that will create a volume when you start a container. The syntax is simply VOLUME <target-directory>. Listing 6.1 shows part of the multi-stage Dockerfile for the image diamol/ch06-todo-list, which is a stateful app that uses a volume.

> **Listing 6.1   Part of a multi-stage Dockerfile using a volume**

```
FROM diamol/dotnet-aspnet
WORKDIR /app
ENTRYPOINT ["dotnet", "ToDoList.dll"]

VOLUME /data
COPY --from=builder /out/ .
```

When you run a container from this image, Docker will automatically create a volume and attach it to the container. The container will have a directory at /data (or C:\data on Windows containers), which it can read from and write to as normal. But the data is actually being stored in a volume, which will live on after the container is removed. You can see that if you run a container from the image and then check the volumes.

> **TRY IT NOW**   Run a container for the to-do list app, and have a look at the volume Docker created:
>
> ```
> docker container run --name todo1 -d -p 8010:80 diamol/ch06-todo-list
>
> docker container inspect --format '{{.Mounts}}' todo1
>
> docker volume ls
> ```

You'll see output like mine in figure 6.5. Docker creates a volume for this container and attaches it when the container runs. I've filtered the volume list to show just the volume for my container.

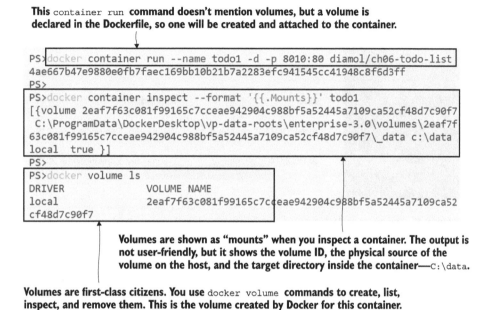

**This** `container run` **command doesn't mention volumes, but a volume is declared in the Dockerfile, so one will be created and attached to the container.**

```
PS>docker container run --name todo1 -d -p 8010:80 diamol/ch06-todo-list
4ae667b47e9880e0fb7faec169bb10b21b7a2283efc941545cc41948c8f6d3ff
PS>
PS>docker container inspect --format '{{.Mounts}}' todo1
[{volume 2eaf7f63c081f99165c7cceae942904c988bf5a52445a7109ca52cf48d7c90f7
 C:\ProgramData\DockerDesktop\vp-data-roots\enterprise-3.0\volumes\2eaf7f
63c081f99165c7cceae942904c988bf5a52445a7109ca52cf48d7c90f7\_data c:\data
local  true }]
PS>
PS>docker volume ls
DRIVER              VOLUME NAME
local               2eaf7f63c081f99165c7cceae942904c988bf5a52445a7109ca52
cf48d7c90f7
```

**Volumes are shown as "mounts" when you inspect a container. The output is not user-friendly, but it shows the volume ID, the physical source of the volume on the host, and the target directory inside the container—**`c:\data`**.**

**Volumes are first-class citizens. You use** `docker volume` **commands to create, list, inspect, and remove them. This is the volume created by Docker for this container.**

**Figure 6.5  Running a container with a volume declared in the Dockerfile**

Docker volumes are completely transparent to the app running in the container. Browse to http://localhost:8010 and you'll see the to-do app. The app stores data in a file at the /data directory, so when you add items through the web page, they are being stored in the Docker volume. Figure 6.6 shows the app in action—it's a special to-do list that works very well for people with workloads like mine; you can add items but you can't ever remove them.

Volumes declared in Docker images are created as a separate volume for each container, but you can also share volumes between containers. If you start a new container running the to-do app, it will have its own volume, and the to-do list will start off being empty. But you can run a container with the volumes-from flag, which attaches another container's volumes. In this example you could have two to-do app containers sharing the same data.

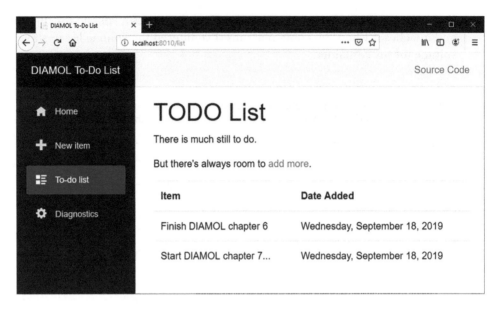

**Figure 6.6   The never-ending to-do list, running in a container using a Docker volume**

**TRY IT NOW**   Run a second to-do list container and check the contents of the data directory. Then compare that to another new container that shares the volumes from the first container (the exec commands are slightly different for Windows and Linux):

```
# this new container will have its own volume
docker container run --name todo2 -d diamol/ch06-todo-list

# on Linux:
docker container exec todo2 ls /data

# on Windows:
docker container exec todo2 cmd /C "dir C:\data"

# this container will share the volume from todo1
docker container run -d --name t3 --volumes-from todo1 diamol/ch06-
    todo-list

# on Linux:
docker container exec t3 ls /data

# on Windows:
docker container exec t3 cmd /C "dir C:\data"
```

The output will look like figure 6.7 (I'm running on Linux for this example). The second container starts with a new volume, so the /data directory is empty. The third container uses the volumes from the first, so it can see the data from the original application container.

**This starts a new container that will have a new volume created for it.**

**The new volume is empty; there are no files at** /data.

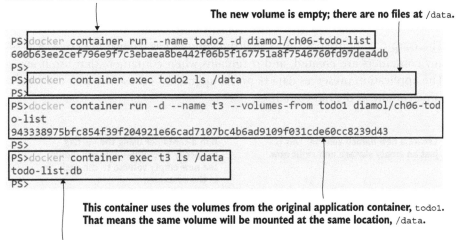

```
PS>docker container run --name todo2 -d diamol/ch06-todo-list
600b63ee2cef796e9f7c3ebaea8be442f06b5f167751a8f7546760fd97dea4db
PS>
PS>docker container exec todo2 ls /data
PS>
PS>docker container run -d --name t3 --volumes-from todo1 diamol/ch06-tod
o-list
943338975bfc854f39f204921e66cad7107bc4b6ad9109f031cde60cc8239d43
PS>
PS>docker container exec t3 ls /data
todo-list.db
PS>
```

**This container uses the volumes from the original application container,** todo1.
**That means the same volume will be mounted at the same location,** /data.

**The new container shares the volume from** todo1, **so it can
see the data written by the original application container.**

**Figure 6.7   Running containers with dedicated and shared volumes**

Sharing volumes between containers is straightforward, but it's probably not what you want to do. Apps that write data typically expect exclusive access to the files, and they may not work correctly (or at all) if another container is reading and writing to the same file at the same time. Volumes are better used to preserve state between application upgrades, and then it's better to explicitly manage the volumes. You can create a named volume and attach that to the different versions of your application container.

**TRY IT NOW**   Create a volume and use it in a container for version 1 of the to-do app. Then add some data in the UI and upgrade the app to version 2. The filesystem paths for the container need to match the operating system, so I'm using variables to make copy and pasting easier:

```
# save the target file path in a variable:
target='/data'    # for Linux containers
$target='c:\data' # for Windows containers

# create a volume to store the data:
docker volume create todo-list

# run the v1 app, using the volume for app storage:
docker container run -d -p 8011:80 -v todo-list:$target --name todo-v1
    diamol/ch06-todo-list

# add some data through the web app at http://localhost:8011

# remove the v1 app container:
docker container rm -f todo-v1
```

```
# and run a v2 container using the same volume for storage:
docker container run -d -p 8011:80 -v todo-list:$target --name todo-v2
    diamol/ch06-todo-list:v2
```

The output in figure 6.8 shows that the volume has its own life cycle. It exists before any containers are created, and it remains when containers that use it are removed. The application preserves data between upgrades because the new container uses the same volume as the old container.

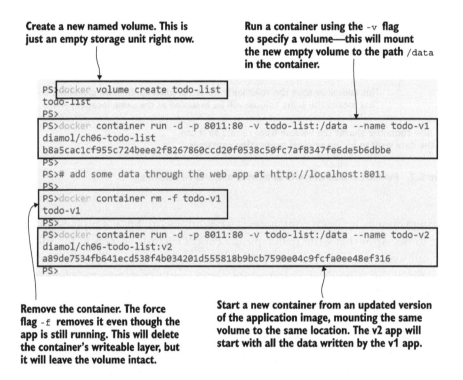

**Create a new named volume. This is just an empty storage unit right now.**

**Run a container using the `-v` flag to specify a volume—this will mount the new empty volume to the path `/data` in the container.**

```
PS>docker volume create todo-list
todo-list
PS>
PS>docker container run -d -p 8011:80 -v todo-list:/data --name todo-v1
diamol/ch06-todo-list
b8a5cac1cf955c724beee2f8267860ccd20f0538c50fc7af8347fe6de5b6dbbe
PS>
PS># add some data through the web app at http://localhost:8011
PS>
PS>docker container rm -f todo-v1
todo-v1
PS>
PS>docker container run -d -p 8011:80 -v todo-list:/data --name todo-v2
diamol/ch06-todo-list:v2
a89de7534fb641ecd538f4b034201d555818b9bcb7590e04c9fcfa0ee48ef316
PS>
```

**Remove the container. The force flag `-f` removes it even though the app is still running. This will delete the container's writeable layer, but it will leave the volume intact.**

**Start a new container from an updated version of the application image, mounting the same volume to the same location. The v2 app will start with all the data written by the v1 app.**

**Figure 6.8   Creating a named volume and using it to persist data between container updates**

Now when you browse to http://localhost:8011 you'll see version 2 of the to-do application, which has had a UI makeover from an expensive creative agency. Figure 6.9 shows this is ready for production now.

There's one thing to make clear about Docker volumes before we move on. The VOLUME instruction in the Dockerfile and the volume (or v) flag for running containers are separate features. Images built with a VOLUME instruction will always create a volume for a container if there is no volume specified in the run command. The volume will have a random ID, so you can use it after the container is gone, but only if you can work out which volume has your data.

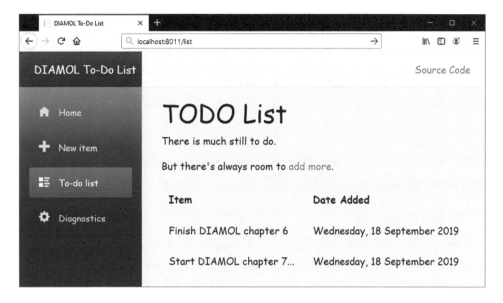

**Figure 6.9  The all-new to-do app UI**

The `volume` flag mounts a volume into a container whether the image has a volume specified or not. If the image does have a volume, the volume flag can override it for the container by using an existing volume for the same target path—so a new volume won't be created. That's what happened with the to-do list containers.

You can use the exact same syntax and get the same results for containers where no volume is specified in the image. As an image author, you should use the `VOLUME` instruction as a fail-safe option for stateful applications. That way containers will always write data to a persistent volume even if the user doesn't specify the `volume` flag. But as an image user, it's better not to rely on the defaults and to work with named volumes.

## 6.3  Running containers with filesystem mounts

Volumes are great for separating out the life cycle of storage and still have Docker manage all the resources for you. Volumes live on the host, so they are decoupled from containers. Docker also provides a more direct way of sharing storage between containers and hosts using *bind mounts*. A bind mount makes a directory on the host available as a path on a container. The bind mount is transparent to the container—it's just a directory that is part of the container's filesystem. But it means you can access host files from a container and vice versa, which unlocks some interesting patterns.

Bind mounts let you explicitly use the filesystems on your host machine for container data. That could be a fast solid-state disk, a highly available array of disks, or even a distributed storage system that's accessible across your network. If you can access that filesystem on your host, you can use it for containers. I could have a server with a RAID array and use that as reliable storage for my to-do list application database.

**TRY IT NOW**   I really do have a server with a RAID array, but you may not, so we'll just create a local directory on your host computer and bind mount it into a container. Again, the filesystem paths need to match the host operating system, so I've declared variables for the source path on your machine and the target path for the container. Note the different lines for Windows and Linux:

```
$source="$(pwd)\databases".ToLower(); $target="c:\data"    # Windows
source="$(pwd)/databases" && target='/data'                # Linux

mkdir ./databases

docker container run --mount type=bind,source=$source,target=$target
    -d -p 8012:80 diamol/ch06-todo-list

curl http://localhost:8012

ls ./databases
```

This exercise uses the curl command (which is on Linux, Mac, and Windows systems) to make an HTTP request to the to-do app. That causes the app to start up, which creates the database file. The final command lists the contents of the local databases directory on your host, and that will show that the application's database file is actually there on your host computer, as you see in figure 6.10.

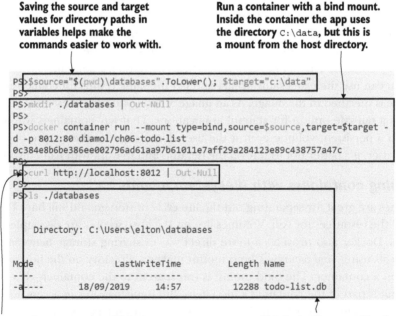

**Saving the source and target values for directory paths in variables helps make the commands easier to work with.**

**Run a container with a bind mount. Inside the container the app uses the directory** c:\data, **but this is a mount from the host directory.**

```
PS>$source="$(pwd)\databases".ToLower(); $target="c:\data"
PS>
PS>mkdir ./databases | Out-Null
PS>
PS>docker container run --mount type=bind,source=$source,target=$target -
d -p 8012:80 diamol/ch06-todo-list
0c384e8b6be386ee002796ad61aa97b61011e7aff29a284123e89c438757a47c
PS>
PS>curl http://localhost:8012 | Out-Null
PS>
PS>ls ./databases


    Directory: C:\Users\elton\databases


Mode                 LastWriteTime         Length Name
----                 -------------         ------ ----
-a----       18/09/2019     14:57           12288 todo-list.db
```

**The container port** 80 **is published to port** 8012 **on the host. Sending an HTTP request to the container with** curl **starts the application, which creates the database file at** c:\data. **The** Out-Null **option silences the output of the command.**

**This is the file created by the container. You can work with it directly from the host, and if you add files to the host directory, they can be seen by the container.**

Figure 6.10   Sharing a directory on the host with a container using a bind mount

The bind mount is bidirectional. You can create files in the container and edit them on the host, or create files on the host and edit them in the container. There's a security aspect here, because containers should usually run as a least-privilege account, to minimize the risk of an attacker exploiting your system. But a container needs elevated permissions to read and write files on the host, so this image is built with the USER instruction in the Dockerfile to give containers administrative rights—it uses the built-in root user in Linux and the ContainerAdministrator user in Windows.

If you don't need to write files, you can bind mount the host directory as read-only inside the container. This is one option for surfacing configuration settings from the host into the application container. The to-do application image is packaged with a default configuration file that sets the logging level for the app to a minimum amount. You can run a container from the same image but mount a local configuration directory into the container, and override the app's configuration without changing the image.

> **TRY IT NOW** The to-do application will load an extra configuration file from the /app/config path if it exists. Run a container that bind-mounts a local directory to that location, and the app will use the host's configuration file. Start by navigating to your local copy of the DIAMOL source code, and then run these commands:

```
cd ./ch06/exercises/todo-list

# save the source path as a variable:
$source="$(pwd)\config".ToLower(); $target="c:\app\config"   # Windows
source="$(pwd)/config" && target='/app/config'               # Linux

# run the container using the mount:
docker container run --name todo-configured -d -p 8013:80 --mount
    type=bind,source=$source,target=$target,readonly diamol/ch06-
    todo-list

# check the application:
curl http://localhost:8013

# and the container logs:
docker container logs todo-configured
```

The config file in the directory on the host is set to use much more detailed logging. When the container starts, it maps that directory, and the application sees the config file and loads the logging configuration. In the final output shown in figure 6.11, there are lots of debug log lines, which the app wouldn't write with the standard configuration.

You can bind-mount any source that your host computer has access to. You could use a shared network drive mounted to /mnt/nfs on a Linux host, or mapped to the X: drive on a Windows host. Either of those could be the source for a bind mount and

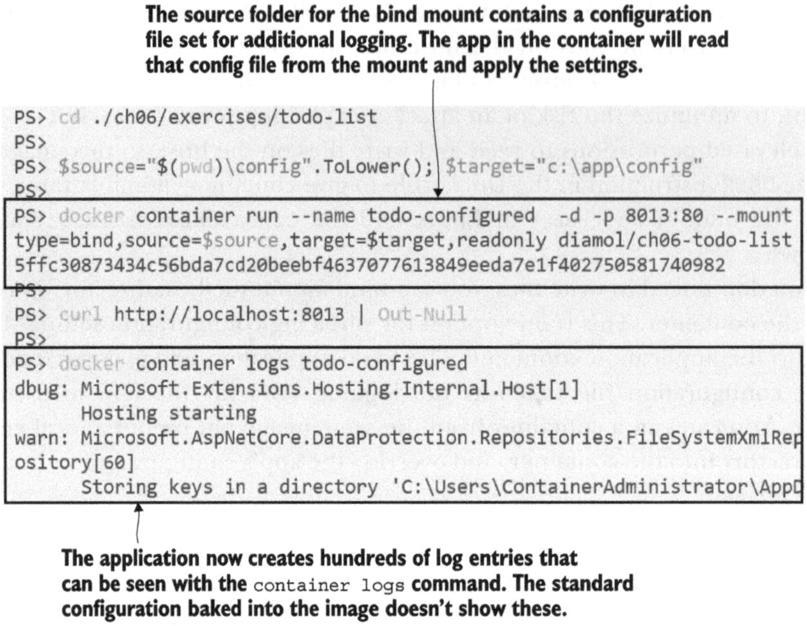

The source folder for the bind mount contains a configuration
file set for additional logging. The app in the container will read
that config file from the mount and apply the settings.

```
PS> cd ./ch06/exercises/todo-list
PS>
PS> $source="$(pwd)\config".ToLower(); $target="c:\app\config"
PS>
PS> docker container run --name todo-configured  -d -p 8013:80 --mount
type=bind,source=$source,target=$target,readonly diamol/ch06-todo-list
5ffc30873434c56bda7cd20beebf4637077613849eeda7e1f402750581740982
PS>
PS> curl http://localhost:8013 | Out-Null
PS>
PS> docker container logs todo-configured
dbug: Microsoft.Extensions.Hosting.Internal.Host[1]
      Hosting starting
warn: Microsoft.AspNetCore.DataProtection.Repositories.FileSystemXmlRep
ository[60]
      Storing keys in a directory 'C:\Users\ContainerAdministrator\AppD
```

The application now creates hundreds of log entries that
can be seen with the `container logs` command. The standard
configuration baked into the image doesn't show these.

Figure 6.11   Using bind mounts to load read-only configuration files into containers

be surfaced into a container in the same way. It's a very useful way to get reliable and
even distributed storage for stateful apps running in containers, but there are some
limitations you need to understand.

## 6.4    *Limitations of filesystem mounts*

To use bind mounts and volumes effectively, you need to understand some key scenarios and limitations, some of which are subtle and will only appear in unusual combinations of containers and filesystems.

The first scenario is straightforward: what happens when you run a container with
a mount, and the mount target directory already exists and has files from the image
layers? You might think that Docker would merge the source into the target. Inside
the container you'd expect to see that the directory has all the existing files from the
image, and all the new files from the mount. But that isn't the case. When you mount
a target that already has data, the source directory *replaces* the target directory—so the
original files from the image are not available.

You can see this with a simple exercise, using an image that lists directory contents
when it runs. The behavior is the same for Linux and Windows containers, but the
filesystem paths in the commands need to match the operating system.

**TRY IT NOW**   Run the container without a mount, and it will list the directory
contents from the image. Run it again with a mount, and it will list the contents

of the source directory (there are variables again here to support Windows and Linux):

```
cd ./ch06/exercises/bind-mount

$source="$(pwd)\new".ToLower(); $target="c:\init"    # Windows
source="$(pwd)/new" && target='/init'                # Linux

docker container run diamol/ch06-bind-mount

docker container run --mount type=bind,source=$source,target=$target
    diamol/ch06-bind-mount
```

You'll see that in the first run the container lists two files: abc.txt and def.txt. These are loaded into the container from the image layers. The second container replaces the target directory with the source from the mount, so those files are not listed. Only the files 123.txt and 456.txt are shown, and these are from the source directory on the host. Figure 6.12 shows my output.

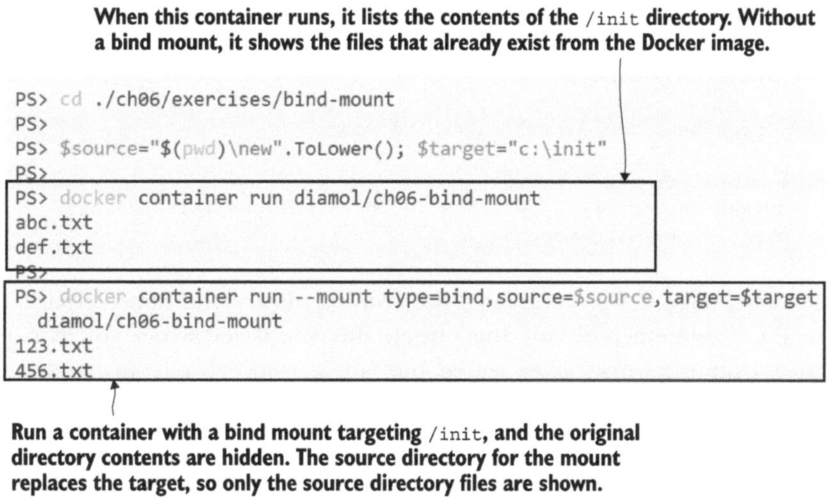

**When this container runs, it lists the contents of the /init directory. Without a bind mount, it shows the files that already exist from the Docker image.**

```
PS> cd ./ch06/exercises/bind-mount
PS>
PS> $source="$(pwd)\new".ToLower(); $target="c:\init"
PS>
PS> docker container run diamol/ch06-bind-mount
abc.txt
def.txt
PS>
PS> docker container run --mount type=bind,source=$source,target=$target
   diamol/ch06-bind-mount
123.txt
456.txt
```

**Run a container with a bind mount targeting /init, and the original directory contents are hidden. The source directory for the mount replaces the target, so only the source directory files are shown.**

Figure 6.12   Bind mount directories shadow the target directory if it exists.

The second scenario is a variation on that: what happens if you mount a single file from the host to a target directory that exists in the container filesystem? This time the directory contents are merged, so you'll see the original files from the image and the new file from the host—unless you're running Windows containers, where this feature isn't supported at all.

The container filesystem is one of the few areas where Windows containers are not the same as Linux containers. Some things do work in the same way. You can use standard Linux-style paths inside Dockerfiles, so /data works for Windows containers and becomes an alias of C:\data. But that doesn't work for volume mounts and bind mounts, which is why the exercises in this chapter use variables to give Linux users /data and Windows C:\data.

The limitation on single-file mounts is more explicit. You can try this yourself if you have Windows and Linux machines available, or if you're running Docker Desktop on Windows, which supports both Linux and Windows containers.

**TRY IT NOW**    The behavior of single-file mounts is different on Linux and Windows. If you have Linux and Windows containers available, you can see that in action:

```
cd ./ch06/exercises/bind-mount

# on Linux:
docker container run --mount
    type=bind,source="$(pwd)/new/123.txt",target=/init/123.txt
    diamol/ch06-bind-mount

# on Windows:
docker container run --mount
    type=bind,source="$(pwd)/new/123.txt",target=C:\init\123.txt
    diamol/ch06-bind-mount

docker container run diamol/ch06-bind-mount

docker container run --mount
    type=bind,source="$(pwd)/new/123.txt",target=/init/123.txt
    diamol/ch06-bind-mount
```

The Docker image is the same, and the commands are the same—apart from the OS-specific filesystem path for the target. But you'll see when you run this that the Linux example works as expected but you get an error from Docker on Windows, as in figure 6.13.

The third scenario is less common. It's very difficult to reproduce without setting up a lot of moving pieces, so there won't be an exercise to cover this—you'll have to take my word for it. The scenario is, what happens if you bind-mount a distributed filesystem into a container? Will the app in the container still work correctly? See, even the question is complicated.

Distributed filesystems let you access data from any machine on the network, and they usually use different storage mechanisms from your operating system's local filesystem. It could be a technology like SMB file shares on your local network, Azure Files, or AWS S3 in the cloud. You can mount locations from distributed storage systems like these into a container. The mount will look like a normal part of the filesystem, but if it doesn't support the same operations, your app could fail.

There's a concrete example in figure 6.14 of trying to run the Postgres database system in a container on the cloud, using Azure Files for container storage. Azure Files

**You can bind-mount a single file with Linux containers. When the target directory already exists, the contents are merged with the bind mount.**

```
PS> cd ./ch06/exercises/bind-mount
PS>
PS> docker container run --mount type=bind,source="$(pwd)/new/123.txt",
target=/init/123.txt diamol/ch06-bind-mount
123.txt
abc.txt
def.txt
PS>
PS> # switch to Windows containers
PS>
PS> docker container run --mount type=bind,source="$(pwd)/new/123.txt",
target=C:\init\123.txt diamol/ch06-bind-mount
C:\Program Files\Docker\Docker\Resources\bin\docker.exe: Error response
 from daemon: invalid mount config for type "bind": source path must be
 a directory.
See C:\Program Files\Docker\Docker\Resources\bin\docker.exe run --help
```

**You can't bind-mount a single file with Windows containers. The feature isn't supported, and you'll get an `invalid mount config` error, telling you the source for the mount must be a directory.**

Figure 6.13   Bind mounts with a single file as the source work on Linux but not on Windows.

supports normal filesystem operations like read and write, but it doesn't support some of the more unusual operations that apps might use. In this case the Postgres container tries to create a file link, but Azure Files doesn't support that feature, so the app crashes.

**The image layers and the writeable layer are stored on an Azure disk, which supports all the usual filesystem features.**

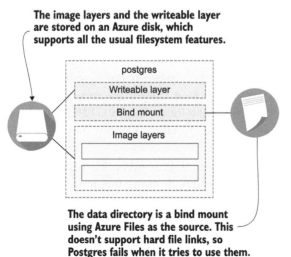

**The data directory is a bind mount using Azure Files as the source. This doesn't support hard file links, so Postgres fails when it tries to use them.**

Figure 6.14   Distributed storage systems may not provide all the usual filesystem features.

This scenario is an outlier, but you need to be aware of it because if it happens there's really no way around it. The source for your bind mount may not support all the filesystem features that the app in your container expects. This is something you can't plan for—you won't know until you try your app with your storage system. If you want to use distributed storage for containers, you should be aware of this risk, and you also need to understand that distributed storage will have very different performance characteristics from local storage. An application that uses a lot of disk may grind to a halt if you run it in a container with distributed storage, where every file write goes over the network.

## 6.5    *Understanding how the container filesystem is built*

We've covered a lot in this chapter. Storage is an important topic because the options for containers are very different from storage on physical computers or virtual machines. I'm going to finish up with a consolidated look at everything we've covered, with some best-practice guidelines for using the container filesystem.

Every container has a single disk, which is a virtual disk that Docker pieces together from several sources. Docker calls this the *union filesystem.* I'm not going to look at how Docker implements the union filesystem, because there are different technologies for different operating systems. When you install Docker, it makes the right choice for your OS, so you don't need to worry about the details.

The union filesystem lets the container see a single disk drive and work with files and directories in the same way, wherever they may be on the disk. But the locations on the disk can be physically stored in different storage units, as figure 6.15 shows.

Applications inside a container see a single disk, but as the image author or container user, you choose the sources for that disk. There can be multiple image layers, multiple volume mounts, and multiple bind mounts in a container, but they will always have a single writeable layer. Here are some general guidelines for how you should use the storage options:

- *Writeable layer*—Perfect for short-term storage, like caching data to disk to save on network calls or computations. These are unique to each container but are gone forever when the container is removed.
- *Local bind mounts*—Used to share data between the host and the container. Developers can use bind mounts to load the source code on their computer into the container, so when they make local edits to HTML or JavaScript files, the changes are immediately in the container without having to build a new image.
- *Distributed bind mounts*—Used to share data between network storage and containers. These are useful, but you need to be aware that network storage will not have the same performance as local disk and may not offer full filesystem features. They can be used as read-only sources for configuration data or a shared cache, or as read-write to store data that can be used by any container on any machine on the same network.

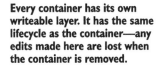

Every container has its own writeable layer. It has the same lifecycle as the container—any edits made here are lost when the container is removed.

Bind mounts surface a storage location on the host computer into the container at a specified directory path. The source could be local disk or network storage like NFS.

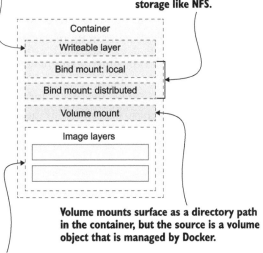

Volume mounts surface as a directory path in the container, but the source is a volume object that is managed by Docker.

The initial state of the container is provided by the image layers. Any files built into the image from the Dockerfile are here. The layers are read-only, but the container can edit files—Docker uses copy-on-write for this.

Figure 6.15 The container filesystem is created from the union of multiple sources.

- *Volume mounts*—Used to share data between the container and a storage object that is managed by Docker. These are useful for persistent storage, where the application writes data to the volume. When you upgrade your app with a new container, it will retain the data written to the volume by the previous version.
- *Image layers*—These present the initial filesystem for the container. Layers are stacked, with the latest layer overriding earlier layers, so a file written in a layer at the beginning of the Dockerfile can be overridden by a subsequent layer that writes to the same path. Layers are read-only, and they can be shared between containers.

## 6.6 Lab

We'll put those pieces together in this lab. It's back to the good old to-do list app, but this time with a twist. The app will run in a container and start with a set of tasks already created. Your job is to run the app using the same image but with different storage options, so that the to-do list starts off empty, and when you save items they get stored to a Docker volume. The exercises from this chapter should get you there, but here are some hints:

- Remember it's docker rm -f $(docker ps -aq) to remove all your existing containers.
- Start by running the app from diamol/ch06-lab to check out the tasks.
- Then you'll need to run a container from the same image with some mounts.
- The app uses a configuration file—there's more in there than settings for the log.

My sample solution is on the book's GitHub repository if you need it, but you should try to work through this one because container storage can trip you up if you haven't had much experience. There are a few ways to solve this. My solution is here: https://github.com/sixeyed/diamol/blob/master/ch06/lab/README.md.

# Part 2

## Running distributed applications in containers

Very few applications do everything in a single component—they're usually distributed across multiple pieces. In this part of the book you'll learn how to use Docker and Docker Compose to define, run, and manage applications that run across multiple containers. You'll learn how to power a continuous integration build pipeline with Docker, configure your apps so you can run multiple environments on a single machine, and isolate workloads with Docker networks. This part will also help get your containers ready for production with health checks and observability.

# Running multi-container apps with Docker Compose

Most applications don't run in one single component. Even large old apps are typically built as frontend and backend components, which are separate logical layers running in physically distributed components. Docker is ideally suited to running distributed applications—from *n*-tier monoliths to modern microservices. Each component runs in its own lightweight container, and Docker plugs them together using standard network protocols. You define and manage multi-container apps like this using Docker Compose.

Compose is a file format for describing distributed Docker apps, and it's a tool for managing them. In this chapter we'll revisit some apps from earlier in the book and see how Docker Compose makes it easier to use them.

## 7.1 The anatomy of a Docker Compose file

You've worked with lots of Dockerfiles, and you know that the Dockerfile is a script for packaging an application. But for distributed apps, the Dockerfile is really just for packaging one part of the application. For an app with a frontend website, a backend API, and a database, you could have three Dockerfiles—one for each component. How would you run that app in containers?

You could use the Docker CLI to start each container in turn, specifying all the options for the app to run correctly. That's a manual process that is likely to become a point of failure, because if you get any of the options wrong, the applications might not work correctly, or the containers might not be able to communicate. Instead you can describe the application's structure with a Docker Compose file.

The Docker Compose file describes the *desired state* of your app—what it should look like when everything's running. It's a simple file format where you place all the options you would put in your `docker container run` commands into the Compose file. Then you use the Docker Compose tool to run the app. It works out what Docker resources it needs, which could be containers, networks, or volumes—and it sends requests to the Docker API to create them.

Listing 7.1 shows a full Docker Compose file—you'll find this in the `exercises` folder for this chapter in the book's source code.

---

**Listing 7.1   A Docker Compose file to run the to-do app from chapter 6**

```
version: '3.7'

services:

  todo-web:
    image: diamol/ch06-todo-list
    ports:
      - "8020:80"
    networks:
      - app-net

networks:
  app-net:
    external:
      name: nat
```

This file describes a simple application with one Docker container plugging into one Docker network. Docker Compose uses YAML, which is a human-readable text format that's widely used because it translates easily to JSON (which is the standard language for APIs). Spaces are important in YAML—indentation is used to identify objects and the child properties of objects.

In this example there are three top-level statements:

- `version` is the version of the Docker Compose format used in this file. The feature set has evolved over many releases, so the version here identifies which releases this definition works with.
- `services` lists all the components that make up the application. Docker Compose uses the idea of *services* instead of actual containers, because a service could be run at scale with several containers from the same image.
- `networks` lists all the Docker networks that the service containers can plug into.

You could run this app with Compose, and it would start a single container to get to the desired state. Figure 7.1 shows the architecture diagram of the app's resources.

There are a couple of things to look at more closely before we actually run this app. The service called `todo-web` will run a single container from the `diamol/ch06-todo-list` image. It will publish port `8020` on the host to port `80` on the container, and it will connect the container to a Docker network referred to as `app-net` inside the Compose file. The end result will be the same as running `docker container run -p 8020:80 --name todo-web --network nat diamol/ch06-todo-list`.

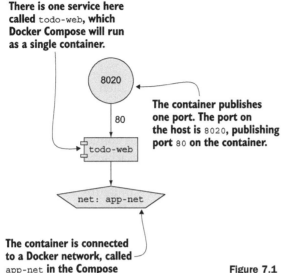

**There is one service here called** todo-web, **which Docker Compose will run as a single container.**

**The container publishes one port. The port on the host is** 8020, **publishing port** 80 **on the container.**

**The container is connected to a Docker network, called** app-net **in the Compose specification.**

**Figure 7.1** **The architecture of a simple Compose file with one service and one network**

Under the service name are the properties, which are a fairly close map to the options in the docker container run command: image is the image to run, ports are the ports to publish, and networks are the networks to connect to. The service name becomes the container name and the DNS name of the container, which other containers can use to connect on the Docker network. The network name in the service is app-net, but under the networks section that network is specified as mapping to an external network called nat. The external option means Compose expects the nat network to already exist, and it won't try to create it.

You manage apps with Docker Compose using the docker-compose command line, which is separate from the Docker CLI. The docker-compose command uses different terminology, so you start an app with the up command, which tells Docker Compose to inspect the Compose file and create anything that's needed to bring the app up to the desired state.

> **TRY IT NOW**   Open a terminal and create the Docker network. Then browse to the folder with the Compose file from listing 7.1, and then run the app using the docker-compose command line:

```
docker network create nat

cd ./ch07/exercises/todo-list

docker-compose up
```

You don't always need to create a Docker network for Compose apps, and you may already have that nat network from running the exercises in chapter 4, in which case you'll get an error that you can ignore. If you use Linux containers, Compose can manage networks for you, but if you use Windows containers, you'll need to use the default network called nat that Docker creates when you install it on Windows. I'm using the nat network, so the same Compose file will work for you whether you're running Linux or Windows containers.

The Compose command line expects to find a file called docker-compose.yml in the current directory, so in this case it loads the to-do list application definition. You won't have any containers matching the desired state for the todo-web service, so Compose will start one container. When Compose runs containers, it collects all the application logs and shows them grouped by containers, which is very useful for development and testing.

My output from running the previous command is in figure 7.2—when you run it yourself you'll also see the images being pulled from Docker Hub, but I'd already pulled them before running the command.

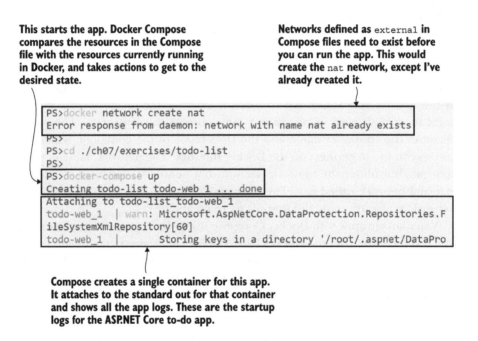

This starts the app. Docker Compose compares the resources in the Compose file with the resources currently running in Docker, and takes actions to get to the desired state.

Networks defined as external in Compose files need to exist before you can run the app. This would create the nat network, except I've already created it.

```
PS>docker network create nat
Error response from daemon: network with name nat already exists
PS>
PS>cd ./ch07/exercises/todo-list
PS>
PS>docker-compose up
Creating todo-list_todo-web_1 ... done
Attaching to todo-list_todo-web_1
todo-web_1  | warn: Microsoft.AspNetCore.DataProtection.Repositories.F
ileSystemXmlRepository[60]
todo-web_1  |       Storing keys in a directory '/root/.aspnet/DataPro
```

Compose creates a single container for this app. It attaches to the standard out for that container and shows all the app logs. These are the startup logs for the ASP.NET Core to-do app.

Figure 7.2   Starting an app using Docker Compose, which creates Docker resources

Now you can browse to http://localhost:8020 and see the to-do list application. It works in exactly the same way as in chapter 6, but Docker Compose gives you a much more robust way to start the app. The Docker Compose file will live in source control alongside the code for the app and the Dockerfiles, and it becomes the single place to describe all the runtime properties of the app. You don't need to document the image name or the published port in a README file, because it's all in the Compose file.

The Docker Compose format records all the properties you need to configure your app, and it can also record other top-level Docker resources like volumes and secrets. This app just has a single service, and even in this case it's good to have a Compose file that you can use to run the app and to document its setup. But Compose really makes sense when you're running multi-container apps.

## 7.2    Running a multi-container application with Compose

Back in chapter 4 we built a distributed app that shows an image from NASA's astronomy picture of the day API. There was a Java frontend website, a REST API written in Go, and a log collector written in Node.js. We ran the app by starting each container in turn, and we had to plug the containers into the same network and use the correct container names so the components could find each other. That's exactly the sort of brittle approach that Docker Compose fixes for us.

In listing 7.2 you can see the `services` section for a Compose file that describes the image gallery application. I've removed the network configuration to focus on the service properties, but the services plug into the `nat` network just like in the to-do app example.

> **Listing 7.2    The Compose services for the multi-container image gallery app**

```
accesslog:
  image: diamol/ch04-access-log

iotd:
  image: diamol/ch04-image-of-the-day
  ports:
    - "80"

image-gallery:
  image: diamol/ch04-image-gallery
  ports:
    - "8010:80"
  depends_on:
    - accesslog
    - iotd
```

This is a good example of how to configure different types of services. The `accesslog` service doesn't publish any ports or use any other properties you would capture from the `docker container run` command, so the only value recorded is the image name. The `iotd` service is the REST API—the Compose file records the image name and also publishes port `80` on the container to a random port on the host. The `image-gallery` service has the image name and a specific published port: `8010` on the host maps to port `80` in the container. It also has a `depends_on` section saying this service has a dependency on the other two services, so Compose should make sure those are running before it starts this one.

Figure 7.3 shows the architecture of this app. I've generated the diagrams in this chapter from a tool that reads the Compose file and generates a PNG image of the

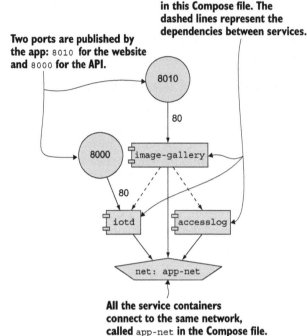

**There are three services in this Compose file. The dashed lines represent the dependencies between services.**

**Two ports are published by the app:** `8010` **for the website and** `8000` **for the API.**

**All the service containers connect to the same network, called** `app-net` **in the Compose file.**

Figure 7.3    A more complex Compose file that specifies three services connected to the same network

architecture. That's a great way to keep your documentation up to date—you can generate the diagram from the Compose file every time there's a change. The diagram tool runs in a Docker container of course—you can find it on GitHub at https://github.com/pmsipilot/docker-compose-viz.

We'll use Docker Compose to run the app, but this time we'll run in *detached mode*. Compose will still collect the logs for us, but the containers will be running in the background so we'll have our terminal session back, and we can use some more features of Compose.

**TRY IT NOW**    Open a terminal session to the root of your DIAMOL source code, and then navigate to the image gallery folder and run the app:

```
cd ./ch07/exercises/image-of-the-day

docker-compose up --detach
```

Your output will be like mine in figure 7.4. You can see that the `accesslog` and `iotd` services are started before the `image-gallery` service, because of the dependencies recorded in the Compose file.

When the app is running, you can browse to http://localhost:8010. It works just like it did in chapter 4, but now you have a clear definition in the Docker Compose

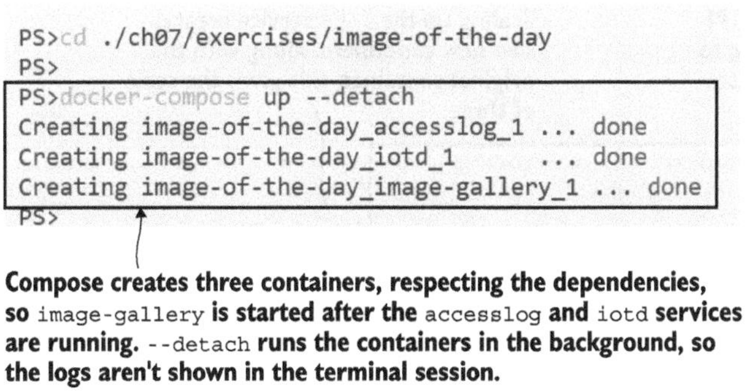

```
PS>cd ./ch07/exercises/image-of-the-day
PS>
PS>docker-compose up --detach
Creating image-of-the-day_accesslog_1 ... done
Creating image-of-the-day_iotd_1       ... done
Creating image-of-the-day_image-gallery_1 ... done
PS>
```

**Compose creates three containers, respecting the dependencies,
so** image-gallery **is started after the** accesslog **and** iotd **services
are running.** --detach **runs the containers in the background, so
the logs aren't shown in the terminal session.**

**Figure 7.4  Starting a multi-container app with dependencies
specified using Docker Compose**

file of how the containers need to be configured for them to work together. You can
also manage the application as a whole using the Compose file. The API service is
effectively stateless, so you can scale it up to run on multiple containers. When the
web container requests data from the API, Docker will share those requests across the
running API containers.

> **TRY IT NOW**  In the same terminal session, use Docker Compose to increase
> the scale of the iotd service, and then refresh the web page a few times and
> check the logs of the iotd containers:

```
docker-compose up -d --scale iotd=3

# browse to http://localhost:8010 and refresh

docker-compose logs --tail=1 iotd
```

You'll see in the output that Compose creates two new containers to run the image
API service, so it now has a scale of three. When you refresh the web page showing the
photograph, the web app requests data from the API, and that request could be handled by any of the API containers. The API writes a log entry when it handles requests,
which you can see in the container logs. Docker Compose can show you all log entries
for all containers, or you can use it to filter the output—the --tail=1 parameter just
fetches the last log entry from each of the iotd service containers.

My output is in figure 7.5—you can see that containers 1 and 3 have been used by
the web app, but container 2 hasn't handled any requests so far.

Docker Compose is now managing five containers for me. I can control the whole
app using Compose; I can stop all the containers to save compute resources, and start
them all again when I need the app running. But these are normal Docker containers
that I can also work with using the Docker CLI. Compose is a separate command-line
tool for managing containers, but it uses the Docker API in the same way that the

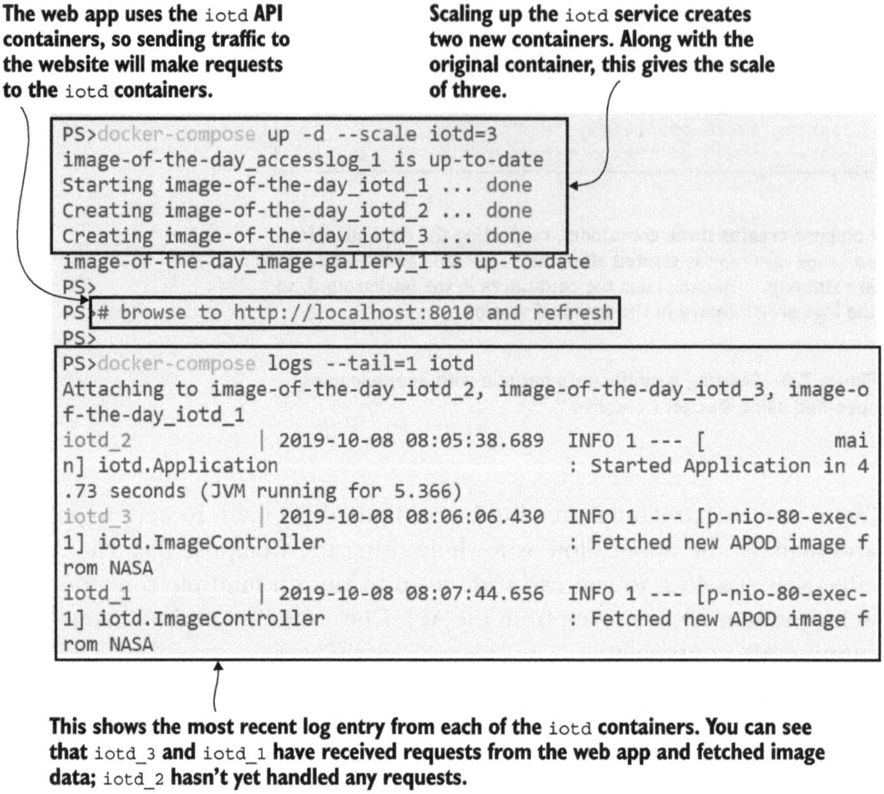

The web app uses the `iotd` API
containers, so sending traffic to
the website will make requests
to the `iotd` containers.

Scaling up the `iotd` service creates
two new containers. Along with the
original container, this gives the scale
of three.

```
PS>docker-compose up -d --scale iotd=3
image-of-the-day_accesslog_1 is up-to-date
Starting image-of-the-day_iotd_1 ... done
Creating image-of-the-day_iotd_2 ... done
Creating image-of-the-day_iotd_3 ... done
image-of-the-day_image-gallery_1 is up-to-date
PS>
PS># browse to http://localhost:8010 and refresh
PS>
PS>docker-compose logs --tail=1 iotd
Attaching to image-of-the-day_iotd_2, image-of-the-day_iotd_3, image-o
f-the-day_iotd_1
iotd_2          | 2019-10-08 08:05:38.689  INFO 1 --- [          mai
n] iotd.Application                       : Started Application in 4
.73 seconds (JVM running for 5.366)
iotd_3          | 2019-10-08 08:06:06.430  INFO 1 --- [p-nio-80-exec-
1] iotd.ImageController                   : Fetched new APOD image f
rom NASA
iotd_1          | 2019-10-08 08:07:44.656  INFO 1 --- [p-nio-80-exec-
1] iotd.ImageController                   : Fetched new APOD image f
rom NASA
```

This shows the most recent log entry from each of the `iotd` containers. You can see
that `iotd_3` and `iotd_1` have received requests from the web app and fetched image
data; `iotd_2` hasn't yet handled any requests.

Figure 7.5   Scaling up an application component and checking its logs with Docker Compose

Docker CLI does. You can use Compose to manage your app, but still use the standard Docker CLI to work with containers that Compose created.

**TRY IT NOW**   In the same terminal session, stop and start the app with Docker Compose commands, and then list all running containers with the Docker CLI:

```
docker-compose stop
```

```
docker-compose start
```

```
docker container ls
```

Your output will be like mine in figure 7.6. You'll see that Compose lists individual containers when it stops the app, but it only lists the services when it starts the app again, and the services are started in the correct dependency order. In the container list you'll see that Compose has restarted the existing containers, rather than creating new ones. All my containers show they were created over 30 minutes ago, but they've only been up for a few seconds.

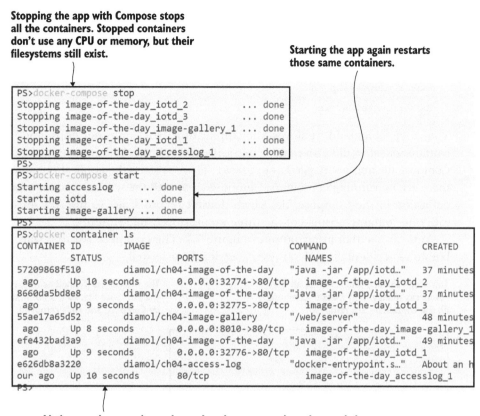

Stopping the app with Compose stops all the containers. Stopped containers don't use any CPU or memory, but their filesystems still exist.

Starting the app again restarts those same containers.

```
PS>docker-compose stop
Stopping image-of-the-day_iotd_2           ... done
Stopping image-of-the-day_iotd_3           ... done
Stopping image-of-the-day_image-gallery_1  ... done
Stopping image-of-the-day_iotd_1           ... done
Stopping image-of-the-day_accesslog_1      ... done
PS>
PS>docker-compose start
Starting accesslog      ... done
Starting iotd           ... done
Starting image-gallery  ... done
PS>
PS>docker container ls
CONTAINER ID      IMAGE                      PORTS               COMMAND               CREATED
                  STATUS                                         NAMES
57209868f510      diamol/ch04-image-of-the-day   "java -jar /app/iotd…"   37 minutes
 ago      Up 10 seconds        0.0.0.0:32774->80/tcp   image-of-the-day_iotd_2
8660da5bd8e8      diamol/ch04-image-of-the-day   "java -jar /app/iotd…"   37 minutes
 ago      Up 9 seconds         0.0.0.0:32775->80/tcp   image-of-the-day_iotd_3
55ae17a65d52      diamol/ch04-image-gallery      "/web/server"           48 minutes
 ago      Up 8 seconds         0.0.0.0:8010->80/tcp    image-of-the-day_image-gallery_1
efe432bad3a9      diamol/ch04-image-of-the-day   "java -jar /app/iotd…"   49 minutes
 ago      Up 9 seconds         0.0.0.0:32776->80/tcp   image-of-the-day_iotd_1
e626db8a3220      diamol/ch04-access-log         "docker-entrypoint.s…"  About an h
our ago   Up 10 seconds        80/tcp                  image-of-the-day_accesslog_1
PS>
```

Listing running containers shows that the app containers have only been up for a few seconds, even though they were created over 30 minutes ago.

**Figure 7.6  Stopping and starting multi-container apps with Docker Compose**

There are many more features to Compose—run `docker-compose` without any options to see the full list of commands—but there's one really important consideration you need to take in before you go much further. Docker Compose is a client-side tool. It's a command line that sends instructions to the Docker API based on the contents of the Compose file. Docker itself just runs containers; it isn't aware that many containers represent a single application. Only Compose knows that, and Compose only knows the structure of your application by looking at the Docker Compose YAML file, so you need to have that file available to manage your app.

It's possible to get your application out of sync with the Compose file, such as when the Compose file changes or you update the running app. That can cause unexpected behavior when you return to manage the app with Compose. We've already done this ourselves—we scaled up the `iotd` service to three containers, but that configuration isn't captured in the Compose file. When you bring the application down and then recreate it, Compose will return it to the original scale.

**TRY IT NOW**   In the same terminal session—because Compose needs to use the same YAML file—use Docker Compose to bring the application down and back up again. Then check the scale by listing running containers:

```
docker-compose down

docker-compose up -d

docker container ls
```

The down command removes the application, so Compose stops and removes containers—it would also remove networks and volumes if they were recorded in the Compose file and not flagged as external. Then up starts the application, and because there are no running containers, Compose creates all the services—but it uses the app definition in the Compose file, which doesn't record scale, so the API service starts with one container instead of the three we previously had running.

You can see that in my output in figure 7.7. The goal here was to restart the app, but we've accidentally scaled the API service down as well.

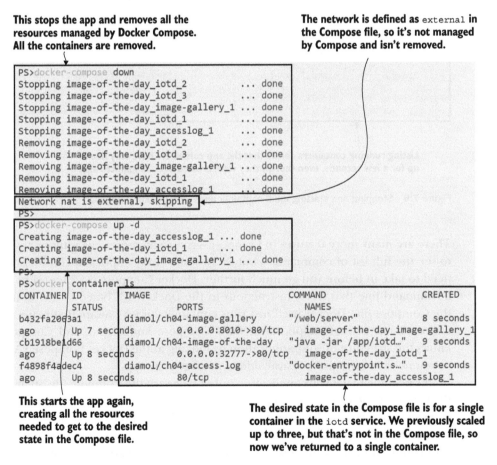

This stops the app and removes all the resources managed by Docker Compose. All the containers are removed.

The network is defined as external in the Compose file, so it's not managed by Compose and isn't removed.

This starts the app again, creating all the resources needed to get to the desired state in the Compose file.

The desired state in the Compose file is for a single container in the iotd service. We previously scaled up to three, but that's not in the Compose file, so now we've returned to a single container.

Figure 7.7   Removing and recreating an app resets it to the state in the Docker Compose file.

Docker Compose is simple to use and powerful, but you need to be mindful that it's a client-side tool, so it's dependent on good management of the app definition YAML files. When you deploy an app with Compose, it creates Docker resources, but the Docker Engine doesn't know those resources are related—they're only an application as long as you have the Compose file to manage them.

## 7.3 *How Docker plugs containers together*

All the components in a distributed application run in Docker containers with Compose, but how do they communicate with each other? You know that a container is a virtualized environment with its own network space. Each container has a virtual IP address assigned by Docker, and containers plugged into the same Docker network can reach each other using their IP addresses. But containers get replaced during the application life cycle, and new containers will have new IP addresses, so Docker also supports service discovery with DNS.

DNS is the Domain Name System, which links names to IP addresses. It works on the public internet and on private networks. When you point your browser to blog.six-eyed.com, you're using a domain name, which gets resolved to an IP address for one of the Docker servers I have hosting my blog. Your machine actually fetches content using the IP address, but you, as the user, work with the domain name, which is much friendlier.

Docker has its own DNS service built in. Apps running in containers make domain lookups when they try to access other components. The DNS service in Docker performs that lookup—if the domain name is actually a container name, Docker returns the container's IP address, and the consumer can work directly across the Docker network. If the domain name isn't a container, Docker passes the request on to the server where Docker is running, so it will make a standard DNS lookup to find an IP address on your organization's network or the public internet.

You can see that in action with the `image-gallery` app. The response from Docker's DNS service will contain a single IP address for services running in a single container, or multiple IP addresses if the service is running at scale across multiple containers.

> **TRY IT NOW** In the same terminal session, use Docker Compose to bring the application up with the API running at a scale of three. Then connect to a session in the web container—choose the Linux or Windows command to run—and perform a DNS lookup:

```
docker-compose up -d --scale iotd=3


# for Linux containers:
docker container exec -it image-of-the-day_image-gallery_1 sh


# for Windows containers:
docker container exec -it image-of-the-day_image-gallery_1 cmd
```

```
nslookup accesslog

exit
```

`nslookup` is a small utility that is part of the base image for the web application—it performs a DNS lookup for the name you provide, and it prints out the IP address. My output is in figure 7.8—you can see there's an error message from `nslookup`, which you can ignore (that's to do with the DNS server itself), and then the IP address for the container. My `accesslog` container has the IP address `172.24.0.2`.

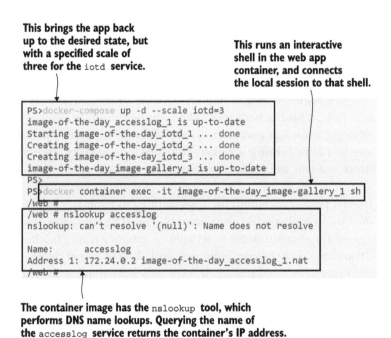

This brings the app back up to the desired state, but with a specified scale of three for the `iotd` service.

This runs an interactive shell in the web app container, and connects the local session to that shell.

```
PS>docker-compose up -d --scale iotd=3
image-of-the-day_accesslog_1 is up-to-date
Starting image-of-the-day_iotd_1 ... done
Creating image-of-the-day_iotd_2 ... done
Creating image-of-the-day_iotd_3 ... done
image-of-the-day_image-gallery_1 is up-to-date
PS>
PS>docker container exec -it image-of-the-day_image-gallery_1 sh
/web #
/web # nslookup accesslog
nslookup: can't resolve '(null)': Name does not resolve

Name:       accesslog
Address 1: 172.24.0.2 image-of-the-day_accesslog_1.nat
/web #
```

The container image has the `nslookup` tool, which performs DNS name lookups. Querying the name of the `accesslog` service returns the container's IP address.

Figure 7.8   Scaling a service with Docker Compose and performing DNS lookups

Containers plugged into the same Docker network will get IP addresses in the same network range, and they connect over that network. Using DNS means that when your containers get replaced and the IP address changes, your app still works because the DNS service in Docker will always return the current container's IP address from the domain lookup.

You can verify that by manually removing the `accesslog` container using the Docker CLI, and then bringing the application back up again using Docker Compose. Compose will see there's no `accesslog` container running, so it will start a new one.

That container may have a new IP address from the Docker network—depending on other containers being created—so when you run a domain lookup, you may see a different response.

> **TRY IT NOW** Still in the same terminal session, use the Docker CLI to remove the `accesslog` container, and then use Docker Compose to bring the app back to the desired state. Then connect to the web container again, using `sh` in Linux or `cmd` in Windows, and run some more DNS lookups:

```
docker container rm -f image-of-the-day_accesslog_1

docker-compose up -d --scale iotd=3

# for Linux containers:
docker container exec -it image-of-the-day_image-gallery_1 sh

# for Windows containers:
docker container exec -it image-of-the-day_image-gallery_1 cmd

nslookup accesslog

nslookup iotd

exit
```

You can see my output in figure 7.9. In my case there were no other processes creating or removing containers, so the same IP address `172.24.0.2` got used for the new `accesslog` container. In the DNS lookup for the `iotd` API, you can see that three IP addresses are returned, one for each of the three containers in the service.

DNS servers can return multiple IP address for a domain name. Docker Compose uses this mechanism for simple load-balancing, returning all the container IP addresses for a service. It's up to the application that makes the DNS lookup how it processes multiple responses; some apps take a simplistic approach of using the first address in the list. To try to provide load-balancing across all the containers, the Docker DNS returns the list in a different order each time. You'll see that if you repeat the `nslookup` call for the `iotd` service—it's a basic way of trying to spread traffic around all the containers.

Docker Compose records all the startup options for your containers, and it takes care of communication between containers at runtime. You can also use it to set up the configuration for your environments.

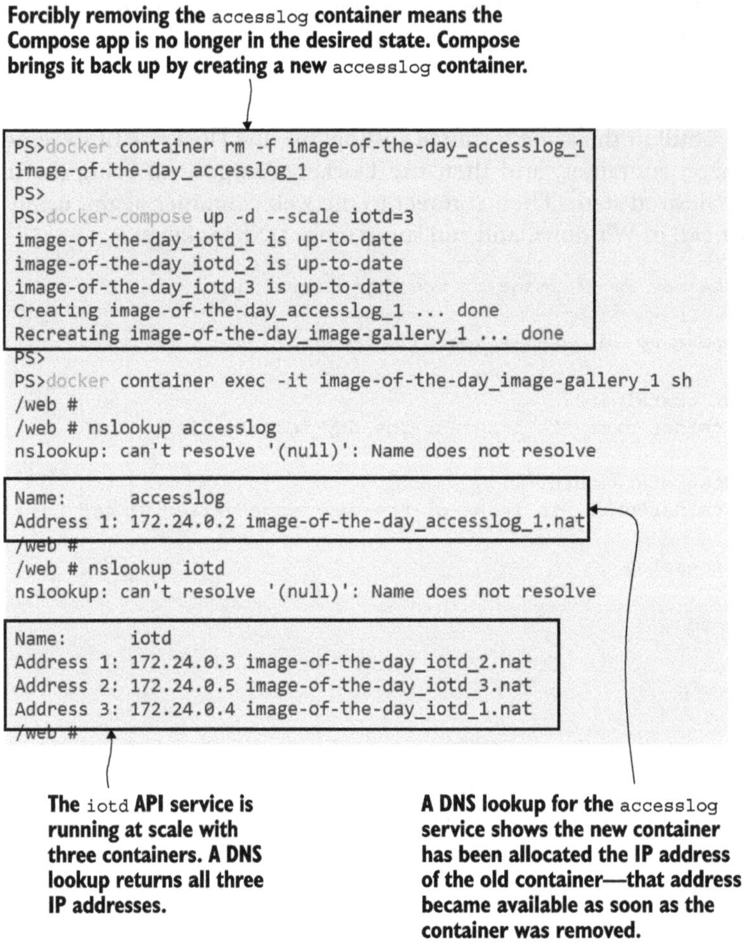

**Forcibly removing the** `accesslog` **container means the Compose app is no longer in the desired state. Compose brings it back up by creating a new** `accesslog` **container.**

```
PS>docker container rm -f image-of-the-day_accesslog_1
image-of-the-day_accesslog_1
PS>
PS>docker-compose up -d --scale iotd=3
image-of-the-day_iotd_1 is up-to-date
image-of-the-day_iotd_2 is up-to-date
image-of-the-day_iotd_3 is up-to-date
Creating image-of-the-day_accesslog_1 ... done
Recreating image-of-the-day_image-gallery_1 ... done
PS>
PS>docker container exec -it image-of-the-day_image-gallery_1 sh
/web #
/web # nslookup accesslog
nslookup: can't resolve '(null)': Name does not resolve

Name:      accesslog
Address 1: 172.24.0.2 image-of-the-day_accesslog_1.nat
/web #
/web # nslookup iotd
nslookup: can't resolve '(null)': Name does not resolve

Name:      iotd
Address 1: 172.24.0.3 image-of-the-day_iotd_2.nat
Address 2: 172.24.0.5 image-of-the-day_iotd_3.nat
Address 3: 172.24.0.4 image-of-the-day_iotd_1.nat
/web #
```

**The** `iotd` **API service is running at scale with three containers. A DNS lookup returns all three IP addresses.**

**A DNS lookup for the** `accesslog` **service shows the new container has been allocated the IP address of the old container—that address became available as soon as the container was removed.**

Figure 7.9   Services scale with multiple containers—every container's IP address is returned in a lookup.

## 7.4   *Application configuration in Docker Compose*

The to-do app from chapter 6 can be used in different ways. You can run it as a single container, in which case it stores data in a SQLite database—which is just a file inside the container. You saw in chapter 6 how to use volumes to manage that database file. SQLite is fine for small projects, but larger apps will use a separate database, and the to-do app can be configured to use a remote Postgres SQL database instead of local SQLite.

Postgres is a powerful and popular open source relational database. It works nicely in Docker, so you can run a distributed application where the app is running in one container and the database is in another container. The Docker image for the to-do app has been built in line with the guidance in this book, so it packages a default set of configuration for the dev environment, but config settings can be applied so they work with other environments. We can apply those config settings using Docker Compose.

Take a look at the services for the Compose file in listing 7.3—these specify a Postgres database service and the to-do application service.

Listing 7.3    The Compose services for the to-do app with a Postgres database

```
services:

  todo-db:
    image: diamol/postgres:11.5
    ports:
      - "5433:5432"
    networks:
      - app-net

  todo-web:
    image: diamol/ch06-todo-list
    ports:
      - "8020:80"
    environment:
      - Database:Provider=Postgres
    depends_on:
      - todo-db
    networks:
      - app-net
    secrets:
      - source: postgres-connection
        target: /app/config/secrets.json
```

The specification for the database is straightforward—it uses the diamol/postgres:11.5 image, publishes the standard Postgres port 5342 in the container to port 5433 on the host, and uses the service name todo-db, which will be the DNS name for the service. The web application has some new sections to set up configuration:

- environment sets up environment variables that are created inside the container. When this app runs, there will be an environment variable called Database:Provider set inside the container, with the value Postgres.
- secrets can be read from the runtime environment and populated as files inside the container. This app will have a file at /app/config/secrets.json with the contents of the secret called postgres-connection.

Secrets are usually provided by the container platform in a clustered environment—that could be Docker Swarm or Kubernetes. They are stored in the cluster database and can be encrypted, so they're useful for sensitive configuration data like database connection strings, certificates, or API keys. On a single machine running Docker, there is no cluster database for secrets, so with Docker Compose you can load secrets from files. There's a secrets section at the end of this Compose file, shown in listing 7.4.

> **Listing 7.4    Loading secrets from local files in Docker Compose**

```
secrets:
  postgres-connection:
    file: ./config/secrets.json
```

This tells Docker Compose to load the secret called `postgres-connection` from the file on the host called `secrets.json`. This scenario is like the bind mounts we covered in chapter 6—in reality the file on the host gets surfaced into the container. But defining it as a secret gives you the option of migrating to a real, encrypted secret in a clustered environment.

Plugging app configuration into the Compose file lets you use the same Docker images in different ways and be explicit about the settings for each environment. You can have separate Compose files for your development and test environments, publishing different ports and triggering different features of the app. This Compose file sets up environment variables and secrets to run the to-do app in Postgres mode and provide it with the details to connect to the Postgres database.

When you run the app, you'll see it behaves in the same way, but now the data is stored in a Postgres database container that you can manage separately from the app.

> **TRY IT NOW**    Open a terminal session at the root of the code for the book, and switch to the directory for this exercise. In that directory you'll see the Docker Compose file and also the JSON file that contains the secret to load into the application container. Start the app using `docker-compose up` in the usual way:
>
> ```
> cd ./ch07/exercises/todo-list-postgres
>
> # for Linux containers:
> docker-compose up -d
>
> # OR for Windows containers (which use different file paths):
> docker-compose -f docker-compose-windows.yml up -d
>
> docker-compose ps
> ```

Figure 7.10 shows my output. There's nothing new in there except the `docker-compose ps` command, which lists all running containers that are part of this Compose application.

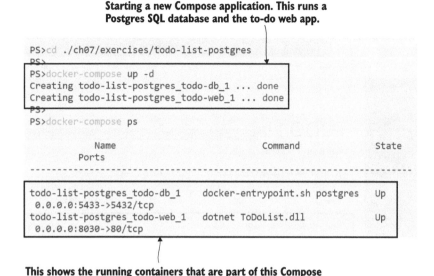

**Starting a new Compose application. This runs a
Postgres SQL database and the to-do web app.**

```
PS>cd ./ch07/exercises/todo-list-postgres
PS>
PS>docker-compose up -d
Creating todo-list-postgres_todo-db_1 ... done
Creating todo-list-postgres_todo-web_1 ... done
PS>
PS>docker-compose ps

        Name                        Command              State
        Ports
-------------------------------------------------------------------
todo-list-postgres_todo-db_1    docker-entrypoint.sh postgres   Up
  0.0.0.0:5433->5432/tcp
todo-list-postgres_todo-web_1   dotnet ToDoList.dll             Up
  0.0.0.0:8030->80/tcp
```

**This shows the running containers that are part of this Compose
application. Other containers from other apps are not shown.**

Figure 7.10   Running a new application with Docker Compose and listing its containers

You can browse to this version of the to-do app at http://localhost:8030. The functionality is the same, but now the data is being saved in the Postgres database container. You can check that with a database client—I use Sqlectron, which is a fast, open source, cross-platform UI for connecting to Postgres, MySQL, and SQL Server databases. The address of the server is `localhost:5433`, which is the port published by the container; the database is called `todo`, the username is `postgres`, and there is no password. You can see in figure 7.11 that I've added some data to the web app, and I can query it in Postgres.

Separating the application package from the runtime configuration is a key benefit of Docker. Your application image will be produced by your build pipeline, and that same image will progress through the test environments until it is ready for production. Each environment will apply its own config settings, using environment variables or bind mounts or secrets—that are easy to capture in Docker Compose files. In every environment, you're working with the same Docker images, so you can be confident you're releasing the exact same binaries and dependencies into production that have passed the tests in all other environments.

The to-do list app works in the same way, but this Compose
app configures it to use a Postgres database for storage.

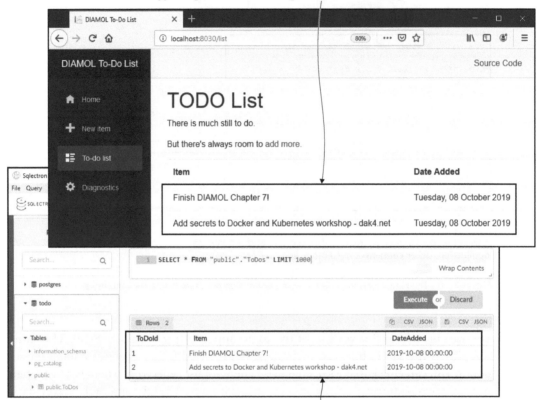

Sqlectron is a database client app; you can use it to query data in Postgres. This is the
same database container the to-do app is using, and you can see how the data is stored.

Figure 7.11    Running the to-do app in containers with a Postgres database and querying the data

## 7.5    *Understanding the problem Docker Compose solves*

Docker Compose is a very neat way of describing the setup for complex distributed
apps in a small, clear file format. The Compose YAML file is effectively a deployment
guide for your application, but it's miles ahead of a guide written as a Word document. In the old days those Word docs described every step of the application release,
and they ran to dozens of pages filled with inaccurate descriptions and out-of-date
information. The Compose file is simple and it's actionable—you use it to run your
app, so there's no risk of it going out of date.

Compose is a useful part of your toolkit when you start making more use of Docker
containers. But it's important to understand exactly what Docker Compose is for, and
what its limitations are. Compose lets you define your application and apply the

definition to a single machine running Docker. It compares the live Docker resources on that machine with the resources described in the Compose file, and it will send requests to the Docker API to replace resources that have been updated and create new resources where they are needed.

You get the desired state of your application when you run `docker-compose up`, but that's where Docker Compose ends. It is not a full container platform like Docker Swarm or Kubernetes—it does not continually run to make sure your application keeps its desired state. If containers fail or if you remove them manually, Docker Compose will not restart or replace them until you explicitly run `docker-compose up` again. Figure 7.12 gives you a good idea of where Compose fits into the application life cycle.

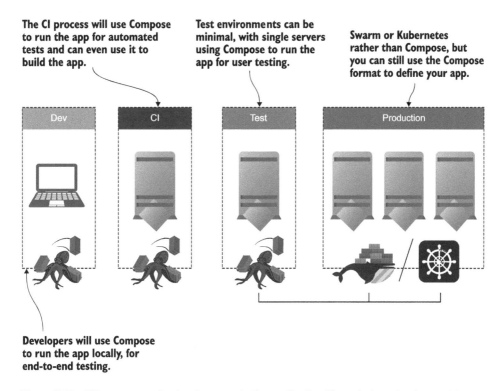

**Figure 7.12  Where you use Docker Compose in the application life cycle from development to production**

That's not to say Docker Compose isn't suitable for production. If you're just starting with Docker and you're migrating workloads from individual VMs to containers, it might be fine as a starting point. You won't get high availability, load balancing, or failover on that Docker machine, but you didn't get that on your individual app VMs either. You will get a consistent set of artifacts for all your applications—everything has Dockerfiles and Docker Compose files—and you'll get consistent tools to deploy and manage your apps. That might be enough to get you started before you look into running a container cluster.

## 7.6   *Lab*

There are some useful features in Docker Compose that add reliability to running your app. In this lab I'd like you to create a Compose definition to run the to-do web app more reliably in a test environment:

- The application containers will restart if the machine reboots, or if the Docker engine restarts.
- The database container will use a bind mount to store files, so you can bring the app down and up again but retain your data.
- The web application should listen on standard port 80 for test.

Just one hint for this one:

- You can find the Docker Compose file specification in Docker's reference documentation at https://docs.docker.com/compose/compose-file. That defines all the settings you can capture in Compose.

My sample solution is on the book's GitHub repository as always. Hopefully this one isn't too complex, so you won't need it: https://github.com/sixeyed/diamol/blob/master/ch07/lab/README.md.

# Supporting reliability with health checks and dependency checks

We're on a journey toward making software production-ready in containers. You've already seen how straightforward it is to package apps in Docker images, run them in containers, and define multi-container apps with Docker Compose. In production you'll run your apps in a container platform like Docker Swarm or Kubernetes, and those platforms have features that help you deploy self-healing apps. You can package your containers with information the platform uses to check if the application inside the container is healthy. If the app stops working correctly, the platform can remove a malfunctioning container and replace it with a new one.

In this chapter you'll learn how to package those checks into your container images to help the platform keep your app online.

## 8.1 Building health checks into Docker images

Docker monitors the health of your app at a basic level every time you run a container. Containers run a specific process when they start, which could be the Java or .NET Core runtime, a shell script, or an application binary. Docker checks that the process is still running, and if it stops, the container goes into the exited state.

That gives you a basic health check that works across all environments. Developers can see that their app is unhealthy if the process fails and the container exits. In a clustered environment, the container platform can restart an exited container or create a replacement container. But it's a very basic check—it ensures the process is running, but not that the app is actually healthy. A web app in a container could hit maximum capacity and start returning HTTP 503 "Service Unavailable" responses to every request, but as long as the process in the container is still running, Docker thinks the container is healthy, even though the app is stalled.

Docker gives you a neat way to build a real application health check right into the Docker image, just by adding logic to the Dockerfile. We'll do that with a simple API container, but first we'll run it without any health checks to be sure we understand the problem.

**TRY IT NOW**    Run a container that hosts a simple REST API that returns a random number. The app has a bug, so after three calls to the API, it becomes unhealthy and every subsequent call fails. Open a terminal, run the container, and use the API—this is a new image, so you'll see Docker pull it when you run the container:

```
# start the API container
docker container run -d -p 8080:80 diamol/ch08-numbers-api

# repeat this three times - it returns a random number
curl http://localhost:8080/rng
curl http://localhost:8080/rng
curl http://localhost:8080/rng

# from the fourth call onwards, the API always fails
curl http://localhost:8080/rng

# check the container status
docker container ls
```

You can see my output in figure 8.1. The API behaves correctly for the first three calls, and then it returns an HTTP 500 "Internal Server Error" response. The bug in the code means it will always return a 500 from now on. (Actually it's not a bug; the app is written deliberately like that. The source code is in the repo for chapter 8 if you want to see how it works.) In the container list, the API container has the status Up. The process inside the container is still running, so it looks good as far as Docker is concerned. The container runtime has no way of knowing what's happening inside that process and whether the app is still behaving correctly.

Enter the HEALTHCHECK instruction, which you can add to a Dockerfile to tell the runtime exactly how to check whether the app in the container is still healthy. The HEALTHCHECK instruction specifies a command for Docker to run inside the container, which will return a status code—the command can be anything you need to check if your app is healthy. Docker will run that command in the container at a timed interval. If the status code says everything is good, then the container is healthy. If the status code is a failure several times in a row, then the container is marked as unhealthy.

Listing 8.1 shows the HEALTHCHECK command in a new Dockerfile for the random number API, which I'll build as version 2 (the full file is in the source for the book at ch08/exercises/numbers/numbers-api/Dockerfile.v2). This health check uses a curl command like I did on my host, but this time it runs inside the container. The /health URL is another endpoint in the application that checks if the bug has been

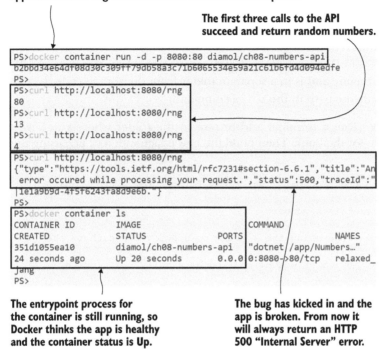

**Runs a container that is a REST API for generating random numbers. The application has a bug that causes it to fail after three requests.**

**The first three calls to the API succeed and return random numbers.**

**The entrypoint process for the container is still running, so Docker thinks the app is healthy and the container status is Up.**

**The bug has kicked in and the app is broken. From now it will always return an HTTP 500 "Internal Server" error.**

**Figure 8.1** Docker checks the app process, so the container is up even if the app is in a failed state.

triggered; it will return a 200 "OK" status code if the app is working and a 500 "Internal Server Error" when it's broken.

**Listing 8.1  The HEALTHCHECK instruction in a Dockerfile**

```
FROM diamol/dotnet-aspnet

ENTRYPOINT ["dotnet", "/app/Numbers.Api.dll"]
HEALTHCHECK CMD curl --fail http://localhost/health

WORKDIR /app
COPY --from=builder /out/ .
```

The rest of the Dockerfile is pretty straightforward. This is a .NET Core application, so the ENTRYPOINT runs the dotnet command, and it's that dotnet process that Docker monitors to check if the application is still running. The health check makes an HTTP call to the /health endpoint, which the API provides to test if the app is healthy. Using the --fail parameter means the curl command will pass the status code on to

Docker—if the request succeeds, it returns the number 0, which Docker reads as a successful check. If it fails, it returns a number other than 0, which means the health check failed.

We'll build a new version of that image so you can see how the build command works with a different file structure. Usually you have a Dockerfile in your application source folder, and Docker finds that and runs the build. In this case, the Dockerfile has a different name and is in a separate folder from the source code, so you need to explicitly specify the path in the build command.

**TRY IT NOW**    Run a terminal and browse to the folder where you have the source code for the book. Then build the new image with a v2 tag, using the v2 Dockerfile:

```
# browse to the root path, which has folders for source code and
    Dockerfiles:
cd ./ch08/exercises/numbers

# build the image using the -f flag to specify the path to the
    Dockerfile:
docker image build -t diamol/ch08-numbers-api:v2 -f ./numbers-
    api/Dockerfile.v2 .
```

Once the image is built, you're ready to run the app with a health check. You can configure how often the health check runs and how many failed checks mean the app is unhealthy. The default is to run every 30 seconds, and for three failures in a row to trigger the unhealthy status. Version v2 of the API image has the health check built in, so when you repeat the test, you'll find the health of the container gets reported.

**TRY IT NOW**    Run the same test but using the v2 image tag, and leave some time between the commands to let Docker fire the health checks inside the container.

```
# start the API container, v2
docker container run -d -p 8081:80 diamol/ch08-numbers-api:v2

# wait 30 seconds or so and list the containers
docker container ls

# repeat this four times - it returns three random numbers and then
    fails
curl http://localhost:8081/rng
curl http://localhost:8081/rng
curl http://localhost:8081/rng
curl http://localhost:8081/rng

# now the app is in a failed state - wait 90 seconds and check
docker container ls
```

My output is in figure 8.2. You can see that the new version of the API container initially shows a healthy status—if images have a health check built in, Docker shows the

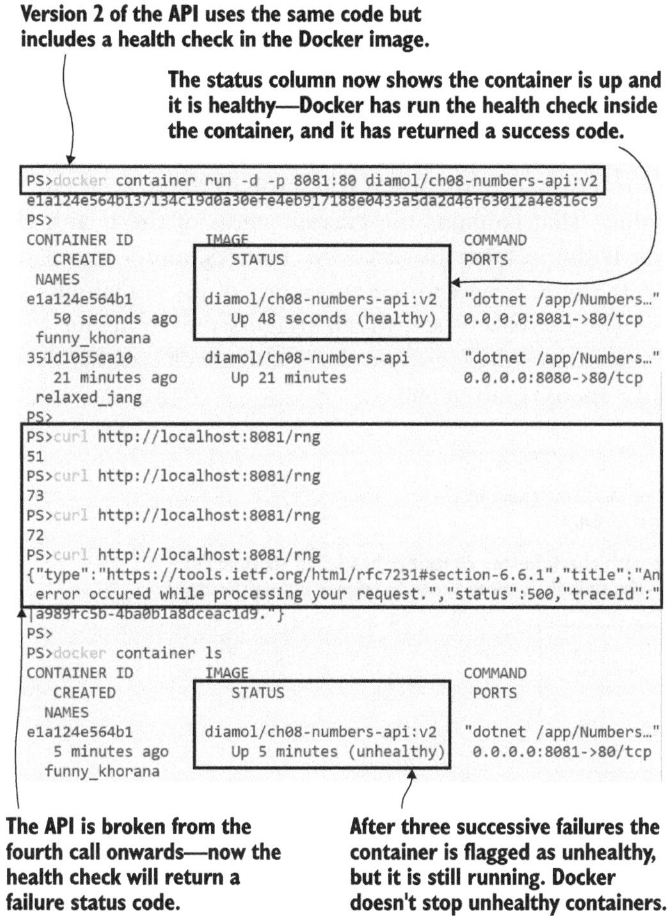

Version 2 of the API uses the same code but
includes a health check in the Docker image.

The status column now shows the container is up and
it is healthy—Docker has run the health check inside
the container, and it has returned a success code.

```
PS>docker container run -d -p 8081:80 diamol/ch08-numbers-api:v2
e1a124e564b137134c19d0a30efe4eb917188e0433a5da2d46f63012a4e816c9
PS>
CONTAINER ID       IMAGE                      COMMAND
  CREATED            STATUS                   PORTS
  NAMES
e1a124e564b1       diamol/ch08-numbers-api:v2 "dotnet /app/Numbers…"
  50 seconds ago     Up 48 seconds (healthy)  0.0.0.0:8081->80/tcp
  funny_khorana
351d1055ea10       diamol/ch08-numbers-api    "dotnet /app/Numbers…"
  21 minutes ago     Up 21 minutes            0.0.0.0:8080->80/tcp
  relaxed_jang
PS>
PS>curl http://localhost:8081/rng
51
PS>curl http://localhost:8081/rng
73
PS>curl http://localhost:8081/rng
72
PS>curl http://localhost:8081/rng
{"type":"https://tools.ietf.org/html/rfc7231#section-6.6.1","title":"An
 error occured while processing your request.","status":500,"traceId":"
|a989fc5b-4ba0b1a8dceac1d9."}
PS>
PS>docker container ls
CONTAINER ID       IMAGE                      COMMAND
  CREATED            STATUS                   PORTS
  NAMES
e1a124e564b1       diamol/ch08-numbers-api:v2 "dotnet /app/Numbers…"
  5 minutes ago      Up 5 minutes (unhealthy) 0.0.0.0:8081->80/tcp
  funny_khorana
```

The API is broken from the
fourth call onwards—now the
health check will return a
failure status code.

After three successive failures the
container is flagged as unhealthy,
but it is still running. Docker
doesn't stop unhealthy containers.

Figure 8.2   A broken app shows as an unhealthy container, but the
container is still up.

status of the health check for running containers. Some time after I've triggered the
bug, the container shows as unhealthy.

That unhealthy status is published as an event from Docker's API, so the platform
running the container is notified and can take action to fix the application. Docker
also records the result of the most recent health checks, which you can see when you
inspect the container. You've already seen the output of docker container inspect,
which shows everything Docker knows about the container. If there's a health check
running, that gets shown too.

**TRY IT NOW**   We have two API containers running and we didn't give a name
when we created them, but we can find the ID of the most recently created

container using `container ls` with the `--last` flag. You can feed that into `container inspect` to see the status of the latest container:

```
docker container inspect $(docker container ls --last 1 --format
     '{{.ID}}')
```

Pages of JSON data are returned here, and if you scroll to the `State` field, you'll see there's a `Health` section. That contains the current status of the health check, the "failing streak," which is the number of successive failures, and a log of the recent health check calls. In figure 8.3 you can see an extract of my container's state. The health check is in a failing streak of six, which triggers the container to be in an unhealthy state, and you can see the logs from the health check commands, which fail when they get an HTTP status result of 500.

**The output from** `docker container inspect`
**includes a detailed** `State` **section.**

The health check for my container has failed six times in a
row—the default is three times to trigger unhealthy status.

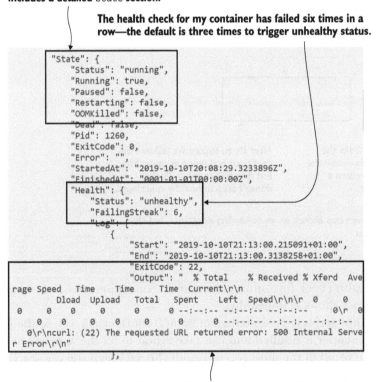

Health check logs are shown too, so I can see the status code
of the check and the log showing an HTTP 500 error code.

**Figure 8.3   Containers with a health check show the health status of the app and
the health check logs.**

The health check is doing what it should: testing the application inside the container and flagging up to Docker that the app is no longer healthy. But you can also see in figure 8.3 that my unhealthy container has a "running" status, so it's still up even though Docker knows it is not working correctly. Why hasn't Docker restarted or replaced that container?

The simple answer is that Docker can't safely do that, because the Docker Engine is running on a single server. Docker could stop and restart that container, but that would mean downtime for your app while it was being recycled. Or Docker could remove that container and start a new one from the same setup, but maybe your app writes data inside the container, so that would mean downtime and a loss of data. Docker can't be sure that taking action to fix the unhealthy container won't make the situation worse, so it broadcasts that the container is unhealthy but leaves it running. The health check continues too, so if the failure is temporary and the next check passes, the container status flips to healthy again.

Health checks become really useful in a cluster with multiple servers running Docker being managed by Docker Swarm or Kubernetes. Then the container platform is notified if the container is unhealthy and it can take action. Because there is additional capacity in a cluster, a replacement container can be started while the unhealthy one is still running, so there shouldn't be any application downtime.

## 8.2 Starting containers with dependency checks

The health check is an ongoing test that helps the container platform keep your application running. A cluster with multiple servers can deal with temporary failures by starting new containers, so there's no loss of service even if some of your containers stop responding. But running across a cluster brings new challenges for distributed apps, because you can no longer control the startup order for containers that may have dependencies on each other.

Our random number generator API has a website to go with it. The web app runs in its own container and uses the API container to generate random numbers. On a single Docker server you can ensure that the API container is created before the web container, so when the web app starts it has all its dependencies available. You can even capture that explicitly with Docker Compose. In a clustered container platform, however, you can't dictate the startup order of the containers, so the web app might start before the API is available.

What happens then depends on your application. The random number app doesn't handle it very well.

**TRY IT NOW** Remove all running containers, so now you have no API container. Then run the web app container and browse to it. The container is up and the app is available, but you'll find it doesn't actually work.

```
docker container rm -f $(docker container ls -aq)

docker container run -d -p 8082:80 diamol/ch08-numbers-web

docker container ls
```

Now browse to http://localhost:8082. You'll see a simple web app that looks OK, but if you click the random number button, you'll see the error shown in figure 8.4.

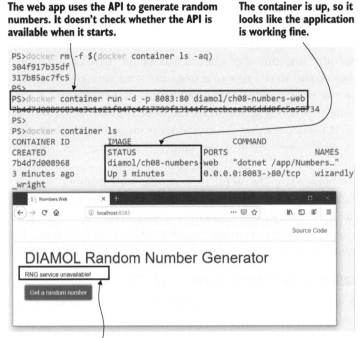

**The web app uses the API to generate random numbers. It doesn't check whether the API is available when it starts.**

**The container is up, so it looks like the application is working fine.**

**The API service isn't available, so the web app doesn't work at all, even though the server process is running and the container is up.**

**Figure 8.4    Apps that don't verify that their dependencies are available may look OK but be in a failed state.**

This is exactly what you don't want to happen. The container looks fine, but the app is unusable because its key dependency is unavailable. Some apps may have logic built into them to verify that the dependencies they need are there when they start, but most apps don't, and the random number web app is one of those. It assumes the API will be available when it's needed, so it doesn't do any dependency checking.

You can add that dependency check inside the Docker image. A dependency check is different from a health check—it runs before the application starts and makes sure everything the app needs is available. If everything is there, the dependency check finishes successfully and the app starts. If the dependencies aren't there, the check fails and the container exits. Docker doesn't have a built-in feature like the HEALTHCHECK instruction for dependency checks, but you can put that logic in the startup command.

Listing 8.2 shows the final application stage of a new Dockerfile for the web application (the full file is at `ch08/exercises/numbers/numbers-web/Dockerfile.v2`)—the CMD instruction verifies that the API is available before it starts the app.

Listing 8.2    A Dockerfile with a dependency check in the startup command

```
FROM diamol/dotnet-aspnet

ENV RngApi:Url=http://numbers-api/rng

CMD curl --fail http://numbers-api/rng && \
    dotnet Numbers.Web.dll

WORKDIR /app
COPY --from=builder /out/ .
```

This check uses the curl tool again, which is part of the base image. The CMD instruction runs when a container starts, and it makes an HTTP call to the API, which is a simple check to make sure it's available. The double-ampersand, `&&`, works the same way in Linux and Windows command shells—it will run the command on the right if the command on the left succeeds.

If my API is available, the `curl` command will succeed and the application gets launched. It's a .NET Core web application, so Docker will monitor the `dotnet` process to verify that the app is still alive (there's no health check in this Dockerfile). If the API is unavailable, the `curl` command will fail, the `dotnet` command won't get run, and nothing happens in the container so it exits.

**TRY IT NOW**    Run a container from the v2 tag of the random number web image. There's still no API container, so when this container starts it will fail and exit:

```
docker container run -d -p 8084:80 diamol/ch08-numbers-web:v2

docker container ls --all
```

You can see my output in figure 8.5. The v2 container exited just a few seconds after it started because the `curl` command failed to find the API. The original web app container is still running, and it's still unusable.

It's counterintuitive, but in this scenario it's better to have an exited container than a running container. This is fail-fast behavior, and it's what you want when you're running at scale. When a container exits, the platform can schedule a new container to come up and replace it. Maybe the API container takes a long time to start up, so it's not available when the web container runs; in that case the web container exits, a replacement is scheduled, and by the time it starts the API is up and running.

With health and dependency checks, we can package an app to be a good citizen in a container platform. The checks we've used so far have been very basic HTTP tests

**Version 2 of the web application image includes a dependency
check, which makes sure the API is available before the app runs.**

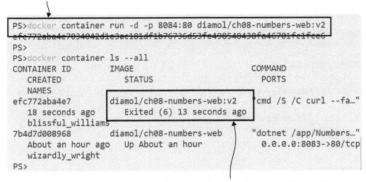

**There's no API container running, so the dependency check fails
and the app doesn't start—the container exits straight away.**

Figure 8.5   A container with dependency checks at startup exits if the checks fail.

using curl. That proves out what we want to do, but it's a simplistic approach, and it's
better not to rely on an external tool for your checks.

## 8.3    *Writing custom utilities for application check logic*

Curl is a very useful tool for testing web apps and APIs. It's cross-platform so it works
on Linux and Windows, and it is part of the .NET Core runtime images that I've used
as the base for my golden images, so I know it will be there to run my checks. I don't
actually need curl in the image for my app to run though, and a security review might
ask for it to be removed.

We covered that in chapter 4—your Docker image should have the bare minimum
in it for your application to run. Any extra tools increase the image size, and they also
increase the frequency of updates and the security attack surface. So although curl is a
great tool for getting started with container checks, it's better to write a custom utility
for your checks using the same language that your application uses—Java for Java
apps, Node.js for Node.js apps, and so on.

There are a whole lot of advantages to this:

- You reduce the software requirements in your image—you don't need to install
  any extra tools, because everything the check utility needs to run is already
  there for the application.
- You can use more complex conditional logic in your checks with retries or
  branches, which are harder to express in shell scripts, especially if you're publishing cross-platform Docker images for Linux and Windows.
- Your utility can use the same application configuration that your app uses, so
  you don't end up specifying settings like URLs in several places, with the risk of
  them getting out of sync.

- You can execute any tests you need, checking database connections or file paths for the existence of certificates that you're expecting the platform to load into the container—all using the same libraries your app uses.

Utilities can also be made generic to work in multiple situations. I've written a simple HTTP check utility in .NET Core that I can use for the health check in the API image and the dependency check in the web image. There are multi-stage Dockerfiles for each app where one stage compiles the application, another stage compiles the check utility, and the final stage copies in the app and the utility. Figure 8.6 shows how that looks.

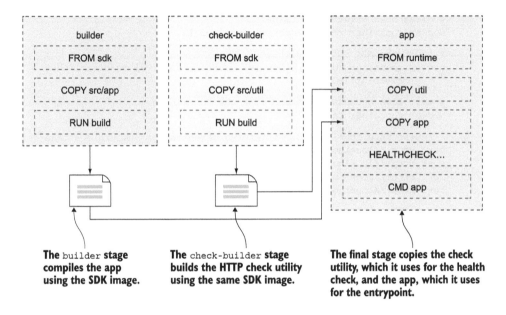

Figure 8.6  Using multi-stage builds to compile and package utilities alongside the application

The final stage of `Dockerfile.v3` for the API is shown in listing 8.3. The command for the health check now uses the check utility, which is a .NET Core app so the check no longer needs curl to be installed in the image.

**Listing 8.3  Using a custom utility for a health check to remove the need for curl**

```
FROM diamol/dotnet-aspnet

ENTRYPOINT ["dotnet", "Numbers.Api.dll"]
HEALTHCHECK CMD ["dotnet", "Utilities.HttpCheck.dll", "-u",
    "http://localhost/health"]

WORKDIR /app
COPY --from=http-check-builder /out/ .
COPY --from=builder /out/ .
```

The behavior of the new health check is pretty much the same; the only difference from the curl version is that you won't see as much verbose logging in the output when you inspect the container. There's just a single line for each check saying whether it was a success or a failure. The app should still report as healthy initially; it will get flagged as unhealthy after you've made a few calls to the API.

> **TRY IT NOW**   Remove all your existing containers and run version 3 of the random number API. This time we'll specify an interval for the health check so it triggers more quickly. Check that the container is listed as healthy, and then use the API and check that the container flips to unhealthy:

```
# clear down existing containers
docker container rm -f $(docker container ls -aq)

# start the API container, v3
docker container run -d -p 8080:80 --health-interval 5s diamol/ch08-
    numbers-api:v3

# wait five seconds or so and list the containers
docker container ls

# repeat this four times - it returns three random numbers and then fails
curl http://localhost:8080/rng
curl http://localhost:8080/rng
curl http://localhost:8080/rng
curl http://localhost:8080/rng

# now the app is in a failed state - wait 15 seconds and check again
docker container ls
```

Figure 8.7 shows my output. The behavior is the same as version 2, with the health check failing once the bug in the API is triggered, so the HTTP check utility is working correctly.

The HTTP check utility has lots of options that make it flexible for different scenarios. In Dockerfile.v3 for the web app, I use the same utility for the dependency check at startup, to see if the API is available.

Listing 8.4 shows the final stage of the Dockerfile. In this case I use the -t flag to set how long the utility should wait for a response, and the -c flag tells the utility to load the same config files as the application and to get the URL for the API from the app config.

> **Listing 8.4   Using a utility for a dependency check at container startup**

```
FROM diamol/dotnet-aspnet

ENV RngApi:Url=http://numbers-api/rng

CMD dotnet Utilities.HttpCheck.dll -c RngApi:Url -t 900 && \
    dotnet Numbers.Web.dll

WORKDIR /app
COPY --from=http-check-builder /out/ .
COPY --from=builder /out/ .
```

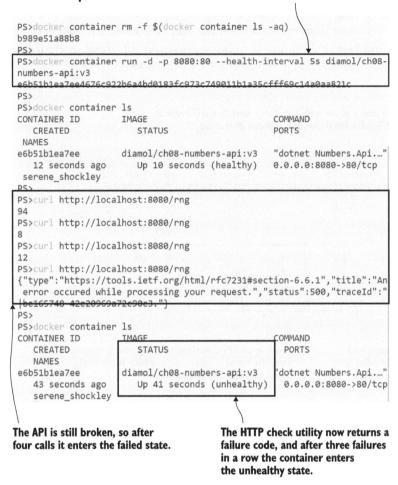

Version 3 of the API uses the .NET HTTP utility app for the health check. This command specifies five seconds as the interval between health checks.

```
PS>docker container rm -f $(docker container ls -aq)
b989e51a88b8
PS>
PS>docker container run -d -p 8080:80 --health-interval 5s diamol/ch08-
numbers-api:v3
e6b51b1ea7ee4676c922b6a4bd0183fc973c749011b1a35cfff69c14a0aa821c
PS>
PS>docker container ls
CONTAINER ID      IMAGE                     COMMAND
   CREATED            STATUS                PORTS
   NAMES
e6b51b1ea7ee      diamol/ch08-numbers-api:v3    "dotnet Numbers.Api...."
   12 seconds ago    Up 10 seconds (healthy)   0.0.0.0:8080->80/tcp
   serene_shockley
PS>
PS>curl http://localhost:8080/rng
94
PS>curl http://localhost:8080/rng
8
PS>curl http://localhost:8080/rng
12
PS>curl http://localhost:8080/rng
{"type":"https://tools.ietf.org/html/rfc7231#section-6.6.1","title":"An
 error occured while processing your request.","status":500,"traceId":"
|be165748-42e20969a72c90e3."}
PS>
PS>docker container ls
CONTAINER ID      IMAGE                     COMMAND
   CREATED            STATUS                PORTS
   NAMES
e6b51b1ea7ee      diamol/ch08-numbers-api:v3    'dotnet Numbers.Api...."
   43 seconds ago    Up 41 seconds (unhealthy)  0.0.0.0:8080->80/tcp
   serene_shockley
```

The API is still broken, so after four calls it enters the failed state.

The HTTP check utility now returns a failure code, and after three failures in a row the container enters the unhealthy state.

**Figure 8.7   A container health check that uses a utility tool packaged into the Docker image**

Again, this removes the requirement for curl in the application image, but the behavior is much the same with the HTTP utility in the startup command.

**TRY IT NOW**   Run version 3 of the web app, and you'll see that the container exits almost immediately because the HTTP check utility fails when it makes the API check:

```
docker container run -d -p 8081:80 diamol/ch08-numbers-web:v3

docker container ls --all
```

Your output will be like mine in figure 8.8. You'll see that the API container is still running, but it's still unhealthy. The web container didn't find it because it's looking for the DNS name numbers-api, and we didn't specify that name when we ran the API container. If we had used that name for the API container, the web app would have connected and been able to use it, although it would still show an error because the bug in the API has been triggered, and it isn't responding.

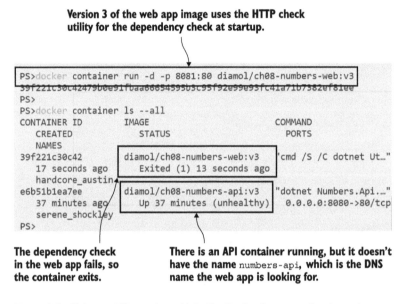

Version 3 of the web app image uses the HTTP check utility for the dependency check at startup.

The dependency check in the web app fails, so the container exits.

There is an API container running, but it doesn't have the name numbers-api, which is the DNS name the web app is looking for.

Figure 8.8    Using a utility packaged into the Docker image as the dependency check tool

One other benefit of writing your own checks in a utility is that it makes your image portable. Different container platforms have different ways of declaring and using health checks and dependency checks, but if you have all the logic you need in a utility in your image, you can have it work in the same way on Docker Compose, Docker Swarm, and Kubernetes.

## 8.4    Defining health checks and dependency checks in Docker Compose

If you're not convinced that it's a good idea for containers to fail and exit when their dependencies aren't available, you're about to see why it works. Docker Compose can go some of the way toward repairing unreliable applications, but it won't replace unhealthy containers for the same reasons that Docker Engine won't: you're running on a single server, and the fix might cause an outage. But it can set containers to restart if they exit, and it can add a health check if there isn't one already in the image.

Listing 8.5 shows the random number API declared as a service in a Docker Compose file (the full file is in `ch08/exercises/numbers/docker-compose.yml`). It specifies the v3 container image, which uses the HTTP utility for its health check, and adds settings to configure how the health check should work.

**Listing 8.5   Specifying health check parameters in a Docker Compose file**

```
numbers-api:
  image: diamol/ch08-numbers-api:v3
  ports:
    - "8087:80"
  healthcheck:
    interval: 5s
    timeout: 1s
    retries: 2
    start_period: 5s
  networks:
    - app-net
```

You have fine-grained control over the health check. I'm using the actual health check command defined in the Docker image but using custom settings for how it runs:

- `interval` is the time between checks—in this case five seconds.
- `timeout` is how long the check should be allowed to run before it's considered a failure.
- `retries` is the number of consecutive failures allowed before the container is flagged as unhealthy.
- `start_period` is the amount of time to wait before triggering the health check, which lets you give your app some startup time before health checks run.

These settings will probably be different for each app and each environment—there's a balance between finding out quickly that your app has failed and allowing for temporary faults so you don't trigger false alarms about unhealthy containers. My setup for the API is quite aggressive; it costs CPU and memory to run health checks, so in a production environment you'd likely run with a longer interval.

You can also add a health check in your Compose file for containers that don't have one declared in the image. Listing 8.6 shows the service for the web app in the same Docker Compose file, and here I'm adding a health check for the service. I'm specifying the same set of options I use for the API service, but there's also the `test` field, which gives Docker the health check command to run.

**Listing 8.6   Adding a health check in Docker Compose**

```
numbers-web:
  image: diamol/ch08-numbers-web:v3
  restart: on-failure
  ports:
    - "8088:80"
  healthcheck:
```

```
      test: ["CMD", "dotnet", "Utilities.HttpCheck.dll", "-t", "150"]
      interval: 5s
      timeout: 1s
      retries: 2
      start_period: 10s
    networks:
      - app-net
```

It's good to add a health check to all containers, but this example comes together with the dependency check in the image and the restart: on-failure setting, which means that if the container exits unexpectedly, Docker will restart it (there's one of the answers to the chapter 7 lab, if you haven't done it yet). There's no depends_on setting, so Docker Compose could start the containers in any order. If the web container starts before the API container is ready, the dependency check will fail and the web container will exit. Meanwhile, the API container will have started, so when the web app container is restarted, the dependency check will succeed and the app will be fully functioning.

> **TRY IT NOW**  Clear your running containers and start the random-number app with Docker Compose. List your containers to see if the web app did start first and then restart:

```
# browse to the Compose file
cd ./ch08/exercises/numbers

# clear down existing containers
docker container rm -f $(docker container ls -aq)

# start the app
docker-compose up -d

# wait five seconds or so and list the containers
docker container ls

# and check the web app logs
docker container logs numbers_numbers-web_1
```

My output is in figure 8.9, and yours should be very similar. Compose creates both containers at the same time, because no dependencies are specified. While the API container is starting up—and before the app is ready to handle requests—the web container's dependency check runs. You can see in my logs that the HTTP check returns a success code, but it takes 3176 ms, and the check is set to require a response within 150 ms, so the check fails and the container exits. The web service is configured to restart on failure, so that same container gets started again. This time the API check gets a success status code in 115 ms, so the check passes and the app is in a working state.

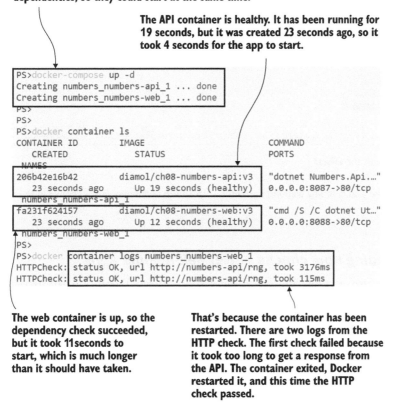

I've removed all my containers, so Docker Compose will start new containers for the API and for the web application, but I have no dependencies, so they could start at the same time.

The API container is healthy. It has been running for 19 seconds, but it was created 23 seconds ago, so it took 4 seconds for the app to start.

```
PS>docker-compose up -d
Creating numbers_numbers-api_1 ... done
Creating numbers_numbers-web_1 ... done
PS>
PS>
PS>docker container ls
CONTAINER ID         IMAGE                STATUS           COMMAND
    CREATED              STATUS                            PORTS
  NAMES
206b42e16b42         diamol/ch08-numbers-api:v3           "dotnet Numbers.Api...."
    23 seconds ago      Up 19 seconds (healthy)           0.0.0.0:8087->80/tcp
  numbers_numbers-api_1
fa231f624157         diamol/ch08-numbers-web:v3           "cmd /S /C dotnet Ut..."
    23 seconds ago      Up 12 seconds (healthy)           0.0.0.0:8088->80/tcp
  numbers_numbers-web_1
PS>
PS>docker container logs numbers_numbers-web_1
HTTPCheck: status OK, url http://numbers-api/rng, took 3176ms
HTTPCheck: status OK, url http://numbers-api/rng, took 115ms
```

The web container is up, so the dependency check succeeded, but it took 11 seconds to start, which is much longer than it should have taken.

That's because the container has been restarted. There are two logs from the HTTP check. The first check failed because it took too long to get a response from the API. The container exited, Docker restarted it, and this time the HTTP check passed.

Figure 8.9   Docker Compose adds resilience—the web container is restarted after its first check fails.

Browse to http://localhost:8088 and you can finally get a random number through the web app. At least, you can click the button three times and get a number—on the fourth you'll trigger the API bug, and you'll just get errors after that. Figure 8.10 shows one of the rare successes.

You might ask, why bother building a dependency check into the container startup when Docker Compose can do it for you with the depends_on flag? The answer is that Compose can only manage dependencies on a single machine, and the startup behavior of your app on a production cluster is far less predictable.

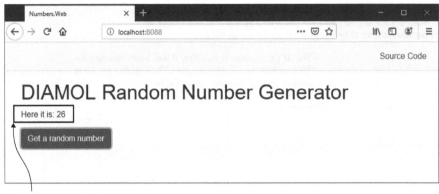

**26. Was it worth the effort?**

**Figure 8.10    The app is finally working correctly, with health and dependency checks in the containers.**

## 8.5    *Understanding how checks power self-healing apps*

Building your app as a distributed system with lots of small components increases your flexibility and agility, but it does make management more complicated. There will be lots of dependencies between components, and it's tempting to want to declare the order in which components get started so you can model the dependencies. But it's really not a great idea to do that.

On a single machine I can tell Docker Compose that my web container depends on my API container, and it will start them in the correct order. In production I could be running Kubernetes on a dozen servers, and I might need 20 API containers and 50 web containers. If I model the startup order, will the container platform start all 20 API containers first, before starting any web containers? What if 19 containers start just fine, but the twentieth container has a problem and takes 5 minutes to start? I have no web containers, so my app isn't running, but all 50 web containers could be running and it would work fine with 1 API container unavailable.

This is where dependency checks and health checks come in. You don't require the platform to guarantee the startup order—you let it spin up as many containers on as many servers as quickly as it can. If some of those containers can't reach their dependencies, they fail quickly and get restarted or replaced with other containers. It might take a few minutes of shuffling before a large app is running at 100% service, but during those minutes the app will have been online and serving users. Figure 8.11 shows an example of the life cycle of a container in a production cluster.

The idea of self-healing apps is that any transient failures can be dealt with by the platform. If your app has a nasty bug that causes it to run out of memory, the platform will shut down the container and replace it with a new one that has a fresh allocation of memory. It doesn't fix the bug, but it keeps the app working correctly.

**This is the startup life cycle. The container starts and then exits because its dependencies are not available. The platform restarts the container, and now its dependencies are available, the app starts correctly, and the health check passes.**

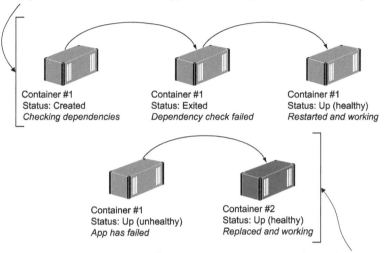

Container #1
Status: Created
*Checking dependencies*

Container #1
Status: Exited
*Dependency check failed*

Container #1
Status: Up (healthy)
*Restarted and working*

Container #1
Status: Up (unhealthy)
*App has failed*

Container #2
Status: Up (healthy)
*Replaced and working*

**This is the ongoing app life cycle. At some point the app fails and the health checks fail repeatedly, so the container is flagged as unhealthy. The platform creates a replacement container—maybe on another server—and when that is running, the original unhealthy container is shut down.**

Figure 8.11 Self-healing applications in a production cluster—containers can be restarted or replaced.

You do need to be careful with your checks though. Health checks run periodically, so they shouldn't do too much work. You need to find the balance so checks are testing that key parts of your app are working without taking too long to run or using too much compute resource. Dependency checks only run at startup, so you don't need to be too concerned about the resources they use, but you need to be careful what you check. Some dependencies are out of your control, and if the platform can't fix things, it won't be helpful if your containers fail.

Working out the logic that goes in your checks is the hard part. Docker makes it easy to capture those checks and execute them for you, and if you get them right, your container platform will keep your app running for you.

## 8.6 Lab

Some applications use resources consistently, so that the initial dependency check and the ongoing health check are testing the same thing. That's the case with this lab. It's an app that simulates a memory hog—it just keeps allocating and holding on to more memory as long as its running. It's a Node.js app and it needs some checks:

- At startup it should check that there's enough memory for it to work; if not, it should exit.

- During runtime it should check every 5 seconds to see if it has allocated more memory than it is allowed; if it has, it needs to flag that it's unhealthy.
- The test logic is already written in the `memory-check.js` script. It just needs to be wired into the Dockerfile.
- The scripts and the initial Dockerfile are in the source folder `ch08/lab`.

**NOTE**   The app doesn't really allocate any memory. Memory management in containers is complicated by different environments—Docker Desktop on Windows behaves differently from Docker Community Edition on Linux. For this lab, the app just pretends to use memory.

This lab is pretty straightforward. I'll just point out that Node.js apps are not compiled, so you don't need multiple stages. My sample is in the same directory, called `Dockerfile.solution`, and you'll find the write-up in the book's GitHub repository: https://github.com/sixeyed/diamol/blob/master/ch08/lab/README.md.

# Adding observability with containerized monitoring

9

Autonomous applications scale themselves up and down to meet incoming traffic, and they heal themselves when there are intermittent faults. It sounds too good to be true—and it probably is. The container platform can do a lot of the operations work for you if you build your Docker images with health checks, but you still need ongoing monitoring and alerting so humans can get involved when things go badly wrong. If you don't have any insight into your containerized application, that's going to be the number one thing that stops you going to production.

Observability is a critical piece of the software landscape when you're running applications in containers—it tells you what your applications are doing and how well they're performing, and it can help you pinpoint the source of problems. In this chapter you'll learn how to use a well-established approach to monitoring with Docker: exposing metrics from your application containers and using Prometheus to collect them and Grafana to visualize them in user-friendly dashboards. These tools are open source and cross-platform, and they run in containers alongside your application. That means you get the same insight into your application performance in every environment, from development to production.

## 9.1 The monitoring stack for containerized applications

Monitoring is different when apps are running in containers. In a traditional environment, you might have a monitoring dashboard showing a list of servers and their current utilization—disk space, memory, CPU—and alerts to tell you if any become overworked and are likely to stop responding. Containerized apps are more dynamic—they may run across dozens or hundreds of containers that are short-lived and are created or removed by the container platform.

137

You need a monitoring approach that is container-aware, with tools that can plug into the container platform for discovery and find all the running applications without a static list of container IP addresses. Prometheus is an open source project that does just that. It's a mature product that is overseen by the Cloud Native Computing Foundation (the same foundation behind Kubernetes and the containerd container runtime). Prometheus runs in a Docker container, so you can easily add a monitoring stack to your applications. Figure 9.1 shows what that stack looks like.

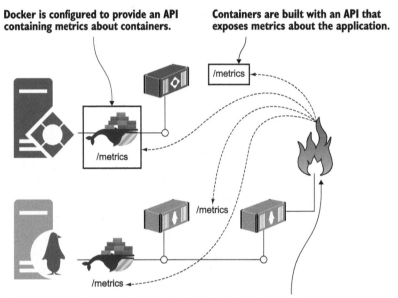

Docker is configured to provide an API containing metrics about containers.

Containers are built with an API that exposes metrics about the application.

Prometheus runs in a container and collects data from the application containers and the Docker Engines. It stores all data with the timestamp when it was collected.

Figure 9.1    Running Prometheus in a container to monitor other containers and Docker itself

Prometheus brings one very important aspect to monitoring: consistency. You can export the same type of metrics for all your applications, so you have a standard way to monitor them whether they're .NET apps in Windows containers or Node.js apps in Linux containers. You only have one query language to learn, and you can apply it for your whole application stack.

Another good reason for using Prometheus is that the Docker Engine can also export metrics in that format, which gives you insight into what's happening in the container platform too. You need to explicitly enable Prometheus metrics in your Docker Engine configuration—you saw how to update the config in chapter 5. You can edit the daemon.json file directly in C:\ProgramData\docker\config on Windows, or /etc/docker on Linux. Alternatively, on Docker Desktop you can right-click the whale icon, choose Settings, and edit the configuration in the Daemon section.

**TRY IT NOW**   Open your configuration settings and add two new values:

```
"metrics-addr" : "0.0.0.0:9323",
"experimental": true
```

These settings enable monitoring and publish metrics on port 9323.

You can see my full configuration file in figure 9.2.

Setting the daemon configuration in Docker Desktop
has the same effect as editing the daemon.json file.

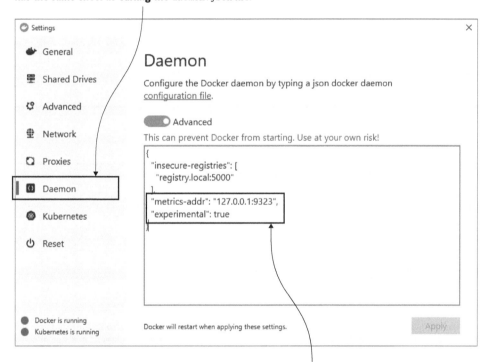

These are the two settings you need to enable metrics. The Docker
Engine needs to be running in experimental mode, and you need
to specify the port where metrics will be published with metrics-addr.

**Figure 9.2   Configuring the Docker Engine to export metrics in Prometheus format**

Docker Engine metrics are currently an experimental feature, which means the details it provides could change. But it's been an experimental feature for a long time, and it's been stable. It's worth including in your dashboards because it adds another layer of detail to the overall health of your system. Now that you have metrics enabled, you can browse to http://localhost:9323/metrics and see all the information Docker provides. Figure 9.3 shows my metrics, which include information about the machine Docker is running on as well as the containers Docker is managing.

**Enabling metrics gives you an HTTP endpoint where you can view data from the Docker Engine.**

**Metrics include static information,
like the amount of memory available
on the machine running Docker.**

**Metrics also include dynamic information,
like the current number of containers in
each state—paused, running, stopped.**

Figure 9.3  Sample metrics captured by Docker and exposed through the HTTP API

This output is in Prometheus format. It's a simple text-based representation where each metric is shown with its name and value, and the metric is preceded by some help text stating what the metric is and the type of data. These basic lines of text are the core of your container-monitoring solution. Each component will expose an endpoint like this providing current metrics; when Prometheus collects them, it adds a timestamp to the data and stores them with all the previous collections, so you can query data with aggregations or track changes over time.

> **TRY IT NOW**  You can run Prometheus in a container to read the metrics from your Docker machine, but first you need to get the machine's IP address. Containers don't know the IP address of the server they're running on, so you need to find it first and pass it as an environment variable to the container:

```
# load your machine's IP address into a variable - on Windows:
$hostIP = $(Get-NetIPConfiguration | Where-Object
    {$_.IPv4DefaultGateway -ne $null }).IPv4Address.IPAddress

# on Linux:
hostIP=$(ip route get 1 | awk '{print $NF;exit}')

# and on Mac:
hostIP=$(ifconfig en0 | grep -e 'inet\s' | awk '{print $2}')

# pass your IP address as an environment variable for the container:
docker container run -e DOCKER_HOST=$hostIP -d -p 9090:9090
    diamol/prometheus:2.13.1
```

The configuration in the diamol/prometheus Prometheus image uses the DOCKER_ HOST IP address to talk to your host machine and collect the metrics you've configured in the Docker Engine. It's rare that you'll need to access a service on the host from inside the container, and if you do, you would usually use your server name and Docker would find the IP address. In a development environment that might not work, but the IP address approach should be fine.

Prometheus is running now. It does several things: it runs a scheduled job to pull the metrics from your Docker host, it stores those metric values alongside a timestamp in its own database, and it has a basic web UI you can use to navigate the metrics. The Prometheus UI shows all the information from Docker's /metrics endpoint, and you can filter the metrics and display them in tables or graphs.

> **TRY IT NOW**  Browse to http://localhost:9090 and you'll see the Prometheus web interface. You can check that Prometheus can access the metrics by browsing to the Status > Targets menu option. Your DOCKER_HOST state should be green, which means Prometheus has found it.
>
> Then switch to the Graph menu and you'll see a dropdown list showing all the available metrics that Prometheus has collected from Docker. One of those is engine_daemon_container_actions_seconds_sum, which is a record of how long different container actions have taken. Select that metric and click Execute, and your output will be similar to mine in figure 9.4, showing the time taken to create, delete, and start containers.

The Prometheus UI is a simple way to see what's being collected and run some queries. Look around the metrics and you'll see that Docker records a lot of information

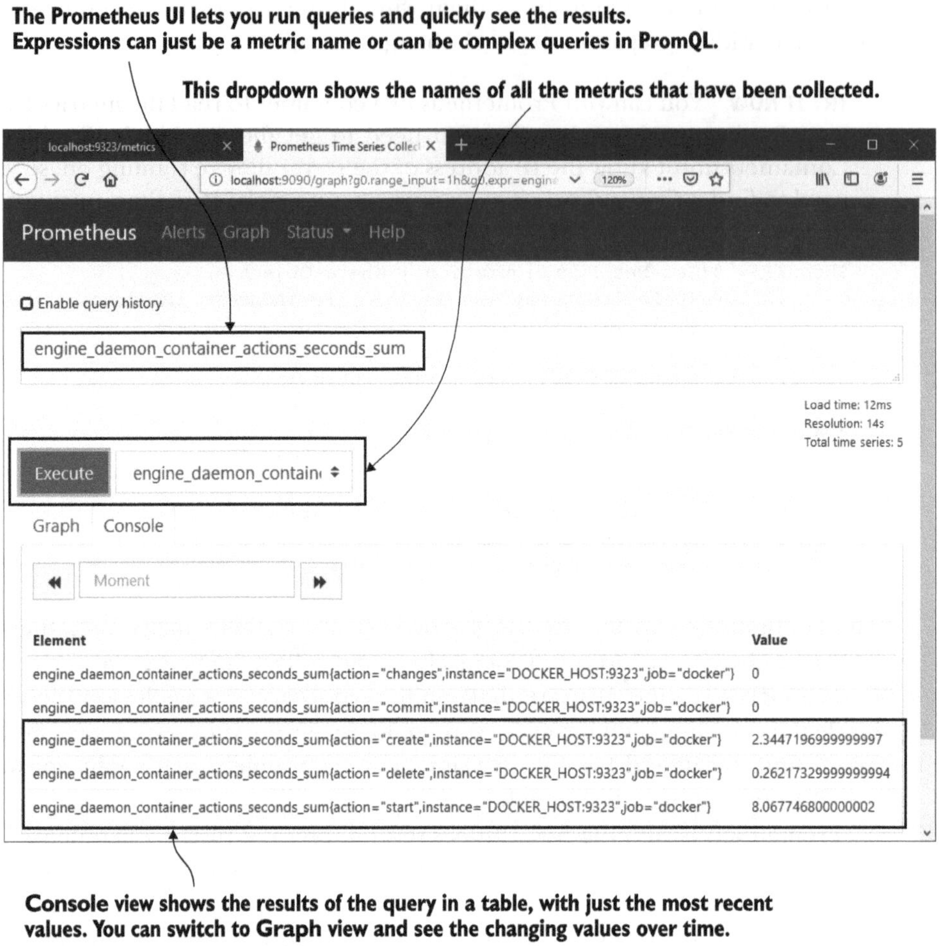

**The Prometheus UI lets you run queries and quickly see the results.**
**Expressions can just be a metric name or can be complex queries in PromQL.**

**This dropdown shows the names of all the metrics that have been collected.**

**Console view shows the results of the query in a table, with just the most recent values. You can switch to Graph view and see the changing values over time.**

**Figure 9.4   Prometheus has a simple web UI that you can use to find metrics and run queries.**

points. Some are high-level readouts, like the number of containers in each state and the number of health checks that have failed; others give low-level details, like the amount of memory the Docker Engine has allocated; and some are static pieces of information, like the number of CPUs Docker has available. These are infrastructure-level metrics, which could all be useful things to include in your status dashboard.

Your applications will expose their own metrics, which will also record details at different levels. The goal is to have a metrics endpoint in each of your containers and have Prometheus collect metrics from them all on a regular schedule. Prometheus will store enough information for you to build a dashboard that shows the overall health of the whole system.

## 9.2    *Exposing metrics from your application*

We've looked at the metrics the Docker Engine exposes, because that's an easy way to get started with Prometheus. Exposing a useful set of metrics from each of your application containers takes more effort, because you need code to capture the metrics and provide the HTTP endpoint for Prometheus to call. It's not as much work as it sounds, because there are Prometheus client libraries for all the main programming languages to do that for you.

In the code for this chapter, I've revisited the NASA image gallery app and added Prometheus metrics to each of my components. I'm using the official Prometheus clients for Java and Go, and the community client library for Node.js. Figure 9.5 shows how each application container is now packaged with a Prometheus client that collects and exposes metrics.

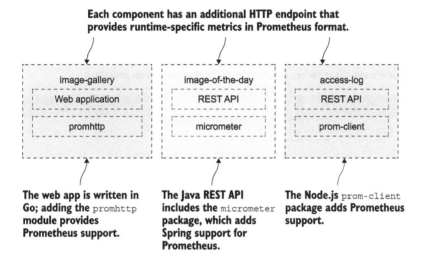

Figure 9.5    Prometheus client libraries in your apps make the metrics endpoints available in the container.

The information points collected from a Prometheus client library are runtime-level metrics. They provide key information regarding what your container is doing and how hard it is working, in terms that are relevant to the application runtime. The metrics for a Go application include the number of active Goroutines; the metrics for a Java application include the memory used in the JVM. Each runtime has its own important metrics, and the client libraries do a great job of collecting and exporting those.

**TRY IT NOW**    There's a Docker Compose file in the exercises for this chapter that spins up a new version of the image gallery app, with metrics in each container. Use the app and then browse to one of the metrics endpoints:

```
cd ./ch09/exercises

# clear down existing containers:
docker container rm -f $(docker container ls -aq)

# create the nat network - if you've already created it
# you'll get a warning which you can ignore:
docker network create nat

# start the project
docker-compose up -d

# browse to http://localhost:8010 to use the app

# then browse to http://localhost:8010/metrics
```

My output is in figure 9.6. These are the metrics from the Go frontend web application—there's no custom code required to produce this data. You can get all this data for free just by adding the Go client library into your application and setting it up.

**Adding the Prometheus client library enables metrics in the application container.**

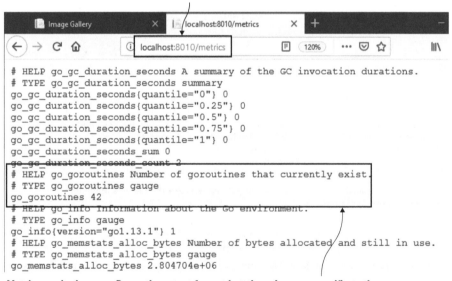

**Metrics are in the same Prometheus text format but the values are specific to the application runtime—this is a count of active Goroutines in the Go application.**

Figure 9.6    Prometheus metrics about the Go runtime from the image gallery web container

You'll see similar metrics for the Java REST API if you browse to http://localhost:8011/actuator/prometheus. The metrics endpoints are a sea of text, but all the key data points are in there to build a dashboard that will show if the containers are running "hot"—if they're using a lot of compute resources like CPU time, memory, or processor threads.

Those runtime metrics are the next level of detail you want after the infrastructure metrics from Docker, but those two levels don't tell you the whole story. The final data points are application metrics that you explicitly capture to record key information about your application. Those metrics could be operations-focused, showing the number of events a component has processed or the average time to process a response. Or they could be business-focused, showing the current number of active users or the number of people signing up to a new service.

Prometheus client libraries let you record these kind of metrics too, but you need to explicitly write the code to capture the information in your app. It's not difficult to do. Listing 9.1 shows an example using the Node.js library, which is in the code for the `access-log` component in the image gallery app. I don't want to throw a whole bunch of code at you, but as you progress further with containers, you're certain to spend more time with Prometheus, and this snippet from the `server.js` file illustrates a couple of key things.

> **Listing 9.1** **Declaring and using custom Prometheus metric values in Node.js**

```
//declare custom metrics:
const accessCounter = new prom.Counter({
  name: "access_log_total",
  help: "Access Log - total log requests"
});

const clientIpGauge = new prom.Gauge({
  name: "access_client_ip_current",
  help: "Access Log - current unique IP addresses"
});

//and later, update the metrics values:
accessCounter.inc();
clientIpGauge.set(countOfIpAddresses);
```

In the source code for the chapter, you'll see how I've added metrics in the `image-gallery` web application written in Go, and in the `image-of-the-day` REST API written in Java. Each Prometheus client library works in a different way. In the `main.go` source file I initialize counters and gauges in a similar way to the Node.js app but then use instrumented handlers from the client library rather than setting metrics explicitly. The Java application is different again—in `ImageController.java` I use the `@Timed` attribute and increment a `registry.counter` object in the source. Each client library works in the most logical way for the language.

There are different types of metrics in Prometheus—I've used the simplest ones in these applications: counters and gauges. They're both numeric values. Counters hold a value that increases or stays the same, and gauges hold values that can increase or decrease. It's down to you or your application developers to choose the metric type and to set its value at the correct time; the rest is taken care of by Prometheus and the client library.

> **TRY IT NOW**   You have the image gallery app running from the last exercise, so these metrics are already being collected. Run some load into the app, and then browse to the Node.js app's metrics endpoint:

```
# loop to make 5 HTTP GET request - on Windows:
for ($i=1; $i -le 5; $i++) { iwr -useb http://localhost:8010 | Out-
    Null }

# or on Linux:
for i in {1..5}; do curl http://localhost:8010 > /dev/null; done

# now browse to http://localhost:8012/metrics
```

You can see my output in figure 9.7—I ran a few more loops to send in traffic. The first two records show my custom metrics, recording the number of access requests received and the total number of IP addresses using the service. These are simple data points (and the IP count is actually fake), but they serve the purpose of collecting and showing metrics. Prometheus lets you record more complex types of metrics, but even with simple counters and gauges you can capture detailed instrumentation in your apps.

**The same metrics endpoint provides my custom values and the standard Node.js data.**

**Node.js runtime metrics are provided by the client library—this shows total amount of CPU time used.**

**Figure 9.7   A metrics endpoint that includes custom data as well as Node.js runtime data**

What you capture depends on your application, but the following list provides some useful guidelines—you can return to these at the end of the month when you're ready to add detailed monitoring to your own apps.

- When you talk to external systems, record how long the call took and whether the response was successful—you'll quickly be able to see if another system is slowing yours down or breaking it.
- Anything worth logging is potentially worth recording in a metric—it's probably cheaper on memory, disk, and CPU to increment a counter than to write a log entry, and it's easier to visualize how often things are happening.
- Any details about application or user behaviors that business teams want to report on should be recorded as metrics—that way you can build real-time dashboards instead of sending historical reports.

## 9.3 Running a Prometheus container to collect metrics

Prometheus uses a pull model to collect metrics. Rather than have other systems send it data, it fetches data from those systems. It calls this *scraping*, and when you deploy Prometheus you configure the endpoints you want it to scrape. In a production container platform, you can configure Prometheus so it automatically finds all the containers across the cluster. In Docker Compose on a single server, you use a simple list of service names, and Prometheus finds the containers through Docker's DNS.

Listing 9.2 shows the configuration I've used for Prometheus to scrape two of the components in my image gallery application. There's a `global` setting that uses a default 10-second interval between scrapes, and then there's a `job` for each component. The job has a name, and the configuration specifies the URL path to the metrics endpoint and a list of targets that Prometheus will query. I use two types here. First, `static_configs` specifies a target hostname, which is fine for a single container. I also use `dns_sd_configs`, which means Prometheus will use DNS service discovery—that will find multiple containers for a service, and it supports running at scale.

> **Listing 9.2 Prometheus configuration for scraping application metrics**

```
global:
  scrape_interval: 10s

scrape_configs:
  - job_name: "image-gallery"
    metrics_path: /metrics
    static_configs:
      - targets: ["image-gallery"]

  - job_name: "iotd-api"
    metrics_path: /actuator/prometheus
    static_configs:
      - targets: ["iotd"]
```

```
- job_name: "access-log"
  metrics_path: /metrics
  dns_sd_configs:
    - names:
        - accesslog
      type: A
      port: 80
```

This configuration sets Prometheus to poll all the containers every 10 seconds. It will use DNS to get the container IP addresses, but for the `image-gallery` it only expects to find a single container, so you'll get unexpected behavior if you scale that component. Prometheus always uses the first IP address in the list if the DNS response contains several, so you'll get metrics from different containers when Docker load balances the request to the metrics endpoint. The `accesslog` component is configured to support multiple IP addresses, so Prometheus will build a list of all the container IP addresses and poll them all on the same schedule. Figure 9.8 shows how the scraping process runs.

**The Docker image is packaged with configuration for Prometheus to scrape the app containers every 10 seconds.**

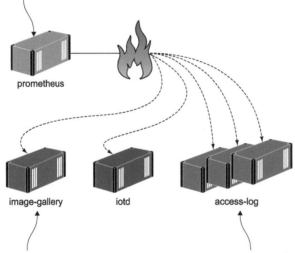

**There are single instances of the Go and Java components. Prometheus is using** `static_config` **so it only expects one IP address for the domain name.**

**The Node.js component is running at scale over three containers. Prometheus is using** `dns_sd_config`, **which means service discovery through DNS, so it will use all the IP addresses Docker returns from the DNS lookup.**

Figure 9.8  Prometheus running in a container, configured to scrape metrics from app containers

I've built a custom Prometheus Docker image for the image gallery application. It's based on the official image that the Prometheus team publish on Docker Hub, and it copies in my own configuration file (you can find the Dockerfile in the source code for this chapter). This approach gives me a preconfigured Prometheus image that I can run without any extra configuration, but I can always override the config file in other environments if I need to.

Metrics are more interesting when lots of containers are running. We can scale up the Node.js component of the image gallery app to run on multiple containers, and Prometheus will scrape and collect metrics from all the containers.

> **TRY IT NOW** There's another Docker Compose file in the chapter's exercises folder that publishes a random port for the access-log service, so that service can be run at scale. Run it with three instances and send some more load into the website:

```
docker-compose -f docker-compose-scale.yml up -d --scale accesslog=3

# loop to make 10 HTTP GET request - on Windows:
for ($i=1; $i -le 10; $i++) { iwr -useb http://localhost:8010 | Out-
    Null }

# or on Linux:
for i in {1..10}; do curl http://localhost:8010 > /dev/null; done
```

The website makes a call to the access-log service every time it processes a request—there are three containers running that service, so the calls should be load-balanced across them all. How can we check that the load balancing is working effectively? The metrics from that component include a label that captures the hostname of the machine sending the metrics—in this case that's the Docker container ID. Open the Prometheus UI and check the access-log metrics. You should see three sets of data.

> **TRY IT NOW** Browse to http://localhost:9090/graph. In the metrics dropdown, select access_log_total and click Execute.

You'll see something similar to my output in figure 9.9—there's one metric value for each of the containers, and the labels contain the hostname. The actual values for each container will show you how evenly spread the load balancing is. In an ideal scenario, the figures would be equal, but there are a lot of network factors in play (like DNS caching and HTTP keep-alive connections), which means you probably won't see that if you're running on a single machine.

Recording extra information with labels is one of the most powerful features of Prometheus. It lets you work with a single metric at different levels of granularity. Right now you're seeing the raw data for the metrics, with one line in the table for each container showing the most recent metric value. You can aggregate across all the containers using a sum() query, ignoring the individual labels and showing a combined total, and you can display that in a graph to see the increasing usage over time.

**This is the custom counter in the Node.js application, which records how many requests it has processed.**

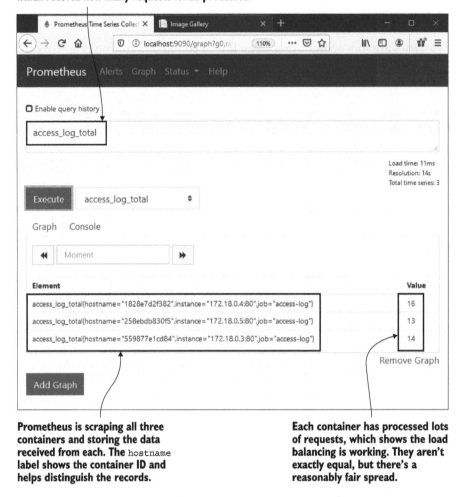

**Prometheus is scraping all three containers and storing the data received from each. The** `hostname` **label shows the container ID and helps distinguish the records.**

**Each container has processed lots of requests, which shows the load balancing is working. They aren't exactly equal, but there's a reasonably fair spread.**

Figure 9.9  Processing metrics can be used to verify that requests are being load-balanced.

**TRY IT NOW**    In the Prometheus UI, click the Add Graph button to add a new query. In the expression text box, paste this query:

```
sum(access_log_total) without(hostname, instance)
```

Click Execute and you'll see a line graph with a time series, which is how Prometheus represents data—a set of metrics, each recorded with a timestamp.

I sent in some more HTTP requests to my local app before I added the new graph—you can see my output in figure 9.10.

**This query aggregates the** `access_log_total` **metric for all containers, summing the values without separating them by** `hostname` **or** `instance`**.**

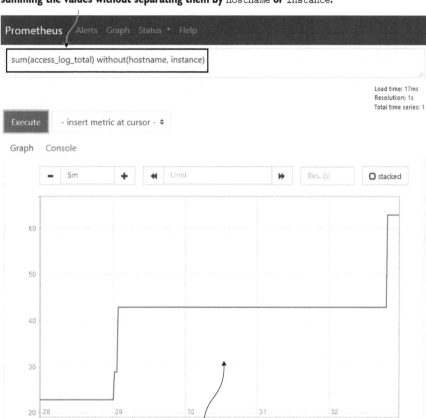

**Switching to Graph view shows the results of the query over time. This is a counter metric, so it will only increase or stay the same.**

**Figure 9.10  Aggregating a metric to sum values from all containers and showing a graph of results**

The `sum()` query is written in Prometheus's own query language called *PromQL*. It's a powerful language with statistical functions that let you query changes over time and rate of change, and you can add subqueries to correlate different metrics. But you don't need to go into any of that complexity to build useful dashboards. The Prometheus format is so well structured that you can visualize key metrics with simple queries. You can use labels to filter values, and sum the results to aggregate, and just those features will give you a useful dashboard.

Figure 9.11 shows a typical query that will feed into a dashboard. This aggregates the value for all the `image_gallery_request` metrics, filtering where the response code is `200`, and summing without the `instance` label, so we will get metrics from all

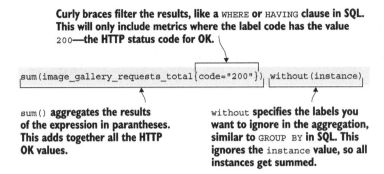

Curly braces filter the results, like a WHERE or HAVING clause in SQL.
This will only include metrics where the label code has the value
200—the HTTP status code for OK.

```
sum(image_gallery_requests_total{code="200"}) without(instance)
```

sum() **aggregates the results
of the expression in parantheses.
This adds together all the HTTP
OK values.**

without **specifies the labels you
want to ignore in the aggregation,
similar to** GROUP BY **in SQL. This
ignores the** instance **value, so all
instances get summed.**

**Figure 9.11   A simple Prometheus query. You don't need to learn much more
PromQL than this.**

the containers. The result will be the total number of 200 "OK" responses sent by
all the containers running the image gallery web application.

The Prometheus UI is fine for checking on your configuration, validating that all
the scrape targets are reachable, and working out queries. But it is not meant to be a
dashboard—that's where Grafana comes in.

## 9.4   *Running a Grafana container to visualize metrics*

We're covering a lot of ground in this chapter because monitoring is a core topic for
containers, but we're going quickly because the finer details are all very application-
dependent. What metrics you need to capture will depend on your business and operational needs, and how you capture them will depend on the application runtime
you're using and the mechanics of the Prometheus client library for that runtime.

Once you have your data in Prometheus, things get simpler—it becomes a pretty
standard approach for all apps. You'll use the Prometheus UI to navigate the metrics
you're recording and work on queries to get the data that you want to see. Then you'll
run Grafana and plug those queries into a dashboard. Each data point shows up as a
user-friendly visualization, and the dashboard as a whole shows you what's happening
with your app.

We've been working toward the Grafana dashboard for the image gallery app all
through this chapter, and figure 9.12 shows the final outcome. It's a very neat way to
show core information from all the application components and the Docker runtime.
These queries are also built to support scale, so the same dashboard can be used in a
production cluster.

The Grafana dashboard conveys key information across many different levels of
the application. It looks complicated, but each visualization is powered by a single
PromQL query, and none of the queries do anything more complex than filtering and
aggregating. The shrunken view in figure 9.12 doesn't give you the full picture, but

The full Grafana dashboard for the application. Each visualization is populated by a simple Prometheus query. There is a dashboard row for each component, showing key metrics.

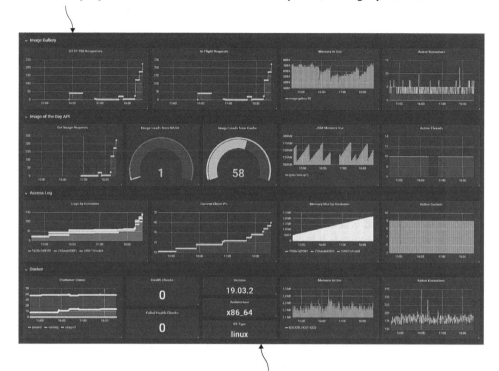

The final row shows information about the Docker Engine, including container metrics and configuration details.

Figure 9.12 The Grafana dashboard for the application. Looks fancy, but it's actually pretty simple to build.

I've packaged the dashboard into a custom Grafana image so you can run it yourself in a container and explore.

**TRY IT NOW** You'll need to capture your computer's IP address again, this time as an environment variable that the Compose file looks for and injects into the Prometheus container. Then run the app with Docker Compose and generate some load:

```
# load your machine's IP address into an environment variable - on
    Windows:
$env:HOST_IP = $(Get-NetIPConfiguration | Where-Object
    {$_.IPv4DefaultGateway -ne $null }).IPv4Address.IPAddress

# on Linux:
export HOST_IP=$(ip route get 1 | awk '{print $NF;exit}')
```

```
# run the app with a Compose file which includes Grafana:
docker-compose -f ./docker-compose-with-grafana.yml up -d --scale
    accesslog=3

# now send in some load to prime the metrics - on Windows:
for ($i=1; $i -le 20; $i++) { iwr -useb http://localhost:8010 |
    Out-Null }

# or on Linux:
for i in {1..20}; do curl http://localhost:8010 > /dev/null; done

# and browse to http://localhost:3000
```

Grafana uses port 3000 for the web UI. When you first browse, you'll need to sign in—the credentials are username `admin`, password `admin`. You'll be asked to change the admin password on the first login, but I won't judge you if you click Skip instead. When the UI loads, you'll be in your "home" dashboard—click on the Home link at the top left, and you'll see the dashboard list in figure 9.13. Click Image Gallery to load the application dashboard.

My application dashboard is a reasonable setup for a production system. There are some key data points you need, to make sure you're monitoring the right things—Google discusses this in the *Site Reliability Engineering* book (http://mng.bz/EdZj). Their focus is on latency, traffic, errors, and saturation, which they call the "golden signals."

I'll go through the first set of my visualizations in detail so you can see that a smart dashboard can be built from basic queries and the right choice of visualization. Figure 9.14

**The Docker image for this container is preconfigured
with Grafana and the dashboard for the application.**

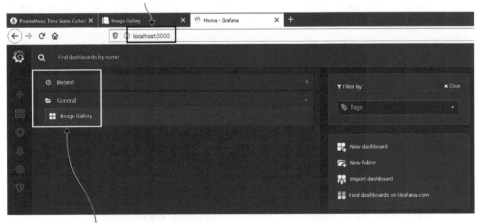

**Grafana can show many dashboards. From the
Home link you can list all available dashboards.**

**Figure 9.13   Navigating dashboards in Grafana—recently used folders are shown here**

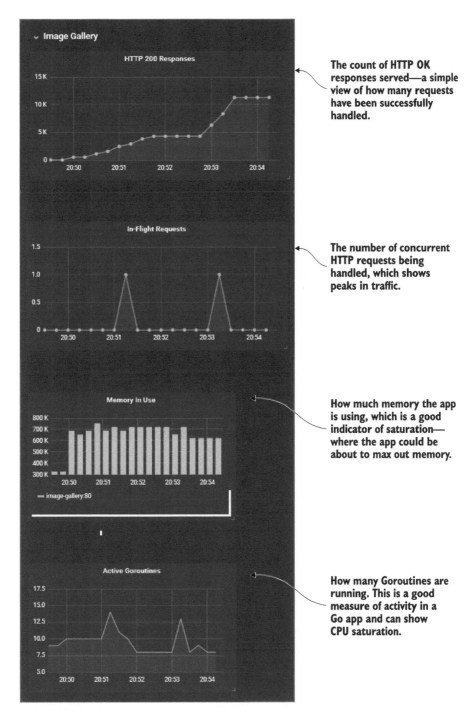

The count of HTTP OK responses served—a simple view of how many requests have been successfully handled.

The number of concurrent HTTP requests being handled, which shows peaks in traffic.

How much memory the app is using, which is a good indicator of saturation—where the app could be about to max out memory.

How many Goroutines are running. This is a good measure of activity in a Go app and can show CPU saturation.

Figure 9.14   A closer look at the application dashboard and how visualizations relate to the golden signals

shows the row of metrics for the Image Gallery web UI—I've chopped the row up to make it easier to see, but these appear on the same line in the dashboard.

There are four metrics here that show how heavily the system is being used, and how hard the system is working to support that level of use:

- *HTTP 200 Responses*—This is a simple count of how many HTTP "OK" responses the website has sent over time. The PromQL query is a sum over the counter metric from the application: `sum(image_gallery_requests_total{code="200"})` `without(instance)`. I could add a similar graph with a query filtering on `code="500"` to show the number of errors.
- *In-Flight Requests*—This shows the number of active requests at any given point. It's a Prometheus gauge, so it can go up or down. There's no filter for this, and the graph will show the total across all containers, so the query is another sum: `sum(image_gallery_in_flight_requests) without(instance)`.
- *Memory In Use*—This shows how much system memory the image gallery containers are using. It's a bar chart, which is easier on the eye for this type of data; it will show a bar for each container when I scale up the web component. The PromQL query filters on the job name: `go_memstats_stack_inuse_bytes{job="image-gallery"}`. I need the filter because this is a standard Go metric, and the Docker Engine job returns a metric with the same name.
- *Active Goroutines*—This is a rough indicator of how hard the component is working—a Goroutine is a unit of work in Go, and many can run concurrently. This graph will show if the web component suddenly has a spike of processing activity. It's another standard Go metric, so the PromQL query filters stats from the web job and sums them: `sum(go_goroutines{job=\"image-gallery\"})` `without(instance)`.

The visualizations in the other rows of the dashboards all use similar queries. There's no need for complex PromQL—choosing the right metrics to show and the right visualization to display them is all you really need.

In these visualizations the actual values are less useful than the trends. It doesn't really matter if my web app uses 200 MB of memory on average or 800 MB—what matters is when there's a sudden spike that deviates from the norm. The set of metrics for a component should help you quickly see anomalies and find correlations. If the graph of error responses is on an upward trend and the number of active Goroutines is doubling every few seconds, it's clear there's something going wrong—the component could be saturated, so you may need to scale up with more containers to handle the load.

Grafana is an extremely powerful tool, but it's straightforward to use. It's the most popular dashboard system for modern applications, so it's worth learning—it can query lots of different data sources, and it can send alerts out to different systems too. Building dashboards is the same as editing existing dashboards—you can add or edit visualizations (called *panels*), resize and move them around, and then save your dashboard to a file.

**TRY IT NOW** The Google SRE approach says that an HTTP error count is a core metric, and that's missing from the dashboard, so we'll add it to the image gallery row now. Run the whole image gallery app again if you don't have it running, browse to Grafana at http://locahost:3000, and log in with username `admin` and password `admin`.

Open the Image Gallery dashboard and click the Add Panel icon at the top right of the screen—it's the bar chart with a plus sign shown in figure 9.15.

This is the navigation bar you see in the top right of the Grafana screen.

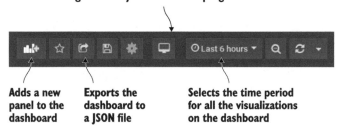

Adds a new panel to the dashboard

Exports the dashboard to a JSON file

Selects the time period for all the visualizations on the dashboard

Figure 9.15 The Grafana toolbar for adding panels, choosing the time period, and saving the dashboard

Now click Add Query in the new panel window, and you'll see a screen where you can capture all the details of the visualization. Select Prometheus as the data source for the query, and in the metrics field paste this PromQL expression:

```
sum(image_gallery_requests_total{code="500"}) without(instance)
```

Your panel should look like mine in figure 9.16. The image gallery application returns an error response around 10% of the time, so if you make enough requests you'll see some errors in your graph.

Press the Escape key to go back to the main dashboard.

You can resize panels by dragging the bottom-right corner, and move them by dragging the title. When you have the dashboard looking how you want, you can click the Share Dashboard icon from the tool panel (see figure 9.15 again), where you have the option to export the dashboard as a JSON file.

The final step with Grafana is packaging your own Docker image, which is already configured with Prometheus as a data source and with the application dashboard. I've done that for the `diamol/ch09-grafana` image. Listing 9.3 shows the full Dockerfile.

**Listing 9.3 The Dockerfile to package a custom Grafana image**

```
FROM diamol/grafana:6.4.3

COPY datasource-prometheus.yaml ${GF_PATHS_PROVISIONING}/datasources/
COPY dashboard-provider.yaml ${GF_PATHS_PROVISIONING}/dashboards/
COPY dashboard.json /var/lib/grafana/dashboards/
```

The Grafana screen to add a new panel. You choose the type of visualization, add the title and the legend, and provide the query that Grafans runs to populate the panel.

This query uses Prometheus as the data source, so the Grafana container will send requests to the Prometheus container.

This is the query to run. It fetches the count of HTTP errors over the selected time period for the dashboard, and Grafana plots the results in a graph.

Figure 9.16   Adding a new panel to the Grafana dashboard to show HTTP errors

The image starts from a specific version of Grafana and then just copies in a set of YAML and JSON files. Grafana follows the configuration pattern I've promoted already in this book—there's some default configuration built in, but you can apply your own. When the container starts, Grafana looks for files in specific folders, and it applies any configuration files it finds. The YAML files set up the Prometheus connection and load any dashboards that are in the /var/lib/Grafana/dashboards folder. The final line copies my dashboard JSON into that folder, so it gets loaded when the container starts.

You can do much more with Grafana provisioning, and you can also use the API to create users and set their preferences. It's not much more work to build a Grafana image with multiple dashboards and a read-only user with access to all those dashboards, which can be put together in a Grafana playlist. Then you can browse to Grafana on a big screen in your office and have it automatically cycle through all your dashboards.

## 9.5 *Understanding the levels of observability*

Observability is a key requirement when you move from simple proof-of-concept containers to getting ready for production. But there's another very good reason I introduced Prometheus and Grafana in this chapter: learning Docker is not just about the mechanics of Dockerfiles and Docker Compose files. Part of the magic of Docker is the huge ecosystem that's grown around containers, and the patterns that have emerged around that ecosystem.

Monitoring was a real headache when containers were first getting popular. My production releases back then were as easy to build and deploy as they are today, but I had no insight into the apps when they were running. I had to rely on external services like Pingdom to check that my APIs were still up, and on user reporting to make sure the app was working correctly. Today the approach to monitoring containers is a tried-and-trusted path. We've followed that path in this chapter, and figure 9.17 summarizes the approach.

I've walked through a single dashboard for the image gallery application, which is an overall view of the app. In a production environment, you'd have additional dashboards that dig into extra levels of detail. There would be an infrastructure dashboard showing free disk space, available CPU, and memory and network saturation for all the servers. Each component might have its own dashboard showing additional information, like a breakdown of response times for serving each page of a web app or each API endpoint.

The summary dashboard is the critical one. You should be able to pull together all the most important data points from your application metrics into a single screen, so you can tell at a glance if something is wrong and take evasive action before it gets worse.

## 9.6 *Lab*

This chapter added monitoring to the image gallery app, and this lab asks you to do the same to the to-do list app. You don't need to dive into source code—I've already built a new version of the application image that contains Prometheus metrics. Run a container from `diamol/ch09-todo-list`, browse to the app, and add some items, and you'll see the metrics available at the `/metrics` URL. For the lab, you want to get that app to the same position we have for the image gallery:

- Write a Docker Compose file that you can use to run the app, which also starts a Prometheus container and a Grafana container.

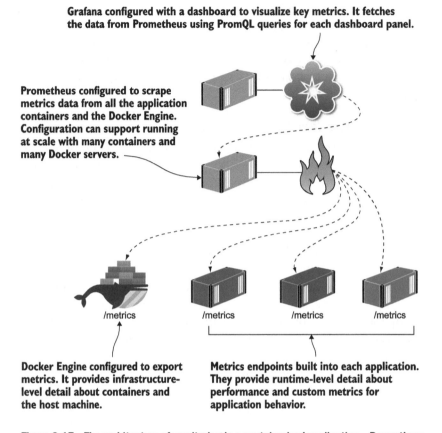

**Grafana configured with a dashboard to visualize key metrics. It fetches the data from Prometheus using PromQL queries for each dashboard panel.**

**Prometheus configured to scrape metrics data from all the application containers and the Docker Engine. Configuration can support running at scale with many containers and many Docker servers.**

/metrics          /metrics          /metrics          /metrics

**Docker Engine configured to export metrics. It provides infrastructure-level detail about containers and the host machine.**

**Metrics endpoints built into each application. They provide runtime-level detail about performance and custom metrics for application behavior.**

Figure 9.17   The architecture of monitoring in a containerized application—Prometheus is at the center.

- The Prometheus container should already be configured to scrape metrics from the to-do list app.
- The Grafana container should be configured with a dashboard to show three key metrics from the app: number of tasks created, total number of HTTP requests processed, and number of HTTP requests currently being processed.

This sounds like a ton of work, but really it's not—the exercises in this chapter cover all the details. It's a good lab to work through, because it will give you experience working with metrics for a new application.

As always, you'll find my solution on GitHub, together with a graphic of my final dashboard: https://github.com/sixeyed/diamol/blob/master/ch09/lab/README.md.

# Running multiple
# environments with
# Docker Compose

We looked at Docker Compose in chapter 7, and you gained a good understanding of how to use YAML to describe a multi-container application and manage it with the Compose command line. Since then we've enhanced our Docker applications to get them ready for production with health checks and monitoring. Now it's time to return to Compose, because we don't need all those production features in every environment. Portability is one of Docker's major benefits. When you package your application to run in containers, it works the same way wherever you deploy it, and that's important because it eliminates drift between environments.

Drift is what always happens when manual processes are used to deploy software. Some updates get missed or some new dependencies are forgotten, so the production environment is different from the user test environment, which is different again from the system test environment. When deployments fail, it's often because of drift, and it takes a huge amount of time and effort to track down the missing pieces and put them right. Moving to Docker fixes that problem because every application is already packaged with its dependencies, but you still need the flexibility to support different behavior for different environments. Docker Compose provides that with the more advanced features we'll cover in this chapter.

## 10.1 Deploying many applications with Docker Compose

Docker Compose is a tool for running multi-container applications on a single Docker Engine. It's great for developers, and it's also heavily used for non-production environments. Organizations often run multiple versions of an app in different environments—maybe version 1.5 is running in production, version 1.5.1 is being tested in a hotfix environment, version 1.6 is finishing up user testing, and version 1.7

is in system test. Those non-production environments don't need the scale and performance of production, so it's a great use case for Docker Compose to run those environments and get maximum utilization from your hardware.

For that to work, there need to be some differences between environments. You can't have several containers trying to listen for traffic on port 80, or writing data to the same files on the server. You can design your Docker Compose files to support that, but first you need to understand how Compose identifies which Docker resources are part of the same application. It does that with naming conventions and labels, and if you want to run several copies of the same application, you need to work around the defaults.

> **TRY IT NOW**  Open a terminal and browse to the exercises for this chapter. Run two of the apps we've already worked with, and then try running another instance of the to-do list application:

```
cd ./ch10/exercises

# run the random number app from chapter 8:
docker-compose -f ./numbers/docker-compose.yml up -d

# run the to-do list app from chapter 6:
docker-compose -f ./todo-list/docker-compose.yml up -d

# and try another copy of the to-do list:
docker-compose -f ./todo-list/docker-compose.yml up -d
```

Your output will be the same as mine in figure 10.1. You can start multiple applications from Compose files in different folders, but you can't start a second instance of an application by running up from the same folder. Docker Compose thinks you're asking it to run an application that is already running, so it doesn't start any new containers.

Docker Compose uses the concept of a *project* to identify that various resources are part of the same application, and it uses the name of the directory that contains the Compose file as the default project name. Compose prefixes the project name when it creates resources, and for containers it also adds a numeric counter as a suffix. So if your Compose file is in a folder called app1, and it defines one service called web and one volume called disk, Compose will deploy it by creating a volume called app1_disk and a container called app1_web_1. The counter at the end of the container name supports scale, so if you scale that up to two instances of the web service, the new container will be called app1_web_2. Figure 10.2 shows how the container name is built for the to-do list application.

You can override the default project name Compose uses, and that's how you can run many copies of the same application in different sets of containers on a single Docker Engine.

**Runs the application specified
in the Compose file in the
`numbers` directory**

**Docker Compose creates containers for
the apps, using the directory name as
the prefix for each container name.**

```
PS>cd ./ch10/exercises
PS>
PS>docker-compose -f .\numbers\docker-compose.yml up -d
Creating numbers_numbers-web_1 ... done
Creating numbers_numbers-api_1 ... done
PS>
PS>docker-compose -f .\todo-list\docker-compose.yml up -d
Creating todo-list_todo-web_1 ... done
PS>
PS>docker-compose -f .\todo-list\docker-compose.yml up -d
todo-list_todo-web_1 is up-to-date
PS>
```

**Runs the application specified
in the `todo-list` directory—
Compose creates the
application container.**

**Repeating the command doesn't create
a second copy of the app; Compose sees
there's already a container running that
matches the app definition.**

**Figure 10.1   Repeating a Docker Compose command to start an app doesn't run a
second copy of the app.**

**TRY IT NOW**   You already have one instance of the to-do app running; you can
start another by specifying a different project name. The website uses random
ports, so you'll need to find the assigned port if you want to actually try the
apps:

```
docker-compose -f ./todo-list/docker-compose.yml -p todo-test up -d

docker container ls

docker container port todo-test_todo-web_1 80
```

**The Compose project name
defaults to the folder name
where the Compose files
are stored.**

**The container index is an
incremented value used
when you scale up to
multiple containers.**

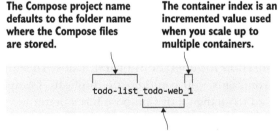

```
todo-list_todo-web_1
```

**The service name in the Compose file. It is also used
as the DNS name for other containers to communicate.**

**Figure 10.2   Docker Compose builds
names for the resources it manages by
including the project name.**

My output is in figure 10.3. Specifying a project name means this is a different application as far as Compose is concerned, and there are no resources that match this project name, so Compose creates a new container. The naming pattern is predictable, so I know the new container will be called `todo-test_todo-web_1`. The Docker CLI has the `container port` command to find the published port for a container, and I can use that with the generated container name to find the application port.

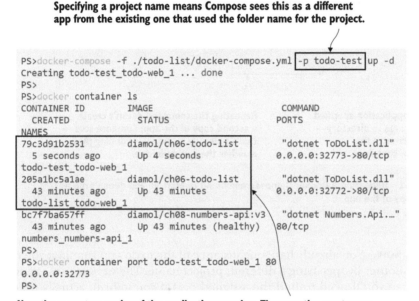

**Specifying a project name means Compose sees this as a different app from the existing one that used the folder name for the project.**

```
PS>docker-compose -f ./todo-list/docker-compose.yml -p todo-test up -d
Creating todo-test_todo-web_1 ... done
PS>
PS>docker container ls
CONTAINER ID        IMAGE                          COMMAND
   CREATED             STATUS                      PORTS
NAMES
79c3d91b2531        diamol/ch06-todo-list          "dotnet ToDoList.dll"
   5 seconds ago       Up 4 seconds                0.0.0.0:32773->80/tcp
todo-test_todo-web_1
205a1bc5a1ae        diamol/ch06-todo-list          "dotnet ToDoList.dll"
   43 minutes ago      Up 43 minutes               0.0.0.0:32772->80/tcp
todo-list_todo-web_1
bc7f7ba657ff        diamol/ch08-numbers-api:v3     "dotnet Numbers.Api...."
   43 minutes ago      Up 43 minutes (healthy)     80/tcp
numbers_numbers-api_1
PS>
PS>docker container port todo-test_todo-web_1 80
0.0.0.0:32773
PS>
```

**Now there are two copies of the application running. They use the exact same Docker Compose file, but the project name makes them separate apps in Compose.**

Figure 10.3  Specifying a project name lets you run multiple copies of the same app with one Compose file.

This approach lets you run many copies of many different applications. I could deploy another instance of my random number application too, using the same Compose file but specifying a different project name. That's useful, but for most situations you'll want a bit more control—having to find out which random port to use for each release isn't a great workflow for operations or test teams. To support different setups in different environments, you could create duplicate Compose files and edit the properties that need to change, but Compose has a better way of managing that with overrides.

## 10.2 Using Docker Compose override files

Teams hit the problem of trying to run different app configurations with Docker Compose and often end up with many Compose files—one for each environment. That works, but it's not maintainable, because those Compose files are often 90% duplicated content, which means they'll get out of sync and you're back to a drift situation. Override files are a much neater approach. Docker Compose lets you merge multiple files together, with properties from later files overriding those from earlier in the merge.

Figure 10.4 shows how you can use overrides to structure an easily maintainable set of Compose files. You start with a core `docker-compose.yml` file that contains the basic structure of the app, with the services defined and configured with properties that are common for all environments. Then each environment has its own override file that adds specific settings, but it doesn't duplicate any of the configuration from the core file.

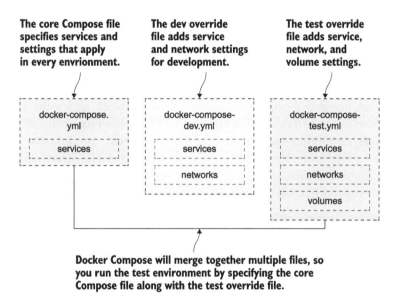

Figure 10.4   Removing duplication with override files that add environment-specific settings

This approach is maintainable. If you need to make a change that applies to all environments—like changing an image tag to use the latest version—you do that once in the core file, and it filters through to every environment. If you just need to change one environment, you only change that single file. The override files you have for each environment also serve as clear documentation of the differences between environments.

Listing 10.1 shows a very simple example where the core Compose file specifies most of the application properties, and the override changes the image tag so this deployment will use v2 of the to-do app.

---

**Listing 10.1   A Docker Compose override file that updates a single property**

```
# from docker-compose.yml - the core app specification:
services:
  todo-web:
    image: diamol/ch06-todo-list
    ports:
      - 80
    environment:
      - Database:Provider=Sqlite
    networks:
      - app-net

# and from docker-compose-v2.yml - the version override file:
services:
  todo-web:
    image: diamol/ch06-todo-list:v2
```

In the override file you just specify the properties you care about, but you need to preserve the structure of the main Compose file so that Docker Compose can link the definitions together. The override file in this example only changes the value of the `image` property, but that needs to be specified in the `todo-web` block under the `services` block, so Compose can match that to the full service definition in the core file.

Docker Compose merges files together when you specify multiple file paths in `docker-compose` commands. The `config` command is very useful here—it validates the contents of the input files, and if the input is valid, it writes out the final output. You can use that to see what will happen when you apply an override file.

> **TRY IT NOW**   In the exercises folder for this chapter, use Docker Compose to merge together the files from listing 10.1 and print the output:

```
docker-compose -f ./todo-list/docker-compose.yml -f ./todo-
    list/docker-compose-v2.yml config
```

The `config` command doesn't actually deploy the app; it just validates the configuration. You'll see in the output that the two files have been merged. All the properties come from the core Docker Compose file, except the `image` tag where the value has been overridden from the second file—you can see that in figure 10.5.

Docker Compose applies overrides in the order that the files are listed in the command, with files to the right overriding files to the left. That's important, because if you get the order wrong, you'll get unexpected results—the `config` command is useful here because it shows you a dry run of the complete Compose file. The output sorts everything by alphabetical order, so you'll see networks, then services, then the

The config command is useful for dry-runs—it merges the input files, validates the final output, and displays it, if it is valid.

```
PS>docker-compose -f .\todo-list\docker-compose.yml
 -f .\todo-list\docker-compose-v2.yml config
networks:
  app-net:
    external: true
    name: nat
services:
  todo-web:
    environment:
      Database:Provider: Sqlite
    image: diamol/ch06-todo-list:v2
    networks:
      app-net: {}
    ports:
    - target: 80
version: '3.7'
```

The `image` tag is the only value that comes from the override file; the rest of the settings come from the base Compose file.

**Figure 10.5  Merging a Compose file with an override file and displaying the output**

Compose version number, which is unsettling at first, but useful. You could automate that command as part of your deployment process and commit the merged files to source control—then the alphabetical order makes it easy to compare releases.

Using overrides for an image tag is just a quick example. There's a more realistic set of compose files for the random number application in the `numbers` folder:

- `docker-compose.yml`—The core application definition. It specifies the web and API services without any ports or network definitions.
- `docker-compose-dev.yml`—For running the app in development. It specifies a Docker network and for the services it adds the ports to publish and disables the health and dependency checks. This is so developers can be up and running quickly.
- `docker-compose-test.yml`—For running in a test environment. This specifies a network, adds health check parameters, and publishes a port for the web app, but it keeps the API service internal by not publishing any ports.
- `docker-compose-uat.yml`—For the User Acceptance Test environment. This specifies a network, publishes standard port 80 for the website, sets the services to always restart, and specifies more stringent health check parameters.

Listing 10.2 shows the contents of the dev override file—it's very clear that it isn't a full app specification because no images are specified. The values in here will be merged into the core Compose file, adding new properties or overriding existing properties if there are matching keys in the core file.

**Listing 10.2   An override file only specifies changes from the main Compose file**

```
services:
  numbers-api:
    ports:
      - "8087:80"
    healthcheck:
      disable: true

  numbers-web:
    entrypoint:
      - dotnet
      - Numbers.Web.dll
    ports:
      - "8088:80"

networks:
  app-net:
    name: numbers-dev
```

The other override files follow the same pattern. Each environment uses different ports for the web application and the API so you can run them all on a single machine.

> **TRY IT NOW**   Start by removing all your existing containers, and then run the random number app in multiple environments. Each environment needs a project name and the correct set of Compose files:

```
# remove any existing containers
docker container rm -f $(docker container ls -aq)

# run the app in dev configuration:
docker-compose -f ./numbers/docker-compose.yml -f ./numbers/docker-
    compose-dev.yml -p numbers-dev up -d

# and the test setup:
docker-compose -f ./numbers/docker-compose.yml -f ./numbers/docker-
    compose-test.yml -p numbers-test up -d

# and UAT:
docker-compose -f ./numbers/docker-compose.yml -f ./numbers/docker-
    compose-uat.yml -p numbers-uat up -d
```

Now you have three copies of the application running, which are all isolated from each other because each deployment is using its own Docker network. In an organization, these would be running on one server, and teams would use the environment they want by browsing to the correct port. For example, you could use port 80 for UAT, port 8080 for system test, and port 8088 for the development team's integration environment. Figure 10.6 shows my output with networks and containers being created.

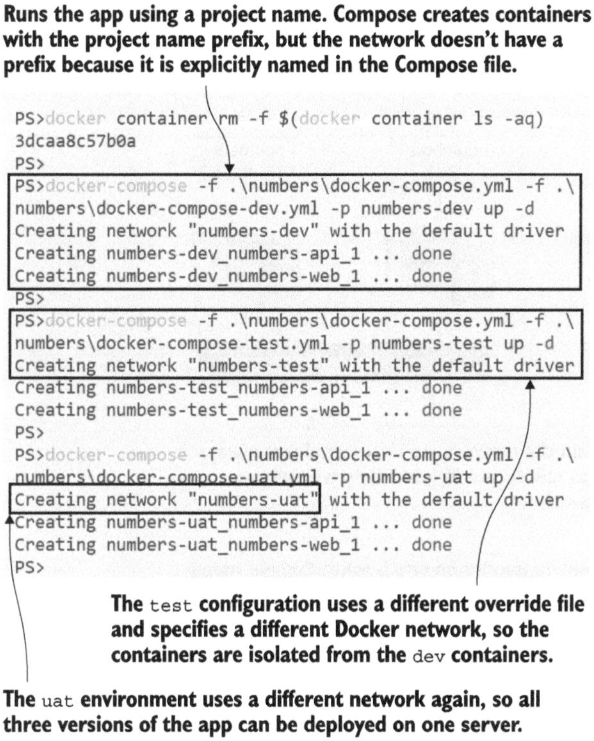

**Runs the app using a project name. Compose creates containers with the project name prefix, but the network doesn't have a prefix because it is explicitly named in the Compose file.**

```
PS>docker container rm -f $(docker container ls -aq)
3dcaa8c57b0a
PS>
PS>docker-compose -f .\numbers\docker-compose.yml -f .\
numbers\docker-compose-dev.yml -p numbers-dev up -d
Creating network "numbers-dev" with the default driver
Creating numbers-dev_numbers-api_1 ... done
Creating numbers-dev_numbers-web_1 ... done
PS>
PS>docker-compose -f .\numbers\docker-compose.yml -f .\
numbers\docker-compose-test.yml -p numbers-test up -d
Creating network "numbers-test" with the default driver
Creating numbers-test_numbers-api_1 ... done
Creating numbers-test_numbers-web_1 ... done
PS>
PS>docker-compose -f .\numbers\docker-compose.yml -f .\
numbers\docker-compose-uat.yml -p numbers-uat up -d
Creating network "numbers-uat" with the default driver
Creating numbers-uat_numbers-api_1 ... done
Creating numbers-uat_numbers-web_1 ... done
PS>
```

**The `test` configuration uses a different override file and specifies a different Docker network, so the containers are isolated from the `dev` containers.**

**The `uat` environment uses a different network again, so all three versions of the app can be deployed on one server.**

Figure 10.6   Running multiple isolated application environments in containers on a single machine

Now you have three deployments that function as separate environments: http:// localhost is UAT, http://localhost:8080 is system test, and http://localhost:8088 is the dev environment. Browse to any of those, and you'll see the same application, but each web container can only see the API container in its own network. This keeps the apps separate, so if you keep fetching random numbers in the dev environment, the API will break, but the system test and UAT environments are still working. The containers in each environment use DNS names to communicate, but Docker restricts traffic within the container network. Figure 10.7 shows how network isolation keeps all your environments separate.

It's time to remind you that Docker Compose is a client-side tool, and you need access to all your Compose files to manage your apps. You also need to remember the project names you used. If you want to clear down the test environment, removing containers and the network, you would normally just run `docker-compose down`, but that won't work for these environments because Compose needs all the same file and project information you used in the `up` command to match the resources.

**Four containers are running on the same Docker Engine, but they connect to different Docker networks. Containers on the** `numbers-test` **network cannot see containers on the** `numbers-uat` **network.**

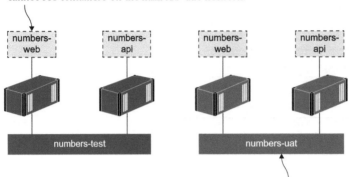

**DNS names are resolved within the network, so web containers always use the name** `numbers-api` **to talk to the API, but they will only see the container from their network.**

Figure 10.7   Running multiple environments on one Docker Engine, using networks for isolation

**TRY IT NOW**   Let's remove that test environment. You can try different variations on the down command, but the only one that will work is the one that has the same file list and project name as the original up command:

```
# this would work if we'd used the default docker-compose.yml file:
docker-compose down

# this would work if we'd used override files without a project name:
docker-compose -f ./numbers/docker-compose.yml -f ./numbers/docker-
    compose-test.yml down

# but we specified a project name, so we need to include that too:
docker-compose -f ./numbers/docker-compose.yml -f ./numbers/docker-
    compose-test.yml -p numbers-test down
```

You can see my output in figure 10.8. You might have guessed that Compose can't identify the running resources for the application unless you provide the matching file and project name, so in the first command it doesn't remove anything. In the second command, Compose does try to delete the container network, even though there are application containers connected to that network.

Those errors happened because the networks were explicitly named in the Compose override files. I didn't specify a project name in the second down command, so it used the default, which is the folder name numbers. Compose looked for containers called numbers_numbers-web_1 and numbers_numbers-api_1, but

**There's no Compose file in this directory and no `-f` flag to point to a Compose file, so the command has nothing to work with.**

```
PS>docker-compose down
ERROR:
        Can't find a suitable configuration file in thi
s directory or any
        parent. Are you in the right directory?

        Supported filenames: docker-compose.yml, docker
-compose.yaml

PS>
PS>docker-compose -f .\numbers\docker-compose.yml -f .\
numbers\docker-compose-test.yml down
Removing network numbers-test
ERROR: error while removing network: network numbers-te
st id df5591c401bb4742263df710dac38a7e6caec411f25c98af9
bda1fd14da4b459 has active endpoints
PS>
PS>docker-compose -f .\numbers\docker-compose.yml -f .\
numbers\docker-compose-test.yml -p numbers-test down
Stopping numbers-test_numbers-api_1 ... done
Stopping numbers-test_numbers-web_1 ... done
Removing numbers-test_numbers-api_1 ... done
Removing numbers-test_numbers-web_1 ... done
Removing network numbers-test
PS>
```

**Because the project name isn't specified, Compose doesn't find the containers. It finds the network, which had an explicit name in the Compose file.**

**This is the matching combination of files and project name for the original `up` command, so Compose finds and removes the resources.**

Figure 10.8   You need to use the same files and project name to manage an application with Compose.

didn't find them because they were actually created with the project prefix `numbers-test`. Compose thought those containers were already gone and it only needed to clean up the network, which it did find because the explicit network name in the Compose file is used without a project prefix. Compose tried to remove that network, but fortunately Docker won't let you remove networks that still have containers attached.

This is a long way of showing you that you need to take care with Docker Compose. It's an excellent tool for non-production environments, where it gets you maximum value from your compute resources by deploying tens or hundreds of applications on single machines. Override files let you reuse application definitions and identify the differences between environments, but you need to be aware of the management overhead. You should look at scripting and automation for your deployments and teardowns.

## 10.3 *Injecting configuration with environment variables and secrets*

You can isolate applications using Docker networks and capture the differences between environments with Compose overrides, but you'll also need to change the application configuration between environments. Most applications can read configuration settings from environment variables or files, and Compose has good support for both those approaches.

I'll cover all the options in this section, so we'll dig a bit deeper into Compose than we have so far. This will help you understand the choices you have for applying configuration settings, and you'll be able to select what works for you.

It's back to the to-do app for these exercises. The Docker image for the app is built to read environment variables and files for configuration settings. There are three items that need to vary between environments:

- *Logging*—How detailed the logging level should be. This will start off being very verbose in the dev environment and become less so in test and production.
- *Database provider*—Whether to use a simple data file inside the application container, or a separate database (which may or may not be running in a container).
- *Database connection string*—The details for connecting to the database, if the app isn't using a local data file.

I'm using override files to inject configuration for different environments, and I'm using different approaches for each item, so I can show you the options Docker Compose has. Listing 10.3 shows the core Compose file; this just has the basic information for the web application with a configuration file set up as a secret.

> **Listing 10.3   The Compose file specifies the web service with a secret**

```
services:
  todo-web:
    image: diamol/ch06-todo-list
    secrets:
      - source: todo-db-connection
        target: /app/config/secrets.json
```

Secrets are a useful way of injecting configuration—they have support in Docker Compose, Docker Swarm, and Kubernetes. In the Compose file you specify the source and target for the secret. The source is the place where the secret is loaded from the container runtime, and the target is the file path where the secret is surfaced inside the container.

This secret is specified as coming from the source `todo-db-connection`, which means there needs to be a secret with that name defined in the Compose file. The contents of the secret will be loaded into the container at the target path `/app/config/secrets.json`, which is one of the locations the application searches for configuration settings.

The preceding Compose file on its own isn't valid because there is no secrets section, and the `todo-db-connection` secret is required because it's used in the service definition. Listing 10.4 shows the override file for development, which sets up some more configuration for the service and specifies the secret.

**Listing 10.4 The development override adds config settings and the secret setup**

```
services:
  todo-web:
    ports:
      - 8089:80
    environment:
      - Database:Provider=Sqlite
    env_file:
      - ./config/logging.debug.env

secrets:
  todo-db-connection:
    file: ./config/empty.json
```

There are three properties in this override file that inject application configuration and change the behavior of the app in the container. You can use any combination of them, but each approach has benefits:

- `environment` adds an environment variable inside the container. This setting configures the app to use the SQLite database, which is a simple data file. This is the easiest way to set configuration values, and it's clear from the Compose file what's being configured.
- `env_file` contains the path to a text file, and the contents of the text file will be loaded into the container as environment variables. Each line in the text file is read as an environment variable, with the name and value separated by an equals sign. The contents of this file set the logging configuration. Using an environment variable file is a simple way to share settings between multiple components, because each component references the file rather than duplicates a list of environment variables.
- `secrets` is a top-level resource in the Compose YAML file, like `services` and `networks`. It contains the actual source of `todo-db-connection`, which is a file on the local filesystem. In this case, there's no separate database for the app to connect to, so it uses an empty JSON file for the secret. The app will read the file, but there are no configuration settings to apply.

**TRY IT NOW** You can run the app in development configuration using the Compose file and the override in the `todo-list-configured` directory. Send a request into the web app with curl and check that the container is logging lots of detail:

```
# remove existing containers:
docker container rm -f $(docker container ls -aq)
```

```
# bring up the app with config overrides - for Linux containers:
docker-compose -f ./todo-list-configured/docker-compose.yml -f ./todo-
    list-configured/docker-compose-dev.yml -p todo-dev up -d

# OR for Windows container, which use different file paths for secrets:
docker-compose -f ./todo-list-configured/docker-compose.yml -f ./todo-
    list-configured/docker-compose-dev.yml -f ./todo-list-
    configured/docker-compose-dev-windows.yml -p todo-dev up -d

# send some traffic into the app:
curl http://localhost:8089/list

# check the logs:
docker container logs --tail 4 todo-dev_todo-web_1
```

You can see my output in figure 10.9. Docker Compose always uses a network for each application, so it creates a default network and connects containers to it even if there's no network specified in the Compose files. In my case, the latest log lines show the

**Runs the app in development configuration, using settings defined in Compose override files, environment files, and secrets.**

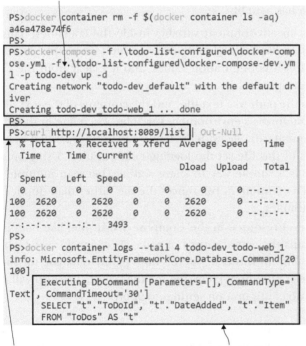

**Using the app causes log entries to be written.**

**The development configuration writes lots of logs, including the SQL statements sent to the database—these aren't produced in the default configuration.**

Figure 10.9  Changing application behavior by applying configuration settings in Docker Compose

SQL database command the app uses. Yours might show something different, but if you check through the whole logs, you should see the SQL statements in there. That shows the enhanced logging configuration is in place.

The developer deployment uses environment variables and secrets for app configuration—the values specified in the Compose files and the config files get loaded into the container.

There's also a test deployment that uses another approach supported by Compose: using environment variables *on the host machine* to provide values for the container. This makes the deployment more portable, because you can alter environments without changing the Compose files themselves. That's useful if you want to spin up a second test environment on a different server with a different configuration. Listing 10.5 shows that in the specification for the todo-web service.

---

**Listing 10.5   Using environment variables as values in Compose files**

```
todo-web:
  ports:
    - "${TODO_WEB_PORT}:80"
  environment:
    - Database:Provider=Postgres
  env_file:
    - ./config/logging.information.env
  networks:
    - app-net
```

The dollar-and-curly-brace setting for the port gets replaced from the environment variable with that name. So if I have a variable set on the machine where I'm running Docker Compose with the name TODO_WEB_PORT and the value 8877, then Compose injects that value, and the port specification actually becomes "8877:80". This service specification is in the file docker-compose-test.yml, which also includes a service for the database and a secret to use for the connection to the database container.

You can run the test environment by specifying the Compose files and project name in the same way as for the development environment, but there's one final configuration feature of Compose that makes things easier. If Compose finds a file called .env in the current folder, it will treat that as an environment file and read the contents as a set of environment variables, populating them before it runs the command.

> **TRY IT NOW**   Navigate to the directory for the configured to-do list application, and run it without specifying any parameters to Docker Compose:

```
cd ./todo-list-configured

# OR for Windows containers - using different file paths:
cd ./todo-list-configured-windows

docker-compose up -d
```

Figure 10.10 shows that Compose has created web and database containers, although the core Compose file doesn't specify a database service. It also used the project name `todo_ch10`, although I didn't specify a name. The `.env` file sets up the Compose configuration to run the test environment by default, without you needing to specify the test override file.

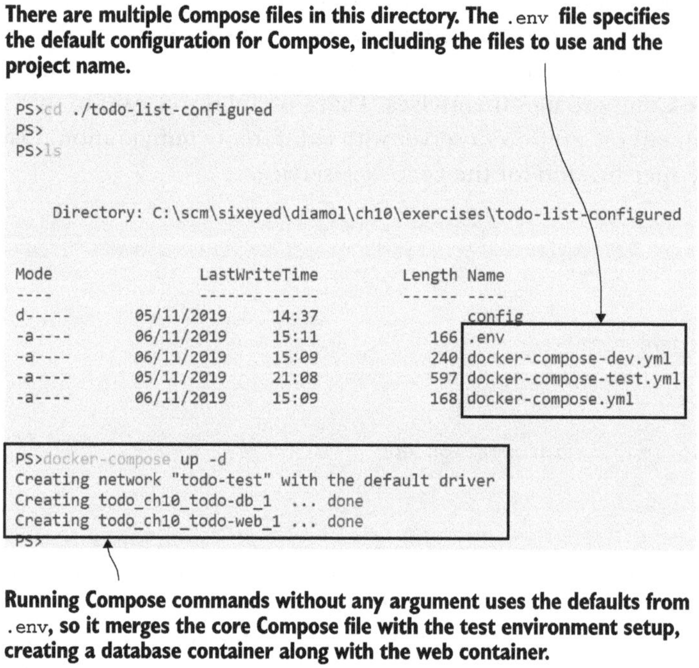

**There are multiple Compose files in this directory. The `.env` file specifies the default configuration for Compose, including the files to use and the project name.**

```
PS>cd ./todo-list-configured
PS>
PS>ls


    Directory: C:\scm\sixeyed\diamol\ch10\exercises\todo-list-configured


Mode                LastWriteTime         Length Name
----                -------------         ------ ----
d-----        05/11/2019     14:37               config
-a----        06/11/2019     15:11            166 .env
-a----        06/11/2019     15:09            240 docker-compose-dev.yml
-a----        05/11/2019     21:08            597 docker-compose-test.yml
-a----        06/11/2019     15:09            168 docker-compose.yml

PS>docker-compose up -d
Creating network "todo-test" with the default driver
Creating todo_ch10_todo-db_1  ... done
Creating todo_ch10_todo-web_1 ... done
PS>
```

**Running Compose commands without any argument uses the defaults from `.env`, so it merges the core Compose file with the test environment setup, creating a database container along with the web container.**

**Figure 10.10   Using an environment file to specify the default for Docker Compose files and project names**

You can use a simple command here without specifying a filename, because the `.env` file contains a set of environment variables that can be used to configure Docker Compose. The first use is for container configuration settings, like the port for the web application; the second is for the Compose command itself, listing the files to use and the project name. Listing 10.6 shows the `.env` file in full.

> **Listing 10.6   Configuring containers and Compose using an environment file**

```
# container configuration - ports to publish:
TODO_WEB_PORT=8877
TODO_DB_PORT=5432

# compose configuration - files and project name:
COMPOSE_PATH_SEPARATOR=;
```

```
COMPOSE_FILE=docker-compose.yml;docker-compose-test.yml
COMPOSE_PROJECT_NAME=todo_ch10
```

The environment file captures the default Compose settings for the app in the test configuration—you could easily modify it so the development configuration was the default. Keeping an environment file alongside your Compose files helps to document which sets of files represent which environment, but be aware that Docker Compose only looks for a file called .env. You can't specify a filename, so you can't easily switch between environments with multiple environment files.

Touring the configuration options in Docker Compose has taken us a little while. You'll be working with a lot of Compose files in your time with Docker, so you need to be familiar with all the options. I'll summarize them all here, but some are more useful than others:

- Using the `environment` property to specify environment variables is the simplest option, and it makes your application configuration easy to read from the Compose file. Those settings are in plain text, though, so you shouldn't use them for sensitive data like connection strings or API keys.
- Loading configuration files with `secret` properties is the most flexible option, because it's supported by all the container runtimes and it can be used for sensitive data. The source of the secret could be a local file when you're using Compose, or it could be an encrypted secret stored in a Docker Swarm or Kubernetes cluster. Whatever the source, the contents of the secret get loaded into a file in the container for the application to read.
- Storing settings in a file and loading them into containers with the `environment _file` property is useful when you have lots of shared settings between services. Compose reads the file locally and sets the individual values as environment properties, so you can use local environment files when you're connected to a remote Docker Engine.
- The Compose environment file, .env, is useful for capturing the setup for whichever environment you want to be the default deployment target.

## 10.4 *Reducing duplication with extension fields*

At this point, you may well be thinking that Docker Compose has enough configuration options to satisfy any situation. But it's actually quite a simple specification, and there are limitations you'll come across as you work with it more. One of the most common problems is how to reduce the bloat of Compose files when you have services that share a lot of the same settings. In this section I'll cover one final feature of Docker Compose that fixes this problem—using extension fields to define blocks of YAML in a single place, which you can reuse throughout the Compose file. Extension fields are a powerful but underused feature of Compose. They remove a lot of duplication and potential for errors, and they're straightforward to use once you get accustomed to the YAML merge syntax.

In the `image-gallery` folder for this chapter's exercises, there's a `docker-compose-prod.yml` file that makes use of extension fields. Listing 10.7 shows how you define extension fields, declaring them outside of any top-level blocks (services, networks, etc.) and giving them a name with the ampersand notation.

---

**Listing 10.7 Defining extension fields at the top of a Docker Compose file**

```
x-labels: &logging
  logging:
    options:
      max-size: '100m'
      max-file: '10'

x-labels: &labels
  app-name: image-gallery
```

Extension fields are custom definitions; in this file there are two called `logging` and `labels`. By convention you prefix the block name with an "x", so the `x-labels` block defines an extension called `labels`. The logging extension specifies settings for container logs, and it can be used inside a service definition. The labels extension specifies a key/value pair for a label that can be used inside an existing `labels` field in a service definition.

You should note the difference between these definitions—the logging field includes the logging property, which means it can be used directly in the service. The labels field does not include the labels property, so it needs to be used inside an existing set of labels. Listing 10.8 makes that clear, with a service definition that uses both extensions.

---

**Listing 10.8 Using extensions inside a service definition with YAML merge**

```
services:

  iotd:
    ports:
      - 8080:80
    <<: *logging
    labels:
      <<: *labels
      public: api
```

Extension fields are used with the YAML merge syntax `<<:` followed by the field name, which is prefixed with an asterisk. So `<<: *logging` will merge in the value of the `logging` extension field at that point in the YAML file. When Compose processes this file, it will add the logging section to the service from the logging extension, and it will add an extra label to the existing labels section, merging in the value from the `labels` extension field.

**TRY IT NOW** We don't need to run this app to see how Compose processes the file. Just running the `config` command will do. That validates all the inputs and prints out the final Compose file, with the extension fields merged into the service definitions:

```
# browse to the image-gallery folder under ch10/exercises:
cd ../image-gallery

# check config for the production override:
docker-compose -f ./docker-compose.yml -f ./docker-compose-prod.yml
    config
```

My output is in figure 10.11—I haven't shown the full output, just enough of the service definitions to show the extension fields being merged in.

**This warning tells you that there is a system environment variable used in the Compose file that doesn't have a value set. This is something to watch out for if you use variable substitution.**

**The** `config` **command merges and processes the input files and validates the result. If it's valid, the merged file is displayed.**

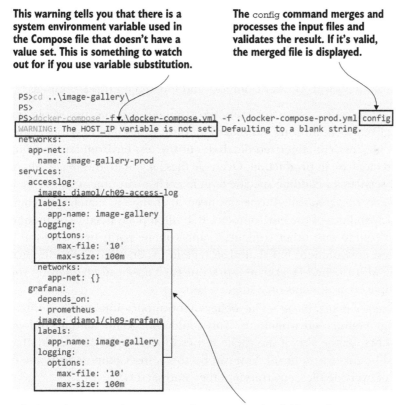

```
PS>cd ..\image-gallery\
PS>
PS>docker-compose -f .\docker-compose.yml -f .\docker-compose-prod.yml config
WARNING: The HOST_IP variable is not set. Defaulting to a blank string.
networks:
  app-net:
    name: image-gallery-prod
services:
  accesslog:
    image: diamol/ch09-access-log
    labels:
      app-name: image-gallery
    logging:
      options:
        max-file: '10'
        max-size: 100m
    networks:
      app-net: {}
  grafana:
    depends_on:
    - prometheus
    image: diamol/ch09-grafana
    labels:
      app-name: image-gallery
    logging:
      options:
        max-file: '10'
        max-size: 100m
```

**Both services merge the** `logging` **and** `labels` **extension fields, so the contents are repeated, but they're not duplicated in the source Compose files.**

**Figure 10.11** Using the `config` command to process files with extension fields and check the result

Extension fields are a useful way of ensuring best practices in your Compose files—using the same logging settings and container labels is a good example of setting standards for all services. It's not something you'll use for every app, but it's good to have in your toolbox for those times when you're about to copy and paste big chunks of YAML. Now you have a better approach. There is one big limitation, though: extension fields don't apply across multiple Compose files, so you can't define an extension in a core Compose file and then use it in an override. That's a restriction of YAML rather than Compose, but it's something to be aware of.

## 10.5   *Understanding the configuration workflow with Docker*

It's incredibly valuable to have the entire deployment configuration for a system captured in a set of artifacts that live in source control. It allows you to deploy any version of your application just by fetching the source at that version and running the deployment scripts. It also allows developers to quickly work on fixes by running the production stack locally and reproducing a bug in their own environment.

There are always variations between environments, and Docker Compose lets you capture the differences between environments while still giving you that set of deployment artifacts that live in source control. In this chapter we've looked at defining different environments with Docker Compose and focused on three key areas:

- *Application composition*—Not every environment will run the whole stack. Features like the monitoring dashboard may not be used by developers, or applications may use containerized databases in the test environment but plug into a cloud database in production. Override files let you do this neatly, sharing common services and adding specific ones in each environment.
- *Container configuration*—Properties need to change to match the requirements and capabilities of the environment. Published ports need to be unique so they don't collide with other containers, and volume paths may use local drives in the test environment but shared storage in production. Overrides enable this, along with isolated Docker networks for each application, allowing you to run multiple environments on a single server.
- *Application configuration*—The behavior of applications inside containers will change between environments. This could change the amount of logging the app does, or the size of the cache it uses to store local data, or whole features could be turned on or off. You can do this using Compose with any combination of override files, environment files, and secrets.

Figure 10.12 shows that with the to-do list app we ran in section 10.3. The development and test environments are completely different: in dev the app is configured to use a local database file, and in test Compose also runs a database container and the app is configured to use that. But each environment uses isolated networks and unique ports, so they can be run on the same machine, which is perfect if developers need to spin up a local test environment and see how it compares to their development version.

**The dev environment uses a local database file and enhanced logging, specified with environment variables, environment files, and secrets.**

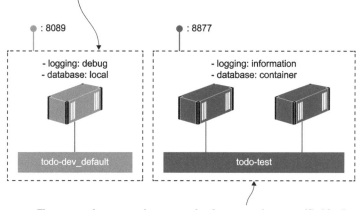

**The test environment also runs a database container, specified in the Compose override file. It uses different ports and networks from dev, so both environments can be run on the same machine.**

**Figure 10.12** Defining very different environments for the same app using Docker Compose

The most important takeaway from this is that the configuration workflow uses the same Docker image in every environment. The build process will produce a tagged version of your container images, which have passed all the automated tests. That's a release candidate that you deploy to the smoke-test environment using the configuration in your Compose files. When it passes the smoke test, it moves on to the next environment, which uses the same set of images and applies new configuration from Compose. Ultimately you'll release that version if the tests all pass, when you'll deploy those same container images to production using your Docker Swarm or Kubernetes deployment manifests. The software that gets released is exactly the same software that has passed all the tests, but now it has production behavior supplied from the container platform.

## 10.6 Lab

In this lab I'd like you to build your own set of environment definitions for the to-do app. You're going to put together a development environment and a test environment, and make sure they can both run on the same machine.

The development environment should be the default, which you can run with `docker-compose up`. The setup should

- Use a local database file
- Publish to port `8089`
- Run v2 of the to-do application

The test environment will need to be run with specific Docker Compose files and a project name. Its setup should

- Use a separate database container
- Use a volume for the database storage
- Publish to port 8080
- Use the latest to-do application image

There are similarities here to the Compose files in the `todo-list-configured` exercises for the chapter. The main difference is the volume—the database container uses an environment variable called `PGDATA` to set where the data files should be written. You can use that along with a volume specification in your Compose files.

As you've seen in this chapter, there are lots of ways you can solve this. My solution is on GitHub here: https://github.com/sixeyed/diamol/blob/master/ch10/lab/README.md.

# Building and testing
# applications with Docker
# and Docker Compose

Automation is at the heart of Docker. You describe the steps to package your component in a Dockerfile and use the Docker command line to execute them; you describe the architecture of your app in a Docker Compose file and use the Compose command line to start and stop the app. Command-line tools fit very neatly with automated processes, like jobs that run on a daily schedule or whenever developers push code changes. It doesn't matter which tool you're using to run those jobs; they all let you run scripted commands so you can easily integrate the Docker workflow with your automation server.

In this chapter you're going to learn how to do continuous integration (CI) with Docker. CI is an automated process that runs regularly to build applications and execute a suite of tests. When the CI job is healthy, it means the latest code for the app is good and has been packaged and is ready to deploy as a release candidate. Setting up and managing CI servers and jobs used to be time consuming and intensive—"build manager" was a full-time role for a human in a large project. Docker simplifies every part of the CI process and frees people up for more interesting work.

## 11.1 How the CI process works with Docker

The CI process is a pipeline that starts with code, executes a set of steps, and finishes with a tested deployable artifact. One of the challenges with CI is that pipelines become unique for each project—different technology stacks do different things in the steps and produce different types of artifacts. The CI server needs to work for all those unique pipelines, so every combination of programming language and build framework can get installed on the server, and it can easily become unmanageable.

Docker brings consistency to the CI process because every project follows the same steps and produces the same type of artifact. Figure 11.1 shows a typical pipeline with Docker—it is triggered by a code change or a timed schedule, and it produces a set of Docker images. Those images contain the latest version of the code—compiled, tested, packaged, and pushed to a registry for distribution.

**The CI job runs whenever developers push code, and usually on a nightly schedule too.**

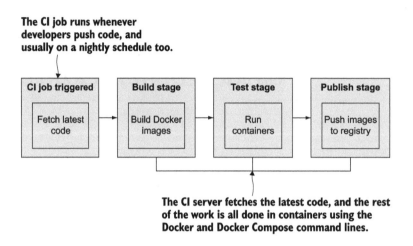

**The CI server fetches the latest code, and the rest of the work is all done in containers using the Docker and Docker Compose command lines.**

Figure 11.1   The basic steps of a CI pipeline to build, test, and publish apps—all executed with Docker.

Each step in the CI pipeline runs with Docker or Docker Compose, and all the work happens inside containers. You use containers to compile applications, so the CI server doesn't need to have any programming languages or build SDKs installed. Automated unit tests run as part of the image build, so if the code is broken, the build fails and the CI job stops. You can also run more sophisticated end-to-end tests by starting the whole application with Docker Compose alongside a separate container that runs tests to simulate user workflows.

In a Dockerized CI process, all the hard work happens in containers, but you still need some infrastructure components to hold everything together: a centralized source code system, a Docker registry to store images, and an automation server to run the CI jobs. There's a huge choice of managed services you can choose from that all support Docker—you can mix and match GitHub with Azure DevOps and Docker Hub, or you could use GitLab, which provides an all-in-one solution. Or you can run your own CI infrastructure in Docker containers.

## 11.2   *Spinning up build infrastructure with Docker*

No one wants to run their own infrastructure components when you can get reliable managed services for free, but running the build system in Docker is a very useful alternative to know. It's ideal if you want to keep your source code and packaged images entirely within your own network—for data sovereignty or transfer speed—but even if you use services for everything, it's great to have a simple backup option for the rare occasions when GitHub or Docker Hub have an outage, or your internet connection goes offline.

The three components you need can easily be run in containers using enterprise-grade open source software. With a single command you can run your own setup using Gogs for source control, the open source Docker registry for distribution, and Jenkins as the automation server.

> **TRY IT NOW**   In the exercises folder for this chapter, there's a Docker Compose file that defines the build infrastructure. One part of the setup is different for Linux and Windows containers, so you'll need to select the right files. You'll also need to add an entry to your hosts file for the DNS name `registry.local` if you didn't do that in section 5.3.

```
cd ch11/exercises/infrastructure

# start the app with Linux containers:
docker-compose -f docker-compose.yml -f docker-compose-linux.yml up -d

# OR start with Windows containers:
docker-compose -f docker-compose.yml -f docker-compose-windows.yml up -d

# add registry domain to local hosts file on Mac or Linux:
echo $'\n127.0.0.1  registry.local' | sudo tee -a /etc/hosts

# OR on Windows:
Add-Content -Value "127.0.0.1  registry.local" -Path
    /windows/system32/drivers/etc/hosts

# check containers:
docker container ls
```

You can see my output in figure 11.2. The commands are different on Linux and Windows, but the outcome is the same—you'll have the Gogs Git server published to port 3000, Jenkins published to port 8080, and the registry published to port 5000.

Those three tools are interesting to work with because they support different levels of automation. The registry server runs in a container without any extra setup, so now you can push and pull images using `registry.local:5000` as the domain in your image tags. Jenkins uses a plugin system to add functionality, and you can set that up

**Starts the build infrastructure—Git, the Docker registry, and the Jenkins automation server. I'm using Docker Desktop for Windows in Linux container mode.**

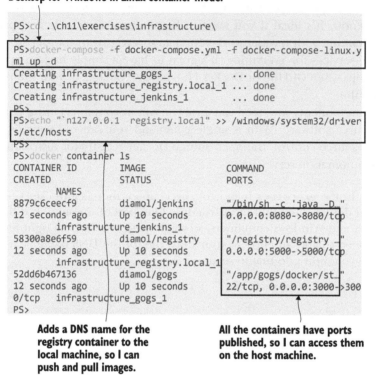

```
PS>cd .\ch11\exercises\infrastructure\
PS>
PS>docker-compose -f docker-compose.yml -f docker-compose-linux.y
ml up -d
Creating infrastructure_gogs_1            ... done
Creating infrastructure_registry.local_1 ... done
Creating infrastructure_jenkins_1         ... done
PS>
PS>echo "`n127.0.0.1  registry.local" >> /windows/system32/driver
s/etc/hosts
PS>
PS>docker container ls
CONTAINER ID        IMAGE               COMMAND
CREATED             STATUS              PORTS
        NAMES
8879c6ceecf9        diamol/jenkins      "/bin/sh -c 'java -D…"
12 seconds ago      Up 10 seconds       0.0.0.0:8080->8080/tcp
        infrastructure_jenkins_1
58300a8e6f59        diamol/registry     "/registry/registry …"
12 seconds ago      Up 10 seconds       0.0.0.0:5000->5000/tcp
        infrastructure_registry.local_1
52dd6b467136        diamol/gogs         "/app/gogs/docker/st…"
12 seconds ago      Up 10 seconds       22/tcp, 0.0.0.0:3000->300
0/tcp    infrastructure_gogs_1
PS>
```

**Adds a DNS name for the registry container to the local machine, so I can push and pull images.**

**All the containers have ports published, so I can access them on the host machine.**

Figure 11.2   Running your whole build infrastructure in containers with one command

manually, or you can bundle a set of scripts in the Dockerfile to automate the setup for you. Gogs doesn't really have a good automation story, so although it's running, it needs some manual configuration.

**TRY IT NOW**   Browse to http://localhost:3000 and you'll see the web UI for Gogs. The first page is the initial installation, shown in figure 11.3. This is shown only on the first use of a new container. All the values are correctly configured; you just need to scroll down and click Install Gogs.

When you first run Gogs, you'll see this installation page—it's an
application that doesn't let you fully automate the deployment.

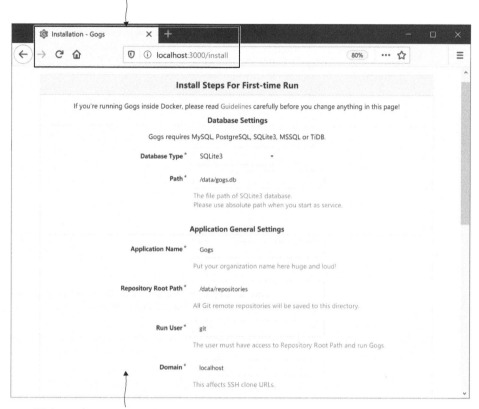

All the settings are preconfigured in the container. You don't need to
change them—just scroll down and click the **Install Gogs** button.

**Figure 11.3   Running Gogs in a container. It's an open source Git server that needs some manual
setup.**

The installation completes very quickly, and you'll come to the sign-on page. There
isn't a default account, so you'll need to click Register to create one. Create a user
with the username `diamol`, as in figure 11.4—you can use any email address or password, but the Jenkins CI job expects the Gogs user to be called `diamol`.

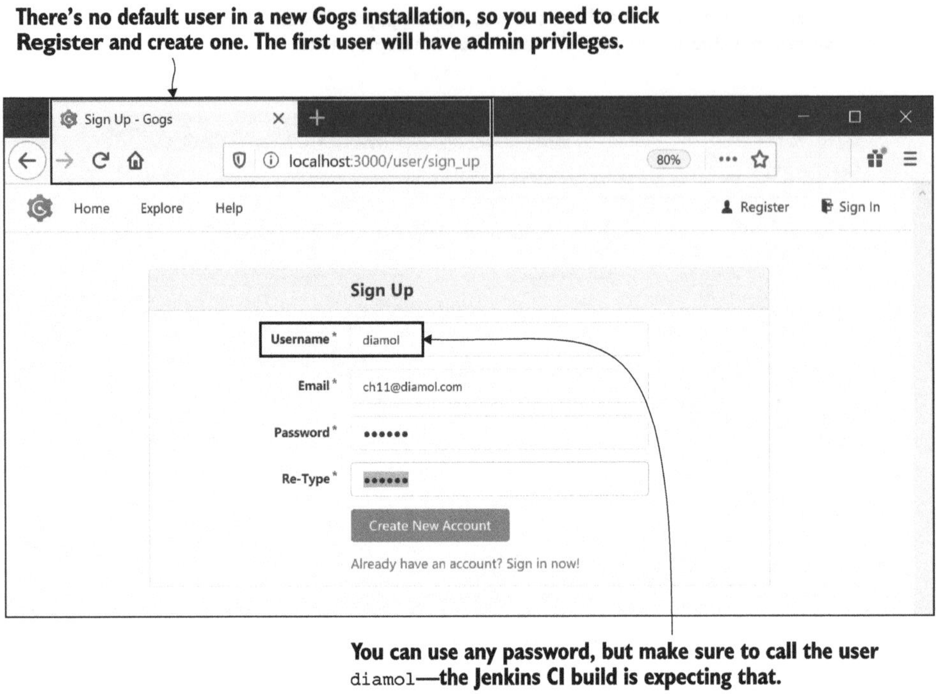

**There's no default user in a new Gogs installation, so you need to click Register and create one. The first user will have admin privileges.**

**You can use any password, but make sure to call the user `diamol`—the Jenkins CI build is expecting that.**

Figure 11.4   Creating a new user in Gogs that you can use to push source code to the server

Click Create New Account, and then sign in with the `diamol` username and your password. The final step is to create a repository—that's where we'll push the code that will trigger the CI job. Browse to http://localhost:3000/repo/create and create a repository called `diamol`—the other details can be left empty, as in figure 11.5.

It's pretty frustrating to have to manually configure software when you're running it in Docker, and it's much more frustrating having to copy and paste screenshots into a book, but not every app lets you fully automate the installation. I could have built a custom image with those setup steps already done, but it's important for you to see that you can't always package things nicely into the docker container run workflow.

Jenkins is a better experience. Jenkins is a Java application, and you can package it as a Docker image with a set of scripts that run when the container starts. Those scripts can do pretty much anything—install plugins, register users, and create pipeline jobs. This Jenkins container does all that, so you can log straight in and start using it.

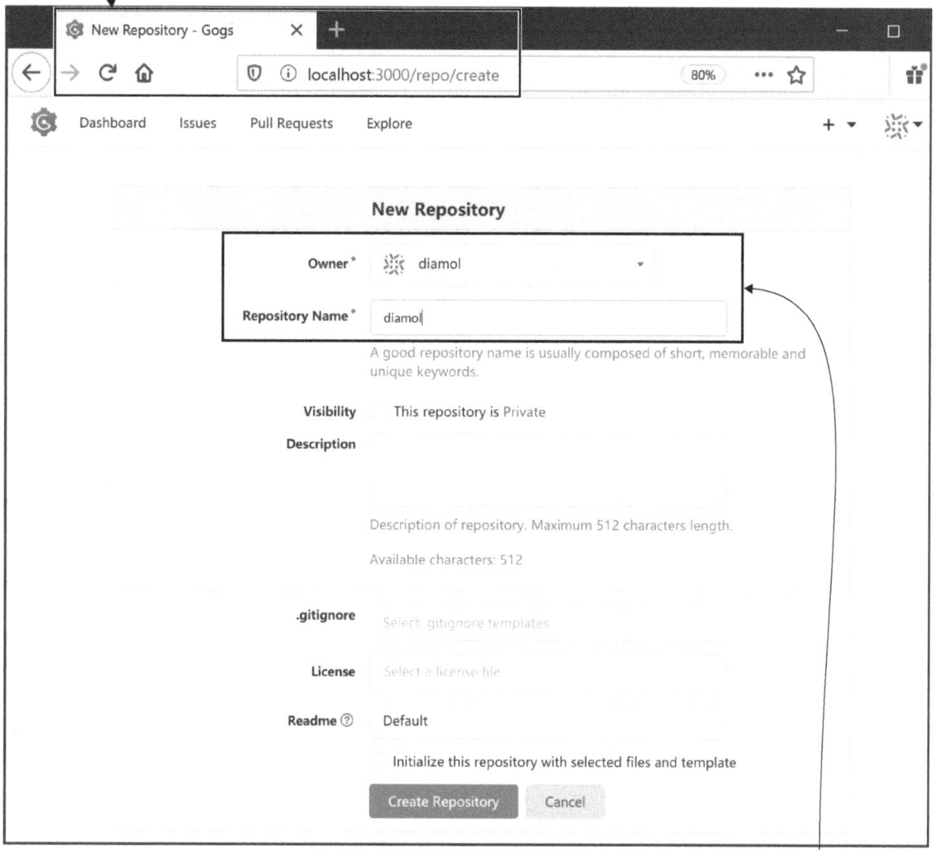

A repository is just like a folder on the Git server for one project or application.
This is where you'll upload your source code, and the upload will trigger the CI job.

Repositories are accessible at specific URLs that contain the user name and repository
name. Jenkins is set up to use the URL for `diamol/diamol` to check for code changes.

**Figure 11.5   Creating a Git repository in Gogs where you can upload the source code for your apps**

**TRY IT NOW**   Browse to http://localhost:8080. You'll see the screen in figure 11.6—there's already a job configured called `diamol` that is in the failed
state. Click the Log In link at the top right and log in with username `diamol`
and password `diamol`.

The Jenkins job failed because it's configured to fetch code from the Gogs Git
server, and there's no code in there yet. The source code for this book is already a
Git repository that you originally cloned from GitHub. You can add your local Gogs

Jenkins has powerful automation support, which I've set up in the
Docker image. When this container starts, the app is ready to use.

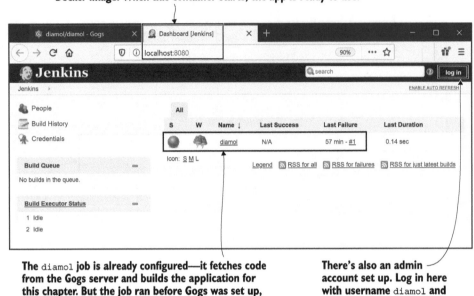

The `diamol` job is already configured—it fetches code
from the Gogs server and builds the application for
this chapter. But the job ran before Gogs was set up,
so it couldn't connect to the Git repository and it failed.

There's also an admin
account set up. Log in here
with username `diamol` and
password `diamol`.

Figure 11.6    Running Jenkins in a container—it is fully configured with a user and CI job already
set up.

container as another Git server for the repo, and push the book's code to your own
infrastructure.

**TRY IT NOW**    You can add an extra Git server using `git remote add` and then
push to the remote. This uploads the code from your local machine to the
Gogs server, which just happens to be a container on your machine too:

```
git remote add local http://localhost:3000/diamol/diamol.git

git push local

# Gogs will ask you to login -
# use the diamol username and password you registered in Gogs
```

Now you have the source code for the whole book in your local Git server. The Jenkins
job is configured to look for changes to the code every minute, and if there are
changes, it will trigger the CI pipeline. The first job run failed because the code repository didn't exist, so Jenkins has put the schedule on hold. You'll need to manually run
the job now to start the schedule working again.

**TRY IT NOW**    Browse to http://localhost:8080/job/diamol. You'll see the screen in figure 11.7, and you can click Build Now in the left-hand menu to run the job. If you don't see the Build Now option, make sure you've logged into Jenkins with the `diamol` credentials.

**The job page is where you can configure the pipeline and see the status of the latest builds.**

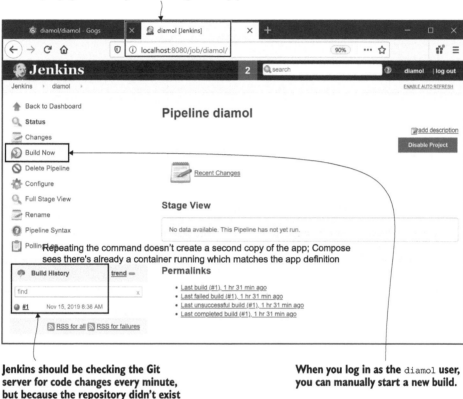

**Jenkins should be checking the Git server for code changes every minute, but because the repository didn't exist on the first run, the job is paused.**

**When you log in as the** `diamol` **user, you can manually start a new build.**

Figure 11.7   The Jenkins job page shows the current status of the job and lets you manually start a build.

After a minute or so, the build will complete successfully, the web page will refresh, and you'll see the output in figure 11.8.

Every part of this pipeline ran using Docker containers, taking advantage of a neat trick: containers running in Docker can connect to the Docker API and start new containers on the same Docker Engine they're running on. The Jenkins image has the Docker CLI installed, and the configuration in the Compose file sets up Jenkins so when it runs Docker commands they get sent to the Docker Engine on your machine.

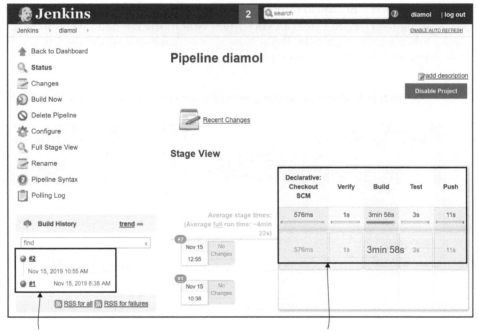

The build history shows the most recent build status—the second build is the one I triggered manually, and it ran successfully.

The pipeline view shows the steps that ran, along with the duration and status of each step. This is similar to the pipeline described in figure 11.1.

**Figure 11.8**  The job page in Jenkins shows the status of the most recent builds, and the pipeline steps.

It sounds odd, but it's really just taking advantage of the fact that the Docker CLI calls into the Docker API, so CLIs from different places can connect to the same Docker Engine. Figure 11.9 shows how that works.

The Docker CLI connects to the local Docker API by default, using a communication channel that is private to your machine—a socket on Linux or a named pipe on Windows. That communication channel can be used as a bind mount for containers, so when the CLI in the container runs, it's actually connecting to the socket or named pipe on your machine. That unlocks some useful scenarios where apps inside containers can query Docker to find other containers, or start and stop new containers. There is also a security concern here, because the app in the container has full access to all the Docker features on the host, so you need to use this carefully with Docker images that you trust—you can trust my `diamol` images, of course.

Listing 11.1 shows part of the Docker Compose files you ran to start the infrastructure containers, focusing on the Jenkins specification. You can see the volumes are binding to the Docker socket in the Linux version and the named pipe in the Windows version—this is the address of the Docker API.

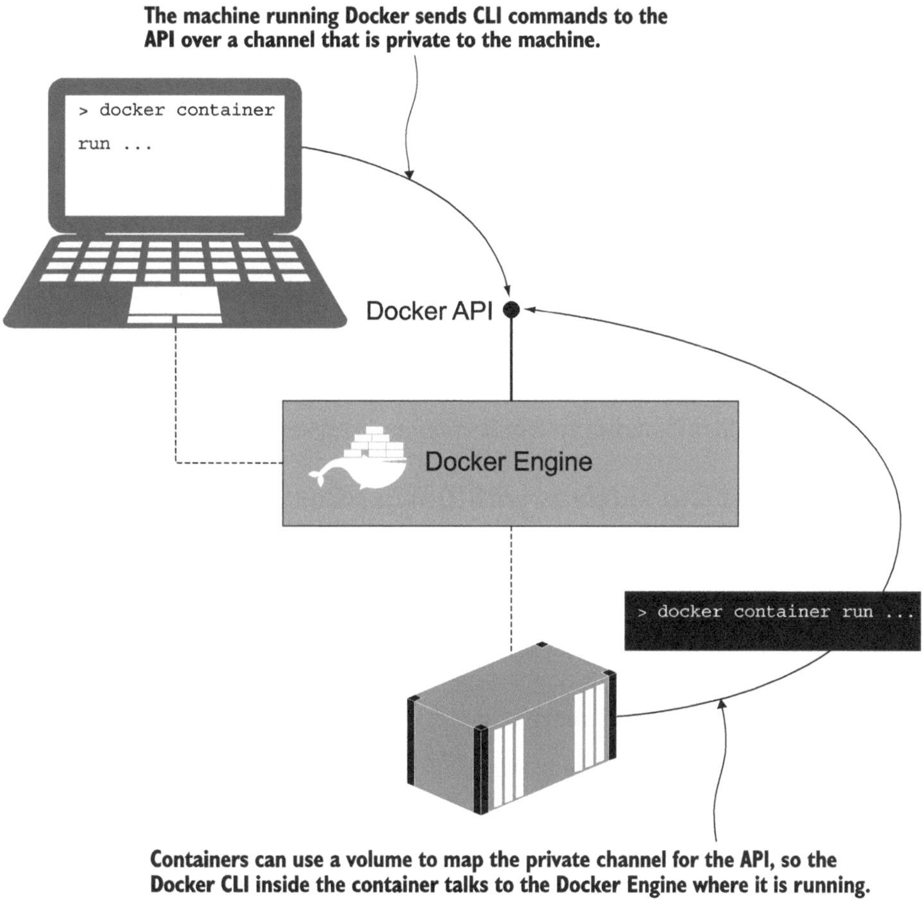

The machine running Docker sends CLI commands to the API over a channel that is private to the machine.

Containers can use a volume to map the private channel for the API, so the Docker CLI inside the container talks to the Docker Engine where it is running.

Figure 11.9 Running containers with a volume to bind the private channel for the Docker API

**Listing 11.1 Binding the Docker CLI in Jenkins to the Docker Engine**

```
# docker-compose.yml
services:
  jenkins:
    image: diamol/jenkins
    ports:
      - "8080:8080"
    networks:
      - infrastructure

# docker-compose-linux.yml
jenkins:
  volumes:
    - type: bind
```

```
        source: /var/run/docker.sock
        target: /var/run/docker.sock

# docker-compose-windows.yml
jenkins:
  volumes:
    - type: npipe
      source: \\.\pipe\docker_engine
      target: \\.\pipe\docker_engine
```

That's all the infrastructure you need. Jenkins connects to the Docker Engine to run Docker and Docker Compose commands, and it can connect to the Git server and the Docker registry by DNS because they're all containers in the same Docker network. The CI process runs a single command to build the application, and all the complexity of the build is captured in Dockerfiles and Docker Compose files.

## 11.3 *Capturing build settings with Docker Compose*

The job that Jenkins ran has built a new version of the random number application from chapter 8. You've seen in chapter 10 how you can break up an application definition across multiple Compose files, and this app uses that approach to capture the details of the build settings. Listing 11.2 is from the base `docker-compose.yml` file in the `ch11/exercises` folder—it contains the web and API service definitions with environment variables in the image name.

> **Listing 11.2   A core Docker Compose file using variables in the image tags**

```
services:
  numbers-api:
    image: ${REGISTRY:-docker.io}/diamol/ch11-numbers-api:v3-build-
      ${BUILD_NUMBER:-local}
    networks:
      - app-net

  numbers-web:
    image: ${REGISTRY:-docker.io}/diamol/ch11-numbers-web:v3-build-
      ${BUILD_NUMBER:-local}
    environment:
      - RngApi__Url=http://numbers-api/rng
    networks:
      - app-net
```

The environment variable syntax here includes a default value set with `:-`, so `${REGISTRY:-docker.io}` tells Compose to replace that token at runtime with the value of the environment variable called `REGISTRY`. If that environment variable doesn't exist or is empty, it will use the default value `docker.io`, which is the domain for Docker Hub. I use the same approach with the image tag, so if the environment variable `BUILD_NUMBER` is set, that value goes into the tag; otherwise `local` gets used.

This is a very useful pattern for supporting a CI process and a local developer build using the same set of artifacts. When a developer builds the API image, they won't have any environment variables set, so the image will be called docker.io/diamol/ ch11-numbers-api:v3-build-local. But docker.io is Docker Hub, which is the default domain, so the image will just be shown as diamol/ch11-numbers-api:v3-build-local. When the same build runs in Jenkins, the variables will be set to use the local Docker registry and the actual build number for the job, which Jenkins sets as an incrementing number, so the image name will be registry.local:5000/ diamol/ ch11-numbers-api:v3-build-2.

Setting a flexible image name is an important part of the CI setup, but the key information is specified in the override file docker-compose-build.yml, which tells Compose where to find the Dockerfiles.

**TRY IT NOW**  You can build the app locally using the same steps as the CI build pipeline. Start from a terminal session, browse to the directory for the chapter, and build the app with Docker Compose:

```
cd ch11/exercises

# build both images:
docker-compose -f docker-compose.yml -f docker-compose-build.yml build

# check the labels for the web image:
docker image inspect -f '{{.Config.Labels}}' diamol/ch11-numbers-
    api:v3-build-local
```

You can see my output in figure 11.10.

Building the application through Docker Compose effectively runs a docker image build command for every service that has build settings specified. That could be a dozen

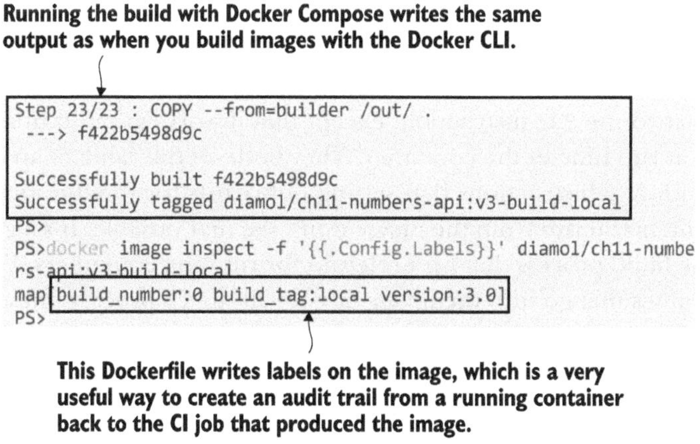

**Running the build with Docker Compose writes the same output as when you build images with the Docker CLI.**

```
Step 23/23 : COPY --from=builder /out/ .
 ---> f422b5498d9c

Successfully built f422b5498d9c
Successfully tagged diamol/ch11-numbers-api:v3-build-local
PS>
PS>docker image inspect -f '{{.Config.Labels}}' diamol/ch11-numbe
rs-api:v3-build-local
map[build_number:0 build_tag:local version:3.0]
PS>
```

**This Dockerfile writes labels on the image, which is a very useful way to create an audit trail from a running container back to the CI job that produced the image.**

**Figure 11.10  Building images with Docker Compose and checking the image labels**

images or a single one—even for one image, it's a good practice to build with Compose because then your Compose file specifies the tag you want when you build the image. There are a few more things in this build that are part of a successful CI pipeline—you can see that in the final inspect command that lists the labels for the image.

Docker lets you apply labels to most resources—containers, images, networks, and volumes. They're simple key/value pairs where you can store additional data about the resource. Labels are very useful on images because they get baked into the image and move with it—when you push or pull the image, the labels go along too. When you build your app with a CI pipeline, it's important to have an audit trail that lets you track back from the running container to the build job that created it, and image labels help you do that.

Listing 11.3 shows part of the Dockerfile for the random number API (you'll find the full file in the exercises for this chapter at numbers/numbers-api/Dockerfile.v4). There are two new Dockerfile instructions here—ARG and LABEL.

Listing 11.3  Specifying image labels and build arguments in the Dockerfile

```
# app image
FROM diamol/dotnet-aspnet

ARG BUILD_NUMBER=0
ARG BUILD_TAG=local

LABEL version="3.0"
LABEL build_number=${BUILD_NUMBER}
LABEL build_tag=${BUILD_TAG}

ENTRYPOINT ["dotnet", "Numbers.Api.dll"]
```

The LABEL instruction just applies the key/value pair from the Dockerfile to the image when it gets built. You can see version=3.0 specified in the Dockerfile, and that matches the label output in figure 11.10. The other two LABEL instructions use environment variables to set the label value, and those environment variables are provided by the ARG instructions.

ARG is very similar to the ENV instruction, except that it works at build time on the image, rather than at run time in the container. They both set the value of an environment variable, but for ARG instructions that setting only exists for the duration of the build, so any containers you run from the image don't see that variable. It's a great way to pass data into the build process that isn't relevant for running containers. I'm using it here to provide values that go into the image labels—in the CI process, these record the number of the build and the full build name. The ARG instruction also sets default values, so when you build the image locally without passing any variables, you see build_number:0 and build_tag:local in the image labels.

You can see how the environment settings in the CI pipeline get passed down into the Docker build command in the Compose override file. Listing 11.4 shows the contents of the docker-compose-build.yml file with all the build settings.

**Listing 11.4 Specifying build settings and reusable arguments in Docker Compose**

```
x-args: &args
  args:
    BUILD_NUMBER: ${BUILD_NUMBER:-0}
    BUILD_TAG: ${BUILD_TAG:-local}

services:
  numbers-api:
    build:
      context: numbers
      dockerfile: numbers-api/Dockerfile.v4
      <<: *args

  numbers-web:
    build:
      context: numbers
      dockerfile: numbers-web/Dockerfile.v4
      <<: *args
```

This Compose file shouldn't be too complicated unless you skipped chapter 10, in which case you should go back and read it. It won't take you more than a lunchtime.

There are three parts to the build block in the Compose specification:

- context—This is the path Docker will use as the working directory for the build. This is usually the current directory, which you pass with a period in the docker image build command, but here it's the numbers directory—the path is relative to the location of the Compose file.
- dockerfile—The path to the Dockerfile, relative to the context.
- args—Any build arguments to pass, which need to match the keys specified as ARG instructions in the Dockerfile. Both the Dockerfiles for this app use the same BUILD_NUMBER and BUILD_TAG arguments, so I'm using a Compose extension field to define those values once, and YAML merge to apply it to both services.

You'll see default values specified in lots of different places, and this is to make sure that support for the CI process doesn't break other workflows. You should always aim for a single Dockerfile that gets built in the same way however the build is run. Default arguments in the Compose file mean the build succeeds when you run it outside of the CI environment, and defaults in the Dockerfile mean the image builds correctly even if you don't use Compose.

**TRY IT NOW** You can build the random number API image with the normal image build command, bypassing the setup in the Compose files. You can call the image whatever you like—the build succeeds and the labels get applied because of the defaults in the Dockerfile:

```
# change to the numbers directory
# (this is done with the context setting in Compose):
cd ch11/exercises/numbers
```

```
# build the image, specifying the Dockerfile path and a build
    argument:
docker image build -f numbers-api/Dockerfile.v4 --build-arg
    BUILD_TAG=ch11 -t numbers-api .

# check the labels:
docker image inspect -f '{{.Config.Labels}}' numbers-api
```

My output is in figure 11.11—you can see in the labels that the value `build_tag:ch11` was set from my build command, but the value `build_number:0` was set from the default for the `ARG` in the Dockerfile.

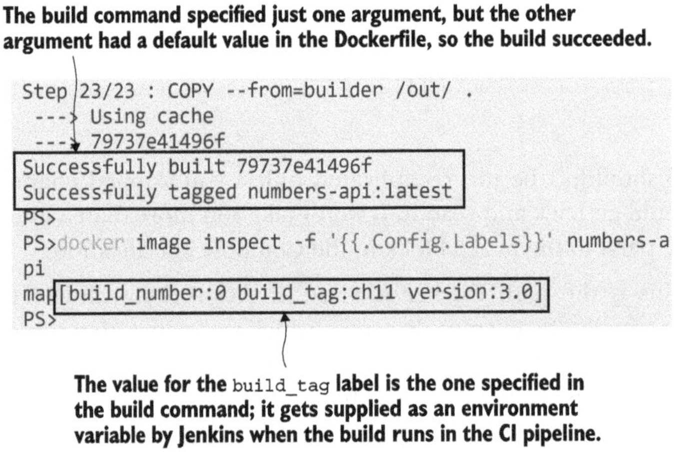

**The build command specified just one argument, but the other argument had a default value in the Dockerfile, so the build succeeded.**

```
Step 23/23 : COPY --from=builder /out/ .
 ---> Using cache
 ---> 79737e41496f
Successfully built 79737e41496f
Successfully tagged numbers-api:latest
PS>
PS>docker image inspect -f '{{.Config.Labels}}' numbers-a
pi
map[build_number:0 build_tag:ch11 version:3.0]
PS>
```

**The value for the `build_tag` label is the one specified in the build command; it gets supplied as an environment variable by Jenkins when the build runs in the CI pipeline.**

Figure 11.11   Including default values for build arguments supports the developer build workflow.

There are quite a few levels of detail here just to get labels into an image, but it's an important thing to get right. You should be able to run `docker image inspect` and find exactly where that image came from, tracking it back to the CI job that produced it, which in turn tracks back to the exact version of code that triggered the build. It's an audit trail from the running container in any environment back to the source code.

## 11.4   *Writing CI jobs with no dependencies except Docker*

You've been happily building images for the random number app in this chapter using Docker and Docker Compose, without needing any other tools installed on your machine. There are two components to the app, and both are written in .NET Core 3.0, but you don't need the .NET Core SDK on your machine to build them. They use the multi-stage Dockerfile approach from chapter 4 to compile and package the app, so Docker and Compose are all you need.

This is a major benefit of containerized CI, and it's supported by all the managed build services like Docker Hub, GitHub Actions, and Azure DevOps. It means you no longer need a build server with lots of tools installed and for the tools to be kept up to date with all the developers. It also means that your build scripts become very simple—developers can use the exact same build scripts locally and get the same output as the CI pipeline, so it becomes easy to move between different build services.

We're using Jenkins for our CI process, and Jenkins jobs can be configured with a simple text file that lives in source control along with the application code, Dockerfiles, and Compose files. Listing 11.5 shows part of the pipeline (from the file `ch11/exercises/Jenkinsfile`) along with the batch script that the pipeline step executes.

> **Listing 11.5    The build step from the Jenkinsfile that describes the CI job**

```
# the build stage in the Jenkinsfile- it switches directory, then runs two
# shell commands - the first sets up a script file so it can be executed
# and the second calls the script:

stage('Build') {
  steps {
    dir('ch11/exercises') {
      sh 'chmod +x ./ci/01-build.bat'
      sh './ci/01-build.bat'
      }
  }
}

# and this is what's in 01-build.bat script:
docker-compose
  -f docker-compose.yml
  -f docker-compose-build.yml
  build --pull
```

Well look at that—it's just the same `docker-compose build` command you ran locally. Except it adds the `pull` flag, which means Docker will pull the latest version of any images it needs during the build. That's a good habit to get into when you do your builds anyway, because it means you'll always build your image from the latest base image with all the recent security fixes. It's especially important in the CI process because there could be a change in an image your Dockerfile uses, which could break your app, and you want to find that out as soon as possible.

The build step runs a simple script file—the filename ends with `.bat` so it runs nicely under Jenkins in a Windows container, but it also works just fine in a Linux container. This step runs the build, and because it's a simple command-line call, all the output from Docker Compose—which is also the output from Docker—gets captured and stored in the build logs.

> **TRY IT NOW**    You can view the logs in the Jenkins UI. Browse to http://localhost :8080/job/diamol to see the jobs, and in the pipeline view click on the Build

step for job #2. Then click Logs. You can expand the steps of the build and you'll see the usual Docker build output; mine is in figure 11.12.

**These are the logs from the build stage. That just runs the build with the Docker Compose CLI, so all the usual image building logs are recorded and shown.**

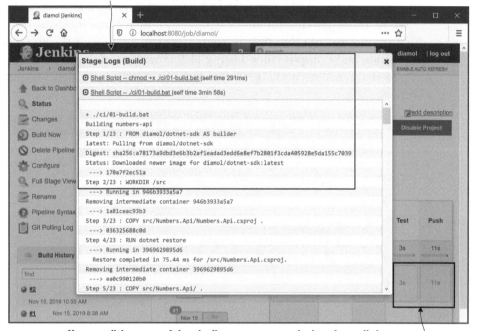

**You can click on any of the pipeline stages to see the logs from all the steps.**

Figure 11.12   Viewing the output from the pipeline build in Jenkins shows the usual Docker logs.

Each step in the build pipeline follows the same pattern; it just calls a batch script that does the actual work by running Docker Compose commands. This approach makes it easy to switch between different build services; instead of writing the logic in a proprietary pipeline syntax, you write it in scripts and use the pipeline to call the scripts. I could add pipeline files to run the build in GitLab or GitHub Actions, and they would call the same batch scripts.

The stages of the Jenkins build are all powered by containers:

- *Verify* calls the script `00-verify.bat`, which just prints out version information for Docker and Docker Compose. This is a useful way to start the pipeline, because it verifies that the Docker dependencies are available and it records the versions of the tools that built the image.

- *Build* calls `01-build.bat`, which you've already seen; it uses Docker Compose to build the images. The `REGISTRY` environment variable is specified in the Jenkinsfile so images will be tagged for the local registry.

- *Test* calls 02-test.bat, which uses Docker Compose to start the whole application, then lists out the containers and brings the application down again. This is just a simple illustration, but it does prove that the containers run without failing. In a real project you would bring up the app and then run end-to-end tests in another container.
- *Push* calls 03-push.bat, which uses Docker Compose to push all the built images. The image tags have the local registry domain, so if the build and test stages are successful, the images get pushed to the registry.

Stages in the CI pipeline are sequential, so if there's a failure at any point, the job ends. That means the registry only stores images for potential release candidates—any image that has been pushed to the registry must have successfully passed the build and test stages.

**TRY IT NOW** You have one successful build from Jenkins—build number 1 failed because there was no source code, and then build number 2 succeeded. You can query your local registry container using the REST API, and you should see just a version 2 tag for each of the random number images:

```
# the catalog endpoint shows all the image repositories:
curl http://registry.local:5000/v2/_catalog

# the tags endpoint shows the individual tags for one repository:
curl http://registry.local:5000/v2/diamol/ch11-numbers-api/tags/list
curl http://registry.local:5000/v2/diamol/ch11-numbers-web/tags/list
```

You can see my output in figure 11.13—there are repositories for the web and API images, but each only has a build-2 tag, because the first build failed and didn't push any images.

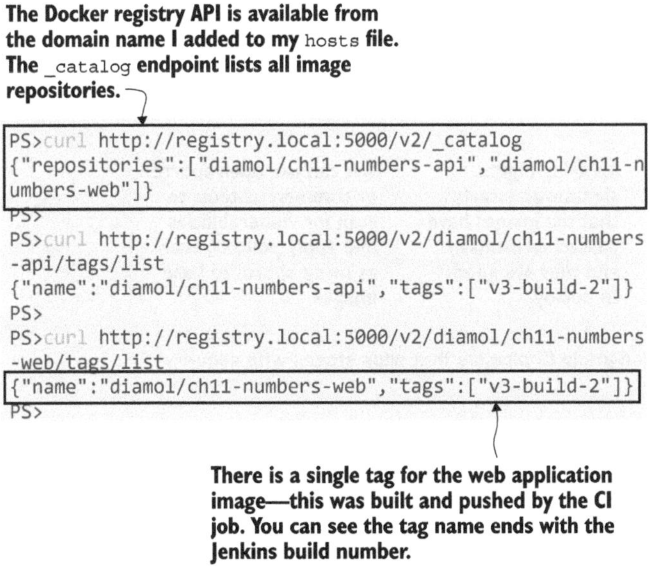

**The Docker registry API is available from the domain name I added to my** hosts **file. The** _catalog **endpoint lists all image repositories.**

```
PS>curl http://registry.local:5000/v2/_catalog
{"repositories":["diamol/ch11-numbers-api","diamol/ch11-n
umbers-web"]}
PS>
PS>curl http://registry.local:5000/v2/diamol/ch11-numbers
-api/tags/list
{"name":"diamol/ch11-numbers-api","tags":["v3-build-2"]}
PS>
PS>curl http://registry.local:5000/v2/diamol/ch11-numbers
-web/tags/list
{"name":"diamol/ch11-numbers-web","tags":["v3-build-2"]}
PS>
```

**There is a single tag for the web application image—this was built and pushed by the CI job. You can see the tag name ends with the Jenkins build number.**

Figure 11.13 Sending web requests to the registry API to query the images stored in the container

This is a fairly simple CI pipeline, but it shows you all the key stages of the build and some important best practices. The key thing is to let Docker do the hard work and to build the stages of your pipeline in scripts. Then you can use any CI tool and just plug your scripts into the tool's pipeline definition.

## 11.5   *Understanding containers in the CI process*

Compiling and running applications in containers is just the start of what you can do with Docker in your CI pipeline. Docker adds a layer of consistency on top of all your application builds, and you can use that consistency to add many useful features to your pipeline. Figure 11.14 shows a more extensive CI process that includes security-scanning container images for known vulnerabilities and digitally signing images to assert their provenance.

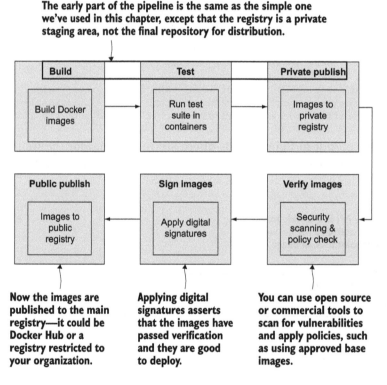

Figure 11.14   A production-grade CI pipeline that adds stages with security gates

Docker calls this approach the *secure software supply chain*, and it's important for all sizes of organizations because it gives you confidence that the software you're about to deploy is safe. You can run tooling in your pipeline to check for known security vulnerabilities and fail the build if there are issues. You can configure your production environment to only run containers from images that have been digitally signed—a process that happens at the end of a successful build. When your containers are deployed to production, you can be certain that they're running from images that came through your build process, and that they contain software that has passed all your tests and is free from security issues.

The checks and balances you add in your pipeline work on containers and images, so they apply in the same way across all your application platforms. If you work with multiple technologies across your projects, you'll be using different base images and different build steps in the Dockerfiles, but the CI pipelines will all be the same.

## 11.6   *Lab*

Lab time! You're going to build your own CI pipeline—but don't run scared. We'll use the ideas and exercises from this chapter, but the pipeline stages will be much simpler.

In the lab folder for this chapter you'll find a copy of the source code for the to-do app from chapter 6. The build for that app is almost ready to go—the Jenkinsfile is there, the CI scripts are there, and the core Docker Compose file is there. There are just a couple of things for you to do:

- Write an override file called `docker-compose-build.yml` with the build settings.
- Create a Jenkins job to run the pipeline.
- Push your changes to Gogs in the `diamol` repository.

Just three tasks, but don't be disheartened if your first few builds fail and you need to check the logs and tweak some things. No one in history has ever written a Jenkins job that passed on the first run, so here are a few hints:

- Your Compose override will be similar to the one in the exercises—specifying the context and a build argument for the build number label.
- In the Jenkins UI, you click New Item to create a job, and you can copy from the existing `diamol` job.
- The new job setup will be the same except for the path to the Jenkinsfile— you'll need to specify the `lab` folder instead of the `exercises` folder.

If you're not getting far with this, you'll find more information in the read-me file in the lab folder, complete with screenshots for the Jenkins steps and sample build configuration for the Docker Compose file: https://github.com/sixeyed/diamol/blob/master/ch11/lab/README.md.

# Part 3

# *Running at scale with a container orchestrator*

Orchestration is about running containerized apps across multiple servers— a cluster of servers. You use the same Docker images, and you can use the same Docker Compose file format, but instead of managing containers yourself, you tell the cluster what you want the end result to be, and it manages containers for you. In this part of the book you'll learn how to use Docker Swarm, which is a simple and powerful orchestrator built into Docker. You'll learn about the application update and rollback process, and how to connect your build pipeline to the cluster to add continuous deployment to your CI pipeline.

# Understanding orchestration: Docker Swarm and Kubernetes

We're halfway through our container journey together, and by now you should be pretty comfortable packaging and running applications with Docker and Docker Compose. The next step is understanding how those applications run in a production environment, where you have many machines running Docker to give you high availability and the power to handle lots of incoming traffic.

In that environment your apps still run in containers using the same Docker images you run locally, but there's a management layer that takes care of coordinating all the machines and running the containers for you. That's called *orchestration* and the two main container orchestrators are Docker Swarm and Kubernetes. They share a lot of the same features and capabilities, but Kubernetes is a complex system with its own learning journey—*Learn Kubernetes in a Month of Lunches* will be your guide there. In this chapter you're going to learn about orchestration using Docker Swarm, which is a powerful production-grade container orchestrator built right into Docker. Even if your ultimate goal is to learn Kubernetes, it's good to start with Swarm—the Kubernetes learning curve is steep, but it's much easier when you already know Swarm.

## 12.1 What is a container orchestrator?

Docker Compose is great for running containers on a single machine, but that doesn't work in a production environment—if that machine goes offline, you lose all your applications. Production systems need high availability, which is where orchestration comes in. An orchestrator is basically a lot of machines all grouped together to form a *cluster*; the orchestrator manages containers, distributing work among all the machines, load-balancing network traffic, and replacing any containers that become unhealthy.

You create a cluster by installing Docker on each of your machines, and then you join them together with the orchestration platform—Swarm or Kubernetes. From then on you manage the cluster remotely using command-line tools or web UIs. Figure 12.1 shows how that looks from the infrastructure view.

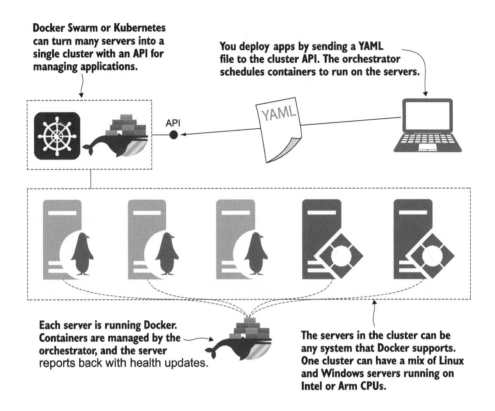

**Docker Swarm or Kubernetes can turn many servers into a single cluster with an API for managing applications.**

**You deploy apps by sending a YAML file to the cluster API. The orchestrator schedules containers to run on the servers.**

API

YAML

**Each server is running Docker. Containers are managed by the orchestrator, and the server reports back with health updates.**

**The servers in the cluster can be any system that Docker supports. One cluster can have a mix of Linux and Windows servers running on Intel or Arm CPUs.**

Figure 12.1   An orchestrator turns many servers into a single cluster, and it manages containers for you.

The orchestrator offers a set of extra capabilities that take your containers to the next level. There's a distributed database in the cluster that stores all the information about the applications you deploy. Then there's a scheduler that works out where to run containers, and a system to send heartbeats between all the servers in the cluster. Those are the basic building blocks for reliability. You deploy applications by sending your YAML file to the cluster; it stores that information and then schedules containers to run the app—distributing the work to servers with available capacity. When the app is running, the cluster makes sure it keeps running. If a server goes offline and you lose a bunch of containers, the cluster will start replacement containers on other servers.

Orchestrators do all the hard work of managing containers; you just define the desired state in your YAML files, and you don't have to know or care how many servers are in the cluster or where your containers are running. The orchestrator also provides features for networking, configuring applications, and storing data. Figure 12.2 shows how network traffic is routed into and within the cluster and how containers can read configuration objects and secrets, and write to shared storage.

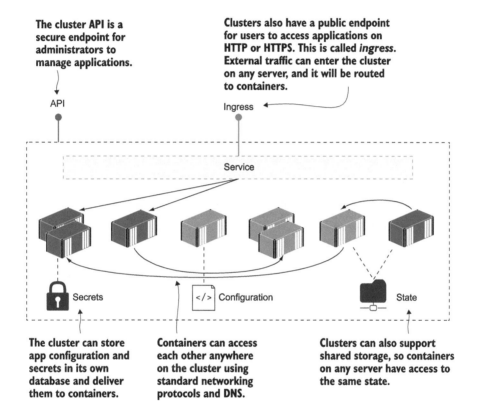

**The cluster API is a secure endpoint for administrators to manage applications.**

**Clusters also have a public endpoint for users to access applications on HTTP or HTTPS. This is called** *ingress.* **External traffic can enter the cluster on any server, and it will be routed to containers.**

API

Ingress

Service

Secrets

</> Configuration

State

**The cluster can store app configuration and secrets in its own database and deliver them to containers.**

**Containers can access each other anywhere on the cluster using standard networking protocols and DNS.**

**Clusters can also support shared storage, so containers on any server have access to the same state.**

Figure 12.2   Orchestrators provide extra features for containers—networking, configuration, and storage.

There's an important thing missing from the diagram in figure 12.2—the servers. The orchestrator hides away the details of the individual machines, networks, and storage devices. You work with the cluster as a single unit, sending commands and running queries through the API, which the command line connects to. The cluster could be 1,000 machines or a single machine—you work with it in the same way and send the same commands and YAML files to manage your apps. Users of your application could connect to any server in the cluster, and the orchestration layer takes care of routing traffic to containers.

## 12.2   Setting up a Docker Swarm cluster

Let's get started now. It's super easy to deploy a container orchestrator with Docker Swarm, because the features are built into the Docker Engine. All you need to do is switch to Swarm mode by initializing the cluster.

> **TRY IT NOW**   The Docker CLI has a set of commands to manage cluster operations. The `swarm init` command switches to Swarm mode. You can usually run it without any arguments, but if your machine is connected to more than one network, you'll get an error and Docker will ask you which IP address to use for the Swarm communication:

```
docker swarm init
```

You can see my output in figure 12.3, which tells me that the Swarm is initialized and my machine is a manager. Machines in a cluster can have different roles: they can either be a manager or a worker. The output from running `swarm init` shows the command you need to run on other machines for them to join the Swarm as workers.

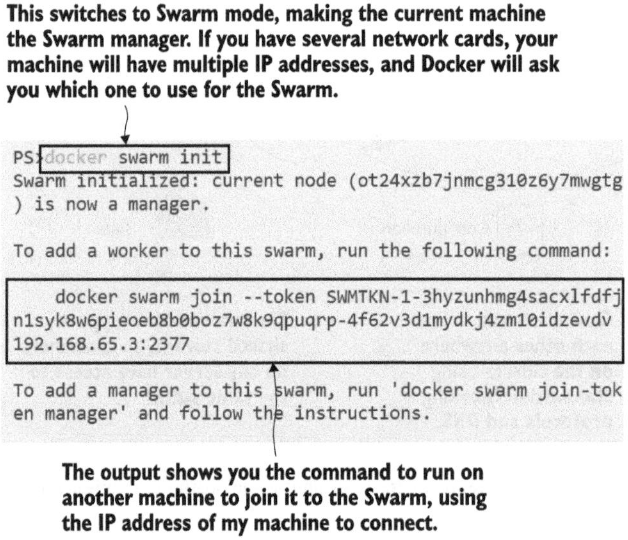

**This switches to Swarm mode, making the current machine the Swarm manager. If you have several network cards, your machine will have multiple IP addresses, and Docker will ask you which one to use for the Swarm.**

```
PS>docker swarm init
Swarm initialized: current node (ot24xzb7jnmcg310z6y7mwgtg
) is now a manager.

To add a worker to this swarm, run the following command:

    docker swarm join --token SWMTKN-1-3hyzunhmg4sacxlfdfj
n1syk8w6pieoeb8b0boz7w8k9qpuqrp-4f62v3d1mydkj4zm10idzevdv
192.168.65.3:2377

To add a manager to this swarm, run 'docker swarm join-tok
en manager' and follow the instructions.
```

**The output shows you the command to run on another machine to join it to the Swarm, using the IP address of my machine to connect.**

**Figure 12.3   Switching to Swarm mode creates a cluster with a single node, which is the manager.**

The difference between managers and workers is that the managers run the show—the cluster database is stored on the managers, you send your commands and YAML files to the API hosted on the managers, and the scheduling and monitoring is all done by the managers. Workers typically just run containers when the managers schedule them, and they report back on their status, although you can have managers running workloads too (insert your own joke here, comparing that to human managers).

Initializing the Swarm is something you do once, and then you can join any number of machines—Docker calls machines in the Swarm *nodes*. To join a node to the

Swarm, it needs to be on the same network, and you need the join token from the manager, which acts like a password to secure the Swarm from rogue nodes. If you have access to the manager, you can print out the tokens for nodes to join as workers or additional managers, and you can list the nodes in the swarm.

**TRY IT NOW** Once you're in Swarm mode, there are a lot more commands available from the Docker CLI. Run these to find the join tokens for worker or manager nodes, and to list all the nodes in the Swarm:

```
# print the command to join a new worker node
docker swarm join-token worker

# print the command to join a new manager node
docker swarm join-token manager

# list all the nodes in the swarm
docker node ls
```

You can see my output in figure 12.4. There's only one node in my Swarm, but I can add any other machines on my network to the Swarm using the manager's IP address in the `join` command.

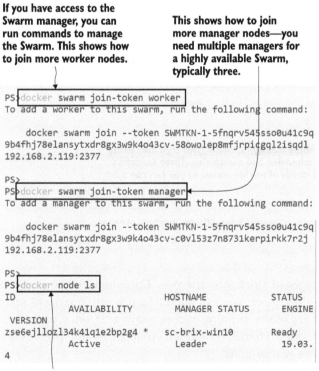

If you have access to the Swarm manager, you can run commands to manage the Swarm. This shows how to join more worker nodes.

This shows how to join more manager nodes—you need multiple managers for a highly available Swarm, typically three.

Lists all the nodes in the Swarm, showing basic details like availability, node type, and the version of Docker on the machine

**Figure 12.4  In Swarm mode you have extra commands to manage the nodes in the cluster.**

A single-node Swarm works in exactly the same way as a multi-node Swarm, except that you don't get high availability from having spare machines, or the option to scale out containers to use the capacity of many machines. Figure 12.5 compares the architecture of a single-node Swarm, which you can use for development and test environments, and a multi-node cluster, which you would use in production.

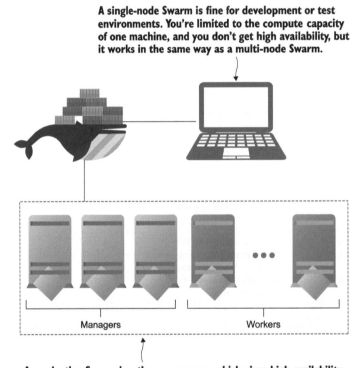

A single-node Swarm is fine for development or test environments. You're limited to the compute capacity of one machine, and you don't get high availability, but it works in the same way as a multi-node Swarm.

Managers

Workers

A production Swarm has three managers, which gives high availability for the cluster database, scheduler, and monitoring. Three managers can run a Swarm with hundreds of worker nodes, so you can run a lot of applications at scale.

Figure 12.5   Test and production Swarms have different numbers of nodes, but the same feature set.

One of the big advantages of Docker Swarm over Kubernetes is the simplicity of setting up and managing the cluster. You can build a Swarm with dozens of nodes just by installing Docker on every server, running `docker swarm init` once, and `docker swarm join` for all the other nodes. There's no hidden complexity—the process is the same for production and test environments.

Now that you have your single-node Swarm, you can explore how applications work when you have an orchestrator managing containers for you.

## 12.3 Running applications as Docker Swarm services

You don't run containers in Docker Swarm—you deploy services, and the Swarm runs containers for you. A service is just an abstraction over the idea of individual containers. Swarm uses the same terminology here as Docker Compose for the same reason: a service could be deployed as multiple containers.

Services are defined with a lot of the same information you use to run containers. You specify the image to use, environment variables to set, ports to publish, and a name for the service that becomes its DNS name on the network. The difference is that a service can have many replicas—individual containers that all use the same specification from the service and can be run on any node in the Swarm.

> **TRY IT NOW** Create a service that runs one container using a simple application image from Docker Hub, and then list the services to check that it's running correctly:

```
docker service create --name timecheck --replicas 1 diamol/ch12-
    timecheck:1.0

docker service ls
```

Services are first-class objects in Docker Swarm, but you need to be running in Swarm mode—or be connected to a Swarm manager—to work with them. My output is in figure 12.6, where you can see that the service gets created and the basic details are shown from the service list command, which shows there is one replica running.

The containers that make up a service are called *replicas*, but they're just ordinary Docker containers. You can connect to the node that's running a replica and work

**Creates a service called** timecheck **that will run in a single container somewhere on the Swarm, using the** diamol/ch12-timecheck:1.0 **image**

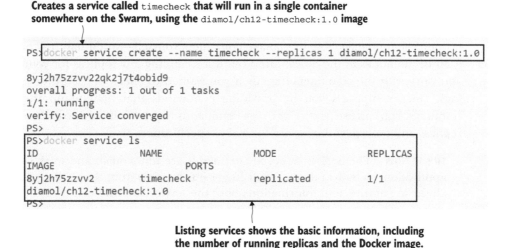

```
PS>docker service create --name timecheck --replicas 1 diamol/ch12-timecheck:1.0

8yj2h75zzvv22qk2j7t4obid9
overall progress: 1 out of 1 tasks
1/1: running
verify: Service converged
PS>
PS>docker service ls
ID                      NAME              MODE          REPLICAS
IMAGE                       PORTS
8yj2h75zzvv2            timecheck         replicated    1/1
diamol/ch12-timecheck:1.0
PS>
```

**Listing services shows the basic information, including the number of running replicas and the Docker image.**

**Figure 12.6  Creating a service is how you ask the Swarm to run containers for you.**

with it using the usual Docker container commands. On a single-node Swarm, every replica will run on that machine, so you can work with the service container you just created. It's not something you would normally do, though, because the containers are being managed by the Swarm. If you try to manage them yourself, what happens may not be what you expect.

> **TRY IT NOW**   The service replica is running on your machine, but it's being managed by the Swarm. You can delete the container, but the Swarm will see that the service is running below the desired replica count, and it will create a replacement.

```
# list the replicas for the service:
docker service ps timecheck

# check the containers on the machine:
docker container ls

# remove the most recent container (which is the service replica):
docker container rm -f $( docker container ls --last 1 -q)

# check the replicas again:
docker service ps timecheck
```

You can see my output in figure 12.7. I had one container running the replica for my service, and I manually removed it. But the service still exists in the Swarm, and it should have a replica level of one. When I removed the container, the Swarm saw there weren't enough replicas running, and it started a replacement. You see in the final replica list that the original container is shown as failed, because the Swarm doesn't know why the container stopped. The running replica is a new container that has only been up for 10 seconds.

When you're running in Swarm mode, you manage your applications as services, and you let the Swarm manage individual containers. That has to be the case because it would be unmanageable to manage containers yourself—you'd have to connect to each of the nodes in the Swarm, find out if it's running any replicas for your service, and work with the containers directly if you wanted to check the status or print out logs. Docker supports you by providing commands that operate on the Swarm resources. You can use docker service commands to print out log entries from all the replicas and to inspect the service to read its specification.

> **TRY IT NOW**   The docker service commands are how you should work with applications in Swarm mode. You can get information from the replicas, like all the log entries, and information about the service as a whole:

```
# print the service logs for the last 10 seconds:
docker service logs --since 10s timecheck

# get the service details, showing just the image:
docker service inspect timecheck -f
    '{{.Spec.TaskTemplate.ContainerSpec.Image}}'
```

**The** `service ps` **command lists the replicas for a service—this shows a single replica running on my Docker Desktop node.**

**Listing containers shows the replica because it's running on my machine. The container name is built from the service name, replica number, and replica ID.**

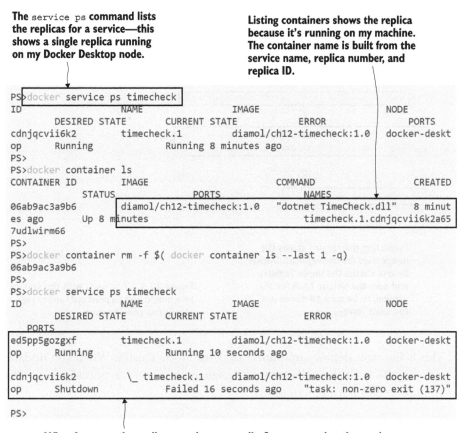

```
PS>docker service ps timecheck
ID                    NAME                 IMAGE                       NODE
      DESIRED STATE        CURRENT STATE           ERROR              PORTS
cdnjqcvii6k2          timecheck.1          diamol/ch12-timecheck:1.0  docker-deskt
op       Running              Running 8 minutes ago
PS>
PS>docker container ls
CONTAINER ID          IMAGE                              COMMAND                CREATED
             STATUS               PORTS               NAMES
06ab9ac3a9b6          diamol/ch12-timecheck:1.0          "dotnet TimeCheck.dll"  8 minut
es ago       Up 8 minutes                              timecheck.1.cdnjqcvii6k2a65
7udlwirm66
PS>
PS>docker container rm -f $( docker container ls --last 1 -q)
06ab9ac3a9b6
PS>
PS>docker service ps timecheck
ID                    NAME                 IMAGE                       NODE
      DESIRED STATE        CURRENT STATE           ERROR
   PORTS
ed5pp5gozgxf          timecheck.1          diamol/ch12-timecheck:1.0   docker-deskt
op       Running              Running 10 seconds ago

cdnjqcvii6k2          \_ timecheck.1       diamol/ch12-timecheck:1.0   docker-deskt
op       Shutdown             Failed 16 seconds ago   "task: non-zero exit (137)"

PS>
```

**When I remove the replica container manually, Swarm sees that the service doesn't have the required number of replicas, and it starts a replacement.**

**Figure 12.7** Service replicas are normal containers, but they're managed by the Swarm—not by you.

My output is in figure 12.8. It shows the most recent log entries from the service replicas and part of the service specification.

The whole specification is saved in the cluster, and you can see it by running that same `service inspect` command but without the format parameter. There's a lot of information there, securely stored in the cluster's database, which is replicated across all the manager nodes. This is one of the big differences between Docker Swarm and Docker Compose, which doesn't have a data store for application definitions. You can only manage applications with Docker Compose if you have the Compose file(s) available, because that's the source of the app definition. In Swarm mode the app definition is stored in the cluster, so you can manage apps without a local YAML file.

You can try that by updating your running service. You can specify a new image version, but you don't need to repeat any of the other information from the service spec.

**Prints out the container logs from all the service replicas. The** `since` **parameter limits the output to logs written in the last 10 seconds.**

**Log entries are shown with the replica ID, so you can track logs back to the container that generated them.**

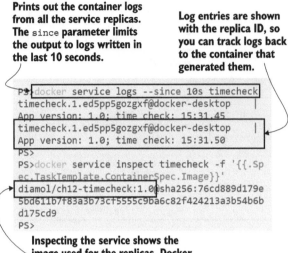

```
PS>docker service logs --since 10s timecheck
timecheck.1.ed5pp5gozgxf@docker-desktop        |
App version: 1.0; time check: 15:31.45
timecheck.1.ed5pp5gozgxf@docker-desktop        |
App version: 1.0; time check: 15:31.50
PS>
PS>docker service inspect timecheck -f '{{.Sp
ec.TaskTemplate.ContainerSpec.Image}}'
diamol/ch12-timecheck:1.0@sha256:76cd889d179e
5bd611b7f83a3b73cf5555c9ba6c82f424213a3b54b6b
d175cd9
PS>
```

**Inspecting the service shows the image used for the replicas. Docker Swarm checks the image registry and uses the unique hash for that version, to be sure all nodes use the same image.**

Figure 12.8  You work with the service as a single unit to print out replica logs or check the specification.

This is how you deploy application updates in the cluster. When you update the service definition, Swarm rolls out the change, replacing the replicas by removing the old containers and starting new ones.

**TRY IT NOW**   Update the timecheck service to use a new image version. It's the same simple app that writes a timestamp every few seconds, but the update prints a new application version in the logs:

```
# update the service to use a new application image:
docker service update --image diamol/ch12-timecheck:2.0 timecheck

# list the service replicas:
docker service ps timecheck

# and check the logs:
docker service logs --since 20s timecheck
```

You'll see when you list the replicas with `service ps` that there are two instances—the old replica running from the image tag 1.0, and the replacement running from the image tag 2.0. Service logs include an ID so you can see which replica produces the log entries. These are just the application logs being written out to the container, collected by the Swarm and shown with the replica ID. You can see mine in figure 12.9.

All container orchestrators use the approach of staged rollouts for application updates, which keeps your app online during the upgrade. Swarm implements this by

**Updating the service rolls out an updated version of the application. The CLI shows you that one out of one replica is running when the rollout is complete.**

**Listing the service replicas shows three: the original version 1.0 container that I manually removed, the 1.0 replacement that the Swarm created, and the current version 2.0 container from the update.**

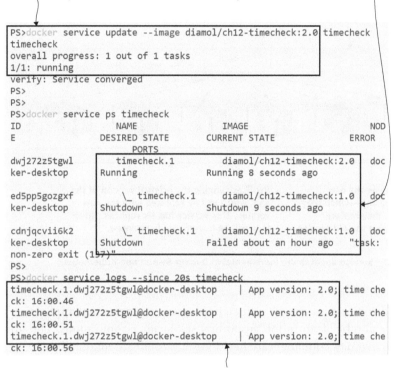

```
PS>docker service update --image diamol/ch12-timecheck:2.0 timecheck
timecheck
overall progress: 1 out of 1 tasks
1/1: running
verify: Service converged
PS>
PS>
PS>docker service ps timecheck
ID                    NAME              IMAGE                   NOD
E                     DESIRED STATE     CURRENT STATE           ERROR
                            PORTS
dwj272z5tgwl          timecheck.1       diamol/ch12-timecheck:2.0  doc
ker-desktop           Running           Running 8 seconds ago

ed5pp5gozgxf            \_ timecheck.1  diamol/ch12-timecheck:1.0  doc
ker-desktop           Shutdown          Shutdown 9 seconds ago

cdnjqcvii6k2            \_ timecheck.1  diamol/ch12-timecheck:1.0  doc
ker-desktop           Shutdown          Failed about an hour ago   "task:
non-zero exit (137)"
PS>
PS>docker service logs --since 20s timecheck
timecheck.1.dwj272z5tgwl@docker-desktop    | App version: 2.0; time che
ck: 16:00.46
timecheck.1.dwj272z5tgwl@docker-desktop    | App version: 2.0; time che
ck: 16:00.51
timecheck.1.dwj272z5tgwl@docker-desktop    | App version: 2.0; time che
ck: 16:00.56
```

**The most recent service logs are from the version 2.0 update of the application, but if I looked further back in time I'd see the version 1.0 log entries too.**

**Figure 12.9   Updating a service starts a gradual rollout of a new application version.**

replacing replicas one at a time, so if you have multiple replicas hosting your application, there are always containers running to service incoming requests. The actual behavior of the rolling upgrade can be configured for your individual service. You might have 10 replicas providing your web application, and when you roll out an upgrade you could have Docker replace two replicas at a time, checking that the new containers are healthy before moving on to replace the next two replicas, until all 10 are replaced.

Figure 12.10 shows how that rolling upgrade looks when it's partway through the deployment—some replicas are running the old version of the application image and some are running the new one. During the rollout, both versions of your app are live and users could hit either one—you need to manage the user experience side of the update yourself.

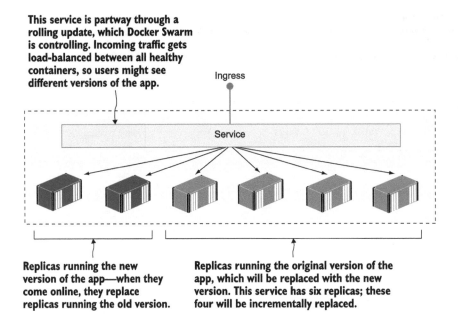

**This service is partway through a rolling update, which Docker Swarm is controlling. Incoming traffic gets load-balanced between all healthy containers, so users might see different versions of the app.**

Ingress

Service

**Replicas running the new version of the app—when they come online, they replace replicas running the old version.**

**Replicas running the original version of the app, which will be replaced with the new version. This service has six replicas; these four will be incrementally replaced.**

Figure 12.10   Service updates are incremental in Docker Swarm and Kubernetes.

Automated rolling updates are a huge improvement on manual application releases, and they're another feature for supporting self-healing applications. The update process checks that new containers are healthy as it is rolling them out; if there's a problem with the new version, and the containers are failing, the update can be automatically paused to prevent breaking the whole application. Swarm also stores the previous specification of a service in its database, so if you need to manually roll back to the previous version, you can do that with a single command.

> **TRY IT NOW**   You normally manage app deployments with YAML files, but if you have a deployment go wrong, it's very useful just to roll back to the previous state. Docker Swarm can do this because it stores the current and previous state of the service in its database:

```
# rollback the previous update:
docker service update --rollback timecheck

# list all the service replicas:
docker service ps timecheck

# print the logs from all replicas for the last 25 seconds:
docker service logs --since 25s timecheck
```

The rollback process works in the same way as the update process, with a staged rollout, but it uses the service specification from before the most recent update, so you don't need to provide the image tag. That's very useful if an update breaks the application in a way that Docker doesn't notice, which could happen if you don't have health checks or if your checks aren't detailed enough. In that case, when you discover the app is broken, you just run the rollback command and you don't need to frantically try and find the details of the previous service spec. My output is in figure 12.11, where you can see the replicas from all the deployments, and the service logs from the most recent replicas—the update to 2.0 and the rollback to 1.0.

Services are the resources you manage when you're in Swarm mode, rather than containers. There are some new types of resources you can manage too, but some of

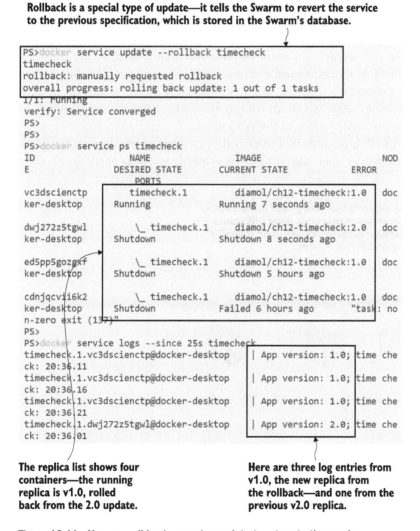

**Rollback is a special type of update—it tells the Swarm to revert the service to the previous specification, which is stored in the Swarm's database.**

```
PS>docker service update --rollback timecheck
timecheck
rollback: manually requested rollback
overall progress: rolling back update: 1 out of 1 tasks
1/1: running
verify: Service converged
PS>
PS>
PS>docker service ps timecheck
ID              NAME              IMAGE                          NOD
E               DESIRED STATE     CURRENT STATE          ERROR
                PORTS
vc3dscienctp       timecheck.1        diamol/ch12-timecheck:1.0   doc
ker-desktop     Running           Running 7 seconds ago

dwj272z5tgwl      \_ timecheck.1      diamol/ch12-timecheck:2.0   doc
ker-desktop     Shutdown          Shutdown 8 seconds ago

ed5pp5gozgxf      \_ timecheck.1      diamol/ch12-timecheck:1.0   doc
ker-desktop     Shutdown          Shutdown 5 hours ago

cdnjqcvii6k2      \_ timecheck.1      diamol/ch12-timecheck:1.0   doc
ker-desktop     Shutdown          Failed 6 hours ago         "task: no
n-zero exit (137)"
PS>
PS>docker service logs --since 25s timecheck
timecheck.1.vc3dscienctp@docker-desktop     | App version: 1.0; time che
ck: 20:36.11
timecheck.1.vc3dscienctp@docker-desktop     | App version: 1.0; time che
ck: 20:36.16
timecheck.1.vc3dscienctp@docker-desktop     | App version: 1.0; time che
ck: 20:36.21
timecheck.1.dwj272z5tgwl@docker-desktop     | App version: 2.0; time che
ck: 20:36.01
```

**The replica list shows four containers—the running replica is v1.0, rolled back from the 2.0 update.**

**Here are three log entries from v1.0, the new replica from the rollback—and one from the previous v2.0 replica.**

Figure 12.11  You can roll back a service update to return to the previous specification with one command.

the key Docker resources work in the same way. When containers need to communicate in Swarm mode, they do it over Docker networks, and you publish ports to let external traffic into your application.

## 12.4 *Managing network traffic in the cluster*

Networking in Swarm mode is standard TCP/IP, as far as the applications inside containers are concerned. Components look for each other by DNS name, the DNS server in Docker returns an IP address, and the container sends network traffic to that IP address. Ultimately the traffic is received by a container and it responds. In Swarm mode, the container sending the request and the container sending the response could be running on different nodes, but that's all transparent to the containers and the applications inside.

There's all sorts of clever networking logic happening behind the scenes to make cross-cluster communication seamless, but you don't need to dig into any of that because it All Just Works. Swarm mode provides a new type of Docker network called the *overlay network*. It's a virtual network that spans all the nodes in the cluster, and when services are attached to an overlay network, they can communicate with each other using the service name as the DNS name.

Figure 12.12 shows how that works with two overlay networks supporting different applications, where each application runs across multiple services on many nodes.

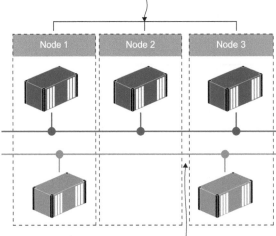

Overlay networks span every node in the Swarm. Containers can communicate using DNS names and standard network channels, even if they're running on different servers.

Docker networks are still isolated in Swarm mode, so containers can only connect if their services are attached to the same network.

Figure 12.12   Networks in the Swarm span the whole cluster and still provide isolation between apps.

The overlay network allows services to communicate when they form part of the same application, but the networks are isolated so services on different networks can't access each other.

There's one other difference with services on overlay networks, compared to containers on ordinary Docker networks. You've seen in chapter 7 that you can use Docker Compose to scale up and run many instances of a container for a single Compose service. A DNS query to Docker for that Compose service will return the IP addresses for all the containers, and it will rely on the consumer to pick one to send the traffic to. That doesn't scale well when you have hundreds of replicas in a Swarm service, so overlay networks use a different approach and return a single virtual IP address for the service.

**TRY IT NOW** Let's remove the simple app from the previous exercises and create a network and the API services for the NASA image of the day application we've used in previous chapters.

```
# remove the original app:
docker service rm timecheck

# create an overlay network for the new app:
docker network create --driver overlay iotd-net

# create the API service, attaching it to the network:
docker service create --detach --replicas 3 --network iotd-net --name
    iotd diamol/ch09-image-of-the-day

# and the log API, attached to the same network:
docker service create --detach --replicas 2 --network iotd-net --name
    accesslog diamol/ch09-access-log

# check the services:
docker service ls
```

Now you have services running the NASA image of the day APIs, and the services are attached to an overlay network. There are three replicas running the image API service and two running the access log service, as you can see from my output in figure 12.13. This is still running on my single-node Swarm using Docker Desktop, but I could run the same set of commands on a Swarm with 500 nodes and the output would be the same—except that the replicas would be running on different nodes.

The easiest way to see the virtual IP address (this is called *VIP networking*) is to connect to a terminal session in any of the container replicas. You can run some network commands to perform DNS queries on the service names and check what IP addresses are returned.

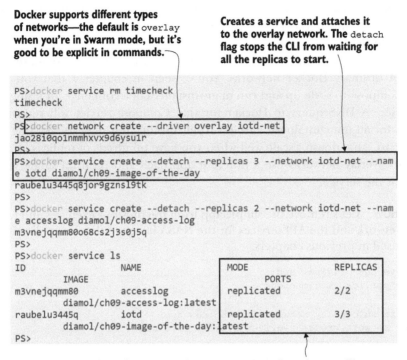

**Docker supports different types of networks—the default is** overlay **when you're in Swarm mode, but it's good to be explicit in commands.**

**Creates a service and attaches it to the overlay network. The** detach **flag stops the CLI from waiting for all the replicas to start.**

```
PS>docker service rm timecheck
timecheck
PS>
PS>docker network create --driver overlay iotd-net
jao28i0qo1nmmhxvx9d6ysu1r
PS>
PS>docker service create --detach --replicas 3 --network iotd-net --nam
e iotd diamol/ch09-image-of-the-day
raubelu3445q8jor9gznsl9tk
PS>
PS>docker service create --detach --replicas 2 --network iotd-net --nam
e accesslog diamol/ch09-access-log
m3vnejqqmm80o68cs2j3s0j5q
PS>
PS>docker service ls
ID              NAME          MODE         PORTS    REPLICAS
      IMAGE
m3vnejqqmm80        accesslog        replicated        2/2
      diamol/ch09-access-log:latest
raubelu3445q        iotd             replicated        3/3
      diamol/ch09-image-of-the-day:latest
PS>
```

**The services are running across many replicas. Swarm will return a single virtual IP address for the service name in DNS lookups.**

Figure 12.13   Running services in Swarm mode and connecting them to an overlay network

**TRY IT NOW**   Execute an interactive terminal session in the most recent container, and run DNS lookups for the API services. The first commands are different for Linux and Windows containers, but once you're connected to the terminal in the container, they're the same:

```
# run a terminal session - Windows containers:
docker container exec -it $(docker container ls --last 1 -q) cmd

# OR on Linux containers:
docker container exec -it $(docker container ls --last 1 -q) sh

# run DNS lookups:
nslookup iotd
nslookup accesslog
```

You can see from my output in figure 12.14 that there is a single IP address for each of the services, even though there are multiple containers running those services. The service IP address is a virtual IP address that is shared across all the replicas.

Fetches the ID of the most recent container, which could be any
of the service replicas, and connects to a shell session inside

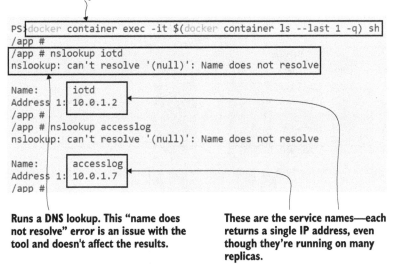

```
PS docker container exec -it $(docker container ls --last 1 -q) sh
/app #
/app # nslookup iotd
nslookup: can't resolve '(null)': Name does not resolve

Name:       iotd
Address 1: 10.0.1.2
/app #
/app # nslookup accesslog
nslookup: can't resolve '(null)': Name does not resolve

Name:       accesslog
Address 1: 10.0.1.7
/app #
```

Runs a DNS lookup. This "name does
not resolve" error is an issue with the
tool and doesn't affect the results.

These are the service names—each
returns a single IP address, even
though they're running on many
replicas.

Figure 12.14  Services use VIP networking, so there's a single IP address for any
number of replicas.

This is VIP networking, which is supported in Linux and Windows and is a much more
efficient way to load-balance network traffic. There is a single IP address from the DNS
lookup, which stays constant even when the service is scaled up or down. Clients send
traffic to that IP address, and the networking layer in the operating system discovers
there are actually multiple destinations for the address, and it decides which one to use.

Docker Swarm uses VIP networking between services to provide reliable and
load-balanced access to services. You only need to know that because it's useful if
you're trying to debug communication issues—otherwise you might run a DNS
lookup for a service with many replicas and be surprised to see a single IP address
returned. Applications running as Swarm services just use DNS names in the usual
way, so the complexity of the overlay network is completely hidden.

Swarm mode takes that same approach of simplifying complex network patterns to
handle traffic coming into the cluster. This is a much more complicated problem, if
you think about the scale of the cluster and the scale of your application. You might
have a web app running with 10 replicas. If there are 20 nodes in your cluster, some
nodes aren't running any of your web containers, and the Swarm needs to direct
requests to nodes that are running containers. If there are only five nodes in your cluster, each node will be running multiple replicas, and the Swarm needs to load-balance
between containers on the node. Swarm uses *ingress networking* to deal with this—the
diagram in figure 12.15 shows how the ingress works, with every node listening on the
same port externally and Docker directing traffic internally within the cluster.

**Ingress networking means every node in the Swarm listens for incoming traffic when a service publishes a port. Any node could receive a request.**

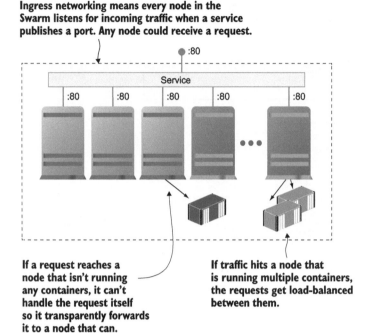

**If a request reaches a node that isn't running any containers, it can't handle the request itself so it transparently forwards it to a node that can.**

**If traffic hits a node that is running multiple containers, the requests get load-balanced between them.**

Figure 12.15   Docker Swarm uses ingress networking to route traffic to containers on nodes.

Ingress networking is the default in Swarm mode when you publish ports for a service, so it's the same as overlay networking—complex technology that is incredibly easy to use. You can publish ports when you create a service, and that's all you need to do to make use of the ingress network.

**TRY IT NOW**   The final component of the image gallery app is the website itself. When you run it as a Swarm service and publish the port, it uses the ingress network:

```
# create the web front end for the app:
docker service create --detach --name image-gallery --network iotd-net
    --publish 8010:80 --replicas 2 diamol/ch09-image-gallery

# list all services:
docker service ls
```

Now you have a service with multiple replicas, listening on a single port. You're not able to do this with Docker Compose because you can't have several containers all listening on the same port, but you can in Docker Swarm because it's the service that listens on the port using the ingress network. When a request comes in to the cluster, the ingress network sends it to one of the service replicas, which could be running on the node that received the request or a different node in the cluster. Figure 12.16 shows the service running with two replicas and the published port.

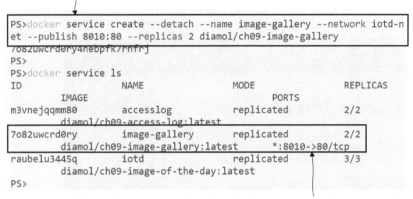

Creates a service with published ports in Docker Swarm, and the ports are published on the ingress network. It's the same simple user experience as publishing ports for containers.

The service has two replicas, but it's listening on a single port—actually it's the ingress that listens on the port and routes traffic to the replicas.

Figure 12.16   Enlisting a service in the ingress network is as simple as publishing a port.

You can browse to the port and you'll see the NASA image app from chapter 4—unless you're running Windows containers. I've managed to avoid any big differences for Windows and Linux readers up till now, other than the odd difference in commands, but there's no getting around this one. If you're running Linux containers—on a Linux machine or a Mac or with Linux container mode on Windows 10—you can go right ahead and browse to http://localhost:8010 to see the app. If you're running Windows containers—either on Windows Server or Windows container mode on Windows 10—you can't do that because Swarm services aren't accessible using localhost.

This is one of the few situations where Windows containers don't work in the same way as Linux containers, and it's down to limitations in the Windows networking stack. In practice, it's not usually an issue because your Swarm clusters will be remote servers in test or production environments, and ingress networking does work when you access a remote machine. But on your local single-node Windows Swarm, you can only access services by browsing to them from a different machine. I know it's not good, but at least we got 12 chapters in before we hit the "this sucks on Windows" moment, and I don't think there are any more coming.

I've switched to Linux containers for this chapter, and in figure 12.17 you can see the image of the day app. My network request is being routed to one of the two replicas for the web service, which is in turn fetching data from one of the three replicas for the API service.

The ingress network is listening on port 8010. Incoming requests get handled by the Swarm and sent to a node running replicas of the service—the traffic gets load-balanced if there are multiple replicas on the node.

**Figure 12.17**  Published ports in services use the ingress network, and Swarm routes requests to replicas.

I've said it before in this chapter, but it's coming once more to make it clear—the size of the cluster doesn't matter as far as deploying and managing applications goes. I could run the exact same commands on a cluster running with 50 nodes in the cloud, and the result would be the same—two replicas of the web service that I can access from any node, working with three replicas of the API service that the web containers can access on any node.

## 12.5 *Understanding the choice between Docker Swarm and Kubernetes*

Docker Swarm was designed to be a simple container orchestrator. It took the concepts of networks and services from Docker Compose, which was already hugely popular, and built them into an orchestrator that became part of the Docker Engine. Other orchestrators have been released as commercial or open source projects, but most of those efforts have been shelved, and now the choice comes down to Docker Swarm and Kubernetes.

Kubernetes is the more popular option because it's offered as a managed service by all the major public clouds. You can spin up a multi-node Kubernetes cluster in Microsoft Azure, Amazon Web Services, or Google Cloud with just a single command from their CLI or a few clicks on their web portal. They take care of initializing the cluster—which is nothing like as simple as with Docker Swarm—and managing the virtual machines that are the nodes. Kubernetes is easily extensible, so the cloud providers can integrate it with their other products, like load balancers and storage, which make it easy to deploy full-featured applications.

Docker Swarm doesn't exist as a managed service from the cloud providers, partly because it has fewer moving parts, so its harder to integrate with other services. If you want to run a Docker Swarm cluster in the cloud, you'll need to provision the VMs and initialize the Swarm yourself. It can all be automated, but it's not as simple as using a managed service. Figure 12.18 shows the main cloud resources you'd need to provision and manage yourself if you wanted to run a Docker Swarm cluster in Azure.

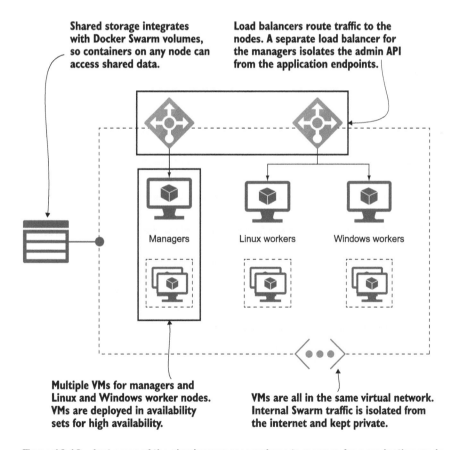

**Shared storage integrates with Docker Swarm volumes, so containers on any node can access shared data.**

**Load balancers route traffic to the nodes. A separate load balancer for the managers isolates the admin API from the application endpoints.**

Managers

Linux workers

Windows workers

**Multiple VMs for managers and Linux and Windows worker nodes. VMs are deployed in availability sets for high availability.**

**VMs are all in the same virtual network. Internal Swarm traffic is isolated from the internet and kept private.**

Figure 12.18   Just some of the cloud resources you have to manage for a production-grade Swarm

You'll deploy clusters less often than you'll deploy applications, though, and for ongoing operations, Docker Swarm is far simpler. It doesn't have all the features of Kubernetes, but it has everything most organizations need with a fraction of the complexity of Kubernetes. The YAML you send to a Swarm cluster is an extension of the Docker Compose syntax, which is concise and logical. The Kubernetes YAML specification is far more complex and verbose, partly because of the additional resources Kubernetes supports. Both orchestrators ultimately have the job of running Docker containers, and they use the same Docker images, but the Kubernetes version of the app definition can easily involve 5 to 10 times as much YAML.

My advice for teams who are new to orchestration is to start with Docker Swarm and move on to Kubernetes if they need a feature that Swarm doesn't have. You have to make some investment in your apps to move them to Docker, and that investment isn't wasted if you move to Kubernetes—you'll be running containers from the same images. It's not always a straightforward decision, though, and there are a few factors you'll need to add in:

- *Infrastructure*—If you're deploying to the cloud, Kubernetes is a simpler option, but if you're in the datacenter, Swarm is far easier to manage. Also, if your team's background is 100% Windows, you can use Swarm without taking on Linux.
- *Learning curve*—Moving to Swarm is straightforward because it's an extension of the Docker and Compose experience that you'll already have. Kubernetes is a whole new set of things to learn, and not everyone on the team will make that investment.
- *Feature set*—The complexity of Kubernetes is partly the result of it being hugely configurable. You can do things with Kubernetes that you can't easily do in Swarm, like blue/green deployments, automatic service scaling, and role-based access control.
- *Future investment*—Kubernetes has one of the largest open source communities, and it's extremely active. Changes and new features are coming all the time, whereas Swarm has been a stable product without large new features for a while now.

Ultimately your roadmap will probably take you to Kubernetes, via *Learn Kubernetes in a Month of Lunches*, but there's no rush to get there. Swarm is a great product that will introduce you to container orchestration in production and make it easy to run your workloads, however large they may be. Visa has talked at Docker's conferences about using their Swarm cluster to power all the payments through their system, including huge spikes on Black Friday.

## 12.6  *Lab*

It's a pretty simple lab this time, just to increase your experience working with applications running as Docker Swarm services. I'd like you to run the random number app from chapter 8 in your Swarm cluster. You'll need two services and a network to connect them, and the services will need to be using these Docker images (which are on Docker Hub, so you don't need to build them yourself):

- `diamol/ch08-numbers-api:v3`
- `diamol/ch08-numbers-web:v3`

My solution is on GitHub in the usual place, but it's only a few commands, so you shouldn't really need to look: https://github.com/sixeyed/diamol/blob/master/ch12/lab/README.md.

# Deploying distributed applications as stacks in Docker Swarm

I have a confession—in the last chapter I had you spend a lot of time learning how to create Docker Swarm services with the command line, but you won't ever do that in a real project. It's a useful way to get started with orchestration and to understand the difference between running containers yourself and having an orchestrator manage them for you. But in a real system you won't connect to the manager and send it commands to run services. Instead, you'll describe your application in a YAML file that you'll send to the manager; it will then decide what actions to take to get your app running. It's the same *desired state* approach that you've seen with Docker Compose—the YAML file specifies what you want the end state to be, and the orchestrator looks at what's currently running and figures out what it needs to do to get to that state.

Docker Swarm and Kubernetes both use the same desired-state approach, but with different YAML syntax. Swarm uses the Docker Compose syntax to define all the components of your app, and when you send your YAML to the manager, it creates networks and services and anything else you declare. The Compose format is very well suited to describing distributed apps for cluster deployment, but there are some concepts that only make sense in Swarm mode and some that only make sense on a single server. The specification is flexible enough to support both, and in this chapter we'll build on your knowledge of Docker Compose and Docker Swarm to run distributed apps in the cluster.

## 13.1  Using Docker Compose for production deployments

The real power of Docker Swarm comes from Compose—your production deployments use the same file format that you use in dev and test environments, so there's consistency across your artifacts and tooling for every environment and every project. The very simplest deployment for a Swarm is identical to a simple Compose file—listing 13.1 shows a basic deployment for the to-do app from chapter 6, which just specifies the image name and the port to publish.

> **Listing 13.1  A Compose file that can be deployed to a Swarm**

```
version: "3.7"

services:
  todo-web:
    image: diamol/ch06-todo-list
    ports:
      - 8080:80
```

You can deploy that on a single server using Docker Compose, and you'll get one container running with a published port to access the app. You can deploy the exact same file on a Swarm, and you'll get a service with a single replica running, using the ingress network for the published port. You deploy applications in Swarm mode by creating a *stack*, which is just a resource that groups together lots of other resources, like services, networks, and volumes.

> **TRY IT NOW**  Deploy that simple Compose file as a stack. You'll need to have initialized your Swarm and then switch to the folder for this chapter's exercises. Deploy the stack and then check what's running:

```
cd ch13/exercises

# deploy the stack from the Compose file:
docker stack deploy -c ./todo-list/v1.yml todo

# list all the stacks and see the new one:
docker stack ls

# list all services and see the service created by the deployment:
docker service ls
```

You can see from my output in figure 13.1 that the behavior is very much like Docker Compose, although you use the standard Docker CLI to deploy to a Swarm. I sent the Compose file to my cluster, and the manager created a default network to plug services into and then created a service for my app. Stacks are a first-class resource in Swarm mode; you can use the CLI to create, list, and remove them. Deploying the stack in this exercise creates a single service.

If you're running Linux containers, you can browse to http://localhost:8080 and see the app, but if you're using Windows containers, you still have the problem that

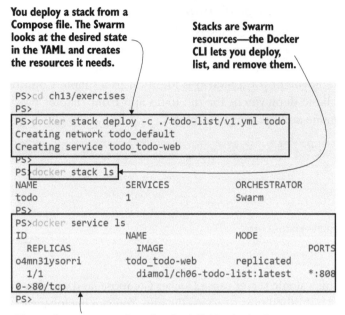

**You deploy a stack from a Compose file. The Swarm looks at the desired state in the YAML and creates the resources it needs.**

**Stacks are Swarm resources—the Docker CLI lets you deploy, list, and remove them.**

```
PS>cd ch13/exercises
PS>
PS>docker stack deploy -c ./todo-list/v1.yml todo
Creating network todo_default
Creating service todo_todo-web
PS>
PS>docker stack ls
NAME                SERVICES           ORCHESTRATOR
todo                1                  Swarm
PS>
PS>docker service ls
ID                  NAME               MODE
  REPLICAS            IMAGE                            PORTS
o4mn31ysorri        todo_todo-web         replicated
  1/1                 diamol/ch06-todo-list:latest    *:808
0->80/tcp
PS>
```

**The stack creates a service using the definition in the Compose file. This service will plug into an overlay network and publish ports using ingress—those are the defaults in Swarm mode.**

Figure 13.1   Deploying a stack in Swarm mode using a standard Docker Compose file

you can't browse to the ingress network locally, so you'll need to browse from another machine. It's the same old to-do app working in the same way, so we'll skip the screenshot. The thing to take away from this exercise is that you've used a standard Docker Compose file with no extra config to deploy to the Swarm. If you had multiple nodes in your Swarm, you'd have high availability—the node running the service replica could go offline, and the Swarm would start a replacement on another node to keep your app available.

Swarm mode has an extra set of features, of course, and you can use them in your app by adding a deploy section to the service in your Compose file. These properties only make sense when you're running in a cluster, so they get applied when you deploy a stack, but you can use the same file with Docker Compose on a single server, and the deploy settings will be ignored. Listing 13.2 shows an updated service definition for the to-do app that includes deployment properties to run multiple replicas and to limit the compute resources each replica can use.

Listing 13.2   **Adding Swarm deployment configuration in your Docker Compose file**

```
services:
  todo-web:
```

```
image: diamol/ch06-todo-list
ports:
  - 8080:80
deploy:
  replicas: 2
  resources:
    limits:
      cpus: "0.50"
      memory: 100M
```

These are the basic properties you'd want to include for a production deployment. Running multiple replicas means your app can manage more load, and it also means one replica will be available to serve traffic if the other goes offline because of a server failure or a service update. You should also specify compute limits for all your services when they go live, to protect your cluster from a rogue replica consuming all the processing power and memory. Working out the limits takes some effort, because you need to know the amount of CPU and memory your app needs when it's working hardest—metrics like those we saw in chapter 9 help with this. The resource limits in this application specification restrict each replica to a maximum of 50% of one CPU core and 100 MB of memory.

Deploying updates to a Swarm stack is the same as deploying a new app—you send the updated YAML file to the manager, and it makes the changes for you. When you deploy the v2 Compose file, the Swarm will create one new replica and replace the existing one.

> **TRY IT NOW** Run a stack deploy command using a new Compose file but the original stack name—this works like an update to the existing stack. List the service tasks and you'll see how the update happened:

```
# deploy an updated Compose file for the stack
docker stack deploy -c ./todo-list/v2.yml todo

# check all the replicas for the web service:
docker service ps todo_todo-web
```

My output is in figure 13.2. You can see that the stack updates the service, and the service has two new replicas. The original replica was replaced because adding resource limits in the Compose file changes the container definition, and that needs to be actioned with a new container.

Docker containers can access all the host machine's CPU and memory if you don't specify a limit. That's the default, and it's fine for non-production environments where you want to cram as many apps on your servers as possible and let them use the resources they need. In production, however, you want limits to safeguard against bad code or malicious users trying to max out your system, but those limits are established when the container starts, so if you update them you get a new container, which is a replica update in Swarm mode.

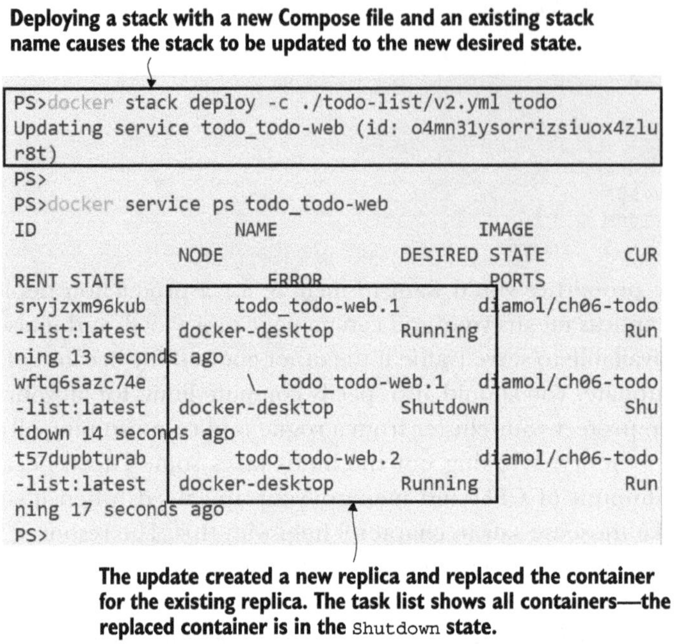

**Deploying a stack with a new Compose file and an existing stack name causes the stack to be updated to the new desired state.**

```
PS>docker stack deploy -c ./todo-list/v2.yml todo
Updating service todo_todo-web (id: o4mn31ysorrizsiuox4zlu
r8t)
PS>
PS>docker service ps todo_todo-web
ID                    NAME                    IMAGE
              NODE            DESIRED STATE          CUR
RENT STATE        ERROR              PORTS
sryjzxm96kub          todo_todo-web.1         diamol/ch06-todo
-list:latest   docker-desktop    Running              Run
ning 13 seconds ago
wftq6sazc74e          \_ todo_todo-web.1      diamol/ch06-todo
-list:latest   docker-desktop    Shutdown             Shu
tdown 14 seconds ago
t57dupbturab          todo_todo-web.2         diamol/ch06-todo
-list:latest   docker-desktop    Running              Run
ning 17 seconds ago
PS>
```

**The update created a new replica and replaced the container for the existing replica. The task list shows all containers—the replaced container is in the** Shutdown **state.**

Figure 13.2   Updating a stack with a new Compose file will update the service if the definition has changed.

Swarm stacks are a neat way of grouping applications, which you need because a cluster will typically run many apps. You can manage applications as a whole using the `stack` commands in the Docker CLI, listing the individual services and the service replicas or removing the app altogether.

**TRY IT NOW**   Stacks are the management unit for applications. They give you a simple way to work with an app that could be running multiple services, each with multiple replicas. Check what's running in the to-do app stack and then remove it:

```
# list all the services in the stack:
docker stack services todo

# list all replicas for all services in the stack:
docker stack ps todo

# remove the stack:
docker stack rm todo
```

This app is a very simple example with a Docker network, one service, and two replicas. Larger distributed apps could run dozens of services across hundreds of replicas in the Swarm, and you still deploy them in the same way with the Compose file and manage them with `docker stack` commands. Figure 13.3 shows my output, finally removing the whole stack.

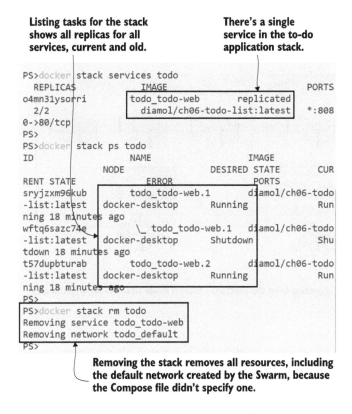

Figure 13.3  Working with the stack using the Docker CLI—you can list resources and remove them.

You can manage all the resources in a stack without needing the Compose file, because all the specifications are stored inside the cluster database. That shared database is replicated between the Swarm managers, so it's a safe place to store other resources too. It's how you'll store application configuration files in the Swarm, which you can make available to services in your Compose file.

## 13.2  *Managing app configuration with config objects*

Apps running in containers need to be able to load their configuration settings from the platform that is running the container. I've covered that with local development and test environments using Docker Compose with environment variables. Now we can round that out with production, which uses Docker config objects stored in the cluster. Figure 13.4 shows how that works, and the important thing here is that it's the exact same Docker image in every environment. It's just the application behavior that changes.

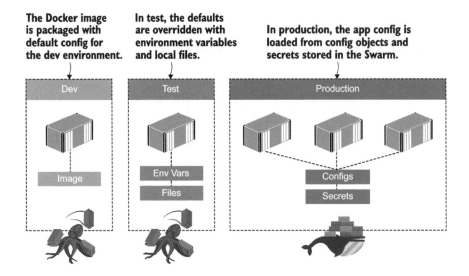

**The Docker image is packaged with default config for the dev environment.**

**In test, the defaults are overridden with environment variables and local files.**

**In production, the app config is loaded from config objects and secrets stored in the Swarm.**

**Figure 13.4**   **Applying configuration from the platform; Swarm mode uses config objects and secrets.**

Configuration is such a critical part of deployment that all the orchestrators have a first-class resource to hold application configuration. In Swarm these are Docker config objects. They're powerful because they let the container load its config from the cluster, but they also decouple the role of application deployment from configuration management.

Organizations often have a config management team that has access to all the secrets—API keys, database server passwords, SSL certificates—and those secrets are all stored in a secure system. That system is often completely separate from the environment where the apps are running, so the team needs a way of applying the config from the central system to the application platform. Docker Swarm supports that workflow with a specific type of resource—config objects—that you load into the cluster from an existing configuration file.

**TRY IT NOW**   The to-do app uses JSON for configuration. The default config in the image uses a local database file for storage, but that doesn't work if you run many replicas—each container will have its own database, and users will see different lists depending on which replica services their request. The first step to fixing that is deploying a new config file in the cluster:

```
# create the config object from a local JSON file:
docker config create todo-list-config ./todo-list/configs/config.json
```

```
# check the configs in the cluster:
docker config ls
```

Config objects are created with a name and the path to the config file contents. This app uses JSON, but config objects can store any type of data—XML, key/value pairs, or even binary files. The Swarm delivers the config object as a file in the container's filesystem, so the application sees the exact same data you uploaded. Figure 13.5 shows my output—the config object is created with a long random ID in addition to the name.

**Creates a config object in the Swarm using the contents of a local file**

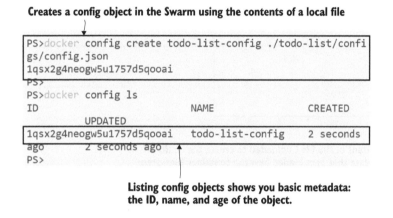

**Listing config objects shows you basic metadata:
the ID, name, and age of the object.**

**Figure 13.5  Loading a local file into the Swarm cluster as a config object**

You work with config objects like other Docker resources—there are commands to remove and inspect them as well as to create them. Inspection is useful because it shows you the contents of the config file. That's an important point about config objects: they're not meant for sensitive data. The file content is not encrypted in the Swarm database, nor is it encrypted in transit as it moves from the managers to the nodes that are running the replicas.

> **TRY IT NOW**  You can inspect a config object to read out the complete contents. This shows you what the replica will see in the container filesystem when it uses the config object:

```
# inspect the config using the pretty flag to show the contents:
docker config inspect --pretty todo-list-config
```

Figure 13.6 shows my output, which contains all the metadata about the config object and the file contents exactly as they were stored, including whitespace.

Managing config objects is a separate workflow from managing the applications that use those config objects. In a DevOps workflow, that could all be done by the

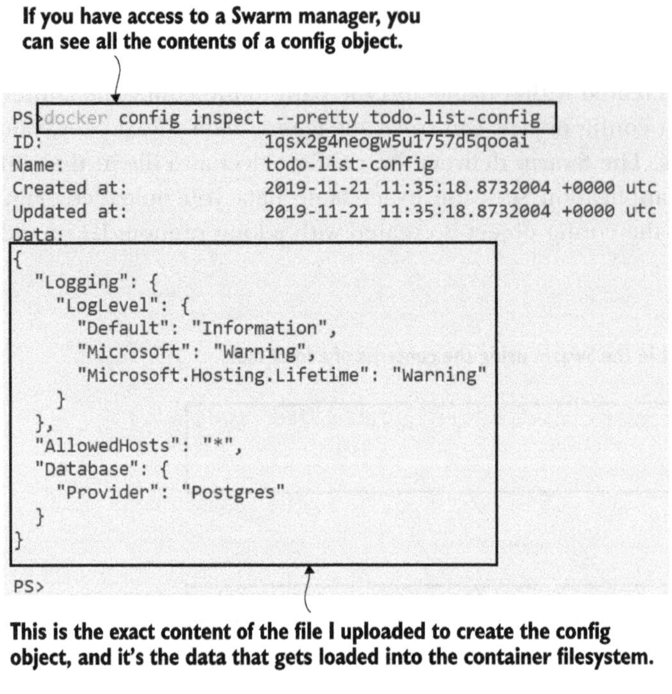

**If you have access to a Swarm manager, you
can see all the contents of a config object.**

```
PS>docker config inspect --pretty todo-list-config
ID:                     1qsx2g4neogw5u1757d5qooai
Name:                   todo-list-config
Created at:             2019-11-21 11:35:18.8732004 +0000 utc
Updated at:             2019-11-21 11:35:18.8732004 +0000 utc
Data:
{
  "Logging": {
    "LogLevel": {
      "Default": "Information",
      "Microsoft": "Warning",
      "Microsoft.Hosting.Lifetime": "Warning"
    }
  },
  "AllowedHosts": "*",
  "Database": {
    "Provider": "Postgres"
  }
}
PS>
```

**This is the exact content of the file I uploaded to create the config
object, and it's the data that gets loaded into the container filesystem.**

Figure 13.6   Config objects are not secure—anyone with access to the
cluster can see the contents.

same team or by one automated pipeline, but in larger enterprises you can keep the
functions separate if that matches your existing processes.

Services consume config objects by specifying them in the Compose file. Listing 13.3
shows part of the updated definition for the to-do list application (the full file is called
v3.yml) that loads configuration from the config object.

Listing 13.3   Config objects in services get surfaced to the container filesystem

```
services:
  todo-web:
    image: diamol/ch06-todo-list
    ports:
      - 8080:80
    configs:
      - source: todo-list-config
        target: /app/config/config.json

#...

configs:
  todo-list-config:
    external: true
```

When a container runs as a replica for this service, it will have the contents of the config object loaded from the Swarm into the file at /app/config/config.json, which is one of the paths the app uses as a configuration source. There's a shorter syntax you can use where you just specify the name of the config object and Docker uses a default target path, but the actual path is different for different operating systems, so it's better to explicitly state where you want the file to be surfaced. (The forward-slash directory paths work in both Windows and Linux containers.)

The second part of the Compose file in listing 13.3 shows the config object itself, with its name and the external flag. External is how you specify that this resource should already exist on the cluster. The deployment workflow is to deploy the config objects first and then the apps that use them. You can do that by deploying the v3 Compose file, which also includes a service for the SQL database, so multiple web containers can share the same database.

**TRY IT NOW** Update the application by deploying the YAML file—the stack command is the same. The Swarm will create a new replica for the database service and new replicas for the web application:

```
# deploy the updated app definition:
docker stack deploy -c ./todo-list/v3.yml todo

# list the services in the stack:
docker stack services todo
```

You removed the old stack in a previous exercise, so this is a new deployment. You'll see a network and two services being created. I've scaled the web component down to a single replica so we can follow the updates more easily; each of the services is now running a single replica. My output is in figure 13.7.

**This is a new deployment, so new resources are created. The config object isn't shown because it's an external resource that already exists.**

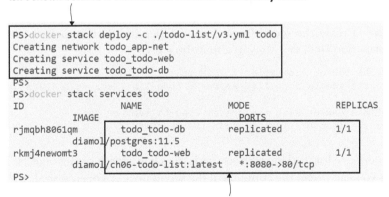

**One replica is running the web service, which should use the single database replica.**

**Figure 13.7  Deploying a stack that uses config objects in services**

Now the app is configured to use Postgres as the database, which is the setting the config object loads into the replicas. If you browse to http://localhost:8080 (or to your machine from another machine if you're on Windows), you'll see the app isn't working. You can check the logs of the web service to see why, and it will show a lot of errors about connecting to the database. This deployment configures the web app to use Postgres, but the config object doesn't provide the connection details for the database, so the connection fails—we'll fix that in the next exercise.

Sensitive data shouldn't be kept in config objects, because they're not encrypted and they can be read by anyone who has access to the cluster. That includes database connection strings that might have usernames and passwords, and also URLs for production services and API keys. You should aim for defense in depth in your production environment, so even if the chances of someone gaining access to your cluster are slim, you should still encrypt sensitive data inside the cluster. Docker Swarm provides secrets for storing this class of config.

## 13.3  *Managing confidential settings with secrets*

Secrets are a resource in the Swarm that the cluster manages, and they work almost exactly like config objects. You create secrets from a local file, and that gets stored in the cluster database. Then you reference the secret in a service specification, and the contents of the secret get loaded into the container filesystem at runtime. The key difference with secrets is that you can only read them in plain text at one point in the workflow: inside the container when they are loaded from the Swarm.

Secrets are encrypted throughout their lifetime in the cluster. The data is stored encrypted in the database shared by the managers, and secrets are only delivered to nodes that are scheduled to run replicas that need the secret. Secrets are encrypted in transit from the manager node to the worker, and they are only unencrypted inside the container, where they appear with the original file contents. We'll use a secret to store the database connection string for the to-do list app.

> **TRY IT NOW**   Create the secret from the local file, and then inspect it to see what information Docker gives you about the secret:
>
> ```
> # create the secret from a local JSON file:
> docker secret create todo-list-secret ./todo-list/secrets/secrets.json
>
> # inspect the secret with the pretty flag to see the data:
> docker secret inspect --pretty todo-list-secret
> ```

The user experience for working with secrets is the same as with config objects. The only difference is you can't read the contents of the secret once it's been stored. You can see my output in figure 13.8—inspecting the secret only shows the metadata about the resource, not the actual data, which you would see if this was a config object.

Now that the secret is stored in the Swarm, we can deploy a new version of the app with a service specification that uses the secret. The Compose syntax for secrets is very

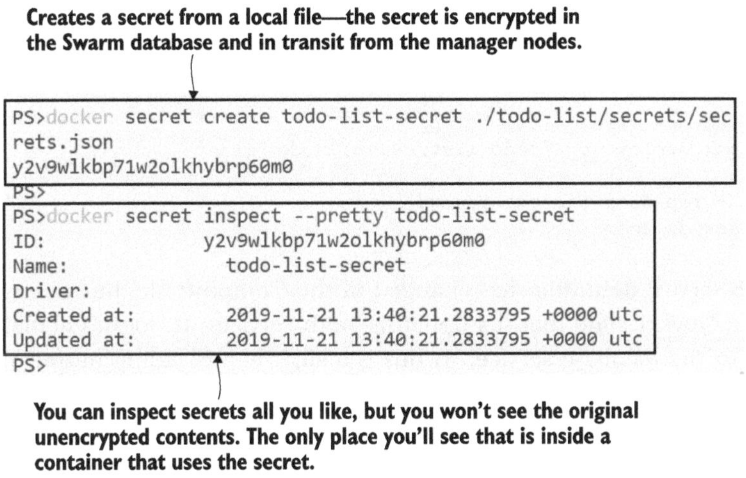

**Creates a secret from a local file—the secret is encrypted in the Swarm database and in transit from the manager nodes.**

```
PS>docker secret create todo-list-secret ./todo-list/secrets/sec
rets.json
y2v9wlkbp71w2olkhybrp60m0
PS>
```

```
PS>docker secret inspect --pretty todo-list-secret
ID:                  y2v9wlkbp71w2olkhybrp60m0
Name:                todo-list-secret
Driver:
Created at:          2019-11-21 13:40:21.2833795 +0000 utc
Updated at:          2019-11-21 13:40:21.2833795 +0000 utc
PS>
```

**You can inspect secrets all you like, but you won't see the original unencrypted contents. The only place you'll see that is inside a container that uses the secret.**

Figure 13.8   Once secrets are stored in the Swarm, you can't read the original unencrypted contents.

similar to config objects; you specify the source and the target path of the secret in the service definition, and then the secret itself gets its own definition. Listing 13.4 shows the key sections of the new deployment, which is in the v4.yml file.

---
**Listing 13.4   Specifying secrets and configs for app configuration**

```
services:
  todo-web:
    image: diamol/ch06-todo-list
    ports:
      - 8080:80
    configs:
      - source: todo-list-config
        target: /app/config/config.json
    secrets:
      - source: todo-list-secret
        target: /app/config/secrets.json

#...

secrets:
  todo-list-secret:
    external: true
```

The content of that secret is more JSON, loaded into another path where the app looks for configuration sources. This sets the app with the connection details to use the Postgres container for its data store, so when you deploy the app, users will get the same list of items whichever web replica serves them.

**TRY IT NOW**   Deploy the latest version of the app, which supplies the missing database connection string and fixes the web application. This updates the service.

```
# deploy the new version of the app:
docker stack deploy -c ./todo-list/v4.yml todo

# check the replicas for the stack:
docker stack ps todo
```

Only the web service definition has changed in the Compose file, but when you run this you'll see Docker state that it's updating both services. It doesn't actually make any updates to the database service, so this is a slightly misleading output from the CLI—it will list all the services in the Compose file as "updating" even though they won't all change. You can see that in my output in figure 13.9.

The Docker CLI shows every service updating in a stack
deployment, but unchanged definitions won't actually change.

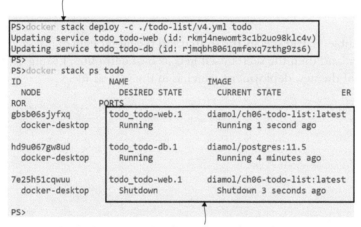

The database service is still running on the original replica; the
web service has the old replica, which is shut down, and the
current one, which uses configs and secrets.

Figure 13.9   Deploying the latest app version will correct the config and fix
the app.

Now the app is working correctly, which you'll see if you browse to port 8080 from a remote machine (if you're using Windows containers) or localhost (if you're using Linux containers). Figure 13.10 shows the infrastructure setup, with the containers connecting on the Docker network and the secret loaded from the Swarm.

The important thing that's missing from figure 13.10 is the hardware view, and that's because this application has the same deployment architecture on Swarms of

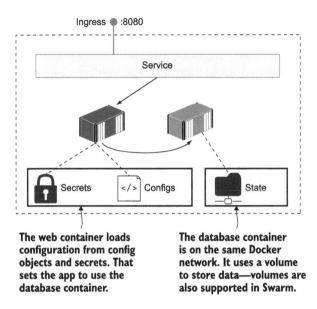

The web container loads configuration from config objects and secrets. That sets the app to use the database container.

The database container is on the same Docker network. It uses a volume to store data—volumes are also supported in Swarm.

Figure 13.10 The to-do app running as a stack uses the key features of Docker Swarm.

any size. Secrets and config objects are stored in the managers' distributed database and are available to every node. The stack creates an overlay network so containers can connect to each other whichever nodes they're running on, and the service uses the ingress network so consumers can send traffic to any node and have it actioned by one of the web replicas.

One thing you do need to understand about config objects and secrets: they can't be updated. When you create them in the cluster, the contents will always be the same, and if you need to update the config for an application, you need to replace it. This will involve three steps:

- Create a new config object or secret with the updated contents and a different name from the previous object.
- Update the name of the config object or secret that your app uses in the Compose file, specifying the new name.
- Deploy the stack from the updated Compose file.

This process means you need to update your service every time you change configuration, which means that running containers get replaced with new ones. This is one area where orchestrators take different approaches—Kubernetes lets you update existing configuration and secret objects in the cluster. That brings its own problems though, because some application platforms watch their config files for changes and others don't, so changes may be ignored and you need to replace containers anyway. Swarm is consistent—you'll always need to update your services when you roll out configuration changes.

Updating services shouldn't scare you, though. You'll be rolling out container updates every time you have new features to deploy in your app, or when there are security updates in the dependencies you use or the operating system your images are based on. At a minimum, you should expect to release updates every month, which is how often most operating-system-based images are updated on Docker Hub.

That brings us to stateful applications in Swarm mode. You're going to be replacing containers regularly, so you'll need to use Docker volumes for persistent storage, and volumes work slightly differently in the Swarm.

## 13.4   *Storing data with volumes in the Swarm*

We covered Docker volumes way back in chapter 6—they're units of storage that have a separate life cycle from containers. Any stateful apps you want to containerize can use volumes for storage. Volumes appear as part of the container's filesystem but they're actually stored outside of the container. Application upgrades replace the container and attach the volume to the new container, so the new container starts with all the data the previous container had.

Volumes are conceptually the same in orchestrators too; you add a volume mount specification for the service in the Compose file, and replicas see that volume as a local directory. There's a big difference in how the data gets stored, though, and that's something you need to understand to make sure your app works as expected. In a cluster you'll have multiple nodes that can run containers, and each node has its own disk where it stores local volumes. The simplest way to maintain state between updates is to use a local volume.

There's a problem with that approach though—a replacement replica may be scheduled to run on a different node from the original, so it won't have access to the original node's data. You can pin services to specific nodes, which means updates will always run on the node that has the data. That works for scenarios where you want application data to be stored outside of the container so it survives updates, but where you don't need to run multiple replicas and you don't need to allow for server failure. You apply a label to your node, and in your Compose file you restrict replicas to running on that node.

> **TRY IT NOW**   You've got a single node Swarm, so every replica will run on this node anyway, but the labeling process works in the same way for multi-node Swarms. Labels can be any key/value pair; we'll use this one to assign a fictitious storage class:

```
# find the ID for your node and update it, adding a label:
docker node update --label-add storage=raid $(docker node ls -q)
```

The output of that command is just the node ID, so we'll skip the screenshot. More interesting is that you now have a way to identify nodes in the cluster, and that can be used to constrain where service replicas get scheduled. Listing 13.5 shows the `constraint` field in the service definition for the to-do database, which also now has a volume specified—this is in the `v5.yml` deployment file.

**Listing 13.5   Configuring constraints and volumes for services in the Swarm**

```
services:
  todo-db:
    image: diamol/postgres:11.5
    volumes:
     - todo-db-data:/var/lib/postgresql/data
    deploy:
      placement:
        constraints:
          - node.labels.storage == raid
#...

volumes:
  todo-db-data:
```

I haven't trimmed down the volume specification at the end of the Compose file in
that listing—the volume name is all there is. This will get created using the default volume driver in the Swarm, which uses the local disk. When you deploy this to your cluster, it will ensure the database replica runs on the node that matches the storage label,
and that node will create a local volume called `todo-db-data`, which is where the data
files get stored.

> **TRY IT NOW**    The constraint in the Compose file matches the label you added
> to your Swarm node, so the database container will run there and use the
> local volume on that node. These commands will explore the volumes on
> your node before and after the deployment:

```
# list all the volumes on your node, showing just IDs:
docker volume ls -q

# update the stack to v5 - for Linux containers:
docker stack deploy -c ./todo-list/v5.yml todo

# OR with Windows containers, using Windows-style paths for the
    volume:
docker stack deploy -c ./todo-list/v5-windows.yml todo

# check the volumes again:
docker volume ls -q
```

You'll see there are lots of volumes (you'll probably have far more than me; I cleared
mine down with the `docker volume prune` command before these exercises). Images
can specify volumes in the Dockerfile, and if services use images with volumes, the
stack creates a default volume for the service. That volume has the same lifetime as
the stack, so if you remove the stack, the volumes get removed, and if you update services, they'll get a new default volume. If you want your data to persist between
updates, you need to use a named volume in your Compose file. You can see my output in figure 13.11; deploying the stack created a new named volume rather than a
default one.

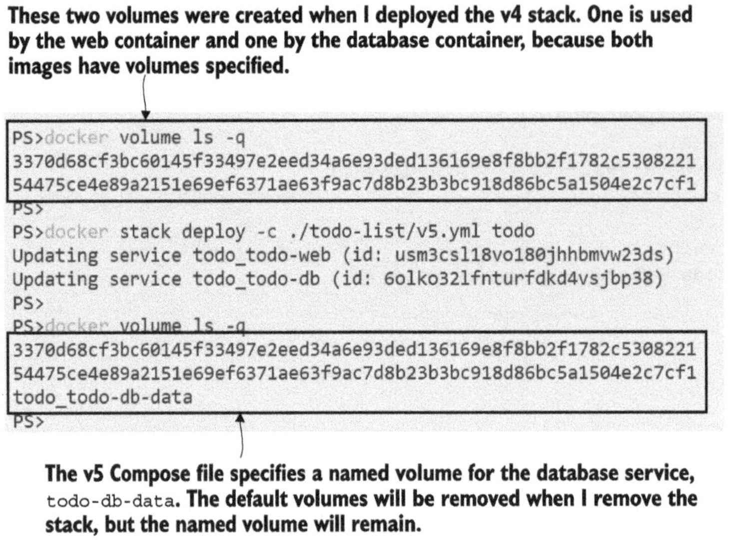

**These two volumes were created when I deployed the v4 stack. One is used by the web container and one by the database container, because both images have volumes specified.**

```
PS>docker volume ls -q
3370d68cf3bc60145f33497e2eed34a6e93ded136169e8f8bb2f1782c5308221
54475ce4e89a2151e69ef6371ae63f9ac7d8b23b3bc918d86bc5a1504e2c7cf1
PS>
PS>docker stack deploy -c ./todo-list/v5.yml todo
Updating service todo_todo-web (id: usm3csl18vo180jhhbmvw23ds)
Updating service todo_todo-db (id: 6olko32lfnturfdkd4vsjbp38)
PS>
PS>docker volume ls -q
3370d68cf3bc60145f33497e2eed34a6e93ded136169e8f8bb2f1782c5308221
54475ce4e89a2151e69ef6371ae63f9ac7d8b23b3bc918d86bc5a1504e2c7cf1
todo_todo-db-data
PS>
```

**The v5 Compose file specifies a named volume for the database service, `todo-db-data`. The default volumes will be removed when I remove the stack, but the named volume will remain.**

**Figure 13.11   Deploying stacks creates volumes too, which can be anonymous or named.**

This deployment provides guarantees for data availability, if the labeled node itself is available. If the container fails its health checks and gets replaced, the new replica will run on the same node as the previous replica and attach to the same named volume. When you update the database service specification, you get the same guarantees. That means the database files are persisted between containers, and your data is safe. You can add items to your to-do list through the web UI, upgrade the database service, and find that the old data is still there in the UI from the new database container.

**TRY IT NOW**   There's been a new release of the Postgres server since I wrote chapter 6, and it's a good idea to stay current, so we'll update the database service. The Compose spec in v6.yml is identical to v5.yml except it uses the updated version of Postgres:

```
# deploy the updated database - for Linux containers:
docker stack deploy -c ./todo-list/v6.yml todo

# OR for Windows containers:
docker stack deploy -c ./todo-list/v6-windows.yml todo

# check the tasks in the stack:
docker stack ps todo

# and check volumes:
docker volume ls -q
```

You can see my output in figure 13.12. The new database replica is running from an updated Docker image, but it attaches to the volume from the previous replica, so all my data is preserved.

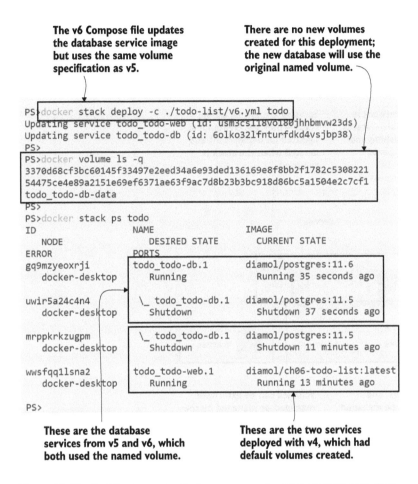

**Figure 13.12** Updating a service that uses a named volume preserves the data for the new container.

This is a simple example, and things get more complex when you have different storage requirements for your applications because the data in local volumes is not replicated across all the nodes. Applications that use disk as a data cache will be fine with local volumes, as the data can be different for each replica, but that won't work for apps that need to access shared state across the cluster. Docker has a plugin system for volume drivers, so Swarms can be configured to provide distributed storage using a cloud storage system or a storage device in the datacenter. Configuring those volumes depends on the infrastructure you're using, but you consume them in the same way, attaching volumes to services.

## 13.5 *Understanding how the cluster manages stacks*

Stacks in Docker Swarm are just groups of resources that the cluster manages for you. A production stack will contain many resources, and they all behave slightly differently in terms of how the orchestrator manages them. Figure 13.13 shows how Swarm manages the typical types of resources.

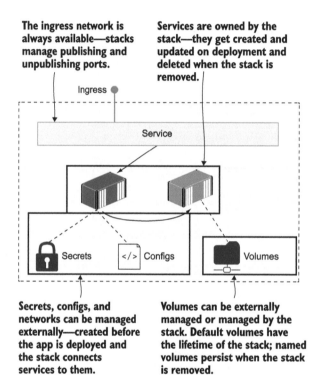

**The ingress network is always available—stacks manage publishing and unpublishing ports.**

**Services are owned by the stack—they get created and updated on deployment and deleted when the stack is removed.**

**Secrets, configs, and networks can be managed externally—created before the app is deployed and the stack connects services to them.**

**Volumes can be externally managed or managed by the stack. Default volumes have the lifetime of the stack; named volumes persist when the stack is removed.**

Figure 13.13   How Docker Swarm resources are managed by stack deployments

There are a few takeaways from this. You've already worked through some of these scenarios in the exercises, but we'll finish up the chapter making them clear:

- Volumes can be created and removed by the Swarm. Stacks will create a default volume if the service image specifies one, and that volume will be removed when the stack is removed. If you specify a named volume for the stack, it will be created when you deploy, but it won't be removed when you delete the stack.
- Secrets and configs are created when an external file gets uploaded to the cluster. They're stored in the cluster database and delivered to containers where the service definition requires them. They are effectively write-once read-many

objects and can't be updated. The admin process for storing app configuration in the Swarm is separate from the app deployment process.

- Networks can be managed independently of applications, with admins explicitly creating networks for applications to use, or they can be managed by the Swarm, which will create and remove them when necessary. Every stack will be deployed with a network to attach services to, even if one is not specified in the Compose file.
- Services are created or removed when stacks are deployed, and while they're running, the Swarm monitors them constantly to ensure the desired service level is being met. Replicas that fail health checks get replaced, as do replicas that get lost when nodes go offline.

The stack is a logical group of components that make up an application, but it doesn't map out a dependency graph between services. When you deploy a stack to the cluster, the managers spin up as many service replicas as quickly as they can across the cluster. You can't constrain the cluster to start one service completely before starting another, and if you could, that would probably ruin deployment performance. Instead you need to assume that your components will start in a random order, and capture health and dependency checks in your images so containers fail fast if the application can't run. That way the cluster can repair the damage by restarting or replacing containers, and that gets you a self-healing app.

## 13.6 *Lab*

Lab! This one will get you some more experience writing Compose files to define apps and deploying them as stacks on the Swarm. I'd like you to write a production deployment for the image gallery app from chapter 9, which should be in a single Compose file that matches these requirements:

- The access log API uses the image `diamol/ch09-access-log`. It's an internal component only accessed by the web app, and it should run on three replicas.
- The NASA API uses the image `diamol/ch09-image-of-the-day`. That should be publicly accessible on port 8088 and run on five replicas to support the expected incoming load.
- The web app uses the image `diamol/ch09-image-gallery`. It should be available at the standard HTTP port 80 and run on two replicas.
- All the components should have sensible CPU and memory limits (this may need a few rounds of deployments to work out safe maximums).
- When you deploy the stack, the app should work.

There are no volumes, configs, or secrets to worry about with this app, so it should be a pretty simple Compose file. As always, you can find my solution on GitHub for reference: https://github.com/sixeyed/diamol/blob/master/ch13/lab/README.md.

# Automating releases with upgrades and rollbacks

Updating containerized applications should be a zero-downtime process that is managed by the container orchestrator. You typically have spare compute power in your cluster that managers can use to schedule new containers during updates, and your container images have health checks so the cluster knows if the new components fail. Those are the enablers for zero-downtime updates, and you've already worked through the process with Docker Swarm stack deployments in chapter 13. The update process is highly configurable, and we'll spend time exploring the configuration options in this chapter.

Tuning update configuration might sound like a topic you can safely skip, but I can tell you from my own experience that it will cause you pain if you don't understand how rollouts work and how you can modify the default behavior. This chapter is focused on Docker Swarm, but all orchestrators have a staged rollout process that works in a similar way. Knowing how updates and rollbacks work lets you experiment to find the settings that fit for your app so you can deploy to production as often as you like, confident that the update will either work successfully or automatically roll back to the previous version.

## 14.1 The application upgrade process with Docker

Docker images are a deceptively simple packaging format. You build your image and run your app in a container, and it feels like you can let that run until you have a new version of your app to deploy, but there are at least four deployment cadences you need to consider. First there's your own application and its dependencies, then the SDK that compiles your app, then the application platform it runs on, and finally

250

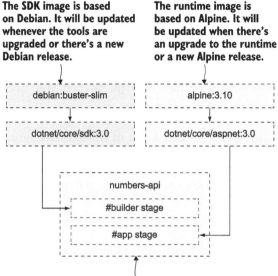

**The SDK image is based on Debian. It will be updated whenever the tools are upgraded or there's a new Debian release.**

**The runtime image is based on Alpine. It will be updated when there's an upgrade to the runtime or a new Alpine release.**

debian:buster-slim

alpine:3.10

dotnet/core/sdk:3.0

dotnet/core/aspnet:3.0

numbers-api

#builder stage

#app stage

**The app image needs to use the latest SDK to be sure of security fixes in the toolchain and the latest runtime image to get the latest platform fixes. It will also be updated when there are new releases of any libraries the app uses, and finally when there are any new features in the app itself.**

Figure 14.1 Your Docker image has a lot of dependencies when you include the other images you use.

the operating system itself. Figure 14.1 shows an example for a .NET Core app built for Linux that actually has six update cadences.

You can see that you should really plan to deploy updates on a monthly schedule to cover OS updates, and you should be comfortable kicking off an ad hoc deployment at any time, to cover security fixes from the libraries your app uses. That's why your build pipeline is the heart of your project. Your pipeline should run every time a change to the source code is pushed—that will take care of new application features and manual updates to your app's dependencies. It should also build every night, which makes sure you always have a potentially releasable image built on the latest SDK, application platform, and operating system updates.

Releasing every month whether your application has changed or not sounds scary, especially in organizations where the release ceremony is so expensive in terms of time and resources that you only do it three times a year. But this approach gets your whole organization into a much healthier mindset: releasing an update is something boring that happens all the time, usually without any humans getting involved. When you have regular automated releases, each update builds confidence in the process, and before you know it you're releasing new features as soon as they're completed, rather than waiting for the next deployment window.

You only get that confidence when releases are successful, and that's where application health checks become critical. Without them, you don't have a self-healing app, and that means you can't have safe updates and rollbacks. We'll follow that through in this chapter using the random number app from chapter 8, making use of the Docker Compose overrides you learned about in chapter 10. That will let us keep a single clean Compose file with the core app definition, a separate Compose file with the production specification, and additional files for the updates. Docker doesn't support stack deployment from multiple Compose files though, so first you need to use Docker Compose to join the override files together.

> **TRY IT NOW**   Let's start by deploying the first build of the random number app. We'll run a single web container and six replicas of the API container, which will help us see how updates get rolled out. You'll need to be running in Swarm mode; then join together some Compose files and deploy the stack:

```
cd ch14/exercises

# join the core Compose file with the production override:
docker-compose -f ./numbers/docker-compose.yml -f ./numbers/prod.yml
    config > stack.yml

# deploy the joined Compose file:
docker stack deploy -c stack.yml numbers

# show the services in the stack:
docker stack services numbers
```

You can see my output in figure 14.2—the Docker Compose command joined the core Compose file with the production override. It's useful to use Docker Compose to join the override files together because it also validates the contents, and that could be part of a continuous deployment pipeline. The stack deployment created an overlay network and two services.

One thing is new about the stack you see in figure 14.2—the API service is running in the normal replicated mode, but the web service is running in *global* mode. Global services run with a single replica on each node of the Swarm, and you can use that configuration to bypass the ingress network. There are scenarios like reverse proxies where that's a good deployment option, but I'm using it here so you can see how it's different from replicated services for rollouts. The settings for the web service are in listing 14.1 (which is an excerpt from the prod.yml override file).

---

**Listing 14.1   A global service that uses host networking rather than ingress**

```
numbers-web:
  ports:
    - target: 80
      published: 80
      mode: host
  deploy:
    mode: global
```

**You need a single Compose file to deploy a stack, which you can generate with the Docker Compose** config **command. The warning tells me there are Swarm-only features in the Compose file.**

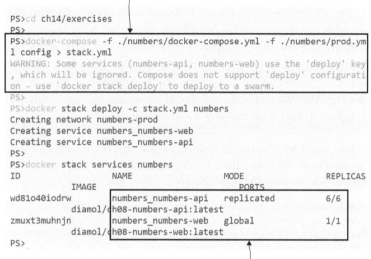

```
PS>cd ch14/exercises
PS>
PS>docker-compose -f ./numbers/docker-compose.yml -f ./numbers/prod.ym
l config > stack.yml
WARNING: Some services (numbers-api, numbers-web) use the 'deploy' key
, which will be ignored. Compose does not support 'deploy' configurati
on - use `docker stack deploy` to deploy to a swarm.
PS>
PS>docker stack deploy -c stack.yml numbers
Creating network numbers-prod
Creating service numbers_numbers-web
Creating service numbers_numbers-api
PS>
PS>docker stack services numbers
ID              NAME              MODE         REPLICAS
      IMAGE                          PORTS
wd81o40iodrw    numbers_numbers-api    replicated     6/6
      diamol/ch08-numbers-api:latest
zmuxt3muhnjn    numbers_numbers-web    global         1/1
      diamol/ch08-numbers-web:latest
PS>
```

**Deploying the stack creates a global service with one replica running on each node, as well as a replicated service with six replicas.**

**Figure 14.2   Deploying a stack from multiple Compose files by joining them together first**

In this new configuration there are two fields which configure the global service:

- mode: global—This setting in the deploy section configures the deployment to run one container on every node in the Swarm. The number of replicas will equal the number of nodes, and if any nodes join, they will also run a container for the service.

- mode: host—This setting in the ports section configures the service to bind directly to port 80 on the host, and not use the ingress network. This can be a useful pattern if your web apps are lightweight enough that you only need one replica per node, but network performance is critical so you don't want the overhead of routing in the ingress network.

This deployment uses the original application images, which don't have any health checks, and this is the app where the API has a bug that means it stops working after a few calls. You can browse to http://localhost (or from an external machine with Windows containers), and you can request lots of random numbers because the calls are load-balanced between six API service replicas. Eventually they'll all break, and then the app will stop working and won't ever repair itself—the cluster doesn't replace containers because it doesn't know they're unhealthy. That's not a safe position to be in, because if you roll out an updated version without any health checks, the cluster won't know if the update has been successful either.

So we'll go on to deploy version 2 of the application images, which have health checks built in. The v2 Compose override file uses the v2 image tag, and there's also an override that adds configuration for health checks to set how often they fire and how many failures trigger corrective action. That's in the normal `healthcheck` block, which works in the same way in Docker Compose, except Compose doesn't take corrective action for you. When this version of the app is deployed to Docker Swarm, the cluster will repair the API. When you break the API containers, they'll fail their health checks and get replaced, and then the app will start working again.

> **TRY IT NOW**  You need to join the new v2 Compose override with the health check and production override files to get your stack deployment YAML. Then you just need to deploy the stack again:

```
# join the healthcheck and v2 overrides to the previous files:
docker-compose -f ./numbers/docker-compose.yml -f ./numbers/prod.yml -f
    ./numbers/prod-healthcheck.yml -f ./numbers/v2.yml --log-level
    ERROR config > stack.yml

# update the stack:
docker stack deploy -c stack.yml numbers

# check the stack's replicas:
docker stack ps numbers
```

This deployment updates both the web and API services to version 2 of their images. Service updates are always done as a staged rollout, and the default is to stop existing containers before starting new ones. This makes sense for global services that are using host-mode ports, because the new container can't start until the old one exits and frees up the port. It might make sense for replicated services too, if your application expects a maximum level of scale, but you need to be aware that during the update the services will be under capacity while old containers are shut down and replacements are starting up. You can see that behavior in figure 14.3.

Docker Swarm uses cautious defaults for the rollout of service updates. It updates one replica at a time and ensures the container starts correctly before moving on to the next replica. Services roll out by stopping existing containers before starting replacements, and if the update fails because new containers don't start correctly, the rollout is paused. That all seems reasonable when it's presented with an authoritative tone in a book, but actually it's pretty strange. Why default to removing old containers before starting new ones, when you don't know if the new ones will work? Why pause a failed rollout, which could leave you with a half-broken system, instead of rolling back automatically? Fortunately the rollout can be configured with more sensible options.

**Specifying the log level for the Compose command suppresses the warning message about Swarm-only values.**

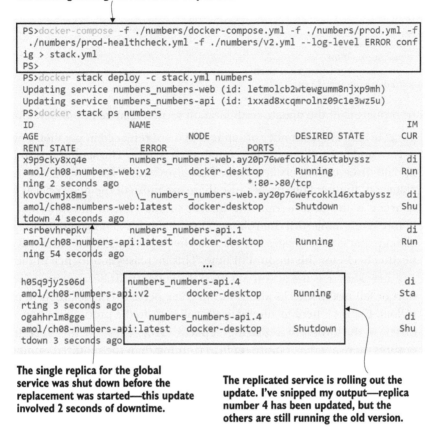

```
PS>docker-compose -f ./numbers/docker-compose.yml -f ./numbers/prod.yml -f
 ./numbers/prod-healthcheck.yml -f ./numbers/v2.yml --log-level ERROR conf
ig > stack.yml
PS>
PS>docker stack deploy -c stack.yml numbers
Updating service numbers_numbers-web (id: letmolcb2wtewgumm8njxp9mh)
Updating service numbers_numbers-api (id: 1xxad8xcqmrolnz09c1e3wz5u)
PS>docker stack ps numbers
ID                      NAME                                            IM
AGE                          NODE            DESIRED STATE       CUR
RENT STATE               ERROR           PORTS
x9p9cky8xq4e            numbers_numbers-web.ay20p76wefcokkl46xtabyssz   di
amol/ch08-numbers-web:v2        docker-desktop      Running     Run
ning 2 seconds ago                       *:80->80/tcp
kovbcwmjx8m5            \_ numbers_numbers-web.ay20p76wefcokkl46xtabyssz di
amol/ch08-numbers-web:latest    docker-desktop      Shutdown    Shu
tdown 4 seconds ago
rsrbevhrepkv            numbers_numbers-api.1                           di
amol/ch08-numbers-api:latest    docker-desktop      Running     Run
ning 54 seconds ago
                                ...
h05q9jy2s06d            numbers_numbers-api.4                           di
amol/ch08-numbers-api:v2        docker-desktop      Running     Sta
rting 3 seconds ago
ogahhrlm8gge            \_ numbers_numbers-api.4                        di
amol/ch08-numbers-api:latest    docker-desktop      Shutdown    Shu
tdown 3 seconds ago
```

**The single replica for the global service was shut down before the replacement was started—this update involved 2 seconds of downtime.**

**The replicated service is rolling out the update. I've snipped my output—replica number 4 has been updated, but the others are still running the old version.**

Figure 14.3  Deploying a service update with default configuration—one replica is updated at a time.

## 14.2  *Configuring production rollouts with Compose*

Version 2 of the random number app is self-repairing because of the health checks. If you request lots of random numbers through the web UI, the API replicas will all break, but wait 20 seconds or so and the Swarm will replace them all and the app will start working again. This is an extreme example, but in a real application with occasional failures, you can see how the cluster monitors containers and keeps the app online based on the health checks.

The rollout of version 2 used the default update configuration, but I want rollouts for the API to be faster and safer. That behavior is set in the `deploy` section for the service in the Compose file. Listing 14.2 shows the `update_config` section I want to apply for the API service (this is an excerpt from the `prod-update-config.yml` file).

**Listing 14.2   Specifying custom configuration for application rollouts**

```
numbers-api:
  deploy:
    update_config:
      parallelism: 3
      monitor: 60s
      failure_action: rollback
      order: start-first
```

The four properties of the update configuration section change how the rollout works:

- `parallelism` is the number of replicas that are replaced in parallel. The default is 1, so updates roll out by one container at a time. The setting shown here will update three containers at a time. That gives you a faster rollout and a greater chance of finding failures, because there are more of the new replicas running.
- `monitor` is the time period the Swarm should wait to monitor new replicas before continuing with the rollout. The default is 0, and you definitely want to change that if your images have health checks, because the Swarm will monitor health checks for this amount of time. This increases confidence in the rollout.
- `failure_action` is the action to take if the rollout fails because containers don't start or fail health checks within the `monitor` period. The default is to pause the rollout; I've set it here to automatically roll back to the previous version.
- `order` is the order of replacing replicas. `stop-first` is the default, and it ensures there are never more replicas running than the required number, but if your app can work with extra replicas, `start-first` is better because new replicas are created and checked before the old ones are removed.

This setup is generally a good practice for most apps, but you'll need to tweak it for your own use case. Parallelism can be set to around 30% of the full replica count so your update happens fairly quickly, but you should have a monitor period long enough to run multiple health checks, so the next set of tasks only get updated if the previous update worked.

There's one important thing to understand: when you deploy changes to a stack, the update configuration gets applied first. Then, if your deployment also includes service updates, the rollout will happen using the new update configuration.

**TRY IT NOW**   The next deployment sets the update config and updates the services to image tag v3. The replica rollout will use the new update configuration:

```
docker-compose -f ./numbers/docker-compose.yml -f ./numbers/prod.yml
    -f ./numbers/prod-healthcheck.yml -f ./numbers/prod-update-
    config.yml   -f ./numbers/v3.yml --log-level ERROR config >
    stack.yml

docker stack deploy -c stack.yml numbers

docker stack ps numbers
```

You'll see that the replica list from `stack ps` gets unmanageably large when you've done a few updates. It shows all the replicas from every deployment, so the original containers and the v2 containers that have been updated are shown as well as the new v3 replicas. I've trimmed my output in figure 14.4, but if you scroll down in yours you'll see three replicas of the API service have been updated and are being monitored before the next set is updated.

**The update configuration for the web service hasn't changed, so the
new v3 replica started after the v2 replica had been shut down.**

```
PS>docker-compose -f ./numbers/docker-compose.yml -f ./numbers/prod.yml -f
 ./numbers/prod-healthcheck.yml -f ./numbers/prod-update-config.yml   -f .
/numbers/v3.yml --log-level ERROR config > stack.yml
PS>
PS>docker stack deploy -c stack.yml numbers
Updating service numbers_numbers-web (id: letmolcb2wtewgumm8njxp9mh)
Updating service numbers_numbers-api (id: 1xxad8xcqmrolnz09c1e3wz5u)
PS>docker stack ps numbers
ID                      NAME                                                   IM
AGE                          NODE                 DESIRED STATE        CUR
RENT STATE           ERROR               PORTS
k2dioh6p7l9k            numbers_numbers-web.ay20p76wefcokkl46xtabyssz     di
amol/ch08-numbers-web:v3       docker-desktop       Running             Run
ning 4 seconds ago                       *:80->80/tcp
x9p9cky8xq4e             \_ numbers_numbers-web.ay20p76wefcokkl46xtabyssz  di
amol/ch08-numbers-web:v2       docker-desktop       Shutdown            Shu
tdown 8 seconds ago
kovbcwmjx8m5             \_ numbers_numbers-web.ay20p76wefcokkl46xtabyssz  di
amol/ch08-numbers-web:latest   docker-desktop       Shutdown            Shu
tdown 14 minutes ago
vzdurp1ra5hh            numbers_numbers-api.1                              di
amol/ch08-numbers-api:v3       docker-desktop       Running             Run
ning 6 seconds ago
```

**Listing all the replicas for a stack takes up a lot of room—if I scrolled
down here I'd see three of the API replicas updated to v3 at the same
time. The rollout will monitor them for one minute, and if they're
healthy it will update the other three.**

Figure 14.4   Updating a stack with a new update config—the rollout settings take
immediate effect.

There's a neater way to report on a Swarm service that identifies the service specification, the update configuration, and the latest update status. That's using the `inspect` command with the `pretty` flag. Services created by a stack use the naming convention `{stack-name}_{service-name}`, so you can work with stack services directly.

**TRY IT NOW**   Inspect the random number API service to view the update status:

```
docker service inspect --pretty numbers_numbers-api
```

You can see my output in figure 14.5. I've trimmed it down again to show just the main pieces of information, but if you scroll in your output you'll also see the health check configuration, resource limits, and update config.

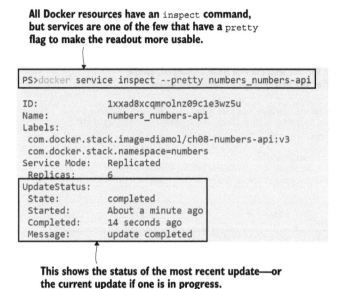

**All Docker resources have an** `inspect` **command, but services are one of the few that have a** `pretty` **flag to make the readout more usable.**

```
PS>docker service inspect --pretty numbers_numbers-api

ID:              1xxad8xcqmrolnz09c1e3wz5u
Name:            numbers_numbers-api
Labels:
 com.docker.stack.image=diamol/ch08-numbers-api:v3
 com.docker.stack.namespace=numbers
Service Mode:    Replicated
 Replicas:       6
UpdateStatus:
 State:          completed
 Started:        About a minute ago
 Completed:      14 seconds ago
 Message:        update completed
```

**This shows the status of the most recent update—or the current update if one is in progress.**

Figure 14.5   Inspecting a service shows the current configuration and the most recent update status.

One important thing you need to be aware of when you change the default update configuration settings is that you need to include those settings in every subsequent deployment. My v3 deployment added the custom settings, but if I don't include the same update override file in the next deployment, Docker will revert the service back to the default update settings. Swarm makes changes to the update configuration first, so it would set the update config back to the defaults and then roll out the next version one replica at a time.

The update config settings for Swarm rollouts have an identical set that applies for rollbacks, so you can also configure how many replicas at a time and how long to wait between sets for an automated rollback. These may seem like minor tweaks, but it's really important to specify the update and rollback process for a production deployment and test it with your app at scale. You need to be confident that you can roll out an update at any time, and that it will be applied quickly but with enough checks in the process for it to roll back automatically if there's a problem. You get that confidence by working through failure scenarios with these config settings.

## 14.3 Configuring service rollbacks

There is no `docker stack rollback` command; only individual services can be rolled back to their previous state. You shouldn't need to manually start a service rollback unless something's gone badly wrong. Rollbacks should happen automatically when the cluster is performing a rollout and it identifies that new replicas are failing within the monitor period. If that happens and you've got your configuration right, you won't realize a rollback has happened until you wonder why your new features aren't showing up.

Application deployments are the main cause of downtime, because even when everything is automated, there are still humans writing the automation scripts and the application YAML files, and sometimes things get forgotten. We can experience that with the random number app—a new version is ready to deploy, but it has a configuration option that must be set. If it isn't set, the API fails immediately.

> **TRY IT NOW** Run v5 of the random number app (v4 was the version we used to demonstrate continuous integration in chapter 11, but it used the same code as v3). This deployment will fail because the configuration setting that v5 needs isn't provided in the Compose files:

```
# join lots of Compose files together
docker-compose -f ./numbers/docker-compose.yml -f ./numbers/prod.yml -
    f ./numbers/prod-healthcheck.yml -f ./numbers/prod-update-
    config.yml -f ./numbers/v5-bad.yml config > stack.yml

# deploy the update:
docker stack deploy -c stack.yml numbers

# wait for a minute and check the service status:
docker service inspect --pretty numbers_numbers-api
```

This is a typical failed deployment. The new API replicas were created and started successfully but they failed their health checks—the health-check configuration is set to run every two seconds with two retries before flagging the container as unhealthy. If any new replicas report as unhealthy during the monitor period of the rollout, that triggers the rollback action, which I've set for this service to automatically roll back. If you wait 30 seconds or so after the deployment before you inspect the service, you'll see output similar to mine in figure 14.6 saying the update has been rolled back and the service is running six replicas of the v3 image.

It's no fun when deployments go wrong, but a failed update like this that automatically rolls back does at least keep your app running. Using the `start-first` rollout strategy helps with that. If I used the default `stop-first`, there would be a period of reduced capacity when three v3 replicas get stopped, then three v5 replicas get started and fail. In the time it takes the new replicas to flag themselves as unhealthy and for the rollback to complete, there would only be three active replicas of the API. Users wouldn't see any errors because Docker Swarm doesn't send any traffic to replicas that aren't healthy, but the API would be running at 50% capacity.

**Merging this many Compose files together is brittle, but the overrides are just there to demonstrate update features. Normally you'd have fewer.**

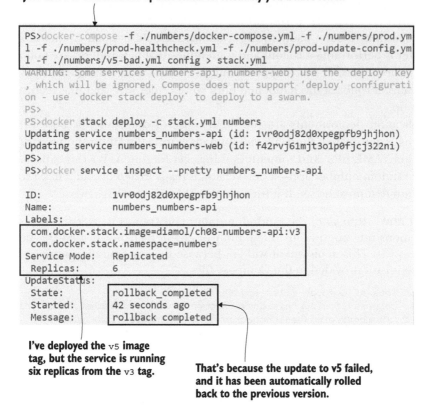

```
PS>docker-compose -f ./numbers/docker-compose.yml -f ./numbers/prod.ym
l -f ./numbers/prod-healthcheck.yml -f ./numbers/prod-update-config.ym
l -f ./numbers/v5-bad.yml config > stack.yml
WARNING: Some services (numbers-api, numbers-web) use the 'deploy' key
, which will be ignored. Compose does not support 'deploy' configurati
on - use `docker stack deploy` to deploy to a swarm.
PS>
PS>docker stack deploy -c stack.yml numbers
Updating service numbers_numbers-api (id: 1vr0odj82d0xpegpfb9jhjhon)
Updating service numbers_numbers-web (id: f42rvj61mjt3o1p0fjcj322ni)
PS>
PS>docker service inspect --pretty numbers_numbers-api

ID:             1vr0odj82d0xpegpfb9jhjhon
Name:           numbers_numbers-api
Labels:
 com.docker.stack.image=diamol/ch08-numbers-api:v3
 com.docker.stack.namespace=numbers
Service Mode:   Replicated
 Replicas:      6
UpdateStatus:
 State:         rollback_completed
 Started:       42 seconds ago
 Message:       rollback completed
```

**I've deployed the v5 image tag, but the service is running six replicas from the v3 tag.**

**That's because the update to v5 failed, and it has been automatically rolled back to the previous version.**

Figure 14.6   When you get your configuration right, a failed update is identified and rolled back.

This deployment uses the default configuration for rollbacks, which is the same as the default configuration for updates: one task at a time with a `stop-first` strategy, zero monitoring time, and the rollback pauses if the replacement replicas fail. I find that too cautious, because in the situation where your app was working fine and a deployment broke it, you usually want to roll back to the previous state as quickly as possible. Listing 14.3 shows my preferred rollback configuration for this service (from `prod-rollback-config.yml`):

**Listing 14.3   Rollback configuration that reverts failed updates quickly**

```
numbers-api:
  deploy:
    rollback_config:
      parallelism: 6
      monitor: 0s
```

```
failure_action: continue
order: start-first
```

The goal here is to revert back as quickly as possible—the parallelism is 6 so all the failed replicas will be replaced in one go, using `start-first` strategy so replicas of the old version will be started before the rollback worries about shutting down replicas of the new version. There's no monitoring period, and if the rollback fails (because replicas don't start) it's set to continue anyway. This is an aggressive rollback policy that assumes the previous version was good and will become good again when the replicas start.

> **TRY IT NOW** We'll try the v5 update again, specifying the custom rollback configuration. This rollout will still fail, but the rollback will happen more quickly, returning the app to full capacity on the v3 API:

```
# join together even more Compose files:
docker-compose -f ./numbers/docker-compose.yml -f ./numbers/prod.yml -f
    ./numbers/prod-healthcheck.yml -f ./numbers/prod-update-config.yml
    -f ./numbers/prod-rollback-config.yml -f ./numbers/v5-bad.yml
    config > stack.yml

# deploy the update again with the new rollback config:
docker stack deploy -c stack.yml numbers

# wait and you'll see it reverts back again:
docker service inspect --pretty numbers_numbers-api
```

This time you'll see the rollback happens more quickly, but only marginally because there are only a small number of replicas in the API service, all running on my single node. You can see how important this would be in a larger deployment that might have 100 replicas running across 20 nodes—rolling back each replica individually would prolong the amount of time your app might be running below capacity or in an unstable state. You can see my output in figure 14.7—I was quick enough this time to catch the rollback just as it had triggered, so the state shows the rollback is starting.

When you run this yourself, take a look at the full service configuration when the rollback has completed—you'll see that the rollback configuration has been reset to the default values. That's guaranteed confusion right there, because you'll be thinking the rollback config wasn't applied. But actually it's because the whole service configuration got rolled back, and that includes the rollback setup—the replicas were rolled back in line with the new policy, and then the rollback policy was rolled back. Next time you deploy, you'll need to make sure you keep adding the update and rollback configs, or they'll be updated back to the default settings.

This is where having multiple override files gets dangerous, because they're all necessary and they all need to be specified in the correct order. Normally you wouldn't split out settings for one environment across multiple files; I've just done that to make our journey through updates and rollbacks easier to follow. Typically you'd have the core

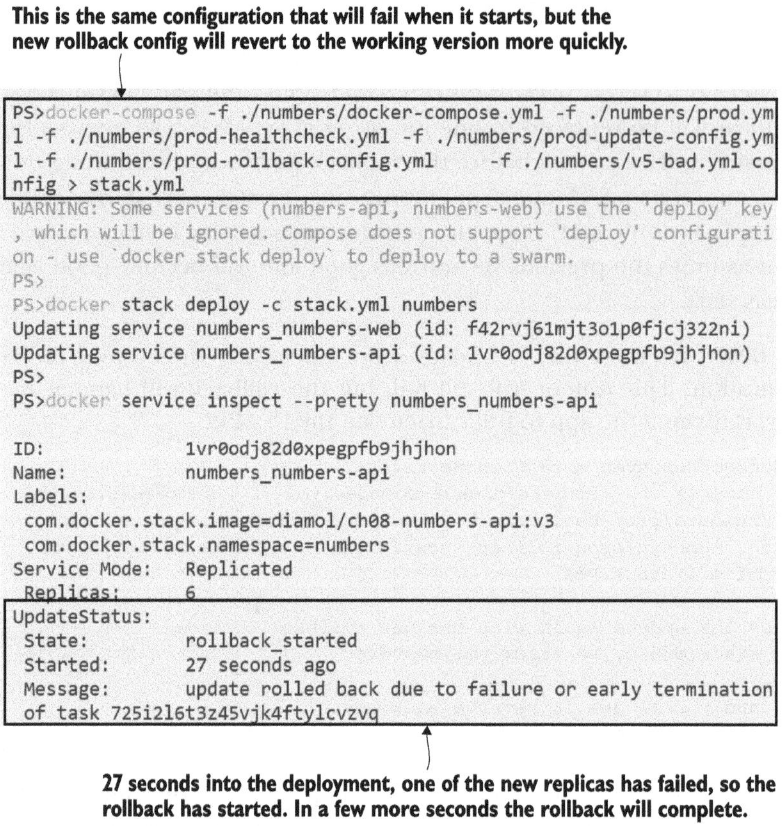

**This is the same configuration that will fail when it starts, but the new rollback config will revert to the working version more quickly.**

```
PS>docker-compose -f ./numbers/docker-compose.yml -f ./numbers/prod.ym
l -f ./numbers/prod-healthcheck.yml -f ./numbers/prod-update-config.ym
l -f ./numbers/prod-rollback-config.yml    -f ./numbers/v5-bad.yml co
nfig > stack.yml
WARNING: Some services (numbers-api, numbers-web) use the 'deploy' key
, which will be ignored. Compose does not support 'deploy' configurati
on - use `docker stack deploy` to deploy to a swarm.
PS>
PS>docker stack deploy -c stack.yml numbers
Updating service numbers_numbers-web (id: f42rvj61mjt3o1p0fjcj322ni)
Updating service numbers_numbers-api (id: 1vr0odj82d0xpegpfb9jhjhon)
PS>
PS>docker service inspect --pretty numbers_numbers-api

ID:             1vr0odj82d0xpegpfb9jhjhon
Name:           numbers_numbers-api
Labels:
 com.docker.stack.image=diamol/ch08-numbers-api:v3
 com.docker.stack.namespace=numbers
Service Mode:   Replicated
 Replicas:      6
UpdateStatus:
 State:         rollback_started
 Started:       27 seconds ago
 Message:       update rolled back due to failure or early termination
 of task 725i2l6t3z45vjk4ftylcvzvq
```

**27 seconds into the deployment, one of the new replicas has failed, so the rollback has started. In a few more seconds the rollback will complete.**

Figure 14.7   Specifying custom rollback settings means a failed rollout gets fixed faster.

Compose file, an environment override file, and possibly a version override file. We'll take that approach for the final deployment, fixing the v5 issue and getting the app working again.

**TRY IT NOW**   The v5 update failed and rolled back, so we got the team together and realized we'd missed a crucial config setting. The v5.yml override file adds that in, and the prod-full.yml override file has all the production settings in one place. Now we can deploy v5 successfully:

```
# this is more like it - all the custom config is in the prod-full file:
docker-compose -f ./numbers/docker-compose.yml -f ./numbers/prod-
    full.yml   -f ./numbers/v5.yml --log-level ERROR config > stack.yml

# deploy the working version of v5:
docker stack deploy -c stack.yml numbers

# wait a while and check the rollout succeeded:
docker service inspect --pretty numbers_numbers-api
```

My output is in figure 14.8. I waited a couple of minutes between the deployment and the service list to be sure that the update had worked and there was no rollback.

**This deployment will work—the v5 override file includes the missing config value from the previous deployment, so now the API replicas will all work.**

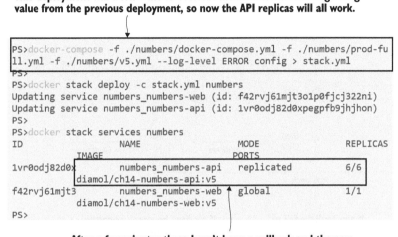

```
PS>docker-compose -f ./numbers/docker-compose.yml -f ./numbers/prod-fu
ll.yml -f ./numbers/v5.yml --log-level ERROR config > stack.yml
PS>
PS>docker stack deploy -c stack.yml numbers
Updating service numbers_numbers-web (id: f42rvj61mjt3o1p0fjcj322ni)
Updating service numbers_numbers-api (id: 1vr0odj82d0xpegpfb9jhjhon)
PS>
PS>docker stack services numbers
ID                 NAME              MODE         REPLICAS
          IMAGE                     PORTS
1vr0odj82d0x        numbers_numbers-api  replicated   6/6
          diamol/ch14-numbers-api:v5
f42rvj61mjt3        numbers_numbers-web  global       1/1
          diamol/ch14-numbers-web:v5
PS>
```

**After a few minutes there hasn't been a rollback and the new deployment has worked. All API replicas are using the v5 image.**

**Figure 14.8   A successful deployment after fixing the app configuration**

Now you have v5 running in all its glory—it's actually the same simple demo app as before, but we can use it to illustrate one final point about rollbacks. The app is working fine now, and the health checks are in place, so if you keep using the API and break the replicas, they'll get replaced and the app will start working again. Failing health checks don't cause a rollback of the last update; they just trigger replacement replicas *unless the failure happens during the monitor period of the update.* If you deploy v5 and during the 60-second monitor period you break the API containers, that will trigger a rollback. Figure 14.9 shows what the update and rollback process would look like for the v3 to v5 update.

That's it for update and rollback configuration. It's really just a case of setting a few values in the deployment section of your Compose file and testing variations to be sure your updates are fast and safe and that they roll back quickly if there's a problem. That helps you maximize the uptime for your application. All that's left is to understand how that uptime is impacted when there's downtime of nodes in the cluster.

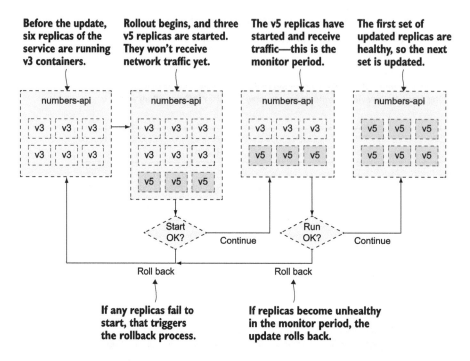

**Before the update, six replicas of the service are running v3 containers.**

**Rollout begins, and three v5 replicas are started. They won't receive network traffic yet.**

**The v5 replicas have started and receive traffic—this is the monitor period.**

**The first set of updated replicas are healthy, so the next set is updated.**

Continue

Continue

Roll back

Roll back

**If any replicas fail to start, that triggers the rollback process.**

**If replicas become unhealthy in the monitor period, the update rolls back.**

Figure 14.9  **This looks suspiciously like a flowchart, but it's just a useful way to model the update process.**

## 14.4  *Managing downtime for your cluster*

Container orchestrators turn a bunch of machines into a powerful cluster, but ultimately it's the machines that run the containers, and they're prone to downtime. Disk, network, and power are all going to fail at some point—the larger your cluster, the more frequently you'll have an outage. The cluster will be able to keep your apps running through most outages, but some unplanned failures need active intervention, and if you have planned outages you can make it easier for the Swarm to work around them.

If you want to follow along with this section, you'll need a multi-node Swarm. You can set up your own if you're happy building virtual machines and installing Docker on them, or you can use an online playground. *Play with Docker* is a great choice for that—you can create a multi-node Swarm and practice deployments and node management without needing any extra machines of your own. Browse to https://labs .play-with-docker.com, sign in with your Docker Hub ID, and click Add New Instance to add a virtual Docker server to your online session. I've added five instances to my session, and I'll use them as my Swarm.

> **TRY IT NOW**  Start your Play with Docker session and create five instances—you'll see them listed in the left navigation, and you can click to select them.

In the main window you'll see a terminal session that is connected to the node you have selected.

```
# select node1 and initialize the Swarm using the node's IP address:
ip=$(hostname -i)
docker swarm init --advertise-addr $ip

# show the commands to join managers and workers to the Swarm:
docker swarm join-token manager
docker swarm join-token worker

# select node2 and paste the manager join command, then the same on
    node3

# select node4 and paste the worker join command, then the same on
    node5

# back on node1 make sure all the nodes are ready:
docker node ls
```

This gives you a completely disposable Swarm. You can do as much damage as you like and then just close your session, and all those nodes will disappear (they're actually containers running Docker-in-Docker with a lot of smarts to manage the sessions and the networking). You can see my output in figure 14.10 with the Swarm all ready to go.

This is Play with Docker—an online playground for working with Linux containers in a browser. It's free to use. Sign in with your Docker ID and you get a dedicated session.

I've created five nodes. The list here shows you the node IP addresses, and you can select a node to switch the terminal session.

My nodes are configured as a highly available Swarm, with three managers and two workers.

**Figure 14.10  Initializing a multi-node Swarm using disposable instances from Play with Docker**

Let's take the simplest scenario first—you need to take a node down for an operating system update on the server or some other infrastructure task. That node might be running containers, and you want them to be gracefully shut down, replaced on other nodes, and for your machine to go into maintenance mode so Docker doesn't try and schedule any new containers during any reboot cycles you need to do. Maintenance mode for nodes in the Swarm is called *drain mode*, and you can put managers or workers into drain.

> **TRY IT NOW**    Switch to the terminal session for your node1 manager, and set two of the other nodes into drain mode:

```
# set a worker and a manager into drain mode:
docker node update --availability drain node5
docker node update --availability drain node3

# check nodes:
docker node ls
```

Drain mode means slightly different things for workers and managers. In both cases all the replicas running on the node are shut down and no more replicas will be scheduled for the node. Manager nodes are still part of the management group though, so they still synchronize the cluster database, provide access to the management API, and can be the leader. Figure 14.11 shows my cluster with two drained nodes.

You change a node's availability from a manager node. Drain means all replicas on the node are removed, and it won't be scheduled for any more work until the availability is changed.

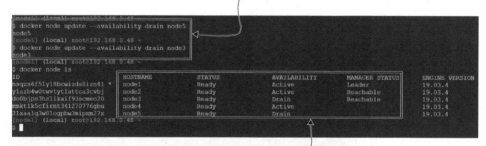

Managers and workers can both be set to drain, but a drained manager is still an active manager node.

**Figure 14.11    Entering drain mode removes all containers and lets you run maintenance on the node.**

What's this about a *leader manager*? You need multiple managers for high availability, but it's an active-passive model. Only one manager is actually controlling the cluster, and that's the leader. The others keep a replica of the cluster database, they can action API requests, and they can take over if the leader fails. That happens with an election process between the remaining managers, which requires a majority vote, and for that you always need an odd number of managers—typically three for smaller clusters and five for large clusters. If you permanently lose a manager node and find yourself with an even number of managers, you can promote a worker node to become a manager instead.

> **TRY IT NOW**  It's not easy to simulate node failure in Play with Docker, but you can connect to the leader and manually remove it from the Swarm. Then one of the remaining managers becomes the leader, and you can promote a worker to keep an odd number of managers:

```
# on node1 - forcibly leave the Swarm:
docker swarm leave --force

# on node 2 - make the worker node available again:
docker node update --availability active node5

# promote the worker to a manager:
docker node promote node5

# check the nodes:
docker node ls
```

There are two ways a node can leave the Swarm—a manager can initiate it with the node rm command or the node itself can do it with swarm leave. If the node leaves by itself, that's a similar situation to the node going offline—the Swarm managers think it should still be there, but it's not reachable. You can see that in my output in figure 14.12. The original node1 is still listed as a manager, but the status is Down and the manager status is Unreachable.

**I've removed node1 from the Swarm, so admin tasks like setting node availability and promoting nodes have to be done from a different manager node.**

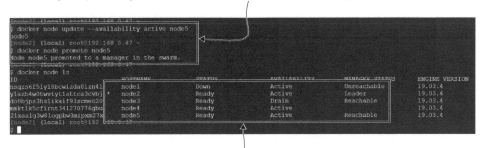

**Now the original manager node is unreachable, but the cluster is still healthy because I have promoted a new manager.**

Figure 14.12  Node management keeps your Swarm fully available even when nodes are offline.

Now the swarm has three managers again, which gives it high availability. If node1 had gone offline unexpectedly, when it came back online I could return one of the other managers to the worker pool by running `node demote`. Those are pretty much the only commands you need to manage a Docker Swarm cluster.

We'll finish up with a couple of less common scenarios, so you know how the Swarm will behave if you encounter them:

- *All managers go offline*—If all your managers go offline but the worker nodes are still running, then your apps are still running. The ingress network and all the service replicas on the worker nodes work in the same way if there are no managers, but now there's nothing to monitor your services, so if a container fails it won't be replaced. You need to fix this and bring managers online to make the cluster healthy again.

- *Leader and all but one manager go offline*—It's possible to lose control of your cluster if all but one manager node goes offline and the remaining manager is not the leader. Managers have to vote for a new leader, and if there are no other managers, a leader can't be elected. You can fix this by running `swarm init` on the remaining manager with the `force-new-cluster` argument. That makes this node the leader but preserves all the cluster data and all the running tasks. Then you can add more managers to restore high availability.

- *Rebalancing replicas for even distribution*—Service replicas don't automatically get redistributed when you add new nodes. If you increase the capacity of your cluster with new nodes but don't update any services, the new nodes won't run any replicas. You can rebalance replicas so they're evenly distributed around the cluster by running `service update --force` without changing any other properties.

## 14.5 Understanding high availability in Swarm clusters

There are multiple layers in your app deployment where you need to consider high availability. We've covered a lot of them in this chapter: health checks tell the cluster if your app is working, and it will replace failed containers to keep the app online; multiple worker nodes provide extra capacity for containers to be rescheduled if a node goes offline; multiple managers provide redundancy for scheduling containers and monitoring workers. There's one final area to consider—the datacenter where the cluster is running.

I'm just going to cover this very briefly to finish up the chapter, because people often try to get high availability between regions by building a single cluster that spans several datacenters. In theory you can do this—you could create managers in datacenter A with workers in datacenters A, B, and C. That certainly simplifies your cluster management, but the problem is network latency. Nodes in a Swarm are very chatty, and if there's a sudden network lag between A and B, the managers might think all the B nodes have gone offline and reschedule all their containers on C nodes. And those scenarios just get worse, with the potential to have split-brain: multiple managers in different regions thinking they're the leader.

If you really need your apps to keep running when there's a regional outage, the only safe way is with multiple clusters. It adds to your management overhead, and there's the risk of drift between the clusters and the apps they're running, but those are manageable issues, unlike network latency. Figure 14.13 shows what that configuration looks like.

You need multiple clusters for true high-availability, and they should be in different data centers or different regions, so your apps keep running even if a whole region is unavailable. An external DNS service can direct users to the nearest cluster if both are online.

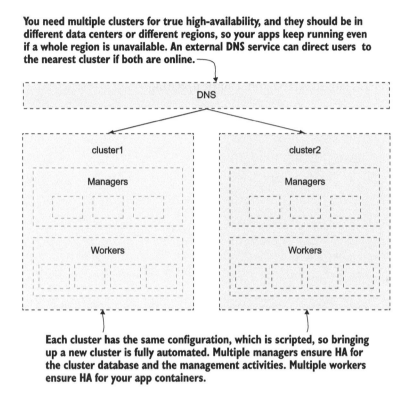

Each cluster has the same configuration, which is scripted, so bringing up a new cluster is fully automated. Multiple managers ensure HA for the cluster database and the management activities. Multiple workers ensure HA for your app containers.

**Figure 14.13  To achieve datacenter redundancy, you need multiple clusters in different regions.**

## 14.6  Lab

It's back to the image gallery app for this lab, and it's your turn to build a stack deployment that has a sensible rollout and rollback configuration for the API service. There's a twist though—the API component doesn't have a health check built into the Docker image, so you'll need to think about how you can add a health check in the service specification. Here are the requirements:

- Write a stack file to deploy the image gallery app using these container images: `diamol/ch04-access-log`, `diamol/ch04-image-of-the-day`, and `diamol/ch04-image-gallery`.

- The API component is `diamol/ch04-image-of-the-day`, and it should run with four replicas, it should have a health check specified, and it should use an update config that is fast but safe and a rollback config that is just fast.
- When you've deployed the app, prepare another stack file that updates the services to these images: `diamol/ch09-access-log`, `diamol/ch09-image-of-the-day`, and `diamol/ch09-image-gallery`.
- Deploy your stack update, and be sure the API component rolls out using your expected policy and doesn't roll back due to an incorrect health check.

This one should be fun, if you find this sort of thing fun. Either way, my solution is up on GitHub for you to check in the usual place: https://github.com/sixeyed/diamol/blob/master/ch14/lab/README.md. Happy updating!

# Configuring Docker for secure remote access and CI/CD

The Docker command line presents a seamless way of working with containers, and it's easy to forget that the command line doesn't really do anything itself—it just sends instructions to the API running on the Docker Engine. Separating the command line from the Engine has two major benefits—other tools can consume the Docker API, so the command line isn't the only way to manage containers, and you can configure your local command line to work with a remote machine running Docker. It's amazingly powerful that you can switch from running containers on your laptop to managing a cluster with dozens of nodes, using all the same Docker commands you're used to, without leaving your desk.

Remote access is how you administer test environments or debug issues in production, and it's also how you enable the *continuous deployment* part of your CI/CD pipeline. After the continuous integration stages of the pipeline have completed successfully, you'll have a potentially releasable version of your app stored in a Docker registry. Continuous deployment is the next stage of the pipeline—connecting to a remote Docker Engine and deploying the new version of the app. That stage could be a test environment that goes on to run a suite of integration tests, and then the final stage could connect to the production cluster and deploy the app to the live environment. In this chapter you'll learn how to expose the Docker API and keep it protected, and how to connect to remote Docker Engines from your machine and from a CI/CD pipeline.

## 15.1 *Endpoint options for the Docker API*

When you install Docker you don't need to configure the command line to talk to the API—the default setup is for the Engine to listen on a local channel, and for the command line to use that same channel. The local channel uses either Linux sockets or Windows named pipes, and those are both network technologies that restrict traffic to the local machine. If you want to enable remote access to your Docker Engine, you need to explicitly set it in the configuration. There are a few different options for setting up the channel for remote access, but the simplest is to allow plain, unsecured HTTP access.

Enabling unencrypted HTTP access is a horribly bad idea. It sets your Docker API to listen on a normal HTTP endpoint, and anyone with access to your network can connect to your Docker Engine and manage containers—without any authentication. You might think that isn't too bad on your dev laptop, but it opens up a nice, easy attack vector. A malicious website could craft a request to http://localhost:2375, where your Docker API is listening, and start up a bitcoin mining container on your machine—you wouldn't know until you wondered where all your CPU had gone.

I'll walk you through enabling plain HTTP access, but only if you promise not to do it again after this exercise. At the end of this section you'll have a good understanding of how remote access works, so you can disable the HTTP option and move on to more secure choices.

> **TRY IT NOW**  Remote access is an Engine configuration option. You can set it easily in Docker Desktop on Windows 10 or Mac by opening Settings from the whale menu and selecting Expose Daemon on tcp://localhost:2375 Without TLS. Figure 15.1 shows that option—once you save the setting, Docker will restart.

If you're using Docker Engine on Linux or Windows Server, you'll need to edit the config file instead. You'll find it at /etc/docker/daemon.json on Linux, or on Windows at C:\ProgramData\docker\config\daemon.json. The field you need to add is hosts, which takes a list of endpoints to listen on. Listing 15.1 shows the settings you need for unsecured HTTP access, using Docker's conventional port, 2375.

**Listing 15.1    Configuring plain HTTP access to the Docker Engine via daemon.json**

```
{
  "hosts": [
  # enable remote access on port 2375:
  "tcp://0.0.0.0:2375",
  # and keep listening on the local channel - Windows pipe:
  "npipe://"
  # OR Linux socket:
  "fd://"
  ],
  "insecure-registries":  [
      "registry.local:5000"
  ]
}
```

**The warning is a helpful reminder that this is a bad idea.**

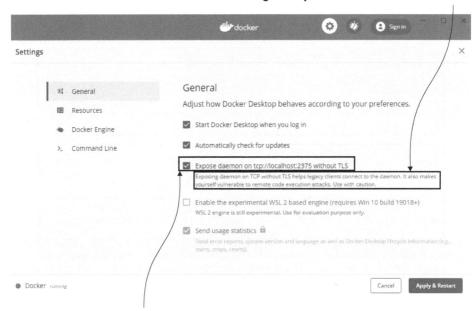

**Docker Desktop makes it easy to expose your Engine API to the network.**

**Figure 15.1  Enabling plain HTTP access to the Docker API—you should try and forget you saw this.**

You can check that the Engine is configured for remote access by sending HTTP requests to the API, and by providing a TCP host address in the Docker CLI.

**TRY IT NOW**  The Docker command line can connect to a remote machine using the host argument. The remote machine could be the localhost, but via TCP rather than the local channel:

```
# connect to the local Engine over TCP:
docker --host tcp://localhost:2375 container ls

# and using the REST API over HTTP:
curl http://localhost:2375/containers/json
```

The Docker and Docker Compose command lines both support a host parameter, which specifies the address of the Docker Engine where you want to send commands. If the Engine is configured to listen on the local address without security, the host parameter is all you need; there's no authentication for users and no encryption of network traffic. You can see my output in figure 15.2—I can list containers using the Docker CLI or the API.

Now imagine the horror of the ops team if you told them you wanted to manage a Docker server, so you needed them to enable remote access—and, by the way, that

**Using the Docker command line with a remote host—this is the local machine, but I could use a server on the network or in the cloud by specifying its IP address or domain name.**

```
PS>docker --host tcp://localhost:2375 container ls
CONTAINER ID        IMAGE               COMMAND                          CREATED
          STATUS                        PORTS
      NAMES
651d1c296e63         diamol/apache          "bin\\httpd.exe -DFOR…"   About a
minute ago   Up About a minute   0.0.0.0:61854->80/tcp, 0.0.0.0:61853->443
/tcp   goofy_williams
PS>
```

```
PS>curl http://localhost:2375/containers/json
[{"Id":"651d1c296e634e1d8693a7a8af979bf0a048e532e4868fab216f537de3f16348",
"Names":["/goofy_williams"],"Image":"diamol/apache","ImageID":"sha256:0303
15a5343f1e24f221554c64ad8f03403721827b9f7ac901d3694bd7fd3e24","Command":"b
in\\httpd.exe -DFOREGROUND","Created":1574867870,"Ports":[{"IP":"0.0.0.0",
"PrivatePort":443,"PublicPort":61853,"Type":"tcp"},{"IP":"0.0.0.0","Privat
ePort":80,"PublicPort":61854,"Type":"tcp"}],"Labels":{},"State":"running",
"Status":"Up About a minute","HostConfig":{"NetworkMode":"default"},"Netwo
rkSettings":{"Networks":{"nat":{"IPAMConfig":null,"Links":null,"Aliases":n
ull,"NetworkID":"d03a7ae545bcbe92f1acf61d971e27426de9d315834874e9108096733
4cc500c","EndpointID":"4d3f961bfa648d66f2e72f028eba57fdb94925eb22bfbd42bbe
bf40af33cee41","Gateway":"172.26.208.1","IPAddress":"172.26.208.210","IPPr
efixLen":16,"IPv6Gateway":"","GlobalIPv6Address":"","GlobalIPv6PrefixLen":
0,"MacAddress":"00:15:5d:cc:80:79","DriverOpts":null}}},"Mounts":[]}]
PS>
```

**The command line is just one client of the Docker API. You can call it directly with curl to perform all the actions the CLI supports.**

Figure 15.2   When the Docker Engine is available over HTTP, anyone with the machine address can use it.

would let anyone do anything with Docker on that machine, with no security and no audit trail. Don't underestimate how dangerous this is. Linux containers use the same user accounts as the host server, so if you run a container as the Linux admin account, root, you've pretty much got admin access to the server. Windows containers work slightly differently, so you don't get unlimited server access from within a container, but you can still do unpleasant things.

When you're working with a remote Docker Engine, any commands you send work in the context of that machine. So if you run a container and mount a volume from the local disk, it's *the remote machine's disk* that the container sees. That can trip you up if you want to run a container on the test server that mounts the source code on your local machine. Either the command will fail because the directory you're mounting doesn't exist on the server (which will confuse you because you know it does exist on your machine), or worse, that path does exist on the server and you won't understand why the files inside the container are different from your disk. It also provides a useful shortcut for someone to browse a remote server's filesystem if they don't have access to the server but they do have access to the Docker Engine.

**TRY IT NOW**   Let's see why unsecured access to the Docker Engine is so bad. Run a container that mounts the Docker machine's disk, and you can browse around the host's filesystem:

```
# using Linux containers:
docker --host tcp://localhost:2375 container run -it -v /:/host-drive
    diamol/base

# OR Windows containers:
docker --host tcp://localhost:2375 container run -it -v C:\:C:\host-
    drive diamol/base

# inside the container, browse the filesystem:
ls
ls host-drive
```

You can see my output in figure 15.3—the user who runs the container has complete access to read and write files on the host.

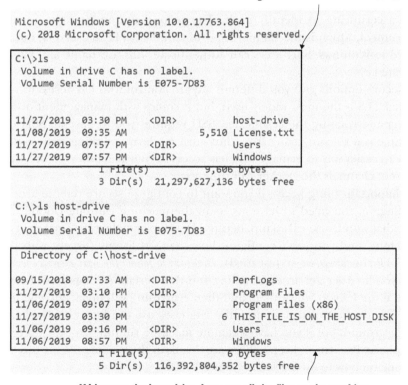

**This is running in an interactive container. I'm using Windows, so I can see the standard Windows folders from the image and the** `host-drive` **mount.**

```
Microsoft Windows [Version 10.0.17763.864]
(c) 2018 Microsoft Corporation. All rights reserved.

C:\>ls
 Volume in drive C has no label.
 Volume Serial Number is E075-7D83


11/27/2019  03:30 PM    <DIR>          host-drive
11/08/2019  09:35 AM             5,510 License.txt
11/27/2019  07:57 PM    <DIR>          Users
11/27/2019  07:57 PM    <DIR>          Windows
               1 File(s)          9,606 bytes
               3 Dir(s)  21,297,627,136 bytes free

C:\>ls host-drive
 Volume in drive C has no label.
 Volume Serial Number is E075-7D83

 Directory of C:\host-drive

09/15/2018  07:33 AM    <DIR>          PerfLogs
11/27/2019  03:10 PM    <DIR>          Program Files
11/06/2019  09:07 PM    <DIR>          Program Files (x86)
11/27/2019  03:30 PM                 6 THIS_FILE_IS_ON_THE_HOST_DISK
11/06/2019  09:16 PM    <DIR>          Users
11/06/2019  08:57 PM    <DIR>          Windows
               1 File(s)              6 bytes
               5 Dir(s)  116,392,804,352 bytes free
```

**If I browse the host drive, I can see all the files on the machine running Docker. This is a read-write mount, so I could edit files too...**

**Figure 15.3   Having access to the Docker Engine means you can get access to the host's filesystem.**

In this exercise you're just connecting to your own machine, so you're not really bypassing security. But if you find out the name or IP address of the server that runs your containerized payroll system, and that server has unsecured remote access to the Docker Engine—well, you might be able to make a few changes and roll up to work in that new Tesla sooner than you expected. This is why you should never enable unsecured access to the Docker Engine, except as a learning exercise.

Before we go on, let's get out of the dangerous situation we've created and go back to the private local channel for the Docker Engine. Either uncheck the local-host box in the settings for Docker Desktop, or revert the config change you made for the Docker daemon, and then we'll go on to look at the more secure options for remote access.

## 15.2 Configuring Docker for secure remote access

Docker supports two other channels for the API to listen on, and both are secure. The first uses Transport Layer Security (TLS)—the same encryption technique based on digital certificates used by HTTPS websites. The Docker API uses mutual TLS, so the server has a certificate to identify itself and encrypt traffic, and the client also has a certificate to identify itself. The second option uses the Secure Shell (SSH) protocol, which is the standard way to connect to Linux servers, but it is also supported in Windows. SSH users can authenticate with username and password or with private keys.

The secure options give you different ways to control who has access to your cluster. Mutual TLS is the most widely used, but it comes with management overhead in generating and rotating the certificates. SSH requires you to have an SSH client on the machine you're connecting from, but most modern operating systems do, and it gives you an easier way to manage who has access to your machines. Figure 15.4 shows the different channels the Docker API supports.

One important thing here—if you want to configure secure remote access to the Docker Engine, you need to have access to the machine running Docker. And you don't get that with Docker Desktop, because Desktop actually runs Docker in a VM on your machine, and you can't configure how that VM listens (except with the unsecured HTTP checkbox we've just used). *Don't try to follow the next exercises using Docker Desktop*—you'll either get an error telling you that certain settings can't be adjusted, or, worse, it will let you adjust them and then everything will break and you'll need to reinstall. For the rest of this section, the exercises use the Play with Docker (PWD) online playground, but if you have a remote machine running Docker (here's where your Raspberry Pi earns its keep), there are details in the readme file for this chapter's source code on how to do the same without PWD.

We'll start by making a remote Docker Engine accessible securely using mutual TLS. For that you need to generate certificate and key file pairs (the key file acts like a password for the certificate)—one for the Docker API and one for the client. Larger organizations will have an internal certificate authority (CA) and a team that owns the

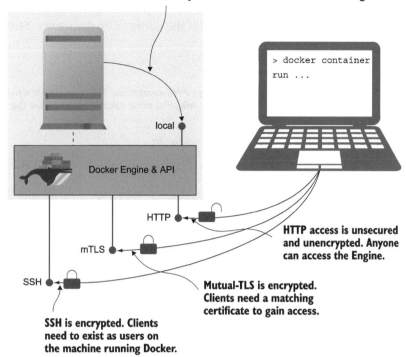

**The local channel is the default. It's only accessible from the machine running Docker.**

local

Docker Engine & API

> docker container
run ...

HTTP

**HTTP access is unsecured and unencrypted. Anyone can access the Engine.**

mTLS

**Mutual-TLS is encrypted. Clients need a matching certificate to gain access.**

SSH

**SSH is encrypted. Clients need to exist as users on the machine running Docker.**

Figure 15.4   There are secure ways of exposing the Docker API, providing encryption and authentication.

certs and can generate them for you. I've already done that, generating certs that work with PWD, so you can use those.

**TRY IT NOW**   Sign in to Play with Docker at https://labs.play-with-docker.com and create a new node. In that session, run a container that will deploy the certs, and configure the Docker Engine on PWD to use the certs. Then restart Docker:

```
# create a directory for the certs:
mkdir -p /diamol-certs

# run a container that sets up the certs & config:
docker container run -v /diamol-certs:/certs -v /etc/docker:/docker
     diamol/pwd-tls:server

# kill docker & restart with new config
pkill dockerd
dockerd &>/docker.log &
```

The container you ran mounted two volumes from the PWD node, and it copied the certs and a new daemon.json file from the container image onto the node. If you

change the Docker Engine configuration, you need to restart it, which is what the
dockerd commands are doing. You can see my output in figure 15.5—at this point
the engine is listening on port 2376 (which is the convention for secure TCP access)
using TLS.

**This container deploys PWD-compatible TLS certs onto the node and updates the Docker config file, using volume mounts from the host.**

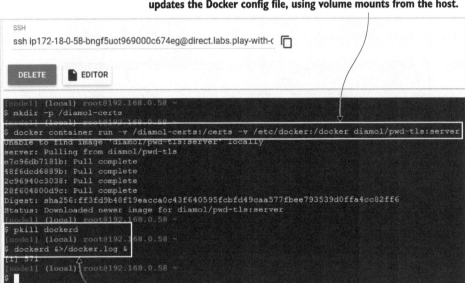

**Restarts the Docker Engine, loading the new configuration. This way of restarting Docker is specific to PWD—on a typical deployment you'd restart the Docker service instead.**

Figure 15.5  Configuring a Play with Docker session so the engine listens using mutual TLS

There's one last step before we can actually send traffic from the local machine into
the PWD node. Click on the Open Port button and open port 2376. A new tab will
open showing an error message. Ignore the message, and copy the URL of that new
tab to the clipboard. *This is the unique PWD domain for your session.* It will be something
like ip172-18-0-62-bo9pj8nad2eg008a76e0-2376.direct.labs.play-with-docker.com,
and you'll use it to connect from your local machine to the Docker Engine in PWD.
Figure 15.6 shows how you open the port.

Your PWD instance is now available to be remotely managed. The certificates
you're using are ones I generated using the OpenSSH tool (running in a container—
the Dockerfile is in the images/cert-generator folder if you're interested in seeing
how it works). I'm not going to go into detail on TLS certificates and OpenSSH
because that's a long detour neither of us would enjoy. But it is important to understand

**Click the Open Port button to configure PWD to listen for incoming traffic.**

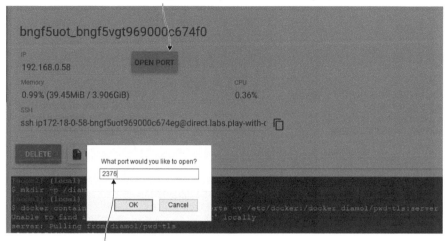

**Port 2376 is the port where the Docker Engine running in PWD is listening for TLS clients. When you click OK, a new tab will launch; you'll need the URL in that tab later.**

Figure 15.6   Opening ports in PWD lets you send external traffic into containers and the Docker Engine.

the relationship between the CA, the server cert, and the client cert. Figure 15.7 shows that.

If you're going to use TLS to secure your Docker Engines, you'll be generating one CA, one server cert for each Engine you want to secure, and one client cert for each user you want to allow access. Certs are created with a lifespan, so you can make short-lived client certs to give temporary access to a remote Engine. All of that can be automated, but there's still overhead in managing certificates.

When you configure the Docker Engine to use TLS, you need to specify the paths to the CA cert, and the server cert and key pair. Listing 15.2 shows the TLS setup that has been deployed on your PWD node.

**Listing 15.2   The Docker daemon configuration to enable TLS access**

```
{
  "hosts": ["unix:///var/run/docker.sock", "tcp://0.0.0.0:2376"],
  "tls": true,
  "tlscacert": "/diamol-certs/ca.pem",
  "tlskey": "/diamol-certs/server-key.pem",
  "tlscert": "/diamol-certs/server-cert.pem"
}
```

Now that your remote Docker Engine is secured, you can't use the REST API with curl or send commands using the Docker CLI unless you provide the CA certificate, client

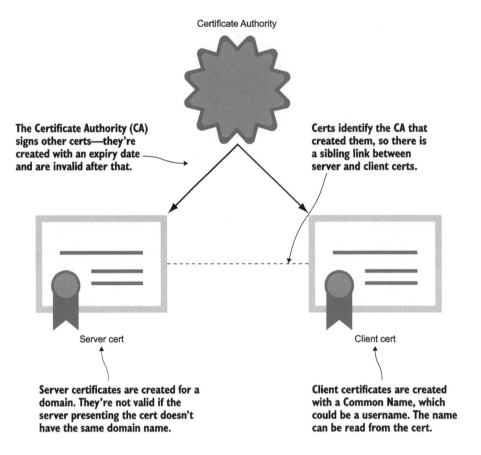

Certificate Authority

**The Certificate Authority (CA) signs other certs—they're created with an expiry date and are invalid after that.**

**Certs identify the CA that created them, so there is a sibling link between server and client certs.**

Server cert

Client cert

**Server certificates are created for a domain. They're not valid if the server presenting the cert doesn't have the same domain name.**

**Client certificates are created with a Common Name, which could be a username. The name can be read from the cert.**

Figure 15.7   A quick guide to mutual TLS—server certs and client certs identify the holder and share a CA.

certificate, and client key. The API won't accept any old client cert either—it needs to have been generated using the same CA as the server. Attempts to use the API without client TLS are rejected by the Engine. You can use a variation of the image you ran on PWD to download the client certs on your local machine, and use those to connect.

**TRY IT NOW**   Make sure you have the URL for port 2376 access to PWD—that's how you'll connect from your local machine to the PWD session. Use the domain for your session that you copied earlier when you opened port 2376. Try connecting to the PWD engine:

```
# grab your PWD domain from the address bar - something like
# ip172-18-0-62-bo9pj8nad2eg008a76e0-6379.direct.labs.play-with-
# docker.com

# store your PWD domain in a variable - on Windows:
$pwdDomain="<your-pwd-domain-from-the-address-bar>"
```

```
# OR Linux:
pwdDomain="<your-pwd-domain-goes-here>"

# try accessing the Docker API directly:
curl "http://$pwdDomain/containers/json"

# now try with the command line:
docker --host "tcp://$pwdDomain" container ls

# extract the PWD client certs onto your machine:
mkdir -p /tmp/pwd-certs
cd ./ch15/exercises
tar -xvf pwd-client-certs -C /tmp/pwd-certs

# connect with the client certs:
docker --host "tcp://$pwdDomain" --tlsverify --tlscacert /tmp/pwd-
    certs/ca.pem --tlscert /tmp/pwd-certs/client-cert.pem --tlskey
    /tmp/pwd-certs/client-key.pem container ls

# you can use any Docker CLI commands:
docker --host "tcp://$pwdDomain" --tlsverify --tlscacert /tmp/pwd-
    certs/ca.pem --tlscert /tmp/pwd-certs/client-cert.pem --tlskey
    /tmp/pwd-certs/client-key.pem container run -d -P diamol/apache
```

It's a little cumbersome to pass the TLS parameters to every Docker command, but you can also capture them in environment variables. If you don't provide the right client cert, you'll get an error, and when you do provide the certs, you have complete control over your Docker Engine running in PWD from your local machine. You can see that in figure 15.8.

The other option for secure remote access is SSH; the advantage here is that the Docker CLI uses the standard SSH client, and there's no need to make any config changes to the Docker Engine. There are no certificates to create or manage, as authentication is handled by the SSH server. On your Docker machine you need to create a system user for everyone you want to permit remote access; they use those credentials when they run any Docker commands against the remote machine.

**TRY IT NOW**  Back in your PWD session, make a note of the IP address for node1, and then click to create another node. Run these commands to manage the Docker Engine that's on node1 from the command line on node2 using SSH:

```
# save the IP address of node1 in a variable:
node1ip="<node1-ip-address-goes-here>"

# open an SSH session to verify the connection:
ssh root@$node1ip
exit

# list the local containers on node2:
docker container ls

# and list the remote containers on node1:
docker -H ssh://root@$node1ip container ls
```

Saving the PWD port 2376 domain name in a variable—the domain is different for every port on every node in every PWD session.

The Engine is configured for TLS—it listens for traffic but rejects requests that don't have the client cert.

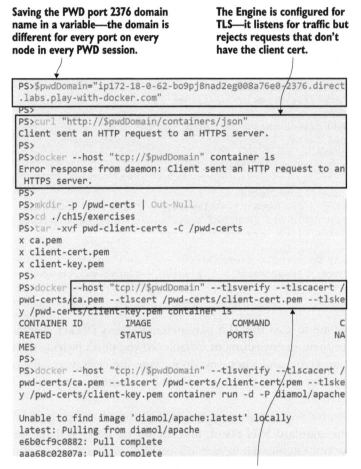

```
PS>$pwdDomain="ip172-18-0-62-bo9pj8nad2eg008a76e0-2376.direct
.labs.play-with-docker.com"
PS>
PS>curl "http://$pwdDomain/containers/json"
Client sent an HTTP request to an HTTPS server.
PS>
PS>docker --host "tcp://$pwdDomain" container ls
Error response from daemon: Client sent an HTTP request to an
 HTTPS server.
PS>
PS>mkdir -p /pwd-certs | Out-Null
PS>cd ./ch15/exercises
PS>tar -xvf pwd-client-certs -C /pwd-certs
x ca.pem
x client-cert.pem
x client-key.pem
PS>
PS>docker --host "tcp://$pwdDomain" --tlsverify --tlscacert /
pwd-certs/ca.pem --tlscert /pwd-certs/client-cert.pem --tlske
y /pwd-certs/client-key.pem container ls
CONTAINER ID         IMAGE                COMMAND              C
REATED               STATUS               PORTS                NA
MES
PS>
PS>docker --host "tcp://$pwdDomain" --tlsverify --tlscacert /
pwd-certs/ca.pem --tlscert /pwd-certs/client-cert.pem --tlske
y /pwd-certs/client-key.pem container run -d -P diamol/apache

Unable to find image 'diamol/apache:latest' locally
latest: Pulling from diamol/apache
e6b0cf9c0882: Pull complete
aaa68c02807a: Pull complete
```

Using the correct TLS certs means you can run any Docker command locally and it executes on the PWD node.

Figure 15.8   You can only work with a TLS-secured Docker Engine if you have the client certs.

Play with Docker makes this very simple, because it provisions nodes with all they need to connect to each other. In a real environment you'd need to create users, and if you want to avoid typing passwords you'd also need to generate keys and distribute the public key to the server and the private key to the user. You can see from my output in figure 15.9 that this is all done in the Play with Docker session, and it works with no special setup.

Ops people will have mixed feelings about using Docker over SSH. On the one hand, it's much easier than managing certificates, and if your organization has a lot of Linux admin experience, it's nothing new. On the other hand, it means giving server

I've created two nodes in this PWD session. The terminal window is currently connected to `node2`.

PWD is already set up so that I can connect to other nodes using SSH without entering a password.

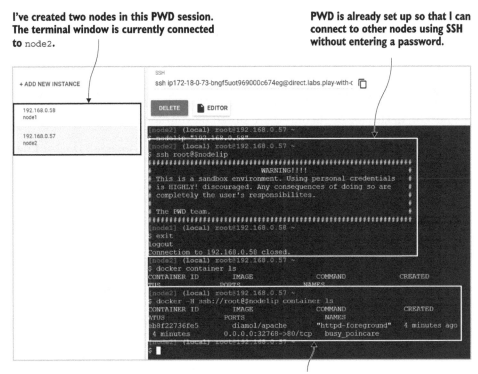

That's it—when SSH is configured, you can use it with the Docker command line without any extra setup on the Docker Engine.

**Figure 15.9    Play with Docker configures the SSH client between nodes so you can use it with Docker.**

access to anyone who needs Docker access, which might be more privilege than they need. If your organization is primarily Windows, you can install the OpenSSH server on Windows and use the same approach, but it's very different from how admins typically manage Windows server access. TLS might be a better option in spite of the certificate overhead because it's all handled within Docker and it doesn't need an SSH server or client.

Securing access to your Docker Engine with TLS or SSH gives you encryption (the traffic between the CLI and the API can't be read on the network) and authentication (users have to prove their identity in order to connect). The security doesn't provide authorization or auditing, so you can't restrict what a user can do, and you don't have any record of what they did do. That's something you'll need to be aware of when you consider who needs access to which environments. Users also need to be careful which environments they use—the Docker CLI makes it super-easy to switch to a remote engine, and it's a simple mistake to delete volumes containing important test data because you thought you were connected to your laptop.

## 15.3   *Using Docker Contexts to work with remote engines*

You can point your local Docker CLI to a remote machine using the host parameter, along with all the TLS cert paths if you're using a secured channel, but it's awkward to do that for every command you run. Docker makes it easier to switch between Docker Engines using Contexts. You create a Docker Context using the CLI, specifying all the connection details for the Engine. You can create multiple contexts, and all the connection details for each context are stored on your local machine.

> **TRY IT NOW**   Create a context to use your remote TLS-enabled Docker Engine running in PWD:
>
> ```
> # create a context using your PWD domain and certs:
> docker context create pwd-tls --docker
>     "host=tcp://$pwdDomain,ca=/tmp/pwd-certs/ca.pem,cert=/tmp/pwd-
>     certs/client-cert.pem,key=/tmp/pwd-certs/client-key.pem"
>
> # for SSH it would be:
> # docker context create local-tls --docker "host=ssh://user@server"
>
> # list contexts:
> docker context ls
> ```

You'll see in your output that there's a default context that points to your local Engine using the private channel. My output in figure 15.10 is from a Windows machine, so the default channel uses named pipes. You'll also see that there's a Kubernetes endpoint option—you can use Docker contexts to store the connection details for Kubernetes clusters too.

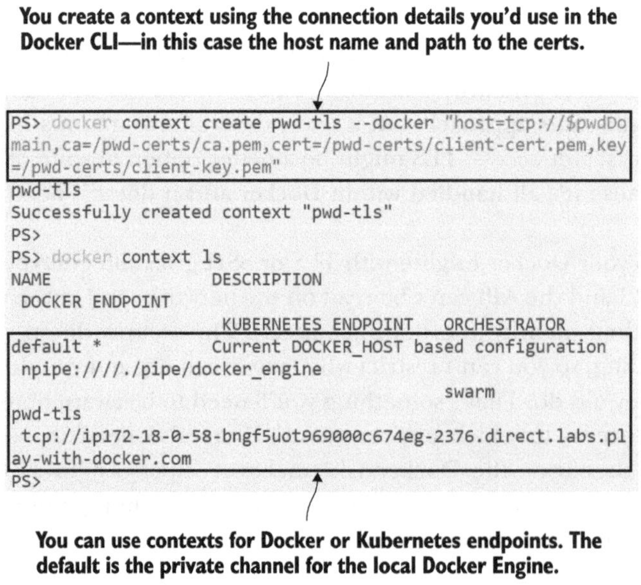

**You create a context using the connection details you'd use in the Docker CLI—in this case the host name and path to the certs.**

```
PS> docker context create pwd-tls --docker "host=tcp://$pwdDo
main,ca=/pwd-certs/ca.pem,cert=/pwd-certs/client-cert.pem,key
=/pwd-certs/client-key.pem"
pwd-tls
Successfully created context "pwd-tls"
PS>
PS> docker context ls
NAME               DESCRIPTION
 DOCKER ENDPOINT
                   KUBERNETES ENDPOINT   ORCHESTRATOR
default *          Current DOCKER_HOST based configuration
 npipe://////./pipe/docker_engine
                                         swarm
pwd-tls
 tcp://ip172-18-0-58-bngf5uot969000c674eg-2376.direct.labs.pl
ay-with-docker.com
PS>
```

**You can use contexts for Docker or Kubernetes endpoints. The default is the private channel for the local Docker Engine.**

Figure 15.10   Adding a new context by specifying the remote host name and the TLS certificate paths

Contexts contain all the information you need to switch between local and remote Docker Engines. This exercise used a TLS-secured engine, but you can run the same command with an SSH-secured engine by replacing the host parameter and cert paths with your SSH connection string.

Contexts can connect your local CLI to other machines on your local network or on the public internet. There are two ways to switch contexts—you can do it temporarily for the duration of one terminal session, or you can do it permanently so it works across all terminal sessions until you switch again.

> **TRY IT NOW**  When you switch contexts, your Docker commands are sent to the selected engine—you don't need to specify host parameters. You can switch temporarily with an environment variable or permanently with the context use command:

```
# switch to a named context with an environment variable - this is the
# preferred way to switch contexts, because it only lasts for this
# session

# on Windows:
$env:DOCKER_CONTEXT='pwd-tls'

# OR Linux:
export DOCKER_CONTEXT='pwd-tls'

# show the selected context:
docker context ls

# list containers on the active context:
docker container ls

# switch back to the default context - switching contexts this way is
# not recommended because it's permanent across sessions:
docker context use default

# list containers again:
docker container ls
```

The output is probably not what you expect, and you need to be careful with contexts because of these different ways of setting them. Figure 15.11 shows my output, with the context still set to the PWD connection, even though I've switched back to the default.

The context you set with `docker context use` becomes the system-wide default. Any new terminal windows you open, or any batch process you have running Docker commands, will use that context. You can override that using the `DOCKER_CONTEXT` environment variable, which takes precedence over the selected context and only applies to the current terminal session. If you regularly switch between contexts, I find that it's a good practice to always use the environment variable option and leave the default context as your local Docker Engine. Otherwise it's easy to start the day by

**You can switch contexts for the current terminal session by setting an environment variable—the value is the name of the context.**

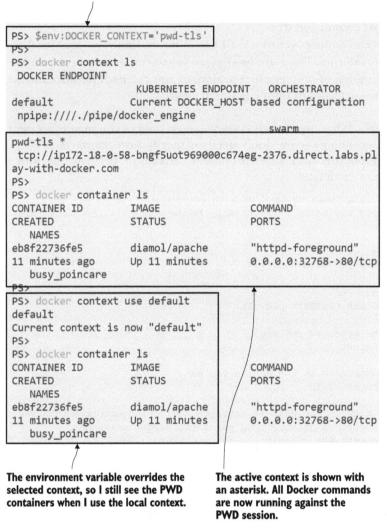

```
PS> $env:DOCKER_CONTEXT='pwd-tls'
PS>
PS> docker context ls
 DOCKER ENDPOINT
                          KUBERNETES ENDPOINT    ORCHESTRATOR
default                   Current DOCKER_HOST based configuration
 npipe://///./pipe/docker_engine
                                                  swarm
pwd-tls *
 tcp://ip172-18-0-58-bngf5uot969000c674eg-2376.direct.labs.pl
ay-with-docker.com
PS>
PS> docker container ls
CONTAINER ID         IMAGE                   COMMAND
CREATED              STATUS                  PORTS
   NAMES
eb8f22736fe5         diamol/apache           "httpd-foreground"
11 minutes ago       Up 11 minutes           0.0.0.0:32768->80/tcp
   busy_poincare
PS>
PS> docker context use default
default
Current context is now "default"
PS>
PS> docker container ls
CONTAINER ID         IMAGE                   COMMAND
CREATED              STATUS                  PORTS
   NAMES
eb8f22736fe5         diamol/apache           "httpd-foreground"
11 minutes ago       Up 11 minutes           0.0.0.0:32768->80/tcp
   busy_poincare
```

**The environment variable overrides the selected context, so I still see the PWD containers when I use the local context.**

**The active context is shown with an asterisk. All Docker commands are now running against the PWD session.**

**Figure 15.11   There are two ways to switch contexts, and if you mix them you'll get confused.**

clearing out all your running containers, forgetting that yesterday you set your context to use the production server.

Of course, you shouldn't need to regularly access the production Docker servers. As you get further along your container journey, you'll take more advantage of the easy automation Docker brings and get to a place where the only users with access to Docker are the uber-admins and the system account for the CI/CD pipeline.

## 15.4 Adding continuous deployment to your CI pipeline

Now that we have a remote Docker machine with secure access configured, we can write a complete CI/CD pipeline, building on the work we did with Jenkins in chapter 11. That pipeline covered the continuous integration (CI) stages—building and testing the app in containers and pushing the built image to a Docker registry. The continuous Deployment (CD) stages add to that, deploying to a testing environment for final signoff and then to production.

The difference between the CI stages and the CD stages is that the CI builds all happen locally using the Docker Engine on the build machine, but the deployment needs to happen with the remote Docker Engines. The pipeline can use the same approach we've taken in the exercises, using Docker and Docker Compose commands with a host argument pointing to the remote machine, and providing security credentials. Those credentials need to live somewhere, and it absolutely must not be in source control—the people who need to work with source code are not the same people who need to work with production servers, so the credentials for production shouldn't be widely available. Most automation servers let you store secrets inside the build server and use them in pipeline jobs, and that separates credential management from source control.

> **TRY IT NOW** We'll spin up a local build infrastructure similar to chapter 11, with a local Git server, Docker registry, and Jenkins server all running in containers. There are scripts that run when this Jenkins container starts to create credentials from the PWD certificate files on your local machine, so the CD stages will deploy to PWD:

```
# switch to the folder with the Compose files:
cd ch15/exercises/infrastructure

# start the containers - using Windows containers:
docker-compose -f ./docker-compose.yml -f ./docker-compose-windows.yml
    up -d

# OR with Linux containers:
docker-compose -f ./docker-compose.yml -f ./docker-compose-linux.yml
    up -d
```

When the containers are running, browse to Jenkins at http://localhost:8080/credentials and log in with username `diamol` and password `diamol`. You'll see that the certificates for the Docker CA and the client connection are already stored in Jenkins—they were loaded from the PWD certs on your machine, and they're available to use in jobs. Figure 15.12 shows the certificates loaded as Jenkins credentials.

This is a fresh build infrastructure running in all-new containers. Jenkins is all configured and ready to go thanks to the automation scripts it uses, but the Git server needs some manual setup. You'll need to browse to http://localhost:3000 and complete the installation, create a user called `diamol`, and then create a repository called

Jenkins supports different types of credentials. These are secret files that can be presented to jobs while they're running. The certs were loaded from my local machine into the container using Jenkins startup scripts.

**Figure 15.12   Using Jenkins credentials to provide TLS certs for pipelines to connect to Docker on PWD**

diamol. If you need a refresher on that, you can flip back to chapter 11—figures 11.3, 11.4, and 11.5 show you what to do.

The pipeline we'll be running in this section builds a new version of the timecheck app from chapter 12, which just prints the local time every 10 seconds. The scripts are all ready to go in the source code for this chapter, but you need to make a change to the pipeline to add your own PWD domain name. Then when the build runs, it will run the CI stages and deploy from your local container to your PWD session. We'll pretend PWD is both the user-acceptance test environment and production.

**TRY IT NOW**   Open up the pipeline definition file in the folder ch15/exercises— use Jenkinsfile if you're running Linux containers and Jenkinsfile.windows if you're using Windows containers. In the environment section there are variables for the Docker registry domain and the User Acceptance Testing (UAT) and production Docker Engines. Replace pwd-domain with your actual PWD domain, and be sure to include the port, :80, after the domain— PWD listens on port 80 externally, and it maps that to port 2376 in the session:

```
environment {
    REGISTRY = "registry.local:5000"
    UAT_ENGINE = "ip172-18-0-59-bngh3ebjagq000ddjbv0-
2376.direct.labs.play-with-docker.com:80"
    PROD_ENGINE = "ip172-18-0-59-bngh3ebjagq000ddjbv0-
2376.direct.labs.play-with-docker.com:80"
}
```

Now you can push your changes to your local Git server:

```
git remote add ch15 http://localhost:3000/diamol/diamol.git

git commit -a -m 'Added PWD domains'

git push ch15

# Gogs will ask you to login -
# use the diamol username and password you registered in Gogs
```

Now browse to Jenkins at http://localhost:8080/job/diamol/ and click Build Now.

This pipeline starts in the same way as the chapter 11 pipeline: fetching the code from Git, building the app with a multi-stage Dockerfile, running the app to test that it starts, and then pushing the image to the local registry. Then come the new deployment stages: first there's a deployment to the remote UAT engine and then the pipeline stops, waiting for human approval to continue. This is a nice way to get started with CD, because every step is automated, but there's still a manual quality gate, and that can be reassuring for organizations that aren't comfortable with automatic deployments to production. You can see in figure 15.13 that the build has passed up to the UAT stage, and now it's stopped at Await Approval.

**The CI stages of the pipeline build and run the app in containers and then push the built image to the registry.**

**The deployment runs containers on the remote engine, which is configured to be PWD.**

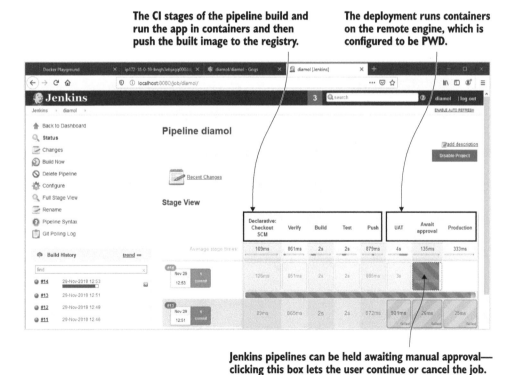

**Jenkins pipelines can be held awaiting manual approval— clicking this box lets the user continue or cancel the job.**

**Figure 15.13**   The CI/CD pipeline in Jenkins has deployed to UAT and is awaiting approval to continue.

Your manual approval stage could involve a whole day of testing with a dedicated team, or it could be a quick sanity check that the new deployment looks good in a production-like environment. When you're happy with the deployment, you go back to Jenkins and signal your approval. Then it goes on to the final stage—deploying to the production environment.

**TRY IT NOW**    Back in your PWD session, check that the timecheck container is running and that it's writing out the correct logs:

```
docker container ls

docker container logs timecheck-uat_timecheck_1
```

I'm sure everything will be fine, so back to Jenkins and click the blue box in the Await Approval stage. A window pops up asking for confirmation to deploy—click Do It! The pipeline will continue.

It's getting exciting now—we're nearly there with our production deployment. You can see my output in figure 15.14, with the UAT test in the background and the approval stage in the foreground.

**On PWD the app is running in the UAT configuration. This was deployed from Jenkins running in Docker on my local machine, using TLS to connect to the PWD session.**

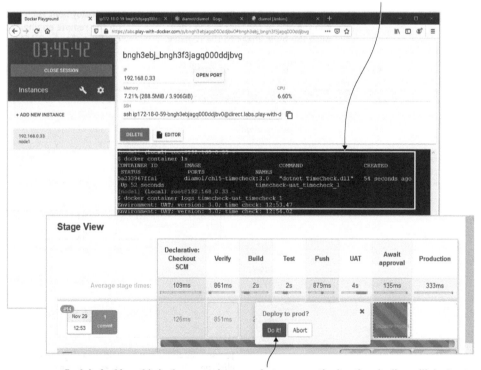

**Back in Jenkins, this is the manual approval stage—continuing the pipeline will deploy to production.**

Figure 15.14    The UAT deployment has worked correctly and the app is running in PWD. On to production!

The CD stages of the pipeline don't do anything more complex than the CI stages. There's a script file for each stage that does the work using a single Docker Compose command, joining together the relevant override files (this could easily be a `docker stack deploy` command if the remote environment is a Swarm cluster). The deployment scripts expect the TLS certificate paths and Docker host domain to be provided in environment variables, and those variables are set up in the pipeline job.

It's important to keep that separation between the actual work that's done with the Docker and Docker Compose CLIs, and the organization of the work done in the pipeline. That reduces your dependency on a particular automation server and makes it easy to switch between them. Listing 15.3 shows part of the Jenkinsfile and the batch script that deploy to UAT.

> **Listing 15.3  Passing Docker TLS certs to the script file using Jenkins credentials**

```
# the deployment stage of the Jenkinsfile:

stage('UAT') {
  steps {
    withCredentials(
      [file(credentialsId: 'docker-ca.pem', variable: 'ca'),
       file(credentialsId: 'docker-cert.pem', variable: 'cert'),
       file(credentialsId: 'docker-key.pem', variable: 'key')]) {
         dir('ch15/exercises') {
           sh 'chmod +x ./ci/04-uat.bat'
           sh './ci/04-uat.bat'
           echo "Deployed to UAT"
      }
    }
  }
}


# and the actual script just uses Docker Compose:

docker-compose \
  --host tcp://$UAT_ENGINE --tlsverify \
  --tlscacert $ca --tlscert $cert --tlskey $key \
  -p timecheck-uat -f docker-compose.yml -f docker-compose-uat.yml \
up -d
```

Jenkins provides the TLS certs for the shell script from its own credentials. You could move this build to GitHub Actions and you'd just need to mimic the workflow using secrets stored in the GitHub repo—the build scripts themselves wouldn't need to change. The production deployment stage is almost identical to UAT; it just uses a different set of Compose files to specify the environment settings. We're using the same PWD environment for UAT and production, so when the job completes you'll be able to see both deployments running.

**TRY IT NOW** Back to the PWD session for one last time, and you can check that your local Jenkins build has correctly deployed to the UAT and production environments:

```
docker container ls
```

```
docker container logs timecheck-prod_timecheck_1
```

My output is in figure 15.15. We have a successful CI/CD pipeline running from Jenkins in a local container and deploying to two remote Docker environments (which just happen to be the same one in this case).

I'm using the same PWD session to represent UAT and production, so both containers are running here. I could use separate nodes in PWD for each environment, but in reality these would be Docker servers or clusters.

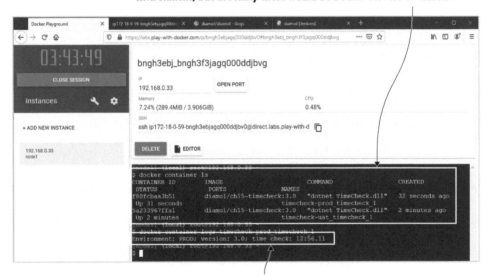

The production environment is running using the latest version 3.0 app, so the pipeline looks good.

Figure 15.15 The deployment on PWD. To use a real cluster, I'd just change the domain name and certs.

This is amazingly powerful. It doesn't take any more than a Docker server to run containers for different environments and a machine running Docker for the CI/CD infrastructure. You can prove this with a pipeline for your own app in a day (assuming you've already Dockerized the components), and the path to production just requires spinning up clusters and changing the deployment targets.

Before you plan out your production pipeline, however, there is one other thing to be aware of when you make your Docker Engine available remotely—even if it is secured. That's the access model for Docker resources.

## 15.5 *Understanding the access model for Docker*

This doesn't really need a whole section because the access model for Docker resources is very simple, but it gets its own section to help it stand out. Securing your Engine is about two things: encrypting the traffic between the CLI and API, and authenticating to ensure the user is allowed access to the API. There's no authorization—the access model is all or nothing. If you can't connect to the API, you can't do anything, and if you can connect to the API, you can do everything.

Whether that frightens you or not depends on your background, your infrastructure, and the maturity of your security model. You might be running internal clusters with no public access, using a separate network for your managers, with restricted IP access to that network, and you rotate the Docker CA every day. That gives you defense in depth, but there's still an attack vector from your own employees to consider (yes, I know Stanley and Minerva are great team players, but are you really sure they aren't crooks? Especially Stanley).

There are alternatives, but they get complicated quickly. Kubernetes has a role-based access control model, as does Docker Enterprise, so you can restrict which users can access resources, and what they can do with those resources. Or there's a GitOps approach that turns the CI/CD pipeline inside out, using a pull-based model so the cluster is aware when a new build has been approved, and the cluster deploys the update itself. Figure 15.16 shows that—there are no shared credentials here because nothing needs to connect to the cluster.

**Changes to source code trigger the pipeline, which builds and pushes images and generates deployment YAML files with the latest versions—they get stored in a separate Git repo.**

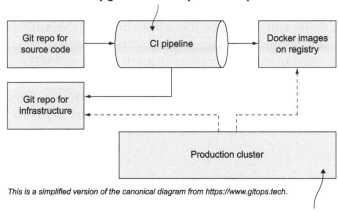

*This is a simplified version of the canonical diagram from https://www.gitops.tech.*

**A component in the production cluster monitors the image registry and the infrastructure repo for any changes. When it sees a change it grabs the latest YAMLs and images and starts the deployment itself.**

**Figure 15.16   The brave new world of GitOps—everything is stored in Git, and clusters start deployments.**

GitOps is a very interesting approach, because it makes everything repeatable and versioned—not just your application source code and the deployment YAML files, but the infrastructure setup scripts too. It gives you the single source of truth for your whole stack in Git, which you can easily audit and roll back. If the idea appeals to you but you're starting from scratch—well, it will take you a chunk of time to get there, but you can start with the very simple CI/CD pipelines we've covered in this chapter and gradually evolve your processes and tools as you gain confidence.

## 15.6   *Lab*

If you followed along with the CD exercise in section 15.4, you may have wondered how the deployment worked, because the CI stage pushed the image to your local registry and PWD can't access that registry. How did it pull the image to run the container? Well, it didn't. I cheated. The deployment override files use a different image tag, one from Docker Hub that I built and pushed myself (sorry if you feel let down, but all the images from this book are built with Jenkins pipelines, so it's the same thing really). In this lab you're going to put that right.

The missing part of the build is in stage 3, which just pushes the image to the local registry. In a typical pipeline there would be a test stage on a local server that could access that image before pushing to the production registry, but we'll skip that and just add another push to Docker Hub. This is the goal:

- Tag your CI image so it uses your account on Docker Hub and a simple "3.0" tag.
- Push the image to Docker Hub, keeping your Hub credentials secure.
- Use your own Docker Hub image to deploy to the UAT and production environments.

There are a few moving pieces here, but go through the existing pipeline carefully and you'll see what you need to do. Two hints: First, you can create a username/password credential in Jenkins and make it available in your Jenkinsfile using the withCredentials block. Second, the open port to a PWD session sometimes stops listening, so you may need to start new sessions that will need new PWD domains in the Jenkinsfile.

My solution on GitHub started as a copy of the exercises folder, so if you want to see what I changed, you can compare the files as well as check the approach: https://github.com/sixeyed/diamol/blob/master/ch15/lab/README.md.

# 16

# Building Docker images that run anywhere: Linux, Windows, Intel, and Arm

There are dozens of try-it-now exercises in this book, and if you've used different machines to follow along, you'll have seen that the exercises work in the same way on Mac, Windows, Linux, and Raspberry Pi. That's not an accident—I've built every Docker image in this book as a *multi-architecture image*. Multi-arch images are built and pushed to registries with multiple variants, each targeting a different operating system or CPU architecture, but all using the same image name. When you use one of these images to run a container or to build another image, Docker pulls the matching variant for the CPU and OS on your machine. If you use the same image name on a different architecture, you'll get a different image variant, but it will be the same app and it will work in the same way. It's a super-easy workflow for the user, but it takes some effort for the image publisher.

In this chapter you'll learn the different ways to produce multi-arch builds, but if you're thinking of skipping this one because you don't use Windows or Arm, you should at least read the first section to learn why this is a game-changing option.

## 16.1   Why multi-architecture images are important

Amazon Web Services provides different classes of compute for VMs that use Intel, AMD, or Arm processors. The Arm options (called A1 instances) are very nearly half the price of the Intel/AMD options. AWS has been the first major cloud to support Arm, but you can be sure that if the others start to lose workloads to AWS because of the savings from Arm CPUs, they'll add support too. If you can take your application and run it at nearly half the price, why wouldn't you? Well, because it's hard to get apps built for Intel to run on Arm.

On the other end of the scale, IoT devices typically run Arm processors because they're highly efficient on power consumption (hence the price reduction in the cloud), and it would be great to ship software to devices as container images too. But Arm CPU instructions are not compatible with the standard x64 instructions that Intel and AMD use. So to support Arm CPUs in the cloud or the edge (or in a datacenter full of Raspberry Pis) you need to use an application platform that can run on Arm, and you need to build your app using an Arm machine. That's the hard part that Docker solves, both for production build farms and for the developer workflow. Docker Desktop supports emulation to build Docker images and run containers with the Arm architecture, even on Intel machines.

**TRY IT NOW**    This one's not for Docker Engine or PWD users I'm afraid, because the engine alone doesn't have Arm emulation—that only comes with Docker Desktop. You can do this on Mac or Windows (in Linux container mode).

First you need to enable experimental mode from the whale icon settings—see figure 16.1.

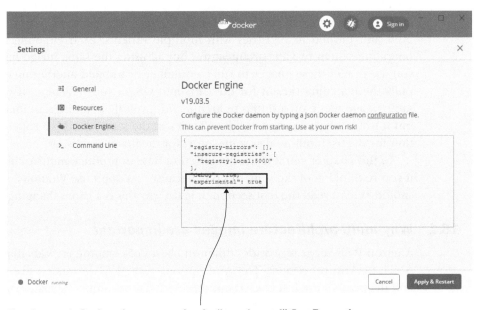

**New features in Docker often come under the "experimental" flag. To use them, you need to explicitly enable experimental mode. Some versions of Docker Desktop have a checkbox for this setting; this one lets you add it in the JSON config.**

Figure 16.1    Enabling experimental mode unlocks features that are still under development.

Now open a terminal and build an image using Arm emulation:

```
# switch to the exercises folder:
cd ch16/exercises

# build for 64-bit Arm:
docker build -t diamol/ch16-whoami:linux-arm64 --platform linux/arm64
    ./whoami

# check the architecture of the image:
docker image inspect diamol/ch16-whoami:linux-arm64 -f
    '{{.Os}}/{{.Architecture}}'

# and the native architecture of your engine:
docker info -f '{{.OSType}}/{{.Architecture}}'
```

You'll see that the image you built is targeted for the 64-bit Arm platform, even though your own machine is running on a 64-bit Intel or AMD machine. This image uses a multi-stage Dockerfile to compile and package a .NET Core application. The .NET Core platform runs on Arm, and the base images in the Dockerfile (for the SDK and the runtime) have Arm variants available. That's all you need to support cross-platform builds.

You could push this image to a registry and run a container from it on a genuine Arm machine (like the Raspberry Pi or an A1 instance in AWS) and it will work just fine. You can see my output in figure 16.2, where I've built an Arm image from an Intel machine.

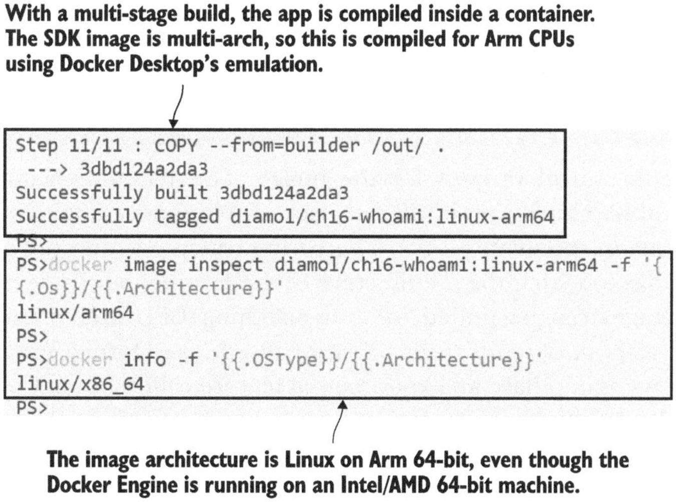

**With a multi-stage build, the app is compiled inside a container. The SDK image is multi-arch, so this is compiled for Arm CPUs using Docker Desktop's emulation.**

```
Step 11/11 : COPY --from=builder /out/ .
 ---> 3dbd124a2da3
Successfully built 3dbd124a2da3
Successfully tagged diamol/ch16-whoami:linux-arm64
PS>

PS>docker image inspect diamol/ch16-whoami:linux-arm64 -f '{
{.Os}}/{{.Architecture}}'
linux/arm64
PS>
PS>docker info -f '{{.OSType}}/{{.Architecture}}'
linux/x86_64
PS>
```

**The image architecture is Linux on Arm 64-bit, even though the Docker Engine is running on an Intel/AMD 64-bit machine.**

**Figure 16.2  Cross-platform support, building Arm images from Intel machines using emulation**

Docker knows many things about your machine, including the operating system and the CPU architecture, and it will use those as a match when you try to pull images. Pulling an image is more than just downloading the layers—there's also optimization to expand the compressed layers and get the image ready to run. That optimization only works if the image you want to use is a match for the architecture you're running on, so if there's no match, you'll get an error—you can't pull the image to even try and run a container.

> **TRY IT NOW**     You can use any Docker Engine running Linux containers to ver-
> ify this—try downloading a Microsoft Windows image:

```
# pull the Windows Nano Server image:
docker image pull mcr.microsoft.com/windows/nanoserver:1809
```

You can see my output in figure 16.3—Docker gets the OS and CPU of the current engine, and checks to see if there's a matching variant in the registry. There is no match, so the image isn't pulled and I get an error.

**This is a multi-arch image with Arm and
Intel variants, but only for Windows.**

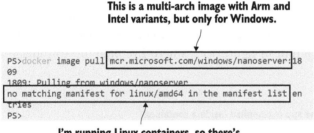

**I'm running Linux containers, so there's
no variant that matches my engine.**

**Figure 16.3   You can't pull an
image from a registry if there's
no variant to match your OS
and CPU.**

The *manifest list* is the set of variants for the image. The Windows Nano Server image isn't truly multi-architecture, it will only run on Windows containers—there are no Linux variants in the manifest list. The basic principle is that the architecture for the image has to match the architecture of the Engine, but there are a few nuances—Linux images can be pulled for non-matching CPU architectures, but containers will fail with an obscure "user process caused 'exec format error'" message. Some Windows engines have an experimental feature called Linux Containers on Windows (LCOW), so they can run Linux containers (but complex apps will fail with even more obscure logs). It's best to stick to the matching architecture for the engine, and multi-arch images let you tailor the image to each OS and CPU if you need to.

## 16.2  Building multi-arch images from one or more Dockerfiles

There are two approaches to building multi-arch images. In the first you follow the example of the `whoami` app in this chapter's exercises: write a multi-stage Dockerfile that compiles the app from source and packages it to run in a container. If the images you use for the SDK and runtime support all the architectures you want to support, you're good to go.

The huge benefit of this approach is that you have a single Dockerfile and you build it on different machines to get the architectures you want to support. I use this approach to build my own golden images for the .NET Core stack; figure 16.4 shows the approach for the SDK.

**The FROM image in the Dockerfile is multi-arch, so Docker will use the matching variant for the engine running the build.**

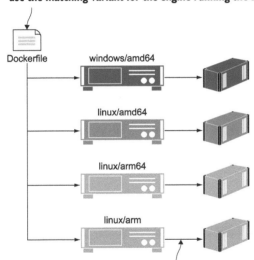

**Building the same Dockerfile on different architectures produces all the image variants ready to push to Docker Hub.**

Figure 16.4  Use a multi-stage Dockerfile based on multi-arch images to build your own multi-arch image

You can't follow this approach if your source image isn't a multi-arch image, or it doesn't support all the images you want to support. Most of the official images on Docker Hub are multi-arch, but they don't all support every variation that you might want. In that case you'll need different Dockerfiles, maybe one for Linux and one for Windows, or maybe additional ones for Arm 32-bit and 64-bit. This approach takes more management, because you have multiple Dockerfiles to maintain, but it gives you a lot more freedom to adapt behavior for each target architecture. I use this approach for my golden image for Maven (a tool to build Java apps)—figure 16.5 shows the stack.

**Multiple Dockerfiles let you tailor the steps for each architecture. Windows and Arm 32-bit images have their own Dockerfile here, but there's a shared Dockerfile for Linux on Intel and Arm 64-bit.**

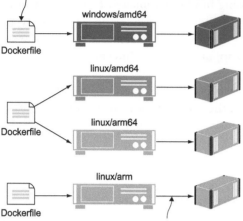

**The approach is the same—build each image variant on the native architecture—but there's a maintenance overhead with multiple Dockerfiles that need to be kept in sync.**

**Figure 16.5    You can also build multi-arch images using Dockerfiles tailored for each architecture.**

In the exercises for this chapter, there's a folder-list app that is very simple—it just prints some basic information about the runtime and then lists the contents of a folder. There are four Dockerfiles, one for each of the architectures supported in this book: Windows on Intel, Linux on Intel, Linux on 32-bit Arm, and Linux on 64-bit Arm. You can use Docker Desktop's CPU emulation with Linux containers to build and test three of those.

**TRY IT NOW**    Build images for different platforms using the Dockerfile for each platform. Each Dockerfile is slightly different, so we can compare the results when we run containers:

```
cd ./folder-list

# build for the native architecture - Intel/AMD:
docker image build -t diamol/ch16-folder-list:linux-amd64 -f
    ./Dockerfile.linux-amd64 .

# build for Arm 64-bit:
docker image build -t diamol/ch16-folder-list:linux-arm64 -f
    ./Dockerfile.linux-arm64 --platform linux/arm64 .

# and for Arm 32-bit:
docker image build -t diamol/ch16-folder-list:linux-arm -f
    ./Dockerfile.linux-arm --platform linux/arm .

# run all the containers and verify the output:
docker container run diamol/ch16-folder-list:linux-amd64
```

```
docker container run diamol/ch16-folder-list:linux-arm64

docker container run diamol/ch16-folder-list:linux-arm
```

The containers print some simple text when they run—a hardcoded string stating the OS and architecture they should be using, followed by the actual OS and CPU reported by the operating system, and then a folder list containing a single file. You can see my output in figure 16.6. Docker uses emulation where necessary, so it uses an Arm emulator when running the Arm-32 and Arm-64 Linux variants in this case.

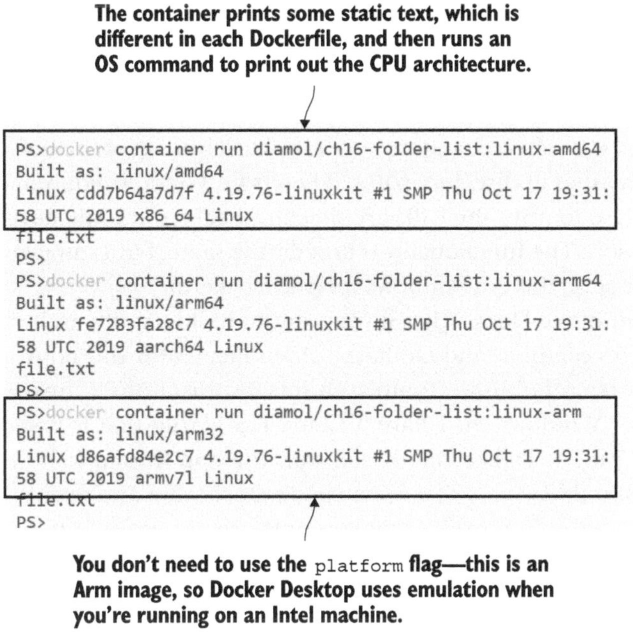

**The container prints some static text, which is different in each Dockerfile, and then runs an OS command to print out the CPU architecture.**

```
PS>docker container run diamol/ch16-folder-list:linux-amd64
Built as: linux/amd64
Linux cdd7b64a7d7f 4.19.76-linuxkit #1 SMP Thu Oct 17 19:31:
58 UTC 2019 x86_64 Linux
file.txt
PS>
PS>docker container run diamol/ch16-folder-list:linux-arm64
Built as: linux/arm64
Linux fe7283fa28c7 4.19.76-linuxkit #1 SMP Thu Oct 17 19:31:
58 UTC 2019 aarch64 Linux
file.txt
PS>
PS>docker container run diamol/ch16-folder-list:linux-arm
Built as: linux/arm32
Linux d86afd84e2c7 4.19.76-linuxkit #1 SMP Thu Oct 17 19:31:
58 UTC 2019 armv7l Linux
file.txt
PS>
```

**You don't need to use the** `platform` **flag—this is an Arm image, so Docker Desktop uses emulation when you're running on an Intel machine.**

Figure 16.6 Images are built for a specific architecture but Docker Desktop supports emulation too.

The Dockerfiles for the Linux variants are all very similar, except for the hardcoded string for the expected architecture. The Windows variant has the same behavior, but Windows has different commands to print the output. This is where multiple Dockerfiles for each architecture become useful; I can have completely different Dockerfile instructions but still get the same desired output. Listing 16.1 compares the Dockerfile for the 64-bit Arm Linux version and the 64-bit Intel Windows version.

**Listing 16.1   Dockerfiles for Linux and Windows image variants**

```
# linux
FROM diamol/base:linux-arm64

WORKDIR /app
COPY file.txt .
```

```
CMD echo "Built as: linux/arm64" && \
    uname -a && \
    ls /app

# windows
# escape=`
FROM diamol/base:windows-amd64

WORKDIR /app
COPY file.txt .

CMD echo Built as: windows/amd64 && `
    echo %PROCESSOR_ARCHITECTURE% %PROCESSOR_IDENTIFIER% && `
    dir /B C:\app
```

Each version starts with a different FROM image, which is specific to the target architecture rather than a multi-arch image. The Windows Dockerfile uses the escape keyword to change the line-break character, changing it to a backtick instead of the default backslash, so I can use backslashes in directory paths. There's no Windows equivalent of the Linux uname command, so to print the CPU architecture I echo out some environment variables that Windows sets. The functionality is broadly the same, but I can take a different path to get there because this is a Windows-specific Dockerfile.

You typically need multiple Dockerfiles if you want to build a multi-arch version of a third-party app. The Prometheus and Grafana golden images for this book are good examples. The project team publishes multi-arch images for all the Linux variants I want to use, but not for Windows. So I have a Linux Dockerfile that is based on the project image and a Windows Dockerfile that installs the app from a web download. For your own apps it should be easy to have a single Dockerfile and avoid the extra maintenance, but you need to be careful that you only use a subset of OS commands that you know work in all the target architectures. It's easy to accidentally include a command (like uname) that doesn't work on one architecture and end up with a broken variant.

> **TRY IT NOW**   There's one other Dockerfile for the folder-list app, which is an attempt at a multi-arch Dockerfile. It uses a multi-arch image as the base, but it mixes Linux and Windows commands, so the image it builds will fail on every architecture.
>
> ```
> # build the multi-arch app:
> docker image build -t diamol/ch16-folder-list .
>
> # and try to run it:
> docker container run diamol/ch16-folder-list
> ```

You'll find that the build completes successfully, so it looks like you have a good image, but the container will fail every time you run it. You can see my output in figure 16.7—I ran both Linux and Windows versions of the image, and both containers fail because the CMD instruction contains invalid commands.

**This is the Linux image variant—the container
fails because** `dir` **is not a Linux command.**

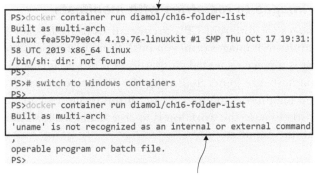

```
PS>docker container run diamol/ch16-folder-list
Built as multi-arch
Linux fea55b79e0c4 4.19.76-linuxkit #1 SMP Thu Oct 17 19:31:
58 UTC 2019 x86_64 Linux
/bin/sh: dir: not found
PS>
PS># switch to Windows containers
PS>
PS>docker container run diamol/ch16-folder-list
Built as multi-arch
'uname' is not recognized as an internal or external command
,
operable program or batch file.
PS>
```

**The Windows variant also fails because**
`uname` **is not a Windows command.**

**Figure 16.7   It's easy to build a
multi-arch image that fails at
runtime on some platforms.**

It's important to bear this in mind, especially if you use complex startup scripts. RUN instructions will fail at build time if you use an unknown OS command, but CMD instructions aren't verified, so you won't know the image is broken until you try to run a container.

One last thing here before we go on to push multi-arch images, and that's to understand which architectures Docker supports, and the various strange codenames you'll encounter when you start using them. Table 16.1 shows the major OS and architecture combinations and aliases for the CPU.

**Table 16.1   Architectures supported by Docker, with their code names**

| OS | CPU | Word Length | CPU Name | CPU Aliases |
|---|---|---|---|---|
| Windows | Intel/AMD | 64-bit | amd64 | x86_64 |
| Linux | Intel/AMD | 64-bit | amd64 | x86_64 |
| Linux | Arm | 64-bit | arm64 | aarch64, armv8 |
| Linux | Arm | 32-bit | arm | arm32v7, armv7, armhf |

Docker supports many more architectures, but these are the main ones you'll find. The amd64 CPU type is the same instruction set in Intel and AMD machines that powers practically every desktop, server, and laptop computer (Docker also supports 32-bit Intel x86 processors). 32-bit and 64-bit Arm CPUs are found in phones, IoT devices, and single-board computers; the most famous is the Raspberry Pi, which was 32-bit up until the release of the Pi4, which is 64-bit. Mainframe users aren't left out either—Docker supports IBM CPU architectures for Linux, so if you have an IBM Z,

POWER, or PowerPC machine in your basement, you can migrate your mainframe apps to Docker containers too.

## 16.3  *Pushing multi-arch images to registries with manifests*

You can build Linux images for different CPU architectures using Docker Desktop, but they don't become multi-arch images until you push them to a registry along with a manifest. The manifest is a piece of metadata that links multiple image variants to the same image tag. Manifests are generated using the Docker command line and pushed to a registry. The manifest contains a list of all the image variants, and they need to exist on the registry first, so the workflow is to create and push all the images, and then create and push the manifest.

> **TRY IT NOW**   Push the image variants of the folder-list app you've built. First you'll need to tag them with your Docker Hub ID so you can push them to your account—you don't have permission to push to the diamol organization:

```
# store your Docker ID in a variable - on Windows:
$dockerId = '<your-docker-hub-id>'

# or on Linux:
dockerId='<your-docker-hub-id>'

# tag the images with your own account name:
docker image tag diamol/ch16-folder-list:linux-amd64 "$dockerId/ch16-
    folder-list:linux-amd64"

docker image tag diamol/ch16-folder-list:linux-arm64 "$dockerId/ch16-
    folder-list:linux-arm64"

docker image tag diamol/ch16-folder-list:linux-arm "$dockerId/ch16-
    folder-list:linux-arm"

# and push to Docker Hub (this pushes all the tags for the image):
docker image push "$dockerId/ch16-folder-list"
```

You'll see all your images get pushed to Docker Hub. Docker registries are architecture-agnostic—the image specification is the same for all architectures, and the registry stores them all in the same way. Registries do know which architecture an image was built for, and they provide that to the Docker Engine as a check before it pulls them. My output is in figure 16.8—the architecture for each image is stored in the image metadata. I've included it in the tags too, but that's not a requirement.

Managing Docker manifests is a feature of the command line, but it's a new addition, so you need to enable experimental features. The CLI and the Docker Engine both support experimental features, but you have to explicitly opt-in to use them. Your engine may already be using them, but you need to enable them for the client too. You can do that in the settings on Docker Desktop, or on the command line for the Docker Engine.

You learned this in chapter 5—you can only push images to
Docker Hub if your account ID is in the image tag. This adds
new tags with my account.

```
PS>$dockerId = 'sixeyed'
PS>
PS>docker image tag diamol/ch16-folder-list:linux-amd64 "$do
ckerId/ch16-folder-list:linux-amd64"
PS>
PS>docker image tag diamol/ch16-folder-list:linux-arm64 "$do
ckerId/ch16-folder-list:linux-arm64"
PS>
PS>docker image tag diamol/ch16-folder-list:linux-arm "$dock
erId/ch16-folder-list:linux-arm"
PS>
PS>docker image push "$dockerId/ch16-folder-list"
The push refers to repository [docker.io/sixeyed/ch16-folder
-list]
ab9f7ec6b26c: Pushed
c2a1b752af4e: Pushed
f1b5933fe4b5: Mounted from diamol/base
linux-amd64: digest: sha256:8c0f5b57bbe9796198a9780c8d3730f4
e3bf7472224b1e1f1412422bc06e58fc size: 942
b423bfad7cab: Pushed
fc8ed974e69b: Pushed
7d5b9c167a1f: Mounted from diamol/base
linux-arm: digest: sha256:988286f0dbc8ac99eecda64e0464acfa52
21d1b9edab63de4335b2d6e09ac9cf size: 942
d0ec2f286967: Pushed
5b124270606a: Pushed
6d626da635fc: Mounted from diamol/base
linux-arm64: digest: sha256:5efa6540e0fb321cb2a1bb033cee10b2
360d20ada2e6da5a39fb0ea86cefa1f4 size: 942
```

You can push multiple images at once if you don't specify a
tag—Docker pushes all the tags for that image name.

Figure 16.8  Pushing all the image
variants is the first stage in making
a multi-arch image available.

**TRY IT NOW**   If you're using Docker Desktop, open Settings from the whale
menu and navigate to the Command Line section. Toggle the Enable Experimental Features flag, as in figure 16.9.

The Docker command line has its own set of experimental
features, and you need to opt in to these to work with manifests.

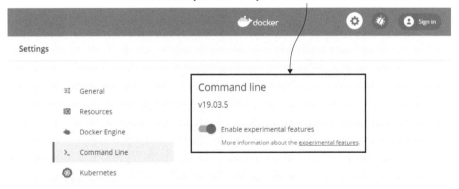

Figure 16.9   Enabling experimental features for the CLI unlocks the Docker manifest commands.

If you're using Docker Community Engine (or Enterprise Engine), edit or create the CLI config file from your home directory: `~/.docker/config.json`. You just need one setting:

```
{ "experimental":"enabled" }
```

Now that your CLI is in experimental mode, you've unlocked docker manifest commands that you can use to create manifests locally, push them to a registry, and also inspect existing manifests on a registry. Inspecting manifests is a great way to see what architectures an image supports without having to navigate the Docker Hub UI. You don't need to have pulled any of the images locally—the command reads all the metadata from the registry.

**TRY IT NOW**    Verify that your CLI is working for manifest commands by checking the published manifest of the base image for this book:

```
docker manifest inspect diamol/base
```

The manifest inspect command doesn't have a filter argument—you can't limit the output. It will show you all the image manifests for the image tag, so it works with single images as well as multi-arch images. In the output you see each image's unique digest, along with the CPU architecture and operating system. My output is in figure 16.10.

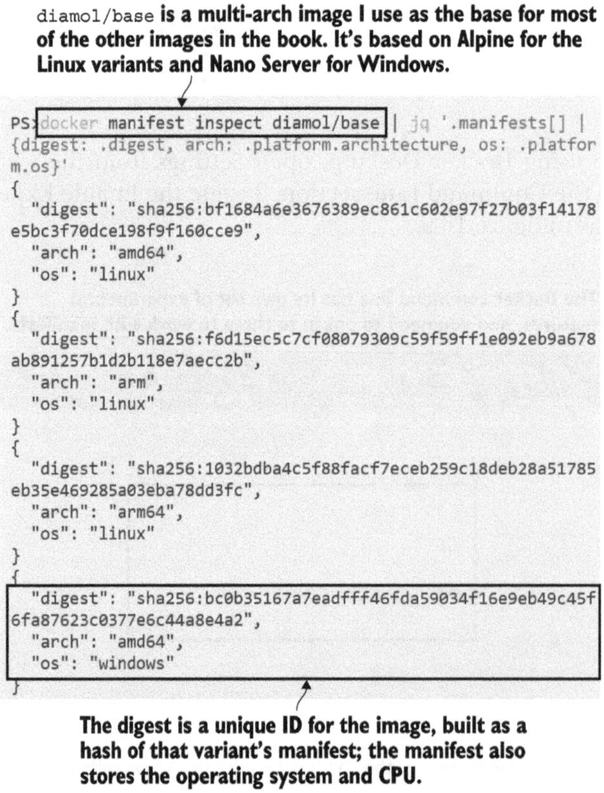

`diamol/base` **is a multi-arch image I use as the base for most of the other images in the book. It's based on Alpine for the Linux variants and Nano Server for Windows.**

```
PS docker manifest inspect diamol/base | jq '.manifests[] |
{digest: .digest, arch: .platform.architecture, os: .platfor
m.os}'
{
  "digest": "sha256:bf1684a6e3676389ec861c602e97f27b03f14178
e5bc3f70dce198f9f160cce9",
  "arch": "amd64",
  "os": "linux"
}
{
  "digest": "sha256:f6d15ec5c7cf08079309c59f59ff1e092eb9a678
ab891257b1d2b118e7aecc2b",
  "arch": "arm",
  "os": "linux"
}
{
  "digest": "sha256:1032bdba4c5f88facf7eceb259c18deb28a51785
eb35e469285a03eba78dd3fc",
  "arch": "arm64",
  "os": "linux"
}
{
  "digest": "sha256:bc0b35167a7eadfff46fda59034f16e9eb49c45f
6fa87623c0377e6c44a8e4a2",
  "arch": "amd64",
  "os": "windows"
}
```

**The digest is a unique ID for the image, built as a hash of that variant's manifest; the manifest also stores the operating system and CPU.**

**Figure 16.10   Multi-arch images have several manifests; each contains the architecture of the image.**

I used the `jq` command to filter the output, but that's just to make it easier to read; you don't need to do that yourself.

Now you can create the manifest, and just like images, it will exist on your local machine first and then you'll push it up to the registry. Technically what you're creating is a *manifest list*, which groups together a set of images under a single image tag. Every image already has its own manifest that you can inspect from the registry, but if multiple manifests are returned, you'll have a multi-architecture image. Figure 16.11 shows the relationship between images, manifests, and manifest lists.

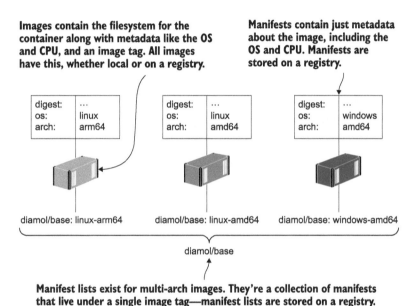

**Images contain the filesystem for the container along with metadata like the OS and CPU, and an image tag. All images have this, whether local or on a registry.**

**Manifests contain just metadata about the image, including the OS and CPU. Manifests are stored on a registry.**

**Manifest lists exist for multi-arch images. They're a collection of manifests that live under a single image tag—manifest lists are stored on a registry.**

**Figure 16.11** Manifests and manifest lists exist on a Docker registry and contain metadata about images.

You can think of a manifest list as a list of image tags, and the name of the manifest list as the name of the multi-arch image. The images you've built so far all have tags to identify the OS and CPU; you can create a manifest using the same image name without a tag, and that will be available as a multi-arch image using the default `latest` tag. You could also push your images with a tag that includes a version number in addition to the OS and CPU, and then the multi-arch tag would just be the version number.

**TRY IT NOW** Create a manifest to link all the Linux variants, and then push it to Docker Hub. The name of the manifest becomes the image tag of the multi-arch image.

```
# create a manifest with a name, followed by all the tags it lists:
docker manifest create "$dockerId/ch16-folder-list" "$dockerId/ch16-
    folder-list:linux-amd64" "$dockerId/ch16-folder-list:linux-arm64"
    "$dockerId/ch16-folder-list:linux-arm"

# push the manifest to Docker Hub:
docker manifest push "$dockerId/ch16-folder-list"

# now browse to your page on Docker Hub and check the image
```

You'll find when you browse to the image on Docker Hub that there's a latest tag with multiple variants—the UI shows the OS and CPU architecture, and the digest that uniquely identifies each image. Anyone with a Linux Docker Engine can run a container from that image, and it will run the amd64 variant on an Intel or AMD machine, the arm64 variant on an AWS A1 machine or the latest Raspberry Pi, and the arm variant on older Pis. You can see my repo on Docker Hub in figure 16.12.

**The manifest lists all the image tags I want as variants for my multi-arch image.**

**Pushing the manifest creates a multi-arch image in the registry—Docker Hub shows that there are Intel and Arm variants of the image.**

**Figure 16.12   A multi-arch image has a single name but many variants. Docker Hub shows all the variants.**

These Arm images were built with emulation in Docker Desktop, and that's only really viable for occasional builds. Emulation is slow, and not every instruction works in the same way under emulation as it does in a real CPU. If you want to support multi-arch images and you want builds to be fast and 100% accurate for the target CPU, you need a build farm. That's what I have to build the images in this book—a handful of single-board computers with different CPU architectures, set up with all the operating systems I want to support. My Jenkins jobs connect to the Docker Engine on each machine to build an image variant for each architecture and push it to Docker Hub, and then the job creates and pushes the manifest.

## 16.4 *Building multi-arch images with Docker Buildx*

There's another way to run a Docker build farm that is more efficient and far easier to use, and that's with a new feature of Docker called *Buildx*. Buildx is an extended version of the Docker build commands, and it uses a new build engine that is heavily optimized to improve build performance. It still uses Dockerfiles as the input and produces images as the output, so you can use it as a straight replacement for `docker image build`. Buildx really shines for cross-platform builds, though, because it integrates with Docker contexts, and it can distribute builds across multiple servers with a single command.

Buildx doesn't work with Windows containers right now, and it only supports building from a single Dockerfile, so it won't cover every scenario (I can't use it for building the images for this book). But if you only need to support CPU variants for Linux, it works very nicely. You use Buildx to create and manage the build farm, as well as for building images.

We'll walk through a full end-to-end example using Play with Docker so you can try out a real distributed build farm. The first step is to create a Docker context for each node in the build farm.

> **TRY IT NOW** Start by setting up your PWD session. Browse to https://play-with-docker.com and add two instances to your session. We'll use node1 for all commands. First store the IP address of node2 and verify the SSH connection; then create contexts for node1 and node2:

```
# store the IP address of node2:
node2ip=<your-node-2-ip>

# verify the ssh connection:
ssh $node2ip

#then exit so you're back in node1
exit

# create a context for node1 using the local socket:
docker context create node1 --docker
    "host=unix:///var/run/docker.sock"
```

```
# and a context for node2 using SSH:
docker context create node2 --docker "host=ssh://root@$node2ip"

# check the contexts are there:
docker context ls
```

Those contexts are there to make the Buildx setup easier. You can see my output in figure 16.13—node1 is the client where I'll run Buildx, so it uses the local channel, and it's configured to connect to node2 over SSH.

**PWD nodes are already set up to use SSH; this step verifies the connection.**

```
$ node2ip=192.168.0.7
[node1] (local) root@192.168.0.8 ~
$ ssh $node2ip
The authenticity of host '192.168.0.7 (192.168.0.7)' can't be established.
RSA key fingerprint is SHA256:ZoNwaA7uSGeRX00ftDttcTr3vSKx1Pdh00SnktPc9fs.
Are you sure you want to continue connecting (yes/no/[fingerprint])? yes
Warning: Permanently added '192.168.0.7' (RSA) to the list of known hosts.
#####################################################################
#                       WARNING!!!!                                 #
# This is a sandbox environment. Using personal credentials         #
# is HIGHLY! discouraged. Any consequences of doing so are          #
# completely the user's responsibilites.                           #
#                                                                   #
# The PWD team.                                                     #
#####################################################################
[node2] (local) root@192.168.0.7 ~
$ exit
logout
Connection to 192.168.0.7 closed.
[node1] (local) root@192.168.0.8 ~
$ docker context create node1 --docker "host=unix:///var/run/docker.sock"
node1
Successfully created context "node1"
[node1] (local) root@192.168.0.8 ~
$ docker context create node2 --docker "host=ssh://root@$node2ip"
node2
Successfully created context "node2"
[node1] (local) root@192.168.0.8 ~
$ docker context ls
NAME              DESCRIPTION                              DOCKER ENDPOINT
default *         Current DOCKER_HOST based configuration  unix:///var/run/docker.sock
node1                                                      unix:///var/run/docker.sock
node2                                                      ssh://root@192.168.0.7
```

**These contexts can be used by buildx to start two simultaneous builds.**

Figure 16.13  Buildx can use Docker contexts to set up a build farm, so creating contexts is the first step.

Setting up your contexts is the first step in creating a build farm. In a real environment your automation server would be the Buildx client, so you'd create your Docker contexts in Jenkins (or whichever system you use). You'd have one or more machines for every architecture you want to support, and you'd create a Docker context for each of them. The machines don't need to be clustered with Swarm or Kubernetes; they can be standalone machines just used for building images.

Next you need to install and configure Buildx. Buildx is a Docker CLI plugin—the client is already installed in Docker Desktop and the latest Docker CE releases (you can check by running `docker buildx`). PWD doesn't have Buildx, so we'll need to manually install it and then set up a builder that uses both our nodes.

**TRY IT NOW** Buildx is a Docker CLI plugin—to use it you need to download the binary and add it to your CLI plugins folder:

```
# download the latest Buildx binary:
wget -O ~/.docker/cli-plugins/docker-buildx
    https://github.com/docker/buildx/releases/download/v0.3.1/buildx-
    v0.3.1.linux-amd64

# set the file to be executable:
chmod a+x ~/.docker/cli-plugins/docker-buildx

# now the plugin is there, use it to create a builder using node1:
docker buildx create --use --name ch16 --platform linux/amd64 node1

# and add node2 to the builder:
docker buildx create --append --name ch16 --platform linux/386 node2

# check the builder setup:
docker buildx ls
```

Buildx is very flexible. It discovers potential build nodes using Docker context, and it connects to see which platforms they support. You create a builder and add nodes to it, and you can either let Buildx work out which platforms each node can build, or you can be specific and limit nodes to particular platforms. That's what I've done here, so node1 will only build x64 images and node2 will only build 386 images. You can see that in figure 16.14.

Now the build farm is ready. It can build multi-arch images that can run as 32-bit or 64-bit Intel Linux containers, as long as the Dockerfile it's building uses images that support those two architectures. Buildx spins up builds concurrently across the builder nodes, sending them the Dockerfile and the folder with the Docker build context (which would normally contain your source code). You can clone the Git repository for this book in your PWD session and then build and push a multi-arch image for this exercise using a single Buildx command.

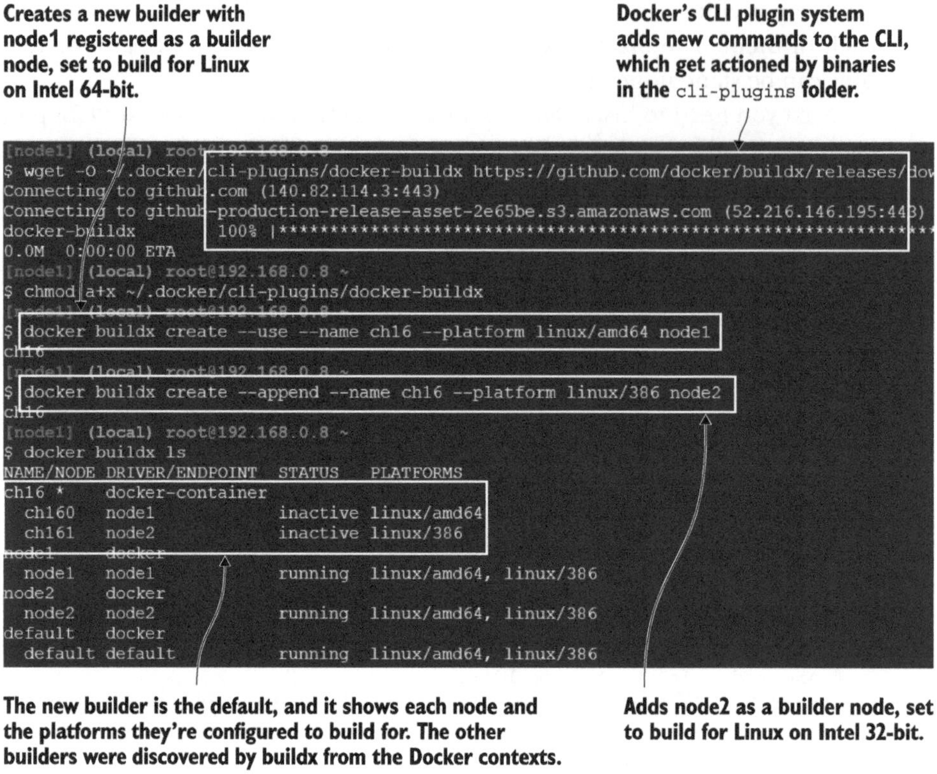

**Creates a new builder with
node1 registered as a builder
node, set to build for Linux
on Intel 64-bit.**

**Docker's CLI plugin system
adds new commands to the CLI,
which get actioned by binaries
in the `cli-plugins` folder.**

```
[node1] (local) root@192.168.0.8 ~
$ wget -O ~/.docker/cli-plugins/docker-buildx https://github.com/docker/buildx/releases/dow
Connecting to github.com (140.82.114.3:443)
Connecting to github-production-release-asset-2e65be.s3.amazonaws.com (52.216.146.195:443)
docker-buildx          100% |*******************************************************
0.0M  0:00:00 ETA
[node1] (local) root@192.168.0.8 ~
$ chmod a+x ~/.docker/cli-plugins/docker-buildx
[node1] (local) root@192.168.0.8 ~
$ docker buildx create --use --name ch16 --platform linux/amd64 node1
ch16
[node1] (local) root@192.168.0.8 ~
$ docker buildx create --append --name ch16 --platform linux/386 node2
ch16
[node1] (local) root@192.168.0.8 ~
$ docker buildx ls
NAME/NODE DRIVER/ENDPOINT   STATUS     PLATFORMS
ch16 *    docker-container
  ch160   node1             inactive  linux/amd64
  ch161   node2             inactive  linux/386
node1     docker
  node1   node1             running   linux/amd64, linux/386
node2     docker
  node2   node2             running   linux/amd64, linux/386
default   docker
  default default           running   linux/amd64, linux/386
```

**The new builder is the default, and it shows each node and
the platforms they're configured to build for. The other
builders were discovered by buildx from the Docker contexts.**

**Adds node2 as a builder node, set
to build for Linux on Intel 32-bit.**

Figure 16.14   Setting up a build farm is easy with Buildx; it uses Docker contexts to connect to engines.

**TRY IT NOW**   Clone the source code and switch to a folder that contains a
multi-arch Dockerfile for the folder-list app. Build and push multiple variants
using Buildx:

```
git clone https://github.com/sixeyed/diamol.git

cd diamol/ch16/exercises/folder-list-2/

# store your Docker Hub ID and log in so Buildx can push images:
dockerId=<your-docker-id>

docker login -u $dockerId

# use Buildx to build and push both variants using node1 and node2:
docker buildx build -t "$dockerId/ch16-folder-list-2" --platform
     linux/amd64,linux/386 --push .
```

The output from a Buildx build is impressive—it's a great thing to have running when
other people can see your screen. The client shows log lines from each builder node,

and you get lots of fast output so it looks like you're doing something immensely technical. Actually Buildx does all the work, and you'll see from the output that it even pushes the images, creates the manifest, and pushes the manifest for you. Figure 16.15 shows the end of my build and the image tags on Docker Hub.

**Buildx manages the builds across all the nodes and collects the output—this would normally be in your CI job, and you'd see these lines in the log.**

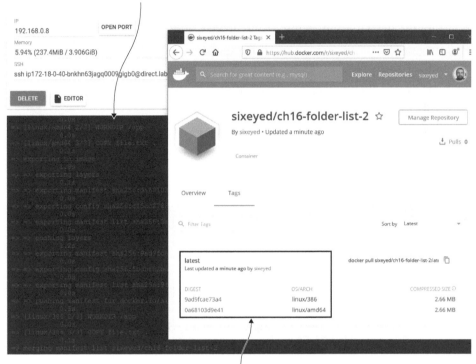

**Buildx pushes the images and the manifest list to Docker Hub—I have Linux 32-bit and 64-bit variants available for this image tag.**

Figure 16.15  Buildx distributes the Dockerfile and build context, collects logs, and pushes images.

Buildx makes these multi-arch builds very simple. You supply the nodes for each architecture you want to support, and Buildx can use them all, so your build commands don't change whether you're building for two architectures or 10. There's an interesting difference with Buildx images on Docker Hub—there are no individual image tags for the variants, there's just the single multi-arch tag. Compare that to the previous section where we manually pushed the variants and then added the manifest—all the variants had their own tags on Docker Hub, and as you build and deploy more image versions, that can get hard for users to navigate. If you don't need to support Windows containers, Buildx is the best way to build multi-arch images right now.

## 16.5   Understanding where multi-arch images fit in your roadmap

Maybe you don't need multi-arch images right now. That's fine—thanks for reading through this chapter anyway. It's definitely worth knowing how multi-arch images work, and how you can build your own, even if you don't plan to do that yet, because they may well come onto your roadmap. You may take on a project that needs to support IoT devices, or you may need to cut cloud running costs, or maybe your customers are clamoring for Windows support. Figure 16.16 shows how projects can evolve with the need to support multi-arch images, adding more variants over years when the need arises.

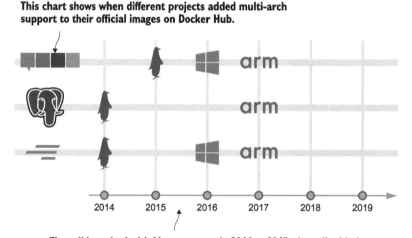

This chart shows when different projects added multi-arch support to their official images on Docker Hub.

They all launched with Linux support in 2014 or 2015; they all added Arm support in 2017. Go and NATS (a message queue) added Windows support in 2016—Postgres is still to support Windows.

Figure 16.16   Projects launch with Linux Intel support and add variants as they become popular.

You can future-proof yourself and make the switch to multi-arch images easy if you stick to two simple rules for all your Dockerfiles: always use multi-arch images in your FROM instructions, and don't include any OS-specific commands in RUN or CMD instructions. If you need some complex deployment or startup logic, you could build that into a simple utility app using the same language as your application, and compile that in another stage of the build.

All the official images on Docker Hub are multi-arch, so it's a good idea to use those as your base images (or create your own golden base images using the official images). All the golden images for this book are multi-arch too, and if you're looking for inspiration you can check the images folder in source for a large suite of examples. As a rough guide, all the modern application platforms support multi-arch (Go, Node.js, .NET Core, Java) and if you're looking for a database, Postgres is the best multi-arch option I've found.

There aren't any managed build services out there that support the full range of architectures—some support Linux and Windows, but if you also want Arm you'll need to set that up yourself. You could run a fairly cheap build farm on AWS using Linux, Windows, and Arm VMs with Docker installed. If you need Linux and Windows but not Arm, you could use a managed service like Azure DevOps or GitHub Actions. The important thing is not to assume you'll never need to support other architectures: follow best practices in your Dockerfiles to make multi-arch support easy, and know what steps you need to take to evolve your build pipeline if you do need to add multi-arch support.

## 16.6 *Lab*

This chapter's lab asks you to fix up a Dockerfile so it can be used to produce multi-arch images. It's the sort of thing you may come across if you have a Dockerfile that didn't follow my best-practice suggestions—this Dockerfile is based on an image for a specific architecture, and it uses OS commands that are not portable. I'd like you to fix the Dockerfile in the lab folder for this chapter so it can build an image targeted for Linux on Intel or Arm, and Windows on Intel. There are lots of ways to solve this; these are just a couple of hints for you:

- Some Dockerfile instructions are cross-platform, while equivalent OS commands in a `RUN` instruction may not be.
- Some Windows commands are the same as Linux, and in the golden base image for the book there are some aliases to make other Linux commands work in Windows.

You'll find my approach in the `Dockerfile.solution` file on GitHub for the chapter: https://github.com/sixeyed/diamol/blob/master/ch16/lab/README.md.

# Part 4

# Getting your containers
# ready for production

Y ou almost know it all, but there are a few more things you should master. This final part of the book focuses on some important practices you'll use before you take your containerized apps to production. You'll learn about optimizing Docker images and integrating your apps with the Docker platform—to read configuration in and write log entries out. You'll also learn some very useful architectural approaches: using a reverse proxy and a message queue. They may sound scary, but they're powerful and straightforward with Docker.

# Optimizing your Docker images for size, speed, and security

Once you have your apps containerized and working well in a cluster, you may think that you're good to go to production, but there are some best practices you still need to invest time in. Optimizing your Docker images is one of the most important, because you need your builds and deployments to be fast, your application content to be secure, and your evenings free to call your own—you do not want to be paged at 2 a.m. when your servers have run out of disk space. The Dockerfile syntax is small and intuitive, but it hides some complexity that you need to understand to make the most of your image builds.

This chapter will take you through the finer details of the image format so you know how and why to optimize it. We'll be building on chapter 3, where you learned that Docker images are actually merged from multiple image layers.

## 17.1 How you optimize Docker images

The Docker image format is heavily optimized. Layers are shared between images wherever possible, which reduces build times, network traffic, and disk usage. But Docker has a conservative approach towards data, and it doesn't automatically remove images that you've pulled—that's something you need to do explicitly. So when you replace containers to update your application, Docker will download the new image layers, but it won't remove any of the old image layers. It's easy for your disk to get swallowed up with lots of old image layers, especially on development or test machines that are regularly updating.

**TRY IT NOW**   You can see how much disk space your images are physically using with the `system df` command, which also shows container, volume, and build cache disk usage:

```
docker system df
```

If you've never cleared out old images from your Docker Engine, you'll probably be surprised at the results. My output is in figure 17.1—you can see there are 185 images totaling 7.5 GB of storage, even though I'm not running any containers.

**Shows how much disk space Docker is using, including the image cache, container writeable layers, volumes, and build cache**

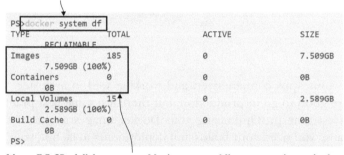

**I have 7.5 GB of disk space used by images, and I'm not running a single container. This is actually a Raspberry Pi with a 16 GB memory card, so that's nearly half the available space on the machine.**

Figure 17.1   It's easy to see your disk swallowed up by Docker images you're not even using.

This example is a mild one—I've seen unloved servers that have been running Docker for years wasting hundreds of gigabytes on unused images. It's a good habit to run `docker system prune` regularly—it clears out image layers and the build cache without removing full images. You can run it with a scheduled job to remove unused layers, but if your images are optimized it will be less of an issue. Optimizing parts of your technology stack is often a cyclical process with many small improvements, but with Docker it's very easy to make big improvements by following some simple best practices.

The first is not to include files in your image unless you need them. It sounds obvious, but you'll often write a Dockerfile that copies in a whole folder structure without realizing that the folder includes documentation or images or other binaries that aren't needed at runtime. Being explicit about the files you copy can be the first big saving you make. Compare the Dockerfiles in listing 17.1—the first example copies in a whole folder, whereas the second example realizes the copy added some extra files and includes a new step to delete them.

**Listing 17.1  Trying to optimize a Dockerfile by removing files**

```
# Dockerfile v1 - copies in the whole directory structure:
FROM diamol/base
CMD echo app- && ls app && echo docs- && ls docs
COPY . .

# Dockerfile v2 - adds a new step to delete unused files
FROM diamol/base
CMD echo app- && ls app && echo docs- && ls docs
COPY . .
RUN rm -rf docs
```

In the v2 Dockerfile, you'd think the image size would be smaller because it deletes the extra `docs` folder, but that's not how image layers work. The image is a merge of all the layers, so the files still exist from the `COPY` layer; they just get hidden in the delete layer, so the total image size doesn't shrink.

**TRY IT NOW**  Build both examples and compare the sizes

```
cd ch17/exercises/build-context

docker image build -t diamol/ch17-build-context:v1 .

docker image build -t diamol/ch17-build-context:v2 -f ./Dockerfile.v2 .

docker image ls -f reference= diamol/ch17*
```

You'll find that the v2 image is exactly the same size as the v1 image, as if the `rm` command to delete the folder hadn't been run at all. You can see my output in figure 17.2—I'm using Linux containers, so the sizes are tiny, but almost half of the size is from unnecessary files in the `docs` folder.

Each instruction in a Dockerfile produces an image layer, and layers are merged together to form the whole image. If you write files in a layer, those files are permanently there; if you delete them in a subsequent layer, all Docker does is hide them in

The v2 image deletes files, but the image size is the same.
The image is a merge of all layers, so the delete layer just
hides files from the previous layer.

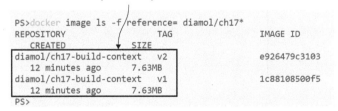

**Figure 17.2  Surprise! Deleting files doesn't reduce the image size if
the delete is in its own layer.**

the filesystem. This is a fundamental thing to understand when you come to image optimization—it's no good trying to remove bloat in later layers—you need to optimize every layer. You can easily see that the delete layer just hides the files by running an image from the previous layer, before the delete happened.

**TRY IT NOW** You can run a container from any image layer if you have those layers in your cache. Compare the final image with the previous image layer:

```
# run a container from the finished image:
docker container run diamol/ch17-build-context:v2

# check the image history to find the previous layer ID:
docker history diamol/ch17-build-context:v2

# run a container from that previous layer:
docker container run <previous-layer-id>
```

There's nothing special about the final layer in an image. You can run a container from a layer partway through the image stack, and you'll see the filesystem merged up to the point of that layer. My output is in figure 17.3—you can see that the deleted files are all available when I run a container from the previous image layer.

**The container just prints out file lists. In the final image there are no contents for the docs directory, because they were deleted in the Dockerfile.**

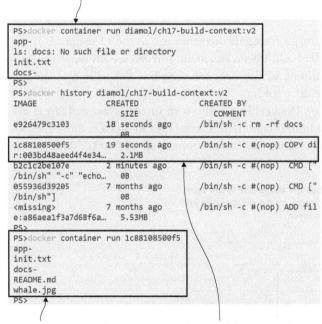

**Running a container from that penultimate layer shows the files are there—the final layer just hides the directory.**

**The penultimate layer is from the** COPY **instruction, and this layer has all the files.**

Figure 17.3 The merged filesystem hides deleted files, but you can get to them from a previous layer.

This is the first point about optimizing—don't copy anything into the image that you don't need to run the app. Even if you try to delete it in later instructions, it will still be there somewhere in the image stack taking up disk space. It's much better to be precise in your COPY instructions to only bring the files you want into the image. That makes for smaller image sizes and also a more clearly documented installation in your Dockerfile. Listing 17.2 shows the optimized v3 Dockerfile for this simple app—the only change from v1 is that it copies the app subfolder rather than the whole of the directory.

**Listing 17.2    An optimized Dockerfile that only copies necessary files**

```
FROM diamol/base
CMD echo app- && ls app && echo docs- && ls docs
COPY ./app ./app
```

When you build this, you'll see that the image size is smaller, but there's another optimization you can make here too. Docker compresses the build context (the folder where you run the build) and sends it to the engine along with the Dockerfile when you run a build. That's how you can build images on a remote engine from files on your local machine. The build context often has files you don't need, so you can exclude them from the build context by listing file paths or wildcards in a file called .dockerignore.

> **TRY IT NOW**    Build the optimized Docker image, and then build it again with a .dockerignore file to reduce the size of the context:
>
> ```
> # build the optimized image; this adds unused files to the context:
> docker image build -t diamol/ch17-build-context:v3 -f ./Dockerfile.v3 .
>
> # now rename the already prepared ignore file and check the contents:
> mv rename.dockerignore .dockerignore
> cat .dockerignore
>
> # run the same build command again:
> docker image build -t diamol/ch17-build-context:v3 -f ./Dockerfile.v3 .
> ```

You'll see that in the first build command, Docker sends 2 MB of build context to the Engine. That's not compressed, so it's the full size of the files in that folder—most of which is a 2 MB picture of a whale. In the second build there's a .dockerignore file in the current directory that tells Docker to exclude the docs folder and the Dockerfiles, so the build context then is only 4 KB. You can see my output in figure 17.4.

A .dockerignore file can save you a lot of time when you count the cost of sending unused data in the build context, and it can save space, even when you're using explicit paths in your Dockerfile. It could be you're building the code locally and also using a multi-stage build to compile in Docker—you can specify the build binaries in your .dockerignore file and be sure they won't get copied into the image. The file

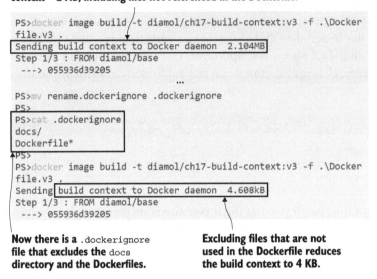

For this build there is no .dockerignore file so the whole of the current directory is sent to the engine as the build context—2 MB, including files not referenced in the Dockerfile.

```
PS>docker image build -t diamol/ch17-build-context:v3 -f .\Docker
file.v3 .
Sending build context to Docker daemon  2.104MB
Step 1/3 : FROM diamol/base
 ---> 055936d39205
                        ...
PS>mv rename.dockerignore .dockerignore
PS>
PS>cat .dockerignore
docs/
Dockerfile*
PS>
PS>docker image build -t diamol/ch17-build-context:v3 -f .\Docker
file.v3 .
Sending build context to Docker daemon  4.608kB
Step 1/3 : FROM diamol/base
 ---> 055936d39205
```

Now there is a .dockerignore file that excludes the docs directory and the Dockerfiles.

Excluding files that are not used in the Dockerfile reduces the build context to 4 KB.

Figure 17.4  Using a .dockerignore file reduces the size of the build context and the time to send it.

format is the same as Git's .gitignore file, and you can use the template for your app platform from GitHub as a good starting point (you should include the Git history folder .git if your Dockerfile is at the root of the repo too).

Now that you've seen the importance of managing which files make it into your Docker image, we're going to take a step back and look at the image you're using as a base.

## 17.2  *Choosing the right base images*

Base image size choice is as much about security as it is about disk space and network transfer time. If your base OS image is large, it probably has all sorts of tools that might be useful on a real machine but can be a security hole in a container. If your OS base image has curl installed, an attacker could use that to download malware or upload your data to their servers, if they manage to break out of your app into the container.

That's also true of application platform base images. If you're running Java apps, the OpenJDK official image is a good base, but there are many tags with different configurations of the Java runtime (the JRE) and the developer SDK (the JDK). Table 17.1 shows the size differences between the multi-arch images for the SDK versus the runtime and the most minimal versions:

**Table 17.1 Size differences between compatible Java 11 images on Docker Hub**

|  | :11-jdk | :11-jre | :11-jre-slim | :11-jre-nanoserver-1809 |
|---|---|---|---|---|
| **Linux** | 296 MB | 103 MB | 69 MB | |
| **Windows** | 2.4 GB | 2.2 GB | | 277 MB |

Linux users can use a 69 MB base image instead of 296 MB, and Windows users can use 277 MB instead of 2.4 GB, just by checking the variants on Docker Hub and picking the ones with the smallest OS image and the smallest Java installation. The Open-JDK team are cautious with their multi-arch images. They select images with the widest compatibility, but it's simple to try your app with a smaller variant. As a good rule, use Alpine or Debian Slim images as the base OS for Linux containers, and Nano Server for Windows containers (the alternative is Windows Server Core, which is pretty much the full Windows Server OS—that's where the gigabytes of disk go). Not every app will work with the smaller variants, but it's easy to switch images in your FROM lines and test it out.

Size isn't just about disk space—it's also about what's using the space. The largest OpenJDK images include the whole Java SDK, so there's a nice attack vector there if someone manages to compromise your container. They could write some Java source code files into the container's disk, compile them with the SDK, and run an app that does anything they want in the security context of your application container.

**TRY IT NOW** Among the exercises for this chapter is a Java app that uses the default JDK image. It runs a very simple REST API that always returns the value true:

```
cd ch17/exercises/truth-app

# build the image - the base image uses the :11-jdk tag:
docker image build -t diamol/ch17-truth-app .

# run the app and try it out:
docker container run -d -p 8010:80 --name truth diamol/ch17-truth-app

curl http://localhost:8010/truth
```

The container you're running has the Java REST API, which is compiled in the image, but it also has all the tools to compile other Java apps. If an attacker manages to break out of the app and run arbitrary commands on the container, they could run their own code to do whatever they liked. In this image I've "accidentally" included a test code file, and a malicious user could find and run that to change the app's behavior.

**TRY IT NOW** Simulate a container breakout by connecting to a shell in your API container. Then use the JDK to compile and run the test code and check the app again afterwards:

```
# connect to the API container - for Linux containers:
docker container exec -it truth sh

# OR for Windows containers:
docker container exec -it truth cmd

# inside the container compile and run the test Java file:
javac FileUpdateTest.java
java FileUpdateTest
exit

# back on your machine, try the API again:
curl http://localhost:8010/truth
```

You'll see that the behavior of the app has changed—the test fixture sets the response to be false instead of true. My output in figure 17.5 shows the original response and the changed response after the "hack."

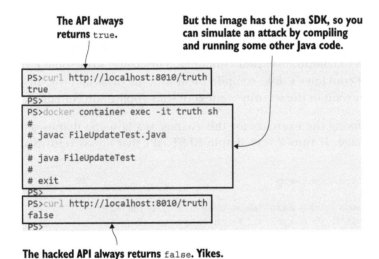

**The API always returns** true.

**But the image has the Java SDK, so you can simulate an attack by compiling and running some other Java code.**

```
PS>curl http://localhost:8010/truth
true
PS>
PS>docker container exec -it truth sh
#
# javac FileUpdateTest.java
#
# java FileUpdateTest
#
# exit
PS>
PS>curl http://localhost:8010/truth
false
PS>
```

**The hacked API always returns** false. **Yikes.**

Figure 17.5  Having the SDK in your app image leaves you open to arbitrary code execution attacks.

This is a slightly contrived example with the handy test file lying around in the image to make things easy, but container breakouts are possible, and this illustrates an interesting attack option. The container could be locked down by the platform to prevent network access, and this attack would still work. The lesson is that your base image should have all you need to run your app, but no extra tooling for building apps (interpreted languages like Node.js and Python are an exception because the build tools are necessary for the app to run).

Golden images are one way around this problem. You have a team that chooses the right base images and builds their own versions for your organization. I use that approach for this book—my Java apps are built from `diamol/openjdk`, which is a multi-arch image that uses the smallest variant for each OS. I can control how often my golden image gets updated, and I can trigger application image builds after the golden image builds. Another advantage of building your own golden image is that you can integrate additional security checks on the base layer in the build process, using a third-party tool like Anchore.

> **TRY IT NOW**    Anchore is an open source project for analyzing Docker images. The analyzer components run in Docker containers, but unfortunately they don't have multi-arch support. If you're running Linux containers on Intel (with Docker Desktop or Community Engine) you're supported; otherwise you can spin up a PWD session and clone the book's GitHub repo for this exercise.

```
cd ch17/exercises/anchore

# start all the Anchore components:
docker-compose up -d

# wait for Anchore to download its database - this can take 15 minutes,
# so you might want to open a new terminal window for this command:
docker exec anchore_engine-api_1 anchore-cli system wait

# now copy the Dockerfile for my Java golden image into the container:
docker container cp "$(pwd)/../../../images/openjdk/Dockerfile"
    anchore_engine-api_1:/Dockerfile

# and add the image and the Dockerfile for Anchore to analyze:
docker container exec anchore_engine-api_1 anchore-cli image add
    diamol/openjdk --dockerfile /Dockerfile

# wait for the analysis to complete:
docker container exec anchore_engine-api_1 anchore-cli image wait
    diamol/openjdk
```

It takes a while for Anchore to fully start up because it downloads a database of known security issues on the first run. Typically you'd integrate Anchore into your CI/CD process, so this hit would only happen when you first deploy it. The `wait` commands will keep your session blocked until Anchore is ready—you can see in figure 17.6 that I've added my OpenJDK image for scanning, but it hasn't been analyzed yet.

When Anchore completes its analysis, it knows an awful lot about your image, including the open source licenses used by all the components in the image, through to the operating system and application platform details, to security issues for any binaries in the image. Those findings could all be part of the quality gate for accepting an updated base image. If the new version uses an OSS license your organization prohibits, or if it includes critical security vulnerabilities, you might skip that update.

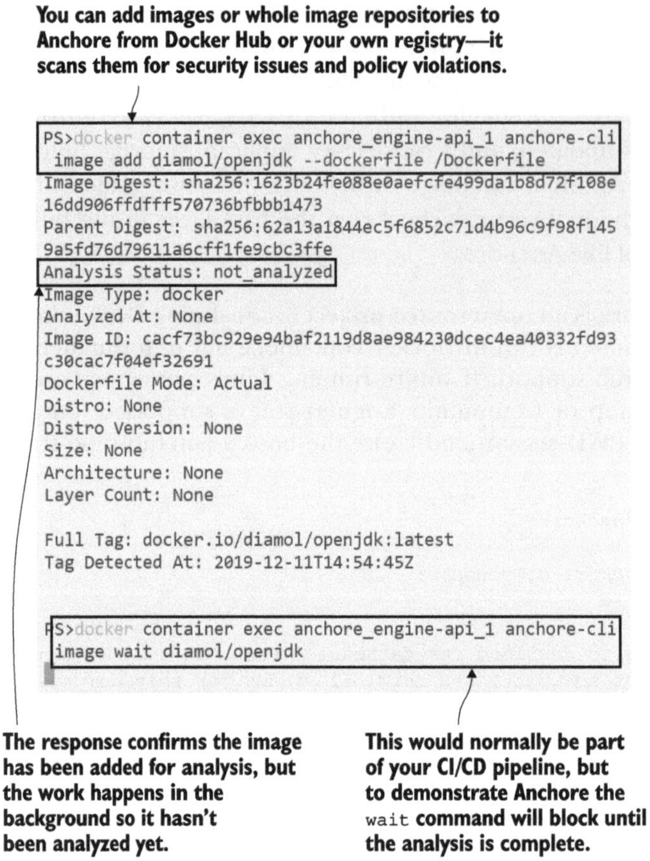

**You can add images or whole image repositories to Anchore from Docker Hub or your own registry—it scans them for security issues and policy violations.**

```
PS>docker container exec anchore_engine-api_1 anchore-cli
  image add diamol/openjdk --dockerfile /Dockerfile
Image Digest: sha256:1623b24fe088e0aefcfe499da1b8d72f108e
16dd906ffdfff570736bfbbb1473
Parent Digest: sha256:62a13a1844ec5f6852c71d4b96c9f98f145
9a5fd76d79611a6cff1fe9cbc3ffe
Analysis Status: not_analyzed
Image Type: docker
Analyzed At: None
Image ID: cacf73bc929e94baf2119d8ae984230dcec4ea40332fd93
c30cac7f04ef32691
Dockerfile Mode: Actual
Distro: None
Distro Version: None
Size: None
Architecture: None
Layer Count: None

Full Tag: docker.io/diamol/openjdk:latest
Tag Detected At: 2019-12-11T14:54:45Z


PS>docker container exec anchore_engine-api_1 anchore-cli
  image wait diamol/openjdk
```

**The response confirms the image has been added for analysis, but the work happens in the background so it hasn't been analyzed yet.**

**This would normally be part of your CI/CD pipeline, but to demonstrate Anchore the `wait` command will block until the analysis is complete.**

Figure 17.6  Using Anchore to analyze Docker images for known issues

Anchore has plugins for CI/CD tools like Jenkins, so you can apply those policies automatically in your pipeline, and you can also query the results directly using the Anchore API container.

**TRY IT NOW**  When the wait command from the previous exercise finishes, the image has been analyzed. Check what Anchore has discovered about the application platform and the image's security issues:

```
# check what Java components Anchore has found in the image:
docker container exec anchore_engine-api_1 anchore-cli image content
    diamol/openjdk java

# and check for known security issues:
docker container exec anchore_engine-api_1 anchore-cli image vuln
    diamol/openjdk all
```

These are just samples of the output that Anchore can give you—in this case it has the details of the Java runtime in the image and a large list of security vulnerabilities. At the time of writing, those vulnerabilities all had negligible severity—meaning they don't pose a significant threat, and you can probably accept them in your image. The output includes a link to the details of the vulnerability so you can read more and decide for yourself. Figure 17.7 shows the partial output from my scan results.

**Anchore knows about the major app platforms. It has found the Java runtime and knows the version details and installation path.**

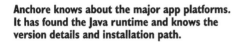

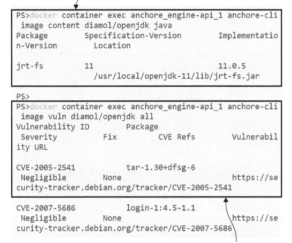

**Security issues are one of the main findings. This is a minimal base image—it has a lot of vulnerabilities but they are all of neglible severity.**

Figure 17.7 Anchore checks all the binaries in the image against its database of security vulnerabilities.

These results are acceptable because I've selected the minimal OpenJDK base image for my golden image. If you add the official `openjdk:11-jdk` image to Anchore and check the results, you'll see it has many more vulnerabilities, a lot with "unknown" severity and one "low" severity for the core SSL security library. That might not be acceptable, so you'll want to stop users basing their apps on that image, even though it's an official one maintained by the OpenJDK team.

Anchore is just one technology in this space—you can get similar features from open source projects you run yourself (like Clair), or commercial projects that can be integrated with your Docker registry (like Aqua). Tools like this really help you understand the security of your images and give you confidence in the set of golden images you build. You can run these tools on your app images too, and one of the policies you should check is that every app is building from one of your own golden images. That enforces the use of your curated, approved images.

## 17.3    *Minimizing image layer count and layer size*

A minimal and secure base image is the prerequisite for getting your app images optimized. The next step is really about setting up your image with everything your app needs and nothing else—which is a much deeper sentence than it sounds. Many processes for installing software leave residues behind because they cache package lists or deploy extra recommended packages. You can keep those under control—the details are different for different operating systems, but the general approach is the same.

> **TRY IT NOW**    Debian Linux uses APT (Advanced Package Tool) to install software. This exercise uses a simple example to show how removing unnecessary packages and clearing out the package list provides big savings (this exercise won't work with Windows containers—Play with Docker is an option instead):

```
cd ch17/exercises/socat

# the v1 image installs packages using standard apt-get commands:
docker image build -t diamol/ch17-socat:v1 .

# v2 installs the same packages but using optimization tweaks:
docker image build -t diamol/ch17-socat:v2 -f Dockerfile.v2 .

# check the image sizes:
docker image ls -f reference=diamol/ch17-socat
```

Both versions of the Dockerfile install the same two tools—curl and socat—on top of the same Debian Slim image, and they're both functionally exactly the same. But you'll see that the v2 image is almost 20 MB smaller, as my output in figure 17.8 shows.

**The v2 image optimizes the commands used to install packages—the** Out-Null **parameter I'm using just hides the build output (the same as** /dev/null **in Linux).**

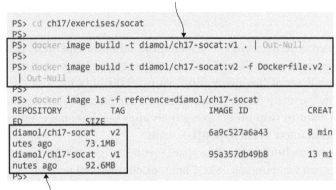

**The optimized image is 20 MB smaller, but it is functionally exactly the same.**

**Figure 17.8   Optimizing software installs reduces the image size in this exercise by over 20%.**

I used just a couple of tweaks to the install commands to get that saving. The first makes use of an APT feature to install only the listed packages and not any recommendations. The second is to combine the install steps into a single RUN instruction, which ends with a command to delete the package list cache and free up that disk space. Listing 17.3 shows the difference between the Dockerfiles.

**Listing 17.3  Installing software packages—the wrong way and the optimized way**

```
# Dockerfile - the naive install with APT:
FROM debian:stretch-slim
RUN apt-get update
RUN apt-get install -y curl=7.52.1-5+deb9u9
RUN apt-get install -y socat=1.7.3.1-2+deb9u1

# Dockerfile.v2 - optimizing the install steps:
FROM debian:stretch-slim
RUN apt-get update \
 && apt-get install -y --no-install-recommends \
    curl=7.52.1-5+deb9u9 \
    socat=1.7.3.1-2+deb9u1 \
 && rm -rf /var/lib/apt/lists/*
```

Another advantage of combining multiple steps in a single RUN instruction is that it produces a single image layer. Reducing the number of image layers isn't really an optimization. There is a maximum layer count, but it should be plenty big enough—typically 127 depending on the OS. But having fewer layers does make it much easier to keep track of your filesystem. It would be easy to put the final rm command to delete the package lists into its own RUN instruction, and arguably that makes the Dockerfile easier to read. But you know from this chapter that deleting files from a previous layer simply hides them from the filesystem, so if you did that there would be no saving on disk space.

Let's look at one more example of this pattern, which applies across all platforms. Often you need to download a package from the internet that is compressed, and then expand it. It's tempting to put the download step in a separate instruction while you're working on the Dockerfile, so you can work with the cached download layer and speed up your development time. That's fine, but once your Dockerfile is working, you need to go through and tidy up afterwards, to combine the download-expand-delete steps into a single instruction.

**TRY IT NOW**  Machine-learning datasets are a good example here, because they are large downloads that expand to even larger folder structures. In the exercises for this chapter there's an example that downloads a dataset from the University of California at Irvine (UCI) archives and extracts just one file from the dataset.

```
cd ch17/exercises/ml-dataset
```

```
# v1 downloads and expands the archive, then deletes unnecessary files:
docker image build -t diamol/ch17-ml-dataset:v1 .
```

```
# v2 downloads the archive but only expands the necessary file:
docker image build -t diamol/ch17-ml-dataset:v2 -f Dockerfile.v2 .

# compare the sizes:
docker image ls -f reference=diamol/ch17-ml-dataset
```

You'll see a massive size difference, which is purely because of the same optimization technique—making sure the layers don't have any more files than they need. My results are in figure 17.9—both images have the same single file from the data download, but one is nearly 2.5 GB and the other is only 24 MB.

**Builds the standard Dockerfile and the
v2 version, which optimizes file extraction**

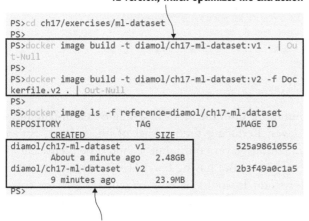

**The optimized version is a staggering 2.46 GB smaller!**

Figure 17.9   Paying close
attention to how you work with
files can save huge amounts of
disk space.

This is not such a contrived example. It's pretty common when you're iterating on a Dockerfile to keep instructions separate because that makes it easier to debug—you can run a container from a layer partway through the build and investigate the filesystem, and you can work on later instructions but keep the cached download. You can't do that when you've compressed multiple commands into one RUN instruction, but it's important to make that optimization once you're happy with your build. Listing 17.4 shows the optimized Dockerfile, which produces a single layer for the data file (the download URL is abbreviated here, but you'll see it in the source code for the chapter).

> **Listing 17.4   An optimized method for downloading and extracting files**

```
FROM diamol/base

ARG DATASET_URL=https://archive.ics.uci.edu/.../url_svmlight.tar.gz

WORKDIR /dataset
```

```
RUN wget -O dataset.tar.gz ${DATASET_URL} && \
    tar -xf dataset.tar.gz url_svmlight/Day1.svm && \
    rm -f dataset.tar.gz
```

The biggest saving here is not actually from deleting the archive; it's from extracting just the single file. The v1 approach expands the whole archive (which is where the 2 GB of disk space goes) and then deletes all the files except the desired one. Knowing how your tools behave and which features minimize disk usage helps you keep your layer size under control, as you've seen with tar in this example and APT in the previous one.

There is an alternative approach to this scenario that gives you the best developer workflow and an optimized final image, and that's using multi-stage Dockerfiles with separate stages for all the disk-hungry steps.

## 17.4 *Taking your multi-stage builds to the next level*

You first saw multi-stage builds in chapter 4 where we used one stage to compile an app from source code, and a later stage to package the compiled binaries for runtime. Multi-stage Dockerfiles should be a best practice for all but the simplest images, because they make it far easier to optimize the final image.

We can revisit the dataset downloader and use separate stages for each of the steps. Listing 17.5 shows we get a much more readable Dockerfile that way (the download URL is abbreviated again).

> **Listing 17.5  Multi-stage Dockerfiles aid readability and simplify optimization**

```
FROM diamol/base AS download
ARG DATASET_URL=https://archive.ics.uci.edu/.../url_svmlight.tar.gz
RUN wget -O dataset.tar.gz ${DATASET_URL}

FROM diamol/base AS expand
COPY --from=download dataset.tar.gz .
RUN tar xvzf dataset.tar.gz

FROM diamol/base
WORKDIR /dataset/url_svmlight
COPY --from=expand url_svmlight/Day1.svm .
```

It's clear in each stage what you're doing, and you don't need to dive into unusual command optimizations to save disk space, because the final image will only have the files explicitly copied in from earlier stages. When you build v3, you'll find it's the same size as the optimized v2 version, but it has the advantage of being easy to debug. Multi-stage Dockerfiles can be built up to a specific stage, so if you need to check the filesystem partway through the build, you can easily do so without trawling image histories to find layer IDs.

**TRY IT NOW** The `target` parameters let you stop a multi-stage build at a specific stage. Try building that v3 image with different targets:

```
cd ch17/exercises/ml-dataset

# build the full v3 image:
docker image build -t diamol/ch17-ml-dataset:v3 -f Dockerfile.v3 .

# build to the 'download' target - same Dockerfile, different tag:
docker image build -t diamol/ch17-ml-dataset:v3-download -f
    Dockerfile.v3  --target download .

# and build to the 'expand' target:
docker image build -t diamol/ch17-ml-dataset:v3-expand -f
    Dockerfile.v3   --target expand .

# check the image sizes:
docker image ls -f reference=diamol/ch17-ml-dataset:v3*
```

Now you'll have three variations of the v3 image. The full build is the same 24 MB as the optimized build, so we haven't lost any optimization moving to a multi-stage Dockerfile. The other variants stop the build at specific stages, and you can run a container from one of those images to navigate the filesystem if you need to debug. The stage builds also show where the disk space is going—you can see in figure 17.10 that the download is around 200 MB, and it expands to over 2 GB.

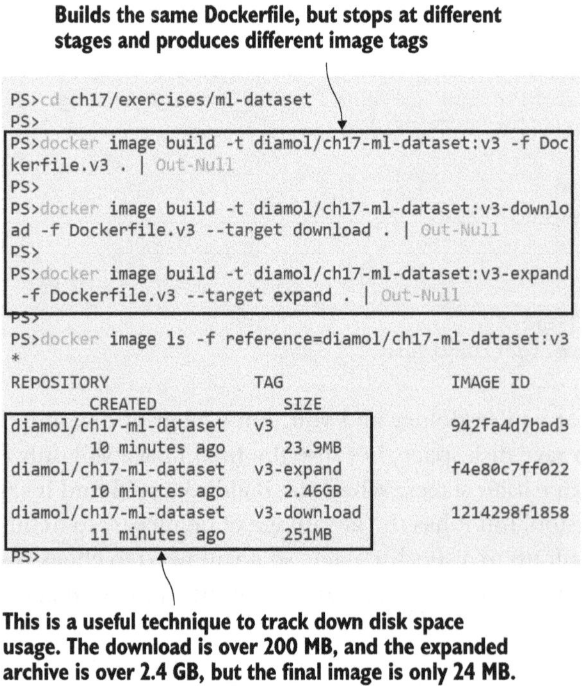

**Builds the same Dockerfile, but stops at different stages and produces different image tags**

```
PS>cd ch17/exercises/ml-dataset
PS>
PS>docker image build -t diamol/ch17-ml-dataset:v3 -f Doc
kerfile.v3 . | Out-Null
PS>
PS>docker image build -t diamol/ch17-ml-dataset:v3-downlo
ad -f Dockerfile.v3 --target download . | Out-Null
PS>
PS>docker image build -t diamol/ch17-ml-dataset:v3-expand
 -f Dockerfile.v3 --target expand . | Out-Null
PS>
PS>docker image ls -f reference=diamol/ch17-ml-dataset:v3
*

REPOSITORY               TAG           IMAGE ID
      CREATED            SIZE
diamol/ch17-ml-dataset   v3            942fa4d7bad3
     10 minutes ago      23.9MB
diamol/ch17-ml-dataset   v3-expand     f4e80c7ff022
     10 minutes ago      2.46GB
diamol/ch17-ml-dataset   v3-download   1214298f1858
     11 minutes ago      251MB
PS>
```

**This is a useful technique to track down disk space usage. The download is over 200 MB, and the expanded archive is over 2.4 GB, but the final image is only 24 MB.**

Figure 17.10  Building multi-stage Dockerfiles to specific stages lets you debug contents and check sizes.

This really is the best approach—you get an optimized image, but you can keep your Dockerfile instructions simple because you don't need to clean up disk in intermediate stages.

One final advantage of multi-stage builds really brings it home: every stage has its own build cache. If you need to tweak the `expand` stage, when you run the build, the `download` stage will still come from the cache. Maximizing the build cache is the final part of optimization, and this is all about the speed of building the image.

The basic way to make the most of the build cache is to order the instructions in your Dockerfile so the things that change least frequently are at the start, and the things that change most frequently are toward the end. This can take a few iterations to get right, because you need to understand how often the steps change, but you can typically put static setup like exposed ports, environment variables, and the application entry point at the beginning of the file. Things that change most are your application binaries and config files, and they can go toward the end. Get this right, and you can drastically reduce build times.

> **TRY IT NOW**   This exercise builds a minimal Jenkins install. It's incomplete, so don't try to run it—we're just using it for builds. The Dockerfile downloads the Jenkins Java file and sets up the initial config. The v2 Dockerfile makes good use of the cache, which you'll see when you make a content change:

```
cd ch17/exercises/jenkins

# build the v1 image and the optimized v2 image:
docker image build -t diamol/ch17-jenkins:v1 .
docker image build -t diamol/ch17-jenkins:v2 -f Dockerfile.v2 .

# now change the config file both Dockerfiles use:
echo 2.0 > jenkins.install.UpgradeWizard.state

# repeat the builds and see how long they run:
docker image build -t diamol/ch17-jenkins:v1 .
docker image build -t diamol/ch17-jenkins:v2 -f Dockerfile.v2 .
```

The second round of builds is where the cache comes in. The v1 Dockerfile copies the config file into the image before downloading the Jenkins file (which is a 75 MB download), so when the config file changes, that busts the cache and the download happens all over again. The v2 Dockerfile uses a multi-stage build and orders the instructions to put the config file copy last. I ran my exercise using the `Measure-Command` function in PowerShell to check the duration of each build (there's an equivalent called `time` in Linux). You can see in figure 17.11 that correctly ordering instructions and using a multi-stage Dockerfile cuts the build time from 10+ seconds to under a second.

Making good use of the cache lets you build and push Docker images from every change to source control without soaking up time in the CI/CD pipeline. You do need to make sure you don't over-cache things, though, because if you install or download

**The first builds with no cached layers take 10+ seconds. The
difference between v1 and v2 is the variability of the network.**

```
PS>Measure-Command { docker image build -t diamol/ch17-je
nkins:v1 . } | Select TotalMilliseconds

TotalMilliseconds
-----------------
       16526.0536


PS>Measure-Command { docker image build -t diamol/ch17-je
nkins:v2 -f Dockerfile.v2 . } | Select TotalMilliseconds

TotalMilliseconds
-----------------
       12149.1303
```

```
PS>echo 2.0 > jenkins.install.UpgradeWizard.state
PS>
```
```
PS>Measure-Command { docker image build -t diamol/ch17-je
nkins:v1 . } | Select TotalMilliseconds

TotalMilliseconds
-----------------
       28675.8448


PS>Measure-Command { docker image build -t diamol/ch17-je
nkins:v2 -f Dockerfile.v2 . } | Select TotalMilliseconds

TotalMilliseconds
-----------------
         391.5283
```

**Changing the input file busts the cache in the v1 Dockerfile, and the
download happens all over again. v2 is correctly structured, so the
cache isn't broken and only the changed layer gets executed.**

**Figure 17.11   Ordering your Dockerfile instructions correctly can
mean huge savings in build time.**

software using RUN instructions, they will be cached until the instruction changes in
the Dockerfile (assuming the cache isn't busted before that instruction). You should
always use explicit versions when you add packages to your image, so you know exactly
what you're running, and you can choose when to update. The socat example in listing 17.3 used explicit version numbers in the APT commands, and the Jenkins example used an ARG instruction for the version to download—both approaches let you use
the cache until you change the versions to install.

## 17.5 *Understanding why optimization counts*

You've seen in this chapter that you can follow some simple best practices and make your Dockerfiles a joy to work with. Those practices boil down to

- Choose the right base image—ideally curate your own set of golden images.
- Use multi-stage Dockerfiles for all but the simplest apps.
- Don't add any unnecessary packages or files—focus on layer size.
- Sort your Dockerfile instructions by change frequency—maximize the cache.

Building, pushing, and pulling images becomes a core part of your organization's workflow as you move more apps to containers. Optimizing those images can remove a lot of pain points, speed up workflows, and prevent more serious issues. Figure 17.12 shows the typical life cycle of an image, and the areas where optimization counts.

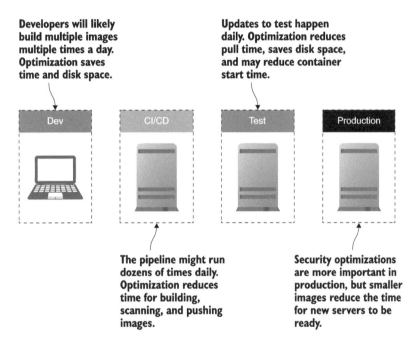

**Developers will likely build multiple images multiple times a day. Optimization saves time and disk space.**

**Updates to test happen daily. Optimization reduces pull time, saves disk space, and may reduce container start time.**

**The pipeline might run dozens of times daily. Optimization reduces time for building, scanning, and pushing images.**

**Security optimizations are more important in production, but smaller images reduce the time for new servers to be ready.**

Figure 17.12 Optimizing your Docker images has beneficial impacts across the life cycle of your projects.

## 17.6 *Lab*

Now it's time to put your optimization skills to the test. Your goal is to optimize an image that installs the Docker command line. There are Linux and Windows examples in the lab folder for this chapter; the Dockerfiles work right now, but they produce unnecessarily large images. Your goals are to

- Optimize the filesystem so the image is under 80 MB for Linux containers, or under 330 MB for Windows containers.
- Make use of the image layer cache, so repeat builds of your image take less than a second.
- Produce an image that writes the Docker CLI version correctly from `docker container run <image> docker version` (the command will give you an error for the server because it's not connected to a Docker Engine, but the CLI version should print correctly).

You shouldn't need any hints, but you'll need to think creatively when you look at the original Dockerfiles. You might not get there optimizing the existing instructions; it might be better to work backwards from the goals for the image.

My optimized files are in the same lab folder—you can also check them on GitHub: https://github.com/sixeyed/diamol/blob/master/ch17/lab/README.md.

You have the knowledge, now go optimize!

# Application configuration management in containers

18

Applications need to load their configuration from the environment they're running in, which is usually a combination of environment variables and files read from disk. Docker creates that environment for apps running in containers, and it can set environment variables and construct a filesystem from many different sources. The pieces are all there to help you build a flexible configuration approach for your apps, so when you deploy to production you're using the same image that passed all the test phases. You just need to do some work to bring the pieces together, setting up your app to merge configuration values from multiple places.

This chapter will take you through the recommended approach (and some alternatives) using examples in .NET Core, Java, Go, and Node.js. Some of the work here lives in the developer space, bringing in libraries to provide config management, and the rest lives in that gray area between dev and ops that relies on communication so both sides know how the configuration model works.

## 18.1 A multi-tiered approach to app configuration

Your configuration model should reflect the structure of the data you're storing, which is typically one of three types:

- Release-level settings, which are the same for every environment for a given release
- Environment-level settings, which are different for every environment
- Feature-level settings, which can be used to change behavior between releases

Some of those are fairly static, some are dynamic with a known set of variables, and others are dynamic with an unknown set of variables. Figure 18.1 shows some sample config settings and where they can be read from the environment.

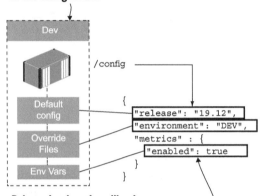

**The app is running in dev configuration. It has a config API that shows the current settings, merged from the layers in the config model.**

```
                        {
  "release": "19.12",
  "environment": "DEV",
  "metrics" : {
    "enabled": true
  }
                        }
```

**Release-level settings like the current release cycle are stored in default config in the image; environment-level settings like the environment name are in override config files loaded into the container filesystem; feature-level settings like enabling metrics can be set by environment variables.**

**Figure 18.1   A config hierarchy with settings from the image, filesystem, and environment variables**

The first example we'll use is Node.js with a popular config management library called node-config. The library lets you read config from multiple file locations in a hierarchy and override them all with environment variables. The access-log sample app in the exercises for this chapter uses the node-config library and sets up two directories to read configuration files from

- config—This will be packaged with default settings in the Docker image.
- config-override—This doesn't exist in the image but can be provisioned in the container filesystem from a volume, config object, or secret.

**TRY IT NOW**   Run the sample app with the default configuration from the image, and then the same image with an override file for the development environment:

```
cd ch18/exercises/access-log

# run a container with the default config in the image:
docker container run -d -p 8080:80 diamol/ch18-access-log
```

```
# run a container loading a local config file override:
docker container run -d -p 8081:80 -v "$(pwd)/config/dev:/app/config-
    override" diamol/ch18-access-log

# check the config APIs in each container:
curl http://localhost:8080/config
curl http://localhost:8081/config
```

The first container only uses the default config file that is packaged in the image—that specifies the name of the release cycle (19.12) and sets the Prometheus metrics to be enabled. There's an UNKNOWN setting for the environment name—if you ever see that, you know the environment-level config settings haven't been correctly applied. The second container loads a local config directory as a volume in the expected location for the app to find overrides—it sets the environment name and flips the metrics feature to off. You'll see when you call the config API that containers from the same image have applied different settings—mine is in figure 18.2.

Loading config overrides from a known path in your app code lets you provide them from any source into the container. I'm using a local bind mount, but the source could be a config object or a secret stored in a container cluster (as we saw in chapters 10

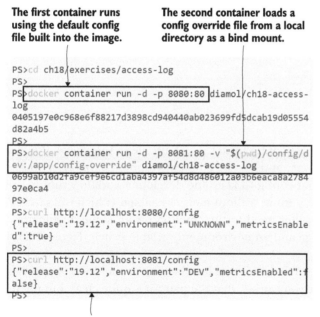

**The first container runs using the default config file built into the image.**

**The second container loads a config override file from a local directory as a bind mount.**

```
PS>cd ch18/exercises/access-log
PS>
PS>docker container run -d -p 8080:80 diamol/ch18-access-
log
0405197e0c968e6f88217d3898cd940440ab023699fd5dcab19d05554
d82a4b5
PS>
PS>docker container run -d -p 8081:80 -v "$(pwd)/config/d
ev:/app/config-override" diamol/ch18-access-log
0699ab10d2fa9cef9e6cd1aba4397af54d8d486012a03b6eaca8a2784
97e0ca4
PS>
PS>curl http://localhost:8080/config
{"release":"19.12","environment":"UNKNOWN","metricsEnable
d":true}
PS>
PS>curl http://localhost:8081/config
{"release":"19.12","environment":"DEV","metricsEnabled":f
alse}
PS>
```

**The app has a config API. In the second container, the settings for environment and metrics have come from the override file—the release name is from the default config file.**

**Figure 18.2   It's straightforward to merge config files using volumes, config objects, or secrets.**

and 13), and the behavior would be the same. There's one nuance to this pattern—your config target can either be a specific file path or a directory. A directory target is more flexible (Windows containers don't support loading volumes from a single file), but the source file names need to match the config file names the app expects. In this example the bind source is the directory config/dev, which has a single file—the container sees /app/config-override/local.json, which is where it looks for overrides.

The node-config package can also load settings from environment variables, and they override any settings loaded from the file hierarchy. This is the configuration approach recommended in "The Twelve-Factor App" (https://12factor.net)—a modern style of application architecture, where environment variables always take precedence over other config sources. It's a useful approach that helps you get into the mindset that containers are ephemeral because changing environment variables to set application config means replacing containers. Node-config has a slightly unusual implementation: rather than specifying individual settings as environment variables, you need to provide the settings as a JSON-formatted string in the environment variable.

> **TRY IT NOW**  Run a third version of the access log container in development mode but with metrics enabled. Use the volume mount to load the dev config and an environment variable to override the metrics setting:

```
cd ch18/exercises/access-log

# run a container with an override file and an environment variable:
docker container run -d -p 8082:80 -v "$(pwd)/config/dev:/app/config-
    override" -e NODE_CONFIG='{\"metrics\": {\"enabled\":\"true\"}}'
    diamol/ch18-access-log

# check the config:
curl http://localhost:8082/config
```

The third container merges config from the default file in the image, the local config override file in the volume, and the specific environment variable setting. This is a good example of building config to keep the developer workflow running smoothly. Devs can run the default settings without metrics enabled (which will save CPU cycles and memory), but when they need to turn metrics on for some debugging, they can do it with the same image and an environment variable switch. Figure 18.3 shows my output.

This is the core pattern for configuration that you should look to apply in all your apps. From this example you can see that the pattern is quite clear, but the details are significant, and that's the gray area where knowledge can break down between delivery and deployment. The access-log app lets you override the default config file with a new one, but that target file has to be in a specific location. You can also override all file settings with environment variables, but the environment variable needs to be in JSON format. Ultimately that will be documented in the YAML files you use for deployment, but you need to be aware that the pattern has the potential for mistakes.

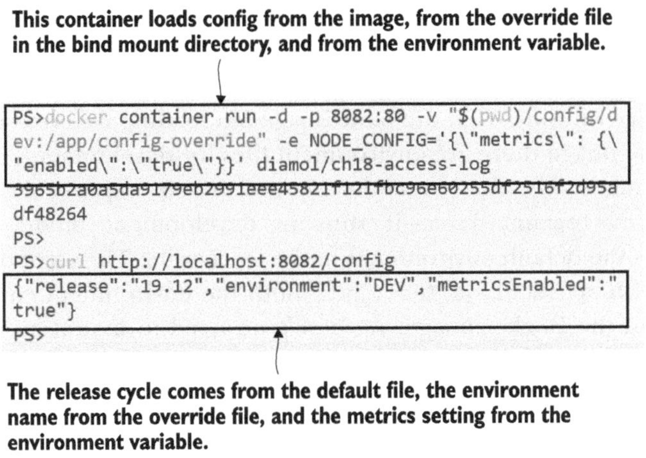

This container loads config from the image, from the override file
in the bind mount directory, and from the environment variable.

```
PS>docker container run -d -p 8082:80 -v "$(pwd)/config/d
ev:/app/config-override" -e NODE_CONFIG='{\"metrics\": {\
"enabled\":\"true\"}}' diamol/ch18-access-log
3965b2a0a5da9179eb2991eee45821f121fbc96e60255df2516f2d95a
df48264
PS>
PS>curl http://localhost:8082/config
{"release":"19.12","environment":"DEV","metricsEnabled":"
true"}
PS>
```

The release cycle comes from the default file, the environment
name from the override file, and the metrics setting from the
environment variable.

Figure 18.3  Merging config from environment variables makes it
easy to change specific features.

An alternative approach removes that risk, at the cost of making config management
less flexible.

## 18.2  *Packaging config for every environment*

Many application frameworks support a config management system where you bundle
all the config files for every environment in your deployment, and at runtime you set a
single value to specify the name of the environment you're running in. The app platform loads the config file with the matching environment name, and your app is fully
configured. .NET Core does this with its default configuration provider setup, where
config settings are merged from these sources:

- appsettings.json—The default values for all environments
- appsettings.{Environment}.json—The overrides for the named environment
- *Environment variables*—Used to specify the environment name, and for setting
  overrides

There's a new version of the to-do list app for this chapter that uses this approach of
packaging all the config files in the Docker image. You use a specific environment
variable to provide the current environment name, and that gets loaded in before the
rest of the configuration files.

> **TRY IT NOW**  Run the to-do list app with the default configuration, which is set
> with the environment name Development, and then with the test environ-
> ment settings:

```
# run the to-do list app with default config:
docker container run -d -p 8083:80 diamol/ch18-todo-list
```

```
# run the app with the config for the test environment:
docker container run -d -p 8084:80 -e DOTNET_ENVIRONMENT=Test
    diamol/ch18-todo-list
```

The two containers are running from the same image but loading different configuration files. Inside the image there are environment files for development, test, and production environments. The first container merges the core `appsettings.json` with `appsettings.Development.json`—it runs in development mode because Development is set as the default environment in the Dockerfile. The second merges `appsettings.json` with `appsettings.Test.json`. Both the environment config files are already present in the Docker image, so there's no need to mount an external source for the new config. Browse to http://localhost:8083/diagnostics to see the dev config and http://localhost:8084/diagnostics to see the test version. My output is in figure 18.4.

**The first container runs in development mode, which is the default for the image.**

**The second container switches to test mode using an environment variable—the test config file is already in the image.**

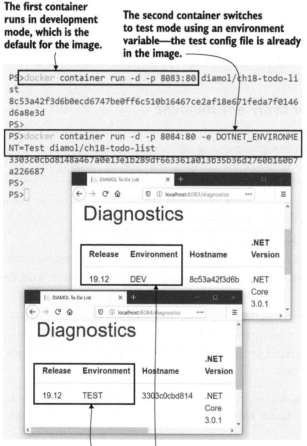

**Each container merges the default config file with the environment override file that matches the specified environment name.**

Figure 18.4  Packaging every environment's config file in the image makes it easy to switch environments.

This approach can work nicely if you have separate systems to manage your configuration files and your source code. The CI/CD pipeline can bring the config files into the Docker image as part of the build, so you keep config management separate from development. The downside is that you still can't package every setting, because you need to keep confidential information out of the Docker image. You need to have a security-in-depth approach and assume that your registry could be compromised—in that case you don't want someone to find all your passwords and API keys in nice plain-text files in your images.

If you like this approach, you still need to allow for override files, and final overrides with environment variables. The to-do list app does that, loading files from a folder called `config-overrides` if it exists, and using the standard .NET Core approach of loading environment variables last. That lets you do useful things like run the production environment locally if you're trying to replicate an issue, but override the environment settings to use a database file instead of a remote database server.

**TRY IT NOW** The to-do list app still supports config overrides, even though all the environment config is bundled in the app. If you run in production mode, the app fails because it's expecting to find a database server, but you can run in production with an override file to use a database file instead:

```
cd ch18/exercises/todo-list
```

```
docker container run -d -p 8085:80 -e DOTNET_ENVIRONMENT=Production -v
    "$(pwd)/config/prod-local:/app/config-override" diamol/ch18-todo-
    list
```

You can browse to http://localhost:8085/diagnostics and see that the app is running in production mode, but the config file override changes the database setting, so the app still works without running a Postgres container. My output is in figure 18.5.

This container merges the default `appsettings.json` file with the environment file `appsettings.Production.json` and the override file `local.json` in the prod-local folder. The setup is similar to the Node.js example, so there's some consistency around folder and file names, but .NET Core takes a different approach to setting overrides with environment variables. In node-config you pass a JSON string as an environment variable to override settings, but in .NET Core you specify individual settings as environment variables.

**TRY IT NOW** Run the same local version of production but with a custom release name by overriding that setting with an environment variable:

```
# run the container with a bind mount and a custom environment variable:
docker container run -d -p 8086:80 -e DOTNET_ENVIRONMENT=Production -e
    release=CUSTOM -v "$(pwd)/config/prod-local:/app/config-override"
    diamol/ch18-todo-list
```

Browse to http://localhost:8086/diagnostics and you'll see the custom release name from the environment variable. My output is in figure 18.6.

The bundled-config approach should still allow for overrides from
additional files and environment variables. This container runs in
production trim but with an override file. ⟍

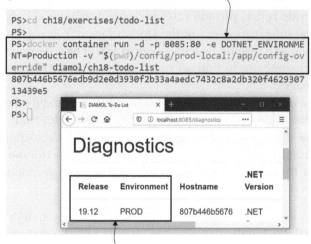

Figure 18.5    Selecting an
environment to run in should
still support config overrides
from additional files.

The config is merged from the default file and the production
override file in the image, and then the new override file in the
bind mount. The result is production-like but with dev features.

This container uses an environment variable to set the release
name—it overrides the setting from all the config files.

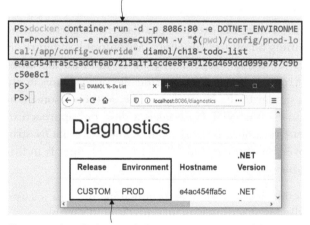

Figure 18.6    The config hierarchy
overrides values from any of the
config files with environment
variables.

The merged config is an entirely custom setup now, with values
coming from three config files and the environment variable.

I have to say I don't like this way of packaging multiple config files, although it's a
common approach across lots of app platforms. There's a danger that you'll include
some config setting in your image that you don't think is sensitive, but your security

team might disagree. Server names, URLs, file paths, logging levels, and even cache sizes could all be useful information to anyone trying to hack your system. By the time you move all the confidential settings to override files that you apply from the runtime, there's probably very little left in those packaged environment files anyway. I also don't like the split, where some settings are managed in source control and others are in a config management system.

The beauty of containers is that you can follow whichever pattern you like, so don't let me decide for you. Some approaches work better, depending on your organization and technology stack. Things get more complicated too if you have multiple stacks to deal with—you'll see that in the next example using a Go application.

## 18.3 Loading configuration from the runtime

Go has a popular configuration module called Viper, which offers much of the same functionality as the .NET Core libraries or node-config. You add the module to your package list, and in your application code you specify the paths to the config directories and whether you want environment variables brought in to override the config files. I've added it to the image gallery app for this chapter, using a similar hierarchy to the other examples:

- Files are loaded from the `config` directory first which is populated in the Docker image.
- Environment-specific files are loaded from the `config-override` directory, which is empty in the image and can be the target for a container filesystem mount.
- Environment variables override the file settings.

Viper supports a wider set of languages for configuration files than the other examples. You can use JSON or YAML, but the popular format in the Go world is TOML (named after its creator, Tom Preston-Werner). TOML is great for configuration files because it maps easily to dictionaries in code, and it's easier to read than JSON or YAML. Listing 18.1 shows the TOML configuration for the image gallery app.

> **Listing 18.1 The TOML format makes for easily managed config files**

```
release = "19.12"
environment = "UNKNOWN"

[metrics]
enabled = true

[apis]

 [apis.image]
 url = "http://iotd/image"

 [apis.access]
 url = "http://accesslog/access-log"
```

You see TOML being used in lots of cloud-native projects because it's so much easier than the alternatives. If you have a choice of formats, TOML is worth considering because "easy to read" also means easy to debug, and easy to see the differences between versions in a merge tool. Other than the file format, this example works in the same way as the Node.js app, with a default `config.toml` file packaged into the Docker image.

**TRY IT NOW**  Run the app without any additional config setup to check the defaults:

```
# run the container:
docker container run -d -p 8086:80 diamol/ch18-image-gallery

# check the config API:
curl http://localhost:8086/config
```

When you run this exercise, you'll see the current app configuration, which all comes from the default TOML file. My output is in figure 18.7, and it shows the release cycle and the default URLs for the APIs that this app consumes.

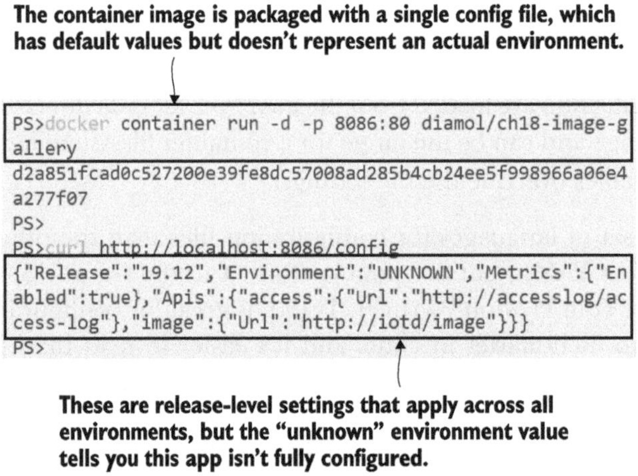

**The container image is packaged with a single config file, which has default values but doesn't represent an actual environment.**

```
PS>docker container run -d -p 8086:80 diamol/ch18-image-g
allery
d2a851fcad0c527200e39fe8dc57008ad285b4cb24ee5f998966a06e4
a277f07
PS>
PS>curl http://localhost:8086/config
{"Release":"19.12","Environment":"UNKNOWN","Metrics":{"En
abled":true},"Apis":{"access":{"Url":"http://accesslog/ac
cess-log"},"image":{"Url":"http://iotd/image"}}}
PS>
```

**These are release-level settings that apply across all environments, but the "unknown" environment value tells you this app isn't fully configured.**

Figure 18.7  You can package your app with default settings that work but aren't a complete environment.

The output is from a config API that returns JSON for the current configuration settings. A config API is a very useful feature in your app when you have multiple layers of config sources; it makes debugging configuration issues much easier, but you need to secure that data. There's no point using secrets for confidential settings if they can be publicly read by anyone who tries browsing to `/config`, so if you're going to add a config API, you need to do three things:

- Don't just publish the whole config; be selective and never include secrets.
- Secure the endpoint so only authorized users can access it.
- Make the config API a feature that can be enabled through config.

The image gallery app takes a slightly different approach from the hierarchical config model—default settings are saved in the image, but not for any specific environment. The expectation is that every environment will specify its own additional config file, which extends or overrides settings in the default file to set up the full environment.

> **TRY IT NOW** Run the same app again with an override file to build a complete environment:

```
cd ch18/exercises/image-gallery

# run the container with a bind mount to the local config directory:
docker container run -d -p 8087:80 -v "$(pwd)/config/dev:/app/config-
    override" diamol/ch18-image-gallery

# check config again:
curl http://localhost:8087/config
```

My output in figure 18.8 shows the app is now fully configured for the dev environment, merging the release-level config file in the image with the environment override file.

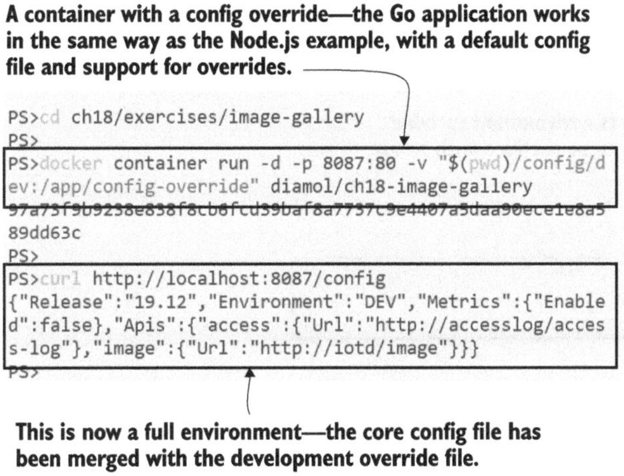

**A container with a config override—the Go application works in the same way as the Node.js example, with a default config file and support for overrides.**

```
PS>cd ch18/exercises/image-gallery
PS>
PS>docker container run -d -p 8087:80 -v "$(pwd)/config/d
ev:/app/config-override" diamol/ch18-image-gallery
97a73f9b9238e838f8cb6fcd39baf8a7737c9e4407a5daa90ece1e8a5
89dd63c
PS>
PS>curl http://localhost:8087/config
{"Release":"19.12","Environment":"DEV","Metrics":{"Enable
d":false},"Apis":{"access":{"Url":"http://accesslog/acces
s-log"},"image":{"Url":"http://iotd/image"}}}
PS>
```

**This is now a full environment—the core config file has been merged with the development override file.**

Figure 18.8 The Go Viper module merges config files in the same way as the node-config package.

Showing you all these slight variations on the config theme isn't just a cheap way to fill out the chapter. When organizations adopt Docker, they tend to find that usage accelerates quickly, and they soon have a lot of apps running in containers that each have their own opinions on configuration. Lots of small variations like this are bound to happen because the app platforms differ in the features they provide and the conventions they expect. You can apply standards at a high level—images must come packaged with default config and must support file and environment variable overrides—but the details of the config file and environment variable formats will be hard to standardize.

We'll see that in a last example with the Go application. The Viper module supports environment variables to override settings in config files, but with a convention that is different again from node-config and from .NET Core.

**TRY IT NOW**    Run the container with an environment variable override. The config model in this app only uses environment variables prefixed with IG:

```
cd ch18/exercises/image-gallery

# run the container with config override and an environment variable:
docker container run -d -p 8088:80 -v "$(pwd)/config/dev:/app/config-
    override" -e IG_METRICS.ENABLED=TRUE diamol/ch18-image-gallery

# check the config:
curl http://localhost:8088/config
```

Viper has the convention that you should prefix environment variable names so they don't clash with other environment variables. In this app, the prefix is IG, followed by an underscore, followed by the config setting name in dot notation (so IG_METRICS .ENABLED matches the enabled value in the metrics group in the TOML file). You can see from my output in figure 18.9 that this setup adds the development environment on top of the default settings but then overrides the metrics settings to enable Prometheus metrics.

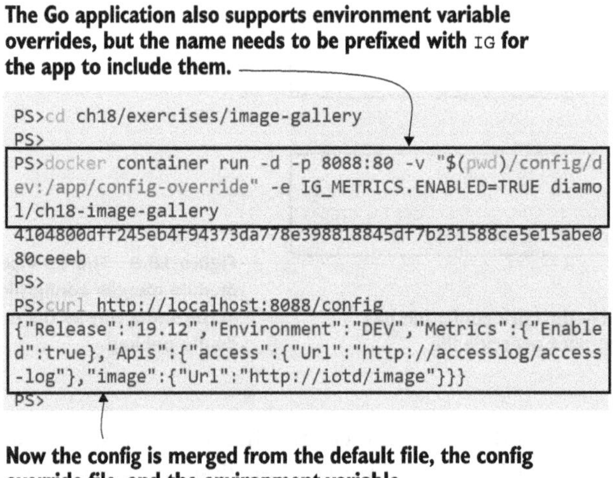

The Go application also supports environment variable overrides, but the name needs to be prefixed with IG for the app to include them. ─────────

```
PS>cd ch18/exercises/image-gallery
PS>
PS>docker container run -d -p 8088:80 -v "$(pwd)/config/d
ev:/app/config-override" -e IG_METRICS.ENABLED=TRUE diamo
l/ch18-image-gallery
4104800dff245eb4f94373da778e398818845df7b231588ce5e15abe0
80ceeeb
PS>
PS>curl http://localhost:8088/config
{"Release":"19.12","Environment":"DEV","Metrics":{"Enable
d":true},"Apis":{"access":{"Url":"http://accesslog/access
-log"},"image":{"Url":"http://iotd/image"}}}
PS>
```

Now the config is merged from the default file, the config override file, and the environment variable.

Figure 18.9    All the example apps support environment variables for config, but with small variations.

We've walked through config modeling with three different apps, and we have three slightly different approaches. The differences are manageable and easy to document in the application manifest files, and they don't actually impact how you build the image or run the container. We'll look at one last example in this chapter that takes the same configuration model and applies it to an application that doesn't have a nice new configuration library, so it needs some extra work to make it behave like a modern app.

## 18.4 *Configuring legacy apps in the same way as new apps*

Legacy apps have their own ideas about configuration, which don't usually involve environment variables or file merges. .NET Framework apps on Windows are a good example—they expect XML configuration files in specific locations. They don't like looking for files outside the application root folder, and they don't look at environment variables at all. You can still take the same configuration approach with those apps, but you need to do some extra work in your Dockerfile.

The approach here is to package a utility app or set of scripts that transform the configuration settings in the container environment into the configuration model the application expects. The exact implementation will depend on your app framework and how it uses config files, but the logic will be something like this:

1 Read in the config override settings from a specified source file in the container.
2 Read in the overrides from environment variables.
3 Merge the two sets of overrides, so environment variables take precedence.
4 Write the merged overrides to the specified target file in the container.

In the exercises for this chapter, there's an updated version of the image of the day Java API that uses this approach. It's not actually a legacy app, but I've built the image with the legacy pattern, as though the app can't use the normal container configuration options. There's a utility app that runs at startup and sets up the configuration, so although the internal configuration mechanism is different, users can configure containers in the same way as the other examples.

> **TRY IT NOW** Run the "legacy" app with default config settings and with a file override:

```
cd ch18/exercises/image-of-the-day

# run a container with default configuration:
docker container run -d -p 8089:80 diamol/ch18-image-of-the-day

# run with a config override file in a bind mount:
docker container run -d -p 8090:80 -v "$(pwd)/config/dev:/config-
    override" -e CONFIG_SOURCE_PATH="/config-
    override/application.properties" diamol/ch18-image-of-the-day

# check the config settings:
curl http://localhost:8089/config
curl http://localhost:8090/config
```

The user experience is very similar to the other apps—mounting a volume with the environment override file (and the source could be a config object or secret)—but you have to additionally specify the override file location in an environment variable so the startup utility knows where to look. You'll see in the output that the default config in the image specifies the release cycle but not the environment—that gets merged in with the override file in the second container. My output is in figure 18.10.

**The image has a settings file, so this container runs with the default config.**

**This container loads an override file in a bind mount, and the environment variable specifies the location of the override file.**

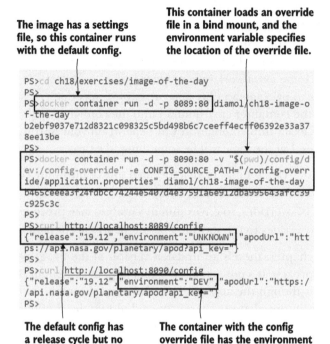

**The default config has a release cycle but no environment name.**

**The container with the config override file has the environment name merged in.**

**Figure 18.10**   This app has a utility to bootstrap the config model, but the user experience is the same.

The magic happens here in a simple Java utility app, which gets compiled and packaged in the same multi-stage build as the rest of the app. Listing 18.2 shows the key parts of the Dockerfile that build the utility and set it to run at startup.

**Listing 18.2   Building and using a config load utility in the Dockerfile**

```
FROM diamol/maven AS builder
# ...
RUN mvn package

# config util
FROM diamol/maven as utility-builder
WORKDIR /usr/src/utilities
COPY ./src/utilities/ConfigLoader.java .
RUN javac ConfigLoader.java

# app
FROM diamol/openjdk
```

```
ENV CONFIG_SOURCE_PATH="" \
    CONFIG_TARGET_PATH="/app/config/application.properties"

CMD java ConfigLoader && \
    java -jar /app/iotd-service-0.1.0.jar

WORKDIR /app
COPY --from=utility-builder /usr/src/utilities/ConfigLoader.class .
COPY --from=builder /usr/src/iotd/target/iotd-service-0.1.0.jar .
```

The important takeaway here is that you can extend your Docker image to make old apps behave in the same way as new apps. You control the startup logic, so you can run any steps you need before starting the actual application. When you do this, you're increasing the amount of time between the container starting and the app being ready, and you're also increasing the risk the container might fail (if the startup logic has an error). You should always have health checks in your image or your application manifests to mitigate that.

My config loader utility app supports the 12-factor approach that has environment variables override other settings. It merges environment variables with the override config file and writes the output as a config file in a location the app expects. The utility takes the same approach as Viper, looking for environment variables with a specific prefix that helps keep app settings separate from other settings in the container.

> **TRY IT NOW**　The legacy app doesn't use environment variables, but the config utility sets them up so the user experience is the same as a modern app.

```
# run a container with an override file and an environment variable:
docker run -d -p 8091:80 -v "$(pwd)/config/dev:/config-override" -e
    CONFIG_SOURCE_PATH="/config-override/application.properties" -e
    IOTD_ENVIRONMENT="custom" diamol/ch18-image-of-the-day

# check the config settings:
curl http://localhost:8091/config
```

The utility lets me work with my old app in the same way as my other apps. It's mostly transparent to the user—they just set environment variables and load override files into volumes. It's transparent to the app, which just reads the config files it expects to see—there are no changes to the original app code here. Figure 18.11 shows that this "legacy" app uses the modern multi-tiered configuration approach.

Now every component in the image gallery app uses the same configuration pattern. There's a level of standardization across all components, but there are also small implementation differences. Every component can be configured with a file override to run in development mode, and every component can be configured with an environment variable to enable Prometheus metrics. How you actually do that differs for each app, which is that gray area I mentioned right at the beginning—it's difficult to enforce a standard to say every component will run a Prometheus endpoint if the environment variable ENABLE_METRICS=true, because app platforms work in different ways.

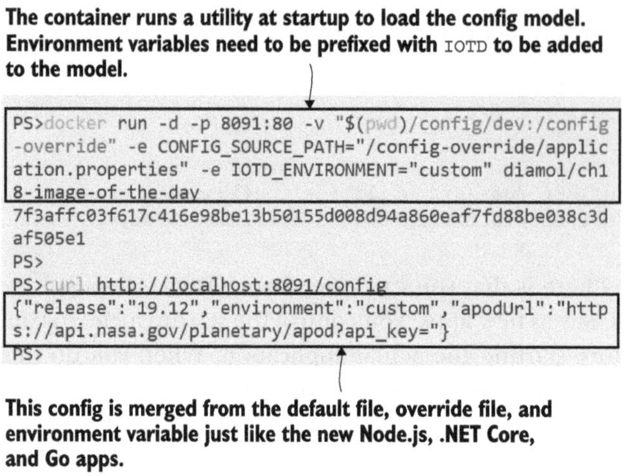

**The container runs a utility at startup to load the config model.**
**Environment variables need to be prefixed with** IOTD **to be added**
**to the model.**

```
PS>docker run -d -p 8091:80 -v "$(pwd)/config/dev:/config
-override" -e CONFIG_SOURCE_PATH="/config-override/applic
ation.properties" -e IOTD_ENVIRONMENT="custom" diamol/ch1
8-image-of-the-day
7f3affc03f617c416e98be13b50155d008d94a860eaf7fd88be038c3d
af505e1
PS>
PS>curl http://localhost:8091/config
{"release":"19.12","environment":"custom","apodUrl":"http
s://api.nasa.gov/planetary/apod?api_key="}
PS>
```

**This config is merged from the default file, override file, and**
**environment variable just like the new Node.js, .NET Core,**
**and Go apps.**

Figure 18.11  Environment
variables make the config
model for this old app behave
like new apps.

Documentation is how you remove that confusion, and in the Docker world, deployment documentation is best done in the application manifest files. There's a Docker Compose file in the exercises for this chapter that does exactly what I've laid out in the previous paragraph—setting every component to development mode, but enabling Prometheus metrics. Listing 18.3 shows the configuration parts of the Compose file.

**Listing 18.3   Documenting config settings in Docker Compose**

```
version: "3.7"

services:
  accesslog:
    image: diamol/ch18-access-log
    environment:
      NODE_CONFIG: '{"metrics": {"enabled":"true"}}'
    secrets:
      - source: access-log-config
        target: /app/config-override/local.json

  iotd:
    image: diamol/ch18-image-of-the-day
    environment:
      CONFIG_SOURCE_PATH: "/config-override/application.properties"
      IOTD_MANAGEMENT_ENDPOINTS_WEB_EXPOSURE_INCLUDE: "health,prometheus"
    secrets:
      - source: iotd-config
        target: /config-override/application.properties

  image-gallery:
    image: diamol/ch18-image-gallery
    environment:
      IG_METRICS.ENABLED: "TRUE"
```

```
    secrets:
      - source: image-gallery-config
        target: /app/config-override/config.toml

secrets:
  access-log-config:
    file: access-log/config/dev/local.json
  iotd-config:
    file: image-of-the-day/config/dev/application.properties
  image-gallery-config:
    file: image-gallery/config/dev/config.toml
```

It's a bit of a lengthy code listing, but I wanted to keep all that in one place so you can see how the patterns are the same, although the details are different. The Node.js app uses a JSON string in an environment variable to enable metrics, and it loads a JSON file as a config override.

The Java application uses an environment variable that lists the management endpoints to include; adding Prometheus in there enables metrics collection. Then it loads a config override from a properties file, which is a series of key/value pairs.

The Go application uses a simple "TRUE" string in an environment variable to enable metrics and loads the config override as a TOML file. I'm using the secret support in Docker Compose for the file sources, but the pattern is the same for volume mounts or config objects in a cluster.

The user experience here is both good and bad. It's good because you can easily load different environments by changing the source paths for the config overrides, and you can change individual settings with environment variables. It's bad because you need to know the quirks of the application. The project team will likely evolve various Docker Compose overrides to cover different configurations, so editing config settings won't be a common activity. Running the app will be far more common, and that's as easy as starting any app with Compose.

**TRY IT NOW**  Let's run the app as a whole with a fixed set of configuration for all the components. Start by removing all running containers, and then run the app with Docker Compose:

```
# clear all containers:
docker container rm -f $(docker container ls -aq)

cd ch18/exercises

# run the app with the config settings:
docker-compose up -d

# check all the config APIs:
curl http://localhost:8030/config
curl http://localhost:8020/config
curl http://localhost:8010/config
```

You can browse to http://localhost:8010 and use the app in the normal way, and browse to the Prometheus endpoints to see the component metrics (on http://localhost:8010/metrics, http://localhost:8030/metrics, and http://localhost:8020/actuator/prometheus). But actually, all the confirmation that the app is configured correctly comes from those config APIs.

You can see my output in figure 18.12. Every component loads the release cycle name from the default config file in the image, the environment name from the config override file, and the metrics setting from the environment variable.

**The compose file specifies the dev environment for every component, with a feature override in an environment variable to enable metrics.**

```
PS>cd ch18/exercises
PS>
PS>docker-compose up -d
Creating network "exercises_iotd-net" with the default dr
iver
Creating exercises_accesslog_1 ... done
Creating exercises_iotd_1        ... done
Creating exercises_image-gallery_1 ... done
PS>
PS>curl http://localhost:8030/config
{"release":"19.12","environment":"DEV","metricsEnabled":"
true"}
PS>
PS>curl http://localhost:8020/config
{"release":"19.12","environment":"DEV","managementEndpoin
ts":"health,prometheus","apodUrl":"https://api.nasa.gov/p
lanetary/apod?api_key="}
PS>
PS>curl http://localhost:8010/config
{"Release":"19.12","Environment":"DEV","Metrics":{"Enable
d":true},"Apis":{"access":{"Url":"http://accesslog/access
-log"},"image":{"Url":"http://iotd/image"}}}
PS>
```

**Each config API shows the settings for the component; all show the same release cycle from default config, the environment name from the dev override file, and the metrics setting from the environment variable.**

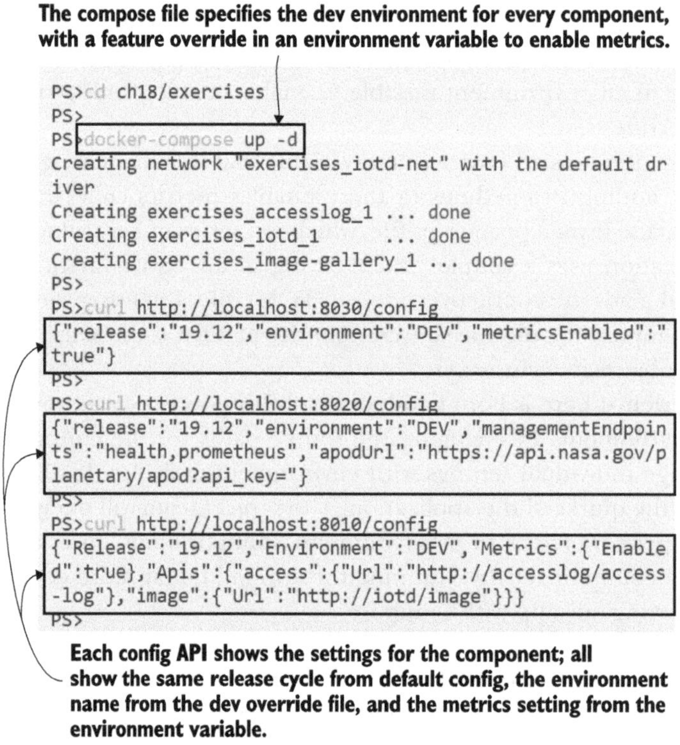

Figure 18.12   Docker Compose can document app config settings and start the app with that configuration.

That's all we really need to cover regarding the patterns for building your applications to fetch configuration from the container environment. We'll wrap up this chapter with some thoughts on where that multi-tiered configuration model can take you.

## 18.5  *Understanding why a flexible configuration model pays off*

I covered the CI/CD pipeline with Docker in chapters 11 and 15, and the core design of that pipeline is that you build one image, and your deployment process is about promoting that image through your environments up to production. Your apps will need to work slightly differently in each environment, and the way to support that while keeping the single-image approach is to use a multi-tiered configuration model.

In practice you'll use the release-level settings built into the container image, with the environment-level override file provided by the container platform in almost all cases, but the ability to set feature-level config with environment variables is a useful addition. It means you can react quickly to production issues—tuning down the level of logging if that's a performance issue, or turning off a feature that has a security hole. It also means you can create a production-like environment on a dev machine to replicate a bug, using the production config override with secrets removed, and using environment variables instead.

That ability to run the exact same image in any environment is the payback for investing time in your config model. Figure 18.13 shows the life cycle of an image from the CI/CD pipeline onwards.

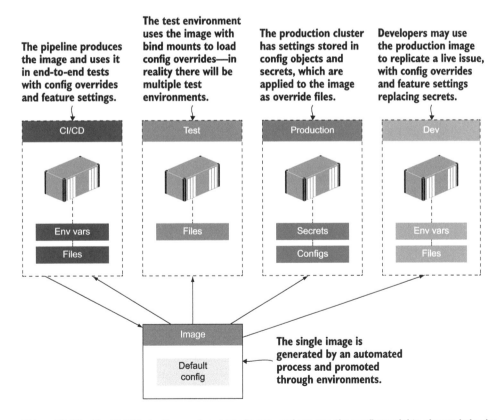

**Figure 18.13   The CI/CD pipeline produces one image, and you use the config model to change behavior.**

The work you do in producing this flexible configuration model will go a long way toward future-proofing your app. All container runtimes support loading files into the container from config objects or secrets and setting environment variables. The Docker images for this chapter's image gallery app will work in the same way with Docker Compose, Docker Swarm, or Kubernetes. And it's not just container runtimes—standard configuration files and environment variables are the models used in platform-as-a-service (PAAS) products and serverless functions too.

## 18.6  *Lab*

It can be tricky to dig into the configuration model for a new app and work out how to set override files and configure feature overrides, so you're going to get some practice in this lab. You'll be using the same image gallery app—in the lab folder for this chapter there's a Docker Compose file with the app components specified but with no configuration. Your job is to set up every component to

- Use volumes to load configuration override files.
- Load the configuration overrides for the test environment.
- Override the release cycle to be "20.01" instead of "19.12".

This should be fairly straightforward, but it will be useful to spend some time tweaking app config without making any changes to the apps. When you run the app with docker-compose up, you should be able to browse to http://localhost:8010 and the app should work. And you should be able to browse to all three config APIs and see that the release name is 20.01 and the environment is TEST.

My solution is in the same folder in the docker-compose-solution.yml file, or you can check it on GitHub here: https://github.com/sixeyed/diamol/blob/master/ch18/lab/README.md.

# Writing and managing application logs with Docker

Logging is usually the most boring part of learning a new technology, but not so with Docker. The basic principle is simple: you need to make sure your application logs are being written to the standard output stream, because that's where Docker looks for them. There are a couple of ways to achieve that, which we'll cover in this chapter, and then the fun begins. Docker has a pluggable logging framework—you need to make sure your application logs are coming out from the container, and then Docker can send them to different places. That lets you build a powerful logging model, where the application logs from all your containers are sent to a central log store with a searchable UI on top of it—all using open source components, all running in containers.

## 19.1  Welcome to stderr and stdout!

A Docker image is the snapshot of a filesystem with all your application binaries and dependencies, and also some metadata telling Docker which process to start when you run a container from the image. That process runs in the foreground, so it's like starting a shell session and then running a command. As long as the command is active, it has control of the terminal input and output. Commands write log entries to the standard output and standard error streams (called *stdout* and *stderr*), so in a terminal session you see the output in your window. In a container, Docker watches stdout and stderr and collects the output from the streams—that's the source of the container logs.

**TRY IT NOW**   You can see this easily if you run the timecheck app from chapter 15 in a container. The application itself runs in the foreground and writes log entries to stdout:

```
# run the container in the foreground:
docker container run diamol/ch15-timecheck:3.0

# exit the container with Ctrl-C when you're done
```

You'll see some log lines in your terminal, and you'll find you can't enter any more commands—the container is running in the foreground, so it's just like running the app itself in your terminal. Every few seconds the app writes another timestamp to stdout, so you'll see another line in your session window. My output is in figure 19.1.

**The container is not detached, so the logs are shown in the terminal.**

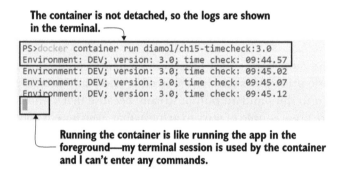

```
PS>docker container run diamol/ch15-timecheck:3.0
Environment: DEV; version: 3.0; time check: 09:44.57
Environment: DEV; version: 3.0; time check: 09:45.02
Environment: DEV; version: 3.0; time check: 09:45.07
Environment: DEV; version: 3.0; time check: 09:45.12
```

**Running the container is like running the app in the foreground—my terminal session is used by the container and I can't enter any commands.**

Figure 19.1   A container in the foreground takes over the terminal session until it exits.

This is the standard operating model for containers—Docker starts a process inside the container and collects the output streams from that process as logs. All the apps we've used in this book follow this same pattern: the application process runs in the foreground—that could be a Go binary or the Java runtime—and the application itself is configured to write logs to stdout (or stderr; Docker treats both streams in the same way). Those application logs are written to the output stream by the runtime, and Docker collects them. Figure 19.2 shows the interaction between the application, the output streams, and Docker.

Container logs are stored as JSON files, so the log entries remain available for detached containers which don't have a terminal session, and for containers that have exited so there is no application process. Docker manages the JSON files for you and they have the same life cycle as the container—when the container is removed, the log files are removed too.

**The application process writes logs
to the standard output streams.**

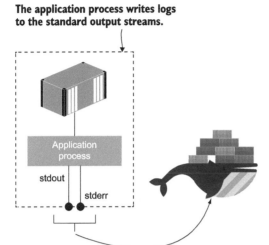

**Docker collects the output from
the streams as container logs.**

Figure 19.2  Docker watches the
application process in the container
and collects its output streams.

**TRY IT NOW**  Run a container from the same image in the background as a
detached container, and check the logs and then the path to the log file:

```
# run a detached container
docker container run -d --name timecheck diamol/ch15-timecheck:3.0

# check the most recent log entry:
docker container logs --tail 1 timecheck

# stop the container and check the logs again:
docker container stop timecheck
docker container logs --tail 1 timecheck

# check where Docker stores the container log file:
docker container inspect --format='{{.LogPath}}' timecheck
```

If you're using Docker Desktop with Linux containers, remember that the Docker
Engine is running inside a VM that Docker manages for you—you can see the path to
the log file for the container, but you don't have access to the VM, so you can't read
the file directly. If you're running Docker CE on Linux or you're using Windows containers, the path to the log file will be on your local machine, and you can open the
file to see the raw contents. You can see my output (using Windows containers) in figure 19.3.

The log file is really just an implementation detail that you don't usually need to
worry about. The format is very simple; it contains a JSON object for each log entry
with the string containing the log, the name of the stream where the log came from

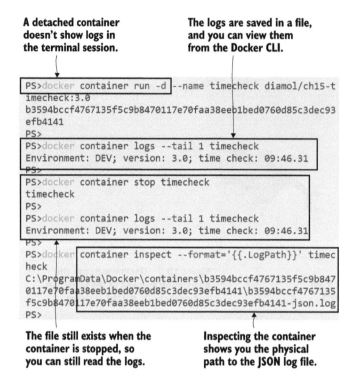

**A detached container doesn't show logs in the terminal session.**

**The logs are saved in a file, and you can view them from the Docker CLI.**

**The file still exists when the container is stopped, so you can still read the logs.**

**Inspecting the container shows you the physical path to the JSON log file.**

Figure 19.3   Docker stores container logs in a JSON file and manages the lifetime of that file.

(stdout or stderr), and a timestamp. Listing 19.1 shows a sample of the logs for my timecheck container.

> **Listing 19.1   The raw format for container logs is a simple JSON object**

```
{"log":"Environment: DEV; version: 3.0; time check:
    09:42.56\r\n","stream":"stdout","time":"2019-12-19T09:42:56.814277Z"}
{"log":"Environment: DEV; version: 3.0; time check:
    09:43.01\r\n","stream":"stdout","time":"2019-12-19T09:43:01.8162961Z"}
```

The only time you will need to think about the JSON is if you have a container that produces lots of logs, and you want to keep all the log entries for a period but have them in a manageable file structure. Docker creates a single JSON log file for each container by default, and will let it grow to any size (until it fills up your disk). You can configure Docker to use rolling files instead, with a maximum size limit, so that when the log file fills up, Docker starts writing to a new file. You also configure how many log files to use, and when they're all full, Docker starts overwriting the first file. You can set those options at the Docker Engine level so the changes apply to every container, or you can set them for individual containers. Configuring logging options for a specific container is a good way to get small, rotated log files for one application but keep all the logs for other containers.

> **TRY IT NOW** Run the same app again, but this time specifying log options to use three rolling log files with a maximum of 5 KB each:

```
# run with log options and an app setting to write lots of logs:
docker container run -d --name timecheck2 --log-opt max-size=5k --log-opt
    max-file=3 -e Timer__IntervalSeconds=1 diamol/ch15-timecheck:3.0

# wait for a few minutes

# check the logs:
docker container inspect --format='{{.LogPath}}' timecheck2
```

You'll see that the log path for the container is still just a single JSON file, but Docker is actually rotating log files using that name as the base but with a suffix for the log file number. If you're running Windows containers or Docker CE on Linux, you can list the contents of the directory where the logs are kept and you'll see those file suffixes. Mine are shown in figure 19.4.

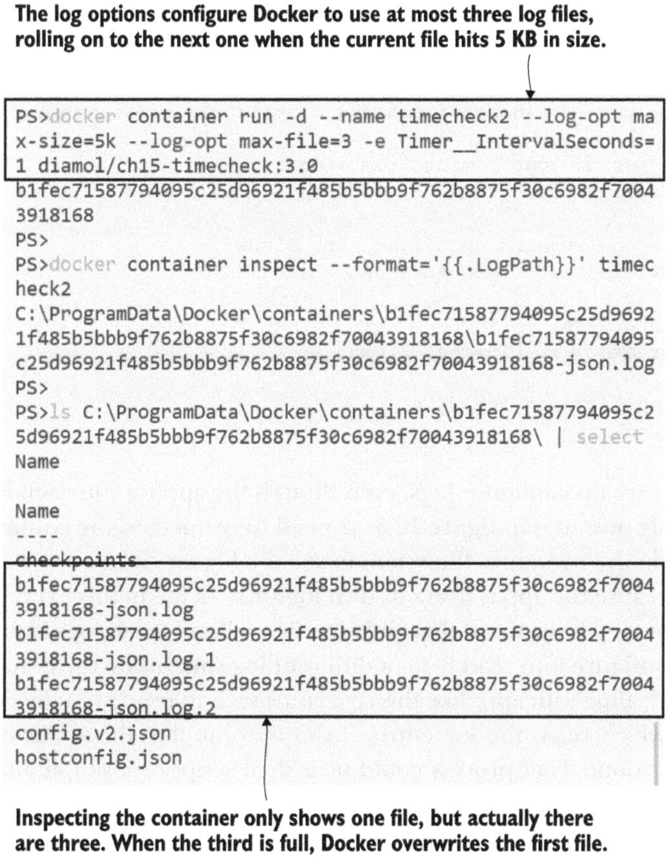

**The log options configure Docker to use at most three log files,
rolling on to the next one when the current file hits 5 KB in size.**

```
PS>docker container run -d --name timecheck2 --log-opt ma
x-size=5k --log-opt max-file=3 -e Timer__IntervalSeconds=
1 diamol/ch15-timecheck:3.0
b1fec71587794095c25d96921f485b5bbb9f762b8875f30c6982f7004
3918168
PS>
PS>docker container inspect --format='{{.LogPath}}' timec
heck2
C:\ProgramData\Docker\containers\b1fec71587794095c25d9692
1f485b5bbb9f762b8875f30c6982f70043918168\b1fec71587794095
c25d96921f485b5bbb9f762b8875f30c6982f70043918168-json.log
PS>
PS>ls C:\ProgramData\Docker\containers\b1fec71587794095c2
5d96921f485b5bbb9f762b8875f30c6982f70043918168\ | select
Name

Name
----
checkpoints
b1fec71587794095c25d96921f485b5bbb9f762b8875f30c6982f7004
3918168-json.log
b1fec71587794095c25d96921f485b5bbb9f762b8875f30c6982f7004
3918168-json.log.1
b1fec71587794095c25d96921f485b5bbb9f762b8875f30c6982f7004
3918168-json.log.2
config.v2.json
hostconfig.json
```

**Inspecting the container only shows one file, but actually there
are three. When the third is full, Docker overwrites the first file.**

**Figure 19.4** Rolling log files let you keep a known amount of log data per container.

There's a collection and processing stage for the application logs coming from stdout, which is where you can configure what Docker does with the logs. In the last exercise we configured the log processing to control the JSON file structure, and there's much more you can do with container logs. To take full advantage of that, you need to make sure every app is pushing logs out of the container, and in some cases that takes a bit more work.

## 19.2   Relaying logs from other sinks to stdout

Not every app fits nicely with the standard logging model; when you containerize some apps, Docker won't see any logs in the output streams. Some applications run in the background as Windows Services or Linux daemons, so the container startup process isn't actually the application process. Other apps might use an existing logging framework that writes to log files or other locations (called *sinks* in the logging world), like syslog in Linux or the Windows Event Log. Either way, there are no application logs coming from the container start process, so Docker doesn't see any logs.

> **TRY IT NOW** There's a new version of the timecheck app for this chapter that writes logs to a file instead of stdout. When you run this version, there are no container logs, although the app logs are being stored in the container filesystem:

```
# run a container from the new image:
docker container run -d --name timecheck3 diamol/ch19-timecheck:4.0

# check - there are no logs coming from stdout:
docker container logs timecheck3

# now connect to the running container, for Linux:
docker container exec -it timecheck3 sh

# OR windows containers:
docker container exec -it timecheck3 cmd

# and read the application log file:
cat /logs/timecheck.log
```

You'll see that there are no container logs, even though the application itself is writing lots of log entries. My output is in figure 19.5—I need to connect to the container and read the log file from the container filesystem to see the log entries.

This happens because the app is using its own log sink—a file in this exercise—and Docker doesn't know anything about that sink. Docker will only read logs from stdout; there's no way to configure it to read from a different log sink inside the container.

The pattern for dealing with apps like this is to run a second process in the container startup command, which reads the log entries from the sink that the application uses and writes them to stdout. That process could be a shell script or a simple utility app, and it is the final process in the start sequence, so Docker reads its output stream and the application logs get relayed as container logs. Figure 19.6 shows how that works.

**This version of the app writes log entries to a file instead of stdout.**

```
PS>docker container run -d --name timecheck3 diamol/ch19-
timecheck:4.0
ce86bf8c303a256c471b058f96d2981f1851198bbf33916bea6cbee40
47a49ca
PS>
```

```
PS>docker container logs timecheck3
PS>
PS>docker container exec -it timecheck3 sh
#
# cat /logs/timecheck.log
2019-12-19 10:30:54.481 +00:00 [INF] Environment: DEV; ve
rsion: 4.0; time check: 10:30.54
2019-12-19 10:30:59.476 +00:00 [INF] Environment: DEV; ve
rsion: 4.0; time check: 10:30.59
```

**There are no container logs. You need to connect to the
container and read the log file to see the application logs.**

Figure 19.5　If the app doesn't write anything to the output streams, you
won't see any container logs.

**The application process writes logs
to a file in the container's filesystem.**

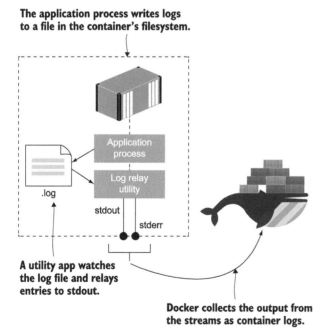

**A utility app watches
the log file and relays
entries to stdout.**

**Docker collects the output from
the streams as container logs.**

Figure 19.6　You need to
package a utility in your
container image to relay
logs from a file.

This is not a perfect solution. Your utility process is running in the foreground, so it
needs to be robust because if it fails, your container exits, even if the actual application is still working in the background. And the reverse is true: if the application fails

but the log relay keeps running, your container stays up even though the app is no longer working. You need health checks in your image to prevent that from happening. And lastly, this is not an efficient use of disk, especially if your app writes a lot of logs—they'll be filling up a file in the container filesystem and filling up a JSON file on the Docker host machine.

Even so, it's a useful pattern to know about. If your app runs in the foreground, and you can tweak your config to write logs to stdout instead, that's a better approach. But if your app runs in the background, there's no other option, and it's better to accept the inefficiency and have your app behave like all other containers.

There's an update for the timecheck app in this chapter that adds this pattern, building a small utility app to watch the log file and relay the lines to stdout. Listing 19.2 shows the final stages of the multi-stage Dockerfile—there are different startup commands for Linux and Windows.

> **Listing 19.2   Building and packaging a log-relay utility with your app**

```
# app image
FROM diamol/dotnet-runtime AS base
...
WORKDIR /app
COPY --from=builder /out/ .
COPY --from=utility /out/ .

# windows
FROM base AS windows
CMD start /B dotnet TimeCheck.dll && dotnet Tail.dll /logs timecheck.log

# linux
FROM base AS linux
CMD dotnet TimeCheck.dll & dotnet Tail.dll /logs timecheck.log
```

The two CMD instructions achieve the same thing, using different approaches for the two operating systems. First the .NET application process is started in the background, using the start command in Windows and suffixing the command with a single ampersand & in Linux. Then the .NET tail utility is started, configured to read the log file the application writes to. The tail utility just watches that file and relays each new line as it gets written, so the logs get surfaced to stdout and become container logs.

**TRY IT NOW**   Run a container from the new image, and verify that logs are coming from the container and that they still get written in the filesystem:

```
# run a container with the tail utility process:
docker container run -d --name timecheck4 diamol/ch19-timecheck:5.0

# check the logs:
docker container logs timecheck4

# and connect to the container - on Linux:
docker container exec -it timecheck4 sh
```

```
# OR with Windows containers:
docker container exec -it timecheck4 cmd

# check the log file:
cat /logs/timecheck.log
```

Now the logs are coming from the container. It's a convoluted approach to get there, with an extra process running to relay the log file contents to stdout, but once the container is running, that's all transparent. The downside to this approach is the extra processing power used by the log relay and the extra disk space for storing the logs twice. You can see my output in figure 19.7, which shows the log file is still there in the container filesystem.

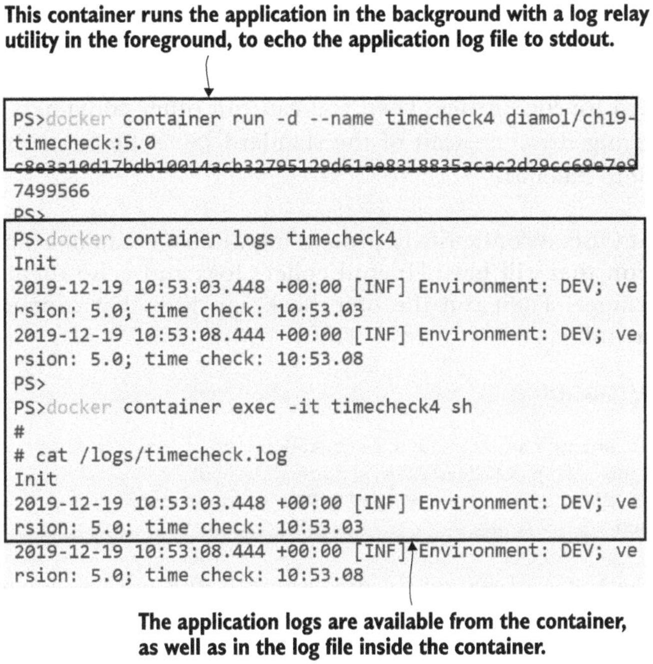

**This container runs the application in the background with a log relay utility in the foreground, to echo the application log file to stdout.**

```
PS>docker container run -d --name timecheck4 diamol/ch19-
timecheck:5.0
c8e3a10d17bdb10014acb32795129d61ae8318835acac2d29cc69e7e9
7499566
PS>
PS>docker container logs timecheck4
Init
2019-12-19 10:53:03.448 +00:00 [INF] Environment: DEV; ve
rsion: 5.0; time check: 10:53.03
2019-12-19 10:53:08.444 +00:00 [INF] Environment: DEV; ve
rsion: 5.0; time check: 10:53.08
PS>
PS>docker container exec -it timecheck4 sh
#
# cat /logs/timecheck.log
Init
2019-12-19 10:53:03.448 +00:00 [INF] Environment: DEV; ve
rsion: 5.0; time check: 10:53.03
2019-12-19 10:53:08.444 +00:00 [INF] Environment: DEV; ve
rsion: 5.0; time check: 10:53.08
```

**The application logs are available from the container, as well as in the log file inside the container.**

**Figure 19.7** A log relay utility gets the application logs out to Docker, but uses twice as much disk space.

I use a custom utility to relay the log entries in this example, because I want the app to work across platforms. I could use the standard Linux `tail` command instead, but there's no Windows equivalent. The custom utility approach is also more flexible, because it could read from any sink and relay to stdout. That should cover any scenario where your application logs are locked away somewhere in the container that Docker doesn't see.

When you have all your container images set up to write application logs as container logs, you can start to make use of Docker's pluggable logging system and consolidate all the logs coming from all your containers.

## 19.3 Collecting and forwarding container logs

Way back in chapter 2 I talked about how Docker adds a consistent management layer over all your apps—it doesn't matter what's happening inside the container; you start, stop, and inspect everything in the same way. That's especially useful with logs when you bring a consolidated logging system into your architecture, and we'll walk through one of the most popular open source examples of that: Fluentd.

Fluentd is a unified logging layer. It can ingest logs from lots of different sources, filter or enrich the log entries, and then forward them on to lots of different targets. It's a project managed by the Cloud Native Computing Foundation (which also manages Kubernetes, Prometheus, and the container runtime from Docker, among other projects), and it's a mature and hugely flexible system. You can run Fluentd in a container, and it will listen for log entries. Then you can run other containers that use Docker's Fluentd logging driver instead of the standard JSON file, and those container logs will be sent to Fluentd.

> **TRY IT NOW**  Fluentd uses a config file to process logs. Run a container with a simple configuration that will have Fluentd collect logs and echo them to stdout in the container. Then run the timecheck app with that container sending logs to Fluentd:

```
cd ch19/exercises/fluentd

# run Fluentd publishing the standard port and using a config file:
docker container run -d -p 24224:24224 --name fluentd -v
    "$(pwd)/conf:/fluentd/etc" -e FLUENTD_CONF=stdout.conf
    diamol/fluentd

# now run a timecheck container set to use Docker's Fluentd log driver:
docker container run -d --log-driver=fluentd --name timecheck5
    diamol/ch19-timecheck:5.0

# check the timecheck container logs:
docker container logs timecheck5

# and check the Fluentd container logs:
docker container logs --tail 1 fluentd
```

You'll see that you get an error when you try to check logs from the timecheck container—not all logging drivers let you see the log entries directly from the container. In this exercise they're being collected by Fluentd, and this configuration writes the output to stdout, so you can see the timecheck container's logs by looking at the logs from Fluentd. My output is in figure 19.8.

**Run Fluentd in a container. This listens on port 24224 for log entries, and the configuration file sets it to echo all the logs it receives to stdout.**

**Run an application container using the Fluentd logging driver—Docker will send all container logs to port 24224.**

```
PS>cd ch19/exercises/fluentd
PS>
PS>docker container run -d -p 24224:24224 --name fluentd
-v "$(pwd)/conf:/fluentd/etc" -e FLUENTD_CONF=stdout.conf
 diamol/fluentd
3bdcebb6b318b0030df77ef603d6bdbe52f87e60bda9d49592fa2af00
7606563
PS>
PS>docker container run -d --log-driver=fluentd --name ti
mecheck5 diamol/ch19-timecheck:5.0
5b950139ff8766414c3a801804a07a70d337a5752606fa7b8e7ce7190
ff61b16
PS>
PS>docker container logs timecheck5
Error response from daemon: configured logging driver doe
s not support reading
PS>
PS>docker container logs --tail 1 fluentd
2019-12-19 11:57:36.000000000 +0000 5b950139ff87: {"conta
iner_name":"/timecheck5","source":"stdout","log":"2019-12
-19 11:57:36.810 +00:00 [INF] Environment: DEV; version:
5.0; time check: 11:57.36","container_id":"5b950139ff8766
414c3a801804a07a70d337a5752606fa7b8e7ce7190ff61b16"}
PS>
```

**The Fluentd logging driver doesn't show application container logs.**

**This Fluentd setup echoes logs to stdout, so I can see my timecheck logs in the Fluentd container.**

Figure 19.8  Fluentd collects logs from other containers, and it can store them or write to stdout.

Fluentd adds its own metadata to each record when it stores logs, including the container ID and name. This is necessary because Fluentd becomes the central log collector for all your containers, and you need to be able to identify which log entries came from which application. Using stdout as a target for Fluentd is just a simple way to see how everything works. Typically you'd forward logs to a central data store. Elasticsearch is a very popular option—it's a no-SQL document database that works well for logs. You can run Elasticsearch in a container for log storage and the companion app Kibana, which is a search UI, in another container. Figure 19.9 shows what the logging model looks like.

It looks like a complicated architecture, but as always with Docker, it's very easy to specify all the parts of your logging setup in a Docker Compose file and spin up the whole stack with one command. When you have your logging infrastructure running in containers, you just need to use the Fluentd logging driver for any container where you want to opt in to centralized logging.

**Application containers write logs to stdout
either directly or using a log relay utility.**

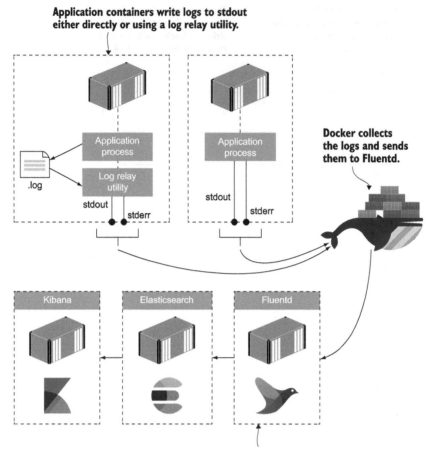

**Docker collects
the logs and sends
them to Fluentd.**

**Fluentd can filter and enrich log records, and then stores them
in Elasticsearch. Kibana is a UI for querying data in Elasticsearch.**

**Figure 19.9  A centralized logging model sends all container logs to Fluentd for
processing and storage.**

**TRY IT NOW**   Remove any running containers and start the Fluentd-Elastic-
search-Kibana logging containers. Then run a timecheck container using the
Fluentd logging driver:

```
docker container rm -f $(docker container ls -aq)

cd ch19/exercises

# start the logging stack:
docker-compose -f fluentd/docker-compose.yml up -d

docker container run -d --log-driver=fluentd diamol/ch19-timecheck:5.0
```

Give Elasticsearch a couple of minutes to be ready, and then browse to
Kibana at http://localhost:5601. Click the Discover tab, and Kibana will ask

for the name of the document collection to search against. Enter `fluentd*` as in figure 19.10.

Kibana queries documents in Elasticsearch, and it first needs to know where to look. The Fluentd logs are stored in indexes with names that begin with `fluentd`.

Figure 19.10   Elasticsearch stores documents in collections called indexes—Fluentd uses its own index.

In the next screen you need to set the field that contains the time filter— select `@timestamp` as in figure 19.11.

Kibana can filter documents based on time ranges if there's a time field in the data. Fluentd adds a timestamp in the field called `@timestamp`.

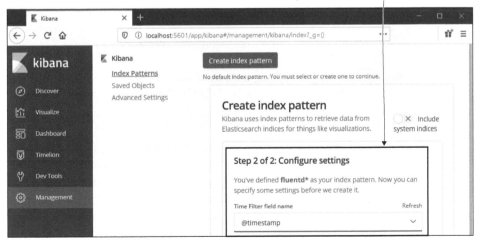

Figure 19.11   Fluentd has already saved data in Elasticsearch, so Kibana can see the field names.

You can automate the Kibana setup, but I haven't because if you're new to the Elastic-search stack, it's worth stepping through it to see how the pieces fit together. Every log entry Fluentd collects is saved as a document in Elasticsearch, in a document collection that's named fluentd-{date}. Kibana gives you a view over all those documents—in the default Discover tab you'll see a bar chart showing how many documents are being created over time, and you can drill into the details for individual documents. In this exercise, each document is a log entry from the timecheck app. You can see the data in Kibana in figure 19.12.

**Run the EFK stack (Elasticsearch,     Run the timecheck app using
Fluentd, and Kibana) in containers.    the Fluentd logging driver.**

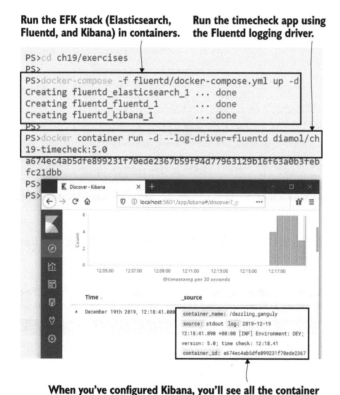

**When you've configured Kibana, you'll see all the container
log entries collected by Fluentd and stored in Elasticsearch.**

Figure 19.12   The EFK stack
in all its glory—container logs
collected and stored for
simple searching

Kibana lets you search across all documents for a specific piece of text, or filter documents by date or another data attribute. It also has dashboard functionality similar to Grafana, which you saw in chapter 9, so you can build charts showing counts of logs per app, or counts of error logs. Elasticsearch is hugely scalable, so it's suitable for large quantities of data in production, and when you start sending it all your container logs via Fluentd, you'll soon find it's a much more manageable approach than scrolling through log lines in the console.

**TRY IT NOW**   Run the image gallery app with each component configured to use the Fluentd logging driver:

```
# from the cd ch19/exercises folder

docker-compose -f image-gallery/docker-compose.yml up -d
```

Browse to http://localhost:8010 to generate some traffic, and the containers will start writing logs. The Fluentd setup for the image gallery app adds a tag to each log, identifying the component that generated it, so log lines can easily be identified—more easily than using the container name or container ID. You can see my output in figure 19.13. I'm running the full image gallery application, but I'm filtering the logs in Kibana to only show the access-log component—the API that records when the app is accessed.

The Compose file for the image gallery application uses the Fluentd driver.

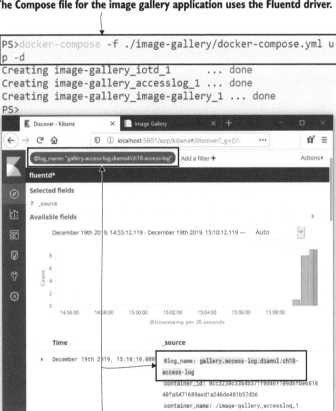

Browsing to the image gallery UI sends logs to Fluentd. In Kibana I've filtered the logs to only show entries from the `access-log` component.

Figure 19.13   Logs are being collected in Elasticsearch for the image gallery and the timecheck container.

It's very easy to add a tag for Fluentd that shows up as the log_name field for filtering; it's an option for the logging driver. You can use a fixed name or inject some useful identifiers—in this exercise I use gallery as the application prefix and then add the component name and image name for the container generating the logs. That's a nice way to identify the application, component, and exact version running for each log line. Listing 19.3 shows the logging options in the Docker Compose file for the image gallery app.

> **Listing 19.3  Using a tag to identify the source of log entries for Fluentd**

```
services:
  accesslog:
    image: diamol/ch18-access-log
        logging:
      driver: "fluentd"
      options:
        tag: " gallery.access-log.{{.ImageName}}"

  iotd:
    image: diamol/ch18-image-of-the-day
    logging:
      driver: "fluentd"
      options:
        tag: "gallery.iotd.{{.ImageName}}"

  image-gallery:
    image: diamol/ch18-image-gallery
    logging:
      driver: "fluentd"
      options:
        tag: "gallery.image-gallery.{{.ImageName}}"
...
```

The model for centralized logging with a searchable data store and a user-friendly UI is one you should definitely consider when you're getting containers ready for production. You're not limited to using Fluentd—there are many other logging drivers for Docker, so you could use other popular tools like Graylog, or commercial tools like Splunk. Remember, you can set the default logging driver and options at the Engine level in the Docker config, but I think there's value in doing it in the application manifests instead—it makes it clear which logging system you're using in each environment.

Fluentd is a good option if you don't already have an established logging system. It's easy to use and it scales from a single dev machine to a full production cluster, and you use it in the same way in every environment. You can also configure Fluentd to enrich the log data to make it easier to work with, and to filter logs and send them to different targets.

## 19.4   *Managing your log output and collection*

Logging is a delicate balance between capturing enough information to be useful in diagnosing problems and not storing huge quantities of data. Docker's logging model gives you some additional flexibility to help with the balance, because you can produce container logs at a more verbose level than you expect to use, but filter them out before you store them. Then if you need to see more verbose logs, you can alter the filter configuration rather than your app configuration so the Fluentd containers get replaced rather than your app containers.

   You can configure this level of filtering in the Fluentd config file. The configuration from the last exercise sends all logs to Elasticsearch, but the updated configuration in listing 19.4 filters out logs from the more verbose access-log component. Those logs go to stdout, and the rest of the app logs go to Elasticsearch.

---

**Listing 19.4   Sending log entries to different targets based on the tag of the record**

```
<match gallery.access-log.**>
  @type copy
  <store>
    @type stdout
  </store>
</match>
<match gallery.**>
  @type copy
  <store>
    @type elasticsearch
...
```

The `match` blocks tell Fluentd what to do with log records, and the filter parameter uses the tag that is set in the logging driver options. When you run this updated configuration, the access-log entries will match the first match block, because the tag prefix is `gallery.access-log`. Those records will stop surfacing in Elasticsearch and will only be available by reading the logs of the Fluentd container. The updated config file also enriches all log entries, splitting the tag into separate fields for app name, service name, and image name, which makes filtering in Kibana much easier.

> **TRY IT NOW**   Update the Fluentd configuration by deploying a Docker Compose override file that specifies a new config file, and update the image gallery application to generate more verbose logs:
>
> ```
> # update the Fluentd config:
> docker-compose -f fluentd/docker-compose.yml -f fluentd/override-
>     gallery-filtered.yml up -d
>
> # update the application logging config:
> docker-compose -f image-gallery/docker-compose.yml -f image-
>     gallery/override-logging.yml up -d
> ```

You can check the contents of those override files, and you'll see they just specify config settings for the applications; all the images are the same. Now when you use the app at http://localhost:8010, the access-log entries are still generated, but they get filtered out by Fluentd so you won't see any new logs in Kibana. You will see the logs from the other components, and these are enriched with the new metadata fields. You can see that in my output in figure 19.14.

The access-log entries are still available because they're writing to stdout inside the Fluentd container. You can see them as container logs—but from the Fluentd container, not the access-log container.

**The new deployment configures Fluentd to filter out access-log records so they won't be stored in Elasticsearch, and it increases the logging level of the image gallery application.**

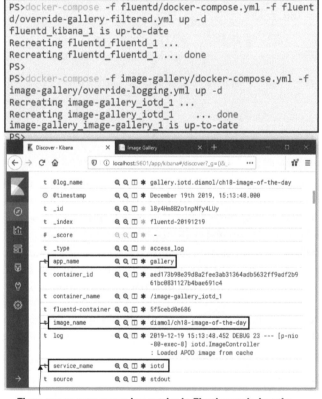

**There are no new access-log entries in Elasticsearch, but the debug logs from the Java app are now recorded, and they have the additional metadata set from Fluentd.**

Figure 19.14  Fluentd uses the tag in the log to filter out records and to generate new fields.

**TRY IT NOW**   Check the Fluentd container logs to be sure the records are still available:

```
docker container logs --tail 1 fluentd_fluentd_1
```

You can see my output in figure 19.15. The access-log entry has been sent to a different target, but it has still been through the same processing to enrich the record with the app, service, and image name:

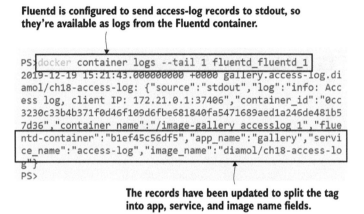

**Fluentd is configured to send access-log records to stdout, so they're available as logs from the Fluentd container.**

**The records have been updated to split the tag into app, service, and image name fields.**

Figure 19.15   These logs are filtered so they're not stored in Elasticsearch but are echoed to stdout.

This is a nice way of separating core application logs from nice-to-have logs. You wouldn't use stdout in production, but you might have different outputs for different classes of logs—performance critical components could send log entries to Kafka, user-facing logs could go to Elasticsearch, and the rest could be filed in Amazon S3 cloud storage. Those are all supported log stores in Fluentd.

There's one final exercise for this chapter to reset the logging and put access-log entries back into Elasticsearch. This approximates a situation in production where you find a system problem and you want to increase the logs to see what's happening. With the logging setup we have, the logs are already being written by the app. We can surface them just by changing the Fluentd configuration file.

**TRY IT NOW**   Deploy a new Fluentd configuration that sends access-log records to Elasticsearch:

```
docker-compose -f fluentd/docker-compose.yml -f fluentd/override-
    gallery.yml up -d
```

This deployment uses a configuration file that removes the `match` block for access-log records, so all the gallery component logs get stored in Elasticsearch. When you refresh the image gallery page in your browser, the logs will get collected and stored. You can see my output in figure 19.16, where the most recent logs are shown from both the API and the access-log components.

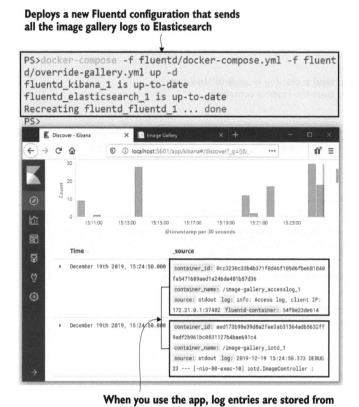

**Deploys a new Fluentd configuration that sends all the image gallery logs to Elasticsearch**

**When you use the app, log entries are stored from the Java API and the access-log component.**

Figure 19.16  A change to the Fluentd config adds logs back into Elasticsearch without any app changes.

You do need to be aware that there's the potential for lost log entries with this approach. During the deployment, containers could be sending logs when there's no Fluentd container running to collect them. Docker continues gracefully in that situation, and your app containers keep running, but the log entries don't get buffered so they'll be lost. It's unlikely to be a problem in a clustered production environment, but even if it did happen, it's preferable to restarting an app container with increased logging configuration—not least because the new container may not have the same issue as the old container, so your new logs won't tell you anything interesting.

## 19.5 *Understanding the container logging model*

The logging approach in Docker is super-flexible, but only when you make your application logs visible as container logs. You can do that directly by having your app write logs to stdout, or indirectly by using a relay utility in your container that copies log entries to stdout. You need to spend some time making sure all your application components write container logs, because once you've got that working, you can process the logs however you like.

We used the EFK stack in this chapter—Elasticsearch, Fluentd, and Kibana—and you've seen how easy it is to pull all your container logs into a centralized database with a user-friendly search UI. All those technologies are swappable, but Fluentd is one of the most used because it's so simple and so powerful. That stack runs nicely in single-machine environments, and it scales for production environments too. Figure 19.17

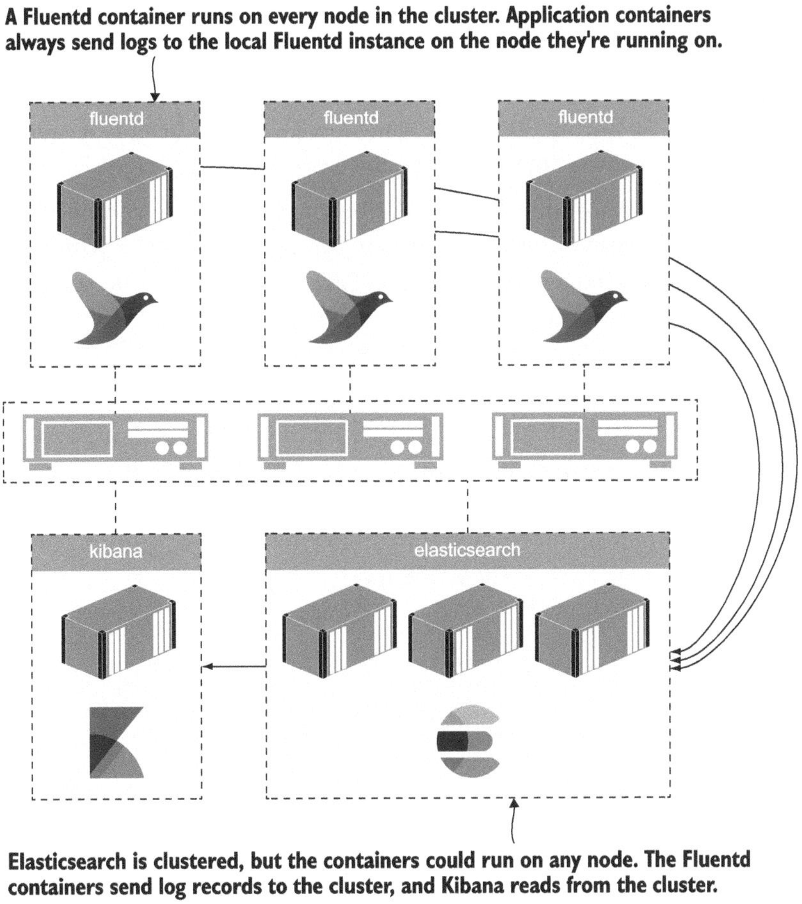

**A Fluentd container runs on every node in the cluster. Application containers always send logs to the local Fluentd instance on the node they're running on.**

**Elasticsearch is clustered, but the containers could run on any node. The Fluentd containers send log records to the cluster, and Kibana reads from the cluster.**

Figure 19.17    The EFK stack works in production with clustered storage and multiple Fluentd instances.

shows how a clustered environment runs a Fluentd container on each node, where the Fluentd container collects logs from the other containers on that node and sends them to an Elasticsearch cluster—also running in containers.

I'll finish with a note of caution before we move on to the lab. Some teams don't like all the processing layers in the container logging model; they prefer to write application logs directly to the final store, so instead of writing to stdout and having Fluentd send data to Elasticsearch, the application writes directly to Elasticsearch. I really don't like that approach. You save some processing time and network traffic in exchange for a complete lack of flexibility. You've hardcoded the logging stack into all your applications, and if you want to switch to Graylog or Splunk, you need to go and rework your apps. I always prefer to keep it simple and flexible—write your application logs to stdout and make use of the platform to collect, enrich, filter, and store the data.

## 19.6 Lab

I didn't focus too much on configuring Fluentd in this chapter, but it's worth getting some experience setting that up, so I'm going to ask you to do it in the lab. In the lab folder for this chapter there's a Docker Compose file for the random number app and a Docker Compose file for the EFK stack. The app containers aren't configured to use Fluentd, and the Fluentd setup doesn't do any enrichment, so you have three tasks:

- Extend the Compose file for the numbers app so all the components use the Fluentd logging driver, and set a tag with the app name, service name, and image.
- Extend the Fluentd configuration file, `elasticsearch.conf`, to split the tag into app name, service name, and image name fields for all records from the numbers app.
- Add a failsafe `match` block to the Fluentd configuration so any records that aren't from the numbers app get forwarded to stdout.

No hints for this one, because this is a case of working through the config setup for the image gallery app and seeing which pieces you need to add for the numbers app. As always, my solution is up on GitHub for you to check: https://github.com/sixeyed/ diamol/blob/master/ch19/lab/README.md.

# *Controlling HTTP traffic to containers with a reverse proxy*

Docker takes care of routing external traffic into your containers, but you can only have one container listening on a network port. It's fine to use any old ports in your non-production environments—in some chapters of this book we've used ten different ports to keep applications separate—but you can't do that when you go live. You'll want lots of applications running on a single cluster, but you need them all to be accessible on the standard HTTP and HTTPS ports, 80 and 443.

That's where a *reverse proxy* comes in. It's a critical piece in the architecture of a containerized environment, and in this chapter you'll learn all about the features it provides and the patterns it enables. We'll use two of the most popular technologies in this space—Nginx (pronounced "engine x") and Traefik—running in containers, of course.

## 20.1   *What is a reverse proxy?*

A proxy is a network component that handles network traffic on behalf of some other component. You might have a proxy in your corporate network that intercepts your browser requests and decides whether you're allowed to access certain sites, logs all your activity, and caches the responses so other users of the same site get a faster experience. A reverse proxy does something similar, but the other way around. You run a reverse proxy as the gateway to several web applications; all traffic goes to the reverse proxy, and it decides which app to get the content from. It can cache responses and mutate them before sending them back to the client. Figure 20.1 shows what a reverse proxy looks like in containers.

A reverse proxy is the only container with published ports—it receives all incoming requests and fetches the responses from other containers. That means all

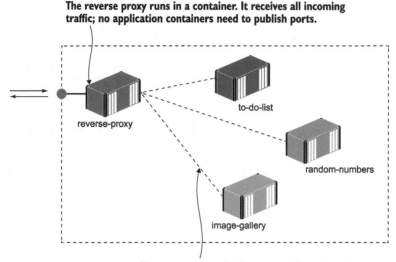

**The reverse proxy runs in a container. It receives all incoming traffic; no application containers need to publish ports.**

reverse-proxy

to-do-list

random-numbers

image-gallery

**The reverse proxy fetches content from the relevant application container and sends it back to the client.**

Figure 20.1    A reverse proxy is the gateway to your apps; application containers are not publicly available.

your application containers become internal components, which can make it easier to scale, update, and secure them. Reverse proxies are not a new technology, but they've shifted left with the container revolution. They used to sit in production and be managed by the ops team, without developers even knowing there was a proxy; now they run in lightweight containers, and you can have the same proxy configuration in every environment.

**TRY IT NOW**    Nginx has been a popular reverse proxy choice for years—it powers over 30% of the internet. It's a very lightweight, fast, and powerful HTTP server that can serve its own content as well as proxying other servers:

```
# create a network for this chapter's apps - for Linux containers:
docker network create ch20

# OR for Windows containers:
docker network create --driver=nat ch20

cd ch20/exercises

# run Nginx with a bind mount to a local configuration folder - on
# Linux:
docker-compose -f nginx/docker-compose.yml -f nginx/override-linux.yml
    up  -d
```

```
# OR on Windows containers:
docker-compose -f nginx/docker-compose.yml -f nginx/override-
    windows.yml up -d

# browse to http://localhost
```

Nginx uses a configuration file for each of the websites it serves. This container has a bind mount to the local folder called `sites-enabled`, but there are no config files in there yet. Nginx has a default site that is a simple HTML page—you can see my output in figure 20.2.

**Runs Nginx in a container. The Compose override file specifies a bind-mount to a local folder, which Nginx uses for website configuration files.**

**There are no website config files yet, so Nginx serves its default web page—the container publishes the standard ports 80 and 443.**

Figure 20.2   Nginx is an HTTP server—it can serve static content and run as a reverse proxy

We're not using Nginx as a reverse proxy yet, but we can set that up by adding a configuration file for another website. When you host multiple apps on the same port, you need a way to differentiate them, and that's usually with the domain name of the website. When you browse to a website like https://blog.sixeyed.com, the browser includes an HTTP header in the client request: `Host=blog.sixeyed.com`. Nginx uses that host header to find the configuration file for the site to serve. On your local machine you can add domains to your hosts file, which is a simple DNS lookup, to serve different apps from your Nginx container.

> **TRY IT NOW**   We'll run the simple who-am-I web app in a container without publishing any ports and make it available through Nginx on the host domain whoami.local:

```
# add the who-am-I domain to local hosts file on Mac or Linux:
echo $'\n127.0.0.1  whoami.local' | sudo tee -a /etc/hosts

# OR on Windows:
Add-Content -Value "127.0.0.1  whoami.local" -Path
    /windows/system32/drivers/etc/hosts

# start the who-am-I container:
docker-compose -f whoami/docker-compose.yml up -d

# copy the app config to the Nginx configuration folder:
cp ./nginx/sites-available/whoami.local ./nginx/sites-enabled/

# and restart Nginx to load the config:
docker-compose -f nginx/docker-compose.yml restart nginx

# browse to http://whoami.local
```

When you browse to http://whoami.local, the entry in your hosts file directs you to your local machine, and the Nginx container receives the request. It uses the HTTP header Host=whoami.local to find the right website configuration, and then it loads the content from the who-am-I container and sends it back. You'll see in figure 20.3 that the response is the same as if the response had come directly from the who-am-I application container.

Nginx is a very powerful server with a huge feature set, but the basic configuration file to proxy a web application is very simple. You need to specify the server's domain name and the location of the content, which can be an internal DNS name. The Nginx container will fetch content from the app container over the Docker network using the container name for DNS. Listing 20.1 shows the full configuration file for the who-am-I site.

> **Listing 20.1**   **Nginx proxy configuration for the who-am-I website**

```
server {
    server_name whoami.local;      # the domain host name

    location / {
        proxy_pass         http://whoami;   # source address for content
        proxy_set_header   Host $host;      # set the host for the source
        add_header         X-Host $hostname; # add proxy name in response
    }
}
```

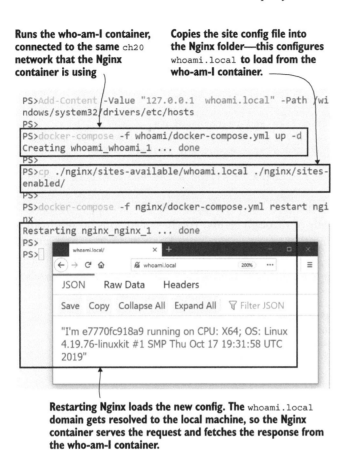

**Runs the who-am-I container, connected to the same** `ch20` **network that the Nginx container is using**

**Copies the site config file into the Nginx folder—this configures** `whoami.local` **to load from the who-am-I container.**

```
PS>Add-Content -Value "127.0.0.1  whoami.local" -Path /wi
ndows/system32/drivers/etc/hosts
PS>
PS>docker-compose -f whoami/docker-compose.yml up -d
Creating whoami_whoami_1 ... done
PS>
PS>cp ./nginx/sites-available/whoami.local ./nginx/sites-
enabled/
PS>
PS>docker-compose -f nginx/docker-compose.yml restart ngi
nx
Restarting nginx_nginx_1 ... done
PS>
PS>
```

JSON  Raw Data  Headers

Save  Copy  Collapse All  Expand All  ⏦ Filter JSON

"I'm e7770fc918a9 running on CPU: X64; OS: Linux 4.19.76-linuxkit #1 SMP Thu Oct 17 19:31:58 UTC 2019"

**Restarting Nginx loads the new config. The** `whoami.local` **domain gets resolved to the local machine, so the Nginx container serves the request and fetches the response from the who-am-I container.**

**Figure 20.3  The reverse proxy in action, loading content from an application container behind the scenes**

Reverse proxies are not just for websites—they're suitable for any HTTP content, so REST APIs are good targets, and there may be support for other types of traffic too (plain TCP/IP or gRPC). This simple configuration makes Nginx work like a pass-through, so for every request it receives, it will call the source container (called the "upstream") and send the response back to the client (called the "downstream"). If the upstream app fails, Nginx sends the failure response back to the downstream client.

**TRY IT NOW**   Add another domain to your hosts file, and run the API for the random-number app, proxying it with Nginx. This is the API that fails after a few calls, and you'll see a 500 response from Nginx after you refresh:

```
# add the API domain to local hosts file on Mac or Linux:
echo $'\n127.0.0.1  api.numbers.local' | sudo tee -a /etc/hosts
```

```
# OR on Windows:
Add-Content -Value "127.0.0.1  api.numbers.local" -Path
    /windows/system32/drivers/etc/hosts

# run the API:
docker-compose -f numbers/docker-compose.yml up -d

# copy the site config file and restart Nginx:
cp ./nginx/sites-available/api.numbers.local ./nginx/sites-enabled/
docker-compose -f nginx/docker-compose.yml restart nginx

# browse to http://api.numbers.local/rng & refresh until it breaks
```

You'll see from this exercise that the user experience for an app is identical whether they're accessing it directly or through Nginx. You have two apps hosted from Nginx, so it is managing the routing to upstream containers, but it doesn't manipulate the traffic, so the response bodies are exactly as they're sent by the app container. Figure 20.4 shows a failure response from the API coming back through the reverse proxy.

**Runs the random-number API container in the same Docker network as Nginx, and loads the config file for the site into the Nginx container**

**This API fails if you call it lots of times, and when that happens it sends a 500 error response. Proxying the app with Nginx gets the same response.**

Figure 20.4  In a simple proxy configuration, Nginx sends the response from the app—even if it's a failure.

Reverse proxies can do much more than this. All your application traffic comes into the proxy, so it can be a central place for configuration, and you can keep a lot of infrastructure-level concerns out of your application containers.

## 20.2　Handling routing and SSL in the reverse proxy

The process we've been following to add new apps to Nginx is to start the app container, copy in the config file, and restart Nginx. That order is important because when Nginx starts, it reads all the server configuration and checks that it can access all the upstreams. If any are unavailable, it exits; if they are all available, it builds an internal routing list, linking host names to IP addresses. That's the first infrastructure concern that the proxy can take care of—it will load-balance requests if there are multiple upstream containers.

> **TRY IT NOW**　We'll run the image gallery app now, proxying the main web app through Nginx. We can scale up the web component, and Nginx will load-balance requests between the containers:

```
# add the domain to the local hosts file on Mac or Linux:
echo $'\n127.0.0.1  image-gallery.local' | sudo tee -a /etc/hosts

# OR on Windows:
Add-Content -Value "127.0.0.1  image-gallery.local" -Path
    /windows/system32/drivers/etc/hosts

# run the app with 3 web containers:
docker-compose -f ./image-gallery/docker-compose.yml up -d --scale
    image-gallery=3

# add the config file and restart Nginx:
cp ./nginx/sites-available/image-gallery.local ./nginx/sites-enabled/
docker-compose -f ./nginx/docker-compose.yml restart nginx

# call the site a few times:
curl -i --head http://image-gallery.local
```

The Nginx configuration for the image gallery website is the same proxy setup as listing 20.1, using a different host name and upstream DNS name. It also adds an extra response header, X-Upstream, which shows the IP address of the container that Nginx fetched the response from. You see in figure 20.5 that the upstream IP address is in the 172.20 range for me, which is the application container's IP address on the Docker network. If you repeat the curl call a few times, you'll see different IP addresses as Nginx load-balances between the web containers.

Now you can run your app with load-balancing on a single Docker machine—you don't need to switch to Swarm mode or spin up a Kubernetes cluster to test your app in a production-like configuration. There are no code changes or config changes to the app either; it's all handled by the proxy.

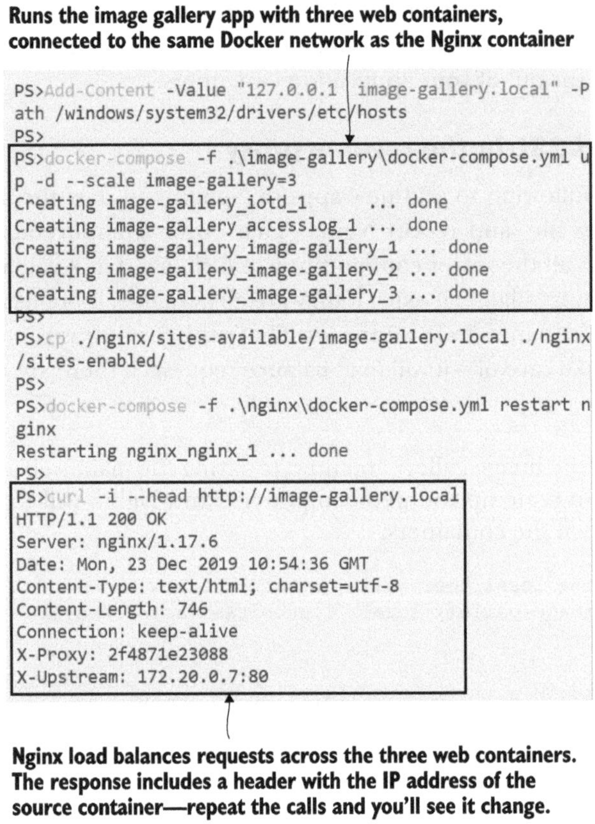

**Runs the image gallery app with three web containers,
connected to the same Docker network as the Nginx container**

```
PS>Add-Content -Value "127.0.0.1  image-gallery.local" -P
ath /windows/system32/drivers/etc/hosts
PS>
PS>docker-compose -f .\image-gallery\docker-compose.yml u
p -d --scale image-gallery=3
Creating image-gallery_iotd_1      ... done
Creating image-gallery_accesslog_1 ... done
Creating image-gallery_image-gallery_1 ... done
Creating image-gallery_image-gallery_2 ... done
Creating image-gallery_image-gallery_3 ... done
PS>
PS>cp ./nginx/sites-available/image-gallery.local ./nginx
/sites-enabled/
PS>
PS>docker-compose -f .\nginx\docker-compose.yml restart n
ginx
Restarting nginx_nginx_1 ... done
PS>
PS>curl -i --head http://image-gallery.local
HTTP/1.1 200 OK
Server: nginx/1.17.6
Date: Mon, 23 Dec 2019 10:54:36 GMT
Content-Type: text/html; charset=utf-8
Content-Length: 746
Connection: keep-alive
X-Proxy: 2f4871e23088
X-Upstream: 172.20.0.7:80
```

**Nginx load balances requests across the three web containers.
The response includes a header with the IP address of the
source container—repeat the calls and you'll see it change.**

Figure 20.5  Nginx takes care of
load-balancing so you can run app
containers at scale.

So far we've used Nginx to route between containers using different host names,
which is how you run multiple apps in one environment. You can also configure fine-
grained paths for Nginx routing, so if you want to selectively expose parts of your
application, you can do that within the same domain name.

**TRY IT NOW**   The image gallery app uses a REST API, and you can configure
Nginx to proxy the API using an HTTP request path. The API appears to be
part of the same application as the web UI, although it's actually coming from
a separate container:

```
# remove the original image-gallery configuration:
rm ./nginx/sites-enabled/image-gallery.local

# copy in the new one, which adds the API, and restart Nginx:
cp ./nginx/sites-available/image-gallery-2.local ./nginx/sites-
    enabled/image-gallery.local

docker-compose -f ./nginx/docker-compose.yml restart nginx

curl -i http://image-gallery.local/api/image
```

This is a very nice pattern for selectively exposing parts of your application stack, assembling one app from many components under the same domain name. Figure 20.6 shows my output—the response is coming from the API container, but the client is making a request on the same `image-gallery.local` domain that it uses for the web UI.

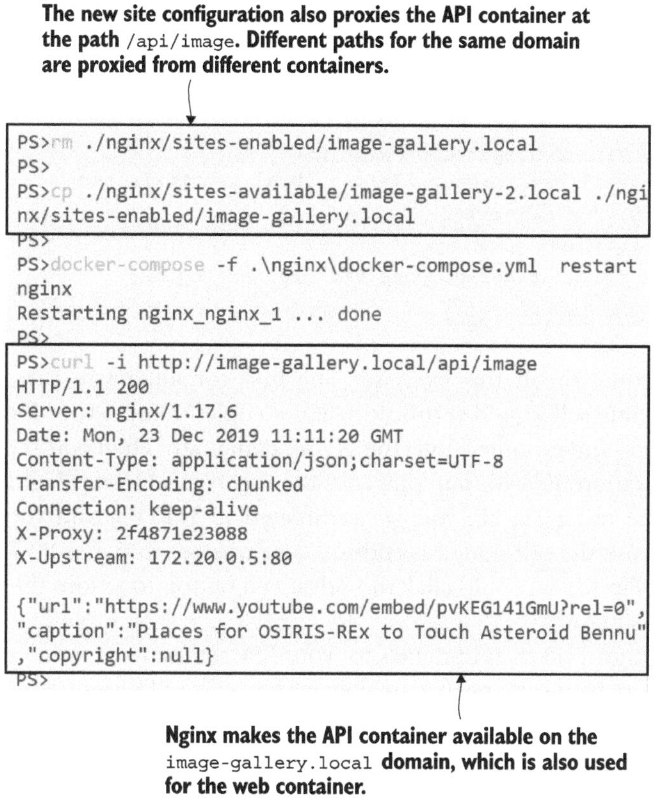

**The new site configuration also proxies the API container at the path** `/api/image`. **Different paths for the same domain are proxied from different containers.**

```
PS>rm ./nginx/sites-enabled/image-gallery.local
PS>
PS>cp ./nginx/sites-available/image-gallery-2.local ./ngi
nx/sites-enabled/image-gallery.local
PS>
PS>docker-compose -f .\nginx\docker-compose.yml restart
nginx
Restarting nginx_nginx_1 ... done
PS>
PS>curl -i http://image-gallery.local/api/image
HTTP/1.1 200
Server: nginx/1.17.6
Date: Mon, 23 Dec 2019 11:11:20 GMT
Content-Type: application/json;charset=UTF-8
Transfer-Encoding: chunked
Connection: keep-alive
X-Proxy: 2f4871e23088
X-Upstream: 172.20.0.5:80

{"url":"https://www.youtube.com/embed/pvKEG141GmU?rel=0",
"caption":"Places for OSIRIS-REx to Touch Asteroid Bennu"
,"copyright":null}
PS>
```

**Nginx makes the API container available on the** `image-gallery.local` **domain, which is also used for the web container.**

Figure 20.6  Nginx can route requests to different containers, based on the domain name or request path

Load-balancing and routing let you get close to the production environment on a single developer or test machine, and one more infrastructure component that the reverse proxy takes care of is SSL termination. If your apps are published as HTTPS sites (which they should be), the configuration and certificates need to live somewhere, and it's far better to put that in your central proxy rather than in every application component. Nginx can be configured with real certificates that you get from a domain provider or a service like Let's Encrypt, but for non-production environments you can create your own self-signed certs and use them.

**TRY IT NOW**   Generate an SSL certificate for the image gallery app, and proxy it through Nginx, using the certificates to serve it as an HTTPS site:

```
# generate a self-signed certificate for the app - on Linux:
docker container run -v "$(pwd)/nginx/certs:/certs" -e
    HOST_NAME=image-gallery.local diamol/cert-generator

# OR Windows containers:
docker container run -v "$(pwd)/nginx/certs:C:\certs" -e
    HOST_NAME=image-gallery.local diamol/cert-generator

# remove the existing image-gallery configuration:
rm ./nginx/sites-enabled/image-gallery.local

# copy in the new site configuration with SSL:
cp ./nginx/sites-available/image-gallery-3.local ./nginx/sites-
    enabled/image-gallery.local

# and restart Nginx:
docker-compose -f nginx/docker-compose.yml  restart nginx

#browse http://image-gallery.local
```

There's quite a bit going on in this exercise. The first container you run uses the OpenSSL tool to generate self-signed certificates, and it copies them to your local certs directory, which is also bind-mounted into the Nginx container. Then you replace the image gallery configuration file with one that uses those certs and restart Nginx. When you browse to the site using HTTP, you get redirected to HTTPS, and you'll get a browser warning because the self-signed certificate isn't trusted. In figure 20.7 you can see the warning from Firefox—I could click the Advanced button to ignore the warning and go on to view the site.

Nginx lets you configure all sorts of details for your SSL setup, down to the protocols and ciphers you support (you can check your site and get a list of best practices to apply from www.ssllabs.com). I won't go into all that detail, but the core part of the HTTPS setup is in listing 20.2—you can see the HTTP site listens on port 80 and returns an HTTP 301 response, which redirects the client to the HTTPS site listening on port 443.

> **Listing 20.2   Serving a site on HTTPS with an HTTP redirect**

```
server {
    server_name image-gallery.local;
    listen 80;
    return 301 https://$server_name$request_uri;
}

server {
    server_name  image-gallery.local;
    listen 443 ssl;

    ssl_certificate         /etc/nginx/certs/server-cert.pem;
    ssl_certificate_key     /etc/nginx/certs/server-key.pem;
    ssl_protocols           TLSv1 TLSv1.1 TLSv1.2;
...
```

**Generating a self-signed certificate and applying the Nginx
site configuration to use HTTPS for the image gallery app**

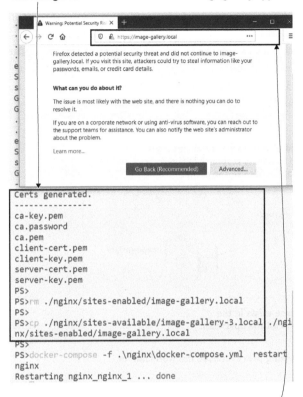

Browsers don't like self-signed certificates, because they
could be fake sites trying to look authentic. They're fine
for testing, and you can ignore the warning and proceed.

**Figure 20.7** Nginx redirects HTTP
requests to HTTPS and serves them
with an SSL certificate.

The configuration loads the certificate and key files from the container's filesystem.
Each certificate and key pair is only good for one domain name, so you'll have one
set of files for each application you use (although you can generate a certificate that
covers multiple subdomains). These are confidential files, so in production you
would use secrets in your cluster to store them. Keeping HTTPS out of your app
containers means less configuration and certificate management—it's an infrastructure concern that now lives in the proxy—and developers can spin up simple HTTP
versions for testing.

There's one last feature of Nginx we'll cover here, which can be a huge performance boost: caching responses from upstream components, which are your own web
applications.

## 20.3    *Improving performance and reliability with the proxy*

Nginx is a very high performance HTTP server. You can use it to serve static HTML for simple sites or single-page applications, and one container can comfortably handle thousands of requests per second. You can use that performance to improve your own applications too—Nginx can work as a caching proxy, so when it fetches content from your application (called the "upstream"), it stores a copy in its local disk or memory store. Subsequent requests for the same content get served directly from the proxy, and the upstream is not used. Figure 20.8 shows how the cache works.

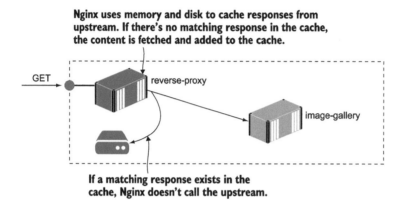

**Figure 20.8   Using Nginx as a caching proxy reduces the workload for application containers.**

There are two benefits to this. First, you reduce the time taken to serve the request, because whatever the application platform does to generate the response is bound to take longer than Nginx takes to read the cached response from memory. Second, you reduce the total amount of traffic to your application, so you should be able to handle more users from the same infrastructure. You can only cache content that is not user-specific, but that could be as simple as bypassing the cache if an authentication cookie is present. Generic sites like the image gallery app can be completely served by the cache.

**TRY IT NOW**   Use Nginx as a caching proxy for the image gallery app. This configuration sets both the web app and the API to use the Nginx cache:

```
# remove the current site config:
rm ./nginx/sites-enabled/image-gallery.local

# copy in the caching config and restart Nginx:
cp ./nginx/sites-available/image-gallery-4.local ./nginx/sites-
    enabled/image-gallery.local

docker-compose -f ./nginx/docker-compose.yml restart nginx
```

```
# make some requests to the site:
curl -i --head --insecure https://image-gallery.local
curl -i --head --insecure https://image-gallery.local
```

The new proxy configuration sets a custom response header, X-Cache, that Nginx populates with the result of the cache lookup. If there's no match in the cache—which will be the case for the first call you make to the site—the response header is X-Cache: MISS, meaning there was no matching response in the cache, and there's an X-Upstream header with the IP address of the container where Nginx fetched the content. When you repeat the call, the response does come from the cache, so you'll see X-Cache: HIT and no X-Upstream header, because Nginx didn't use an upstream. My output is in figure 20.9.

**This site configuration uses Nginx as a caching proxy for the image gallery app.**

**The cache starts empty, so Nginx fetches content from upstream and adds it to the cache.**

```
PS>rm ./nginx/sites-enabled/image-gallery.local
PS>
PS>cp ./nginx/sites-available/image-gallery-4.local ./ngi
nx/sites-enabled/image-gallery.local
PS>
PS>docker-compose -f .\nginx\docker-compose.yml  restart
nginx
Restarting nginx_nginx_1 ... done
PS>
PS>curl -i --head --insecure https://image-gallery.local
HTTP/1.1 200 OK
Server: nginx/1.17.6
Date: Mon, 23 Dec 2019 13:27:06 GMT
Content-Type: text/html; charset=utf-8
Content-Length: 746
Connection: keep-alive
X-Cache: MISS
X-Proxy: 2f4871e23088
X-Upstream: 172.20.0.9:80
```

```
PS>curl -i --head --insecure https://image-gallery.local
HTTP/1.1 200 OK
Server: nginx/1.17.6
Date: Mon, 23 Dec 2019 13:27:13 GMT
Content-Type: text/html; charset=utf-8
Content-Length: 746
Connection: keep-alive
X-Cache: HIT
X-Proxy: 2f4871e23088
```

**On the second call there's a cache hit for the request. Nginx serves the response directly without using the upstream at all.**

**Figure 20.9** If the proxy has the response in its cache, it sends it without using the upstream.

Nginx lets you fine-tune how you use the cache. In the latest configuration I've set the API to use a short-lived cache, so responses are stale after one minute and then Nginx fetches the latest content from the API container. That's a good setup for content that needs to be fresh but where you have a very high load—if your API gets 5,000 requests per second, even a one-minute cache saves 300,000 requests from reaching your API. The web app is set to use a longer cache, so responses stay fresh for six hours. Listing 20.3 shows the cache configuration.

---

**Listing 20.3   Nginx as a caching reverse proxy for API and web content**

```
...
location = /api/image {
    proxy_pass              http://iotd/image;
    proxy_set_header        Host $host;
    proxy_cache             SHORT;
    proxy_cache_valid       200  1m;
    ...
}

location / {
    proxy_pass              http://image-gallery;
    proxy_set_header        Host $host;
    proxy_cache             LONG;
    proxy_cache_valid       200  6h;
    proxy_cache_use_stale   error timeout invalid_header updating
                            http_500 http_502 http_503 http_504;
    ...
}
```

The caches, named LONG and SHORT, are defined in the core Nginx configuration in the diamol/nginx image. The cache specs set how much memory and disk to use for responses, and the eviction time for stale items.

I don't want to dig into Nginx configuration too deeply, but there's one very useful feature you can use to improve app reliability, which is defined for the web app in the proxy_cache_use_stale setting. That tells Nginx that it can use cached responses even when they're stale if the upstream is not available. Serving content from stale items in the cache means your app stays online (although it may not be fully functional) even if the application containers are down. This is a very useful backup for working around transient failures in your app, or application rollouts that need to be rolled back. You need to think carefully about the paths that can be served successfully from the cache, but in a nice simple demo app you can serve the whole thing.

> **TRY IT NOW**   Make a couple of calls to the image gallery app and API so Nginx saves those responses in its cache. Then kill the containers and try requesting the content again:

```
# call the site and the API:
curl -s --insecure https://image-gallery.local
curl -s --insecure https://image-gallery.local/api/image

# remove all the web containers:
docker container rm -f $(docker container ls -f name=image-
    gallery_image-gallery_* -q)
```

```
# try the web app again:
curl -i --head --insecure https://image-gallery.local

# remove the API container:
docker container rm -f image-gallery_iotd_1

# try the API again:
curl -i --head --insecure  https://image-gallery.local/api/image
```

You'll see the different cache configurations in action here. The web cache is set to expire after six hours, so even when there are no web containers available, the content keeps getting served from Nginx's cache. The API response cache expires after one minute, and it's not set to use the stale cache, so you'll get an HTTP 502 error from Nginx, meaning it was unable to reach the upstream component. My output is in figure 20.10.

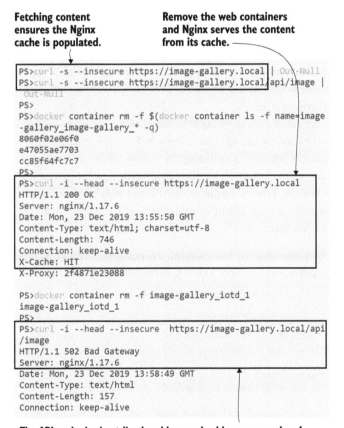

**Fetching content ensures the Nginx cache is populated.**

**Remove the web containers and Nginx serves the content from its cache.**

```
PS>curl -s --insecure https://image-gallery.local | Out-Null
PS>curl -s --insecure https://image-gallery.local/api/image |
Out-Null
PS>
PS>docker container rm -f $(docker container ls -f name=image
-gallery_image-gallery_* -q)
8060f02e06f0
e47055ae7703
cc85f64fc7c7
PS>
PS>curl -i --head --insecure https://image-gallery.local
HTTP/1.1 200 OK
Server: nginx/1.17.6
Date: Mon, 23 Dec 2019 13:55:50 GMT
Content-Type: text/html; charset=utf-8
Content-Length: 746
Connection: keep-alive
X-Cache: HIT
X-Proxy: 2f4871e23088

PS>docker container rm -f image-gallery_iotd_1
image-gallery_iotd_1
PS>
PS>curl -i --head --insecure  https://image-gallery.local/api
/image
HTTP/1.1 502 Bad Gateway
Server: nginx/1.17.6
Date: Mon, 23 Dec 2019 13:58:49 GMT
Content-Type: text/html
Content-Length: 157
Connection: keep-alive
```

**The API cache is short-lived and has expired by now, so when I remove the container I get an error instead of the cached response.**

Figure 20.10  Nginx caching can be fine-tuned to keep content fresh or to add reliability to your app.

That's as far as we'll go with exercises for Nginx. It's a very capable reverse proxy, and there's plenty more you can do with it—like enabling GZip compression for HTTP responses and adding client cache headers—which can improve end-user performance and reduce the load on your app containers. It's a technology that existed before containers, so it doesn't actually integrate with the container platform; it just works at the network level looking up IP addresses for DNS names, which is where Docker provides the container IP address. It works well, but you need to maintain a configuration file for each app and reload Nginx whenever the configuration changes.

We'll finish the chapter by looking at a modern alternative that's container-aware and integrates nicely with Docker.

## 20.4  *Using a cloud-native reverse proxy*

Back in chapter 11 we built a CI pipeline using Jenkins, running in a container. That container connected to the Docker Engine it was running on, so it could build and push images. Connecting a container to the Docker Engine also lets applications query the Docker API to learn about other containers, and that's exactly what powers the cloud-native reverse proxy Traefik (approximately pronounced "traffic"). There's no static configuration file for each app you want to make available in the proxy; instead, you add labels to your containers, and Traefik uses those labels to build its own configuration and routing maps.

Dynamic configuration is one of the major benefits of a container-aware proxy like Traefik. You don't need to start your upstream apps before you run Traefik because it watches for new containers while it's running. You don't have to restart Traefik or reload configuration to make a change to your application setup—that's all part of your application deployment. Traefik has its own API and web UI that shows the rules, so you can run Traefik without any other containers and then deploy an application and see how the config gets built.

> **TRY IT NOW**  Start by removing all the existing containers; then run Traefik and check the UI to get a feel for how Traefik manages components:

```
docker container rm -f $(docker container ls -aq)

# start Traefik - connecting to a Linux Docker Engine:
docker-compose -f traefik/docker-compose.yml -f traefik/override-
    linux.yml up -d

# OR using Windows containers:
docker-compose -f traefik/docker-compose.yml -f traefik/override-
    windows.yml up -d

# browse to http://localhost:8080
```

There are different override files for Linux and Windows because they use different private channels for the container to connect to the Docker Engine. Other than that, the behavior of Traefik is exactly the same on all platforms. The dashboard is your view over the applications that Traefik is proxying and how each is configured. You can see the resources Traefik uses to configure proxies in figure 20.11.

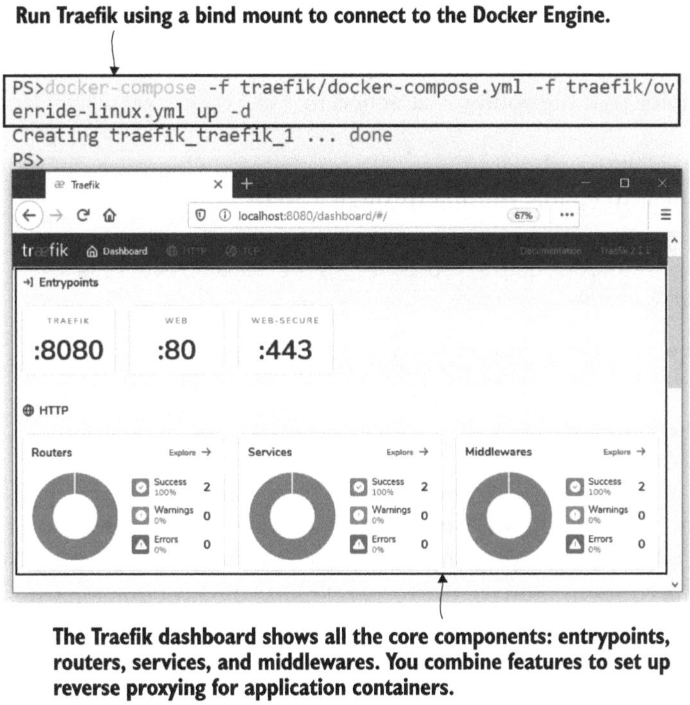

**Run Traefik using a bind mount to connect to the Docker Engine.**

The Traefik dashboard shows all the core components: entrypoints, routers, services, and middlewares. You combine features to set up reverse proxying for application containers.

Figure 20.11 The Traefik dashboard shows you the configuration for all the apps being proxied.

Traefik is very widely used, and it has a similar operational model to Nginx—there's a free, open source product that is published as an official image in Docker Hub, and there's a commercial variant if you want to run with support. If you're new to reverse proxies, Nginx and Traefik are the two options I'd recommend; it will become a major part of your infrastructure, so you should look to spend some time comparing the two. Let's dig a little bit into how Traefik works:

- *Entrypoints*—These are the ports Traefik listens on for external traffic, so these map to the published ports for the container. I'm using 80 and 443 for HTTP and HTTPS, and 8080 for the Traefik dashboard.
- *Routers*—These are the rules for matching an incoming request to a target container. HTTP routers have rules like host name and path to identify client requests.

- *Services*—These are the upstream components—the application containers that actually serve the content to Traefik so it can pass the response back to the client.
- *Middlewares*—These are components that can modify requests from a router before they get sent to the service. You can use middleware components to change the request path or headers, or even to enforce authentication.

The simplest configuration just needs a router set up with rules to match client requests to the service that the router is attached to.

> **TRY IT NOW**   Deploy the who-am-I app with an updated Compose definition that includes labels to enable routing through Traefik:

```
# deploy the app with Traefik labels in the override file:
docker-compose -f whoami/docker-compose.yml -f whoami/override-
    traefik.yml up -d

# browse to the Traefik configuration for the router:
# http://localhost:8080/dashboard/#/http/routers/whoami@docker

# and check the routing:
curl -i http://whoami.local
```

This is a very simple configuration—the route just links the entrypoint port to the upstream service, which is the who-am-I container. You can see in figure 20.12 that Traefik has built the configuration for the router, linking the host domain whoami.local to the whoami service.

That's all done by applying two labels on the container: one to enable Traefik for the app, and the other to specify the host name to match on. Listing 20.4 shows those labels in the override Compose file.

> **Listing 20.4   Configuring Traefik by adding labels to application containers**

```
services:
  whoami:
    labels:
      - "traefik.enable=true"
      - "traefik.http.routers.whoami.rule=Host(`whoami.local`)"
```

Traefik supports some very sophisticated routing options. You can match by host name and path, or a path prefix, and then use a middleware component to strip prefixes. That sounds complicated, but it's just what we need for the image gallery API, so we can expose it as a path in the main image gallery domain. We can configure Traefik to listen for incoming requests with the "api" path prefix, and then strip the prefix from the request URL before it calls the service, because the service itself doesn't use that prefix.

**Starts the image gallery containers, with Traefik labels applied
to the web container to configure proxy routing rules**

```
PS>docker-compose -f whoami/docker-compose.yml -f whoami/over
ride-traefik.yml up -d
Creating whoami_whoami_1 ... done
PS>
PS># browse to the Traefik configuration for the router:
```

```
PS>curl http://whoami.local
"I'm 7cf243035a4d running on CPU: X64; OS: Linux 4.19.76-linu
xkit #1 SMP Thu Oct 17 19:31:58 UTC 2019"
PS>
```

**Traefik is running and connected to the Docker Engine, so it sees the
new containers and uses the labels to build up the router configuration.**

**Figure 20.12** Traefik uses the Docker API to find containers and labels,
using them to build configuration.

**TRY IT NOW** The image gallery app just needs an override file with labels
specified to enable Traefik support. Deploy the app, and Traefik will add the
configuration to its routing rules:

```
# start the app with the new Traefik labels:
docker-compose -f image-gallery/docker-compose.yml -f image-
    gallery/override-traefik.yml up -d

# check the web application:
curl --head http://image-gallery.local

# and the API:
curl -i http://image-gallery.local/api/image
```

You'll see in the output that you get a correct response from the API call—Traefik receives an external request on http://image-gallery.local/api/image and uses the router and middleware configuration to make an internal call to the container at http://iotd/image. The configuration for that is slightly cryptic. You define the router and then the middleware component, and then attach the middleware to the router— it's in the file `image-gallery/override-traefik.yml` if you want to check it out.

That complexity is all transparent to the consumer. You can see in figure 20.13 that the response looks like it's coming direct from the API.

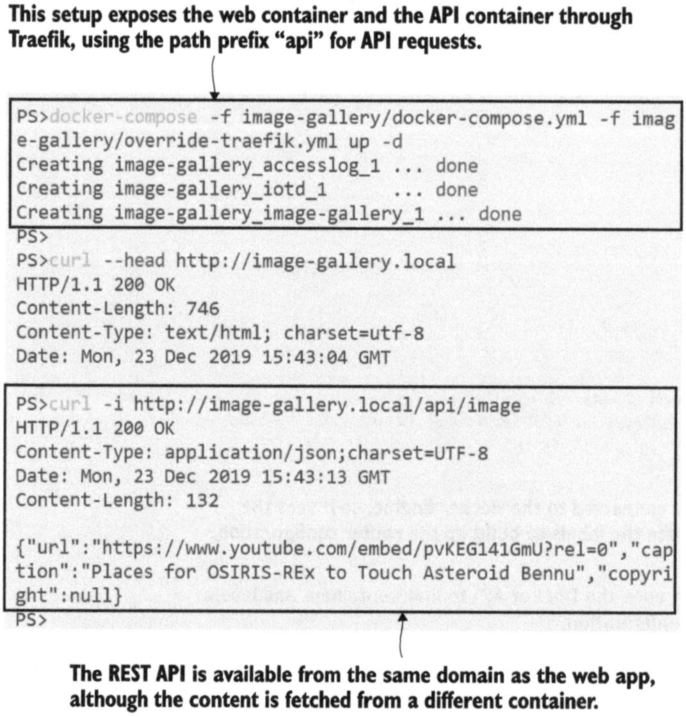

**This setup exposes the web container and the API container through Traefik, using the path prefix "api" for API requests.**

```
PS>docker-compose -f image-gallery/docker-compose.yml -f imag
e-gallery/override-traefik.yml up -d
Creating image-gallery_accesslog_1 ... done
Creating image-gallery_iotd_1      ... done
Creating image-gallery_image-gallery_1 ... done
PS>
PS>curl --head http://image-gallery.local
HTTP/1.1 200 OK
Content-Length: 746
Content-Type: text/html; charset=utf-8
Date: Mon, 23 Dec 2019 15:43:04 GMT

PS>curl -i http://image-gallery.local/api/image
HTTP/1.1 200 OK
Content-Type: application/json;charset=UTF-8
Date: Mon, 23 Dec 2019 15:43:13 GMT
Content-Length: 132

{"url":"https://www.youtube.com/embed/pvKEG141GmU?rel=0","cap
tion":"Places for OSIRIS-REx to Touch Asteroid Bennu","copyri
ght":null}
PS>
```

**The REST API is available from the same domain as the web app, although the content is fetched from a different container.**

Figure 20.13   Routing rules let you present a multi-container app at a single domain.

Reverse proxies don't all support the same feature set. Traefik doesn't have a cache (as of version 2.1), so if you need a caching proxy, Nginx is the way to go. But when it comes to SSL, Traefik has much better support—it integrates with certificate providers out of the box, so you can have it automatically connect to Let's Encrypt and update certs for you. Or you can use the default self-signed certificate provider and add SSL to your sites in non-production environments without any cert management.

**TRY IT NOW**   Adding SSL support to the image gallery app and API needs a more complex Traefik setup. It needs to listen on the HTTPS entry point as well as HTTP, but redirect HTTP calls to HTTPS. It's all still done with labels, so the deployment is just an application update:

```
# run the app with Traefik labels for HTTPS:
docker-compose -f image-gallery/docker-compose.yml -f image-
    gallery/override-traefik-ssl.yml up -d

# check the website using HTTPS:
curl --head --insecure https://image-gallery.local

# and the API:
curl --insecure https://image-gallery.local/api/image
```

If you browse to the site or the API, you'll see the same warning message in the browser that we had using SSL with Nginx—the certificate isn't trusted by a known certificate authority. But this time we didn't need to create our own certificate and carefully manage the certificate and key files—Traefik did it all. You can see my output in figure 20.14. Using curl with the insecure flag tells it to carry on even though the cert is untrusted.

Routing, load-balancing, and SSL termination are the main features of a reverse proxy, and Traefik supports them all with dynamic configuration through container labels. If you're evaluating it against Nginx, you need to remember that Traefik doesn't

**This configuration sets up HTTPS with Traefik's default certificate provider—it will generate self-signed certificates for the site.**

```
PS>docker-compose -f image-gallery/docker-compose.yml -f imag
e-gallery/override-traefik-ssl.yml up -d
image-gallery_accesslog_1 is up-to-date
Recreating image-gallery_iotd_1 ... done
Recreating image-gallery_image-gallery_1 ... done
PS>
PS>curl --head --insecure https://image-gallery.local
HTTP/1.1 200 OK
Content-Length: 746
Content-Type: text/html; charset=utf-8
Date: Mon, 23 Dec 2019 16:00:19 GMT

PS>curl --insecure https://image-gallery.local/api/image
{"url":"https://www.youtube.com/embed/pvKEG141GmU?rel=0","cap
tion":"Places for OSIRIS-REx to Touch Asteroid Bennu","copyri
ght":null}
```

**The certificate isn't trusted, so I need to use curl's** insecure **flag, and then I see the web and API content over HTTPS.**

Figure 20.14   Using Traefik for HTTPS—it can generate certificates or fetch them from third-party providers

give you a cache—that's a much-requested feature that may come into Traefik in a later release.

There's one last feature we'll try which is easy in Traefik and much harder in Nginx: sticky sessions. Modern apps are built to have as many stateless components as possible—it's important when you're running at scale that client requests can be routed to any container so you benefit from load-balancing and see immediate results when you scale up. Old apps tend not to be built from stateless components, and you may find when you migrate those apps to run in containers that you want the user to be routed to the same container each time. That's called a *sticky session*, and you can enable that in Traefik with a setting for the service.

**TRY IT NOW**    The whoami app is an easy example of sticky sessions. You can scale up the current deployment and make repeated calls—they'll be load-balanced between the containers by Traefik. Deploy a new version with sticky sessions, and all your requests will be handled by the same container:

```
# run the who-am-I app with multiple containers:
docker-compose -f whoami/docker-compose.yml -f whoami/override-
    traefik.yml up -d --scale whoami=3

# check that requests are load-balanced between containers:
curl -c c.txt -b c.txt http://whoami.local
curl -c c.txt -b c.txt http://whoami.local

# now deploy the same app with sticky session support:
docker-compose -f whoami/docker-compose.yml -f whoami/override-
    traefik-sticky.yml up -d --scale whoami=3

# and check that requests are served by the same container:
curl -c c.txt -b c.txt http://whoami.local
curl -c c.txt -b c.txt http://whoami.local
```

With sticky sessions enabled, your requests get served by the same container each time because Traefik sets a cookie identifying which container it should use for that client (you'll see the same behavior with the browser too). If you're interested, you can examine the cookies in your browser session or in the c.txt file, and you'll see Traefik puts the container's IP address in that cookie. The next time you make a call, it uses the IP address to access the same container. My output is in figure 20.15.

Sticky sessions are one of the major asks from teams moving old apps to containers, and Traefik makes it pretty easy. It's not quite the same as a sticky session for a physical server or VM, because containers are replaced more frequently, so clients could be stuck to a container that no longer exists. If the cookie directs Traefik to an unavailable container, it will pick another one, so the user will see a response, but their session will have ended.

**Running without sticky sessions, requests are load balanced by Traefik between the application containers.**

```
PS>docker-compose -f whoami/docker-compose.yml -f whoami/over
ride-traefik.yml up -d --scale whoami=3
Recreating whoami_whoami_1 ... done
Creating whoami_whoami_2  ... done
Creating whoami_whoami_3  ... done
PS>
```

```
PS>curl -c c.txt -b c.txt http://whoami.local
"I'm bf520136449c running on CPU: X64; OS: Linux 4.19.76-linu
xkit #1 SMP Thu Oct 17 19:31:58 UTC 2019"
PS>
PS>curl -c c.txt -b c.txt http://whoami.local
"I'm cba81f8d6bfd running on CPU: X64; OS: Linux 4.19.76-linu
xkit #1 SMP Thu Oct 17 19:31:58 UTC 2019"
PS>
```

```
PS>docker-compose -f whoami/docker-compose.yml -f whoami/over
ride-traefik-sticky.yml up -d --scale whoami=3
Recreating whoami_whoami_1 ... done
Recreating whoami_whoami_2 ... done
Recreating whoami_whoami_3 ... done
PS>
```

```
PS>curl -c c.txt -b c.txt http://whoami.local
"I'm 4a38665b433f running on CPU: X64; OS: Linux 4.19.76-linu
xkit #1 SMP Thu Oct 17 19:31:58 UTC 2019"
PS>
PS>curl -c c.txt -b c.txt http://whoami.local
"I'm 4a38665b433f running on CPU: X64; OS: Linux 4.19.76-linu
xkit #1 SMP Thu Oct 17 19:31:58 UTC 2019"
```

**Traefik uses cookies to tie the client to one container, so the next client request is served by the same container. Curl uses text files to store and present cookies, so this simulates browser behavior.**

Figure 20.15    Enabling sticky sessions in Traefik—it uses cookies to send the client to the same container.

## 20.5  *Understanding the patterns a reverse proxy enables*

A reverse proxy is pretty much essential when you start running many containerized apps in production. We've covered some of the more advanced features in this chapter—SSL, caching, and sticky sessions—but even without those you'll find you need a reverse proxy sooner or later. There are three major patterns that a reverse proxy enables, and we'll finish up by walking through them.

The first is hosting several web applications on the standard HTTP and HTTPS ports, using the host name in the client request to fetch the correct content, as in figure 20.16.

The second is for microservice architectures, where a single application runs across multiple containers. You can use a reverse proxy to selectively expose individual microservices, routed by HTTP request path. Externally your app has a single domain, but different paths are served by different containers. Figure 20.17 shows this pattern.

**The reverse proxy is the single external-facing component, publishing ports 80 and 443 from the container to the server (or all the servers in a cluster). All app containers are internal components.**

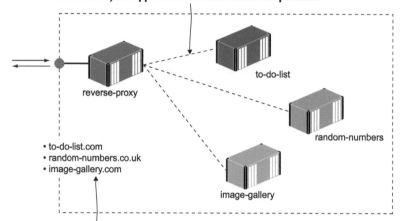

reverse-proxy

to-do-list

random-numbers

image-gallery

• to-do-list.com
• random-numbers.co.uk
• image-gallery.com

**The routing rules in the reverse proxy use the host domain from the client request to load the content from the application container.**

Figure 20.16   Using a reverse proxy to host many applications with different domain names in one cluster

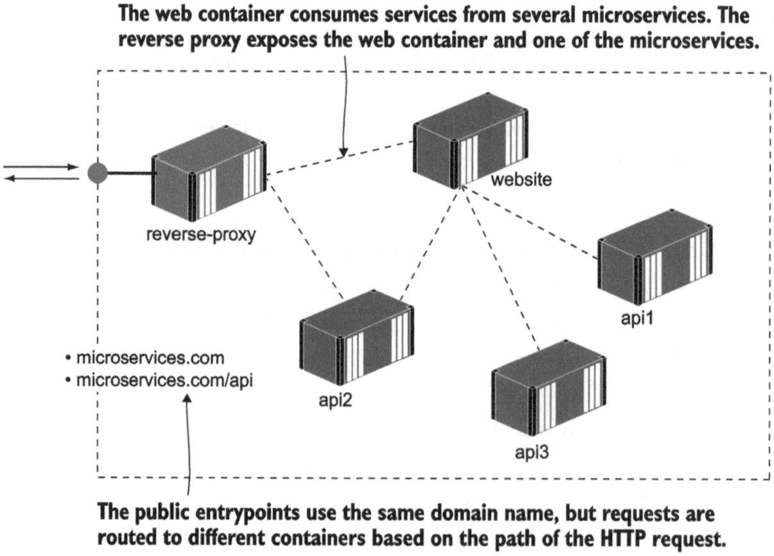

**The web container consumes services from several microservices. The reverse proxy exposes the web container and one of the microservices.**

reverse-proxy

website

api1

api2

api3

• microservices.com
• microservices.com/api

**The public entrypoints use the same domain name, but requests are routed to different containers based on the path of the HTTP request.**

Figure 20.17   Microservices exposed by the reverse proxy are part of the same application domain.

The final pattern is very powerful if you have old monolithic applications that you want to migrate to containers. You can use a reverse proxy to start breaking up the monolithic frontend of your old app, splitting features out into new containers. Those new features are routed by the reverse proxy, and because they're in separate containers, they can use a different, modern technology stack. Figure 20.18 shows this.

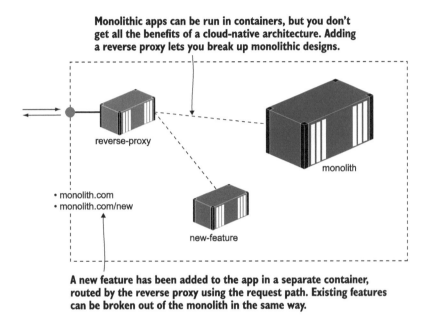

Monolithic apps can be run in containers, but you don't get all the benefits of a cloud-native architecture. Adding a reverse proxy lets you break up monolithic designs.

reverse-proxy

monolith

• monolith.com
• monolith.com/new

new-feature

A new feature has been added to the app in a separate container, routed by the reverse proxy using the request path. Existing features can be broken out of the monolith in the same way.

**Figure 20.18  The reverse proxy hides the monolithic architecture so it can be broken into smaller services.**

These patterns are not mutually exclusive—in a single cluster you could have a reverse proxy powering all three patterns, hosting multiple domains with a mixture of microservices and monolithic applications running in containers.

## 20.6  *Lab*

We've got a whole new app for this lab—one that will clearly show the power of a caching reverse proxy. It's a simple website that calculates pi to a specified number of decimal places. In the lab folder for this chapter, you can run the app with Docker Compose and browse to http://localhost:8031/?dp=50000 to see what pi looks like to 50,000 decimal places. Refresh the browser and you'll see it takes just as long to compute the same response. Your job is to run the app behind a reverse proxy:

- The app should be available at the domain `pi.local` on the standard HTTP port.

- The proxy should cache responses so when users repeat the same request, the response is served from the cache and is much faster than from the app.
- The proxy should add resilience, so if you kill the app container, any cached responses are still available from the proxy.

My solution is up on GitHub, and you'll find there are huge time savings from caching proxies with compute-intensive work like this: https://github.com/sixeyed/diamol/blob/master/ch20/lab/README.md.

# 21
# *Asynchronous communication with a message queue*

This is the final full chapter of the book, and it introduces a new way for the components of a system to communicate: sending and receiving messages using a queue. Message queues have been around for a very long time—they're a way of decoupling components so instead of making a direct connection to communicate with each other, they send messages to the queue. The queue can deliver messages to one or many recipients, and that adds a lot of flexibility to your architecture.

In this chapter we'll focus on two scenarios that are enabled when you add a message queue to your application: improving system performance and scalability, and adding new features with zero downtime. We'll use two modern message queues that run very nicely in Docker: Redis and NATS.

## 21.1 What is asynchronous messaging?

Software components usually communicate synchronously—the client makes a connection to the server, sends a request, waits for the server to send a response, and then closes the connection. That's true for REST APIs, SOAP web services, and gRPC, which all use HTTP connections.

Synchronous communication is like making a telephone call: it needs both parties to be available at the same time, so it needs careful management. Servers might be offline or running at full capacity, so they can't accept connections. Services may take a long time to process, and client connections might time out waiting for the response. Connections can fail at the network level, and the client needs to know if they can safely repeat the request. You need a lot of logic in your application code or libraries to deal with all the failure modes.

Asynchronous communication adds a layer between the client and the server. If the client needs a server to do something, it sends a message to the queue. The server is listening on the queue, picks up the message, and processes it. The server can send a response message to the queue, and if the client wants a response, it will be listening on the queue and will pick it up. Asynchronous messaging is like communicating by email—parties can join in when they have free time. If the server is offline or out of capacity, the message sits in the queue until a server is available to pick it up. If the message takes a long time to process, that doesn't affect the client or the queue. If there's a failure when the client sends a message, the message isn't in the queue and the client can safely send it again. Figure 21.1 shows communication with asynchronous messaging.

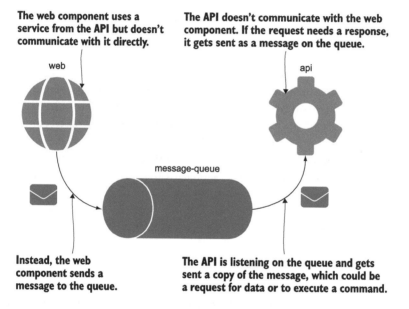

**Figure 21.1   Message queues decouple components so they don't communicate with each other directly.**

Messaging has always been a favorite option for integration architects, but it used to raise some difficult issues—the queue technology needs to be super-reliable, but enterprise queues are too expensive to run in test environments, so can we use different queues in different environments, or skip the queues altogether in dev? Docker fixes that, making it easy to add enterprise-grade open source queues to your application. Running queues in lightweight containers means you can run a dedicated queue for each application, and free open source software means you can use the same technology in every environment. Redis is a popular message queue option (which you can also use as a data store), and you can easily try it out to get a feel for asynchronous messaging.

**TRY IT NOW** Run the Redis server in a container, connected to a network where you can run other containers to send and receive messages:

```
# create the network - on Linux containers:
docker network create ch21

# OR Windows containers:
docker network create -d nat ch21

# run the Redis server:
docker container run -d --name redis --network ch21 diamol/redis

# check that the server is listening:
docker container logs redis --tail 1
```

Message queues are server components that just run until you stop them. Redis listens for connections on port 6379, and that same address is used by clients to send messages and by servers to listen for messages. You'll see from your container logs that Redis is up and running just a few seconds after you start the container—my output is in figure 21.2.

Clients need to open a connection to the queue to send their message—and if you're wondering how that's better than just calling a REST API directly, it's all down to speed. Queues usually have their own custom communication protocol, which is highly optimized, so when the client sends a message, it just transmits the bytes of the

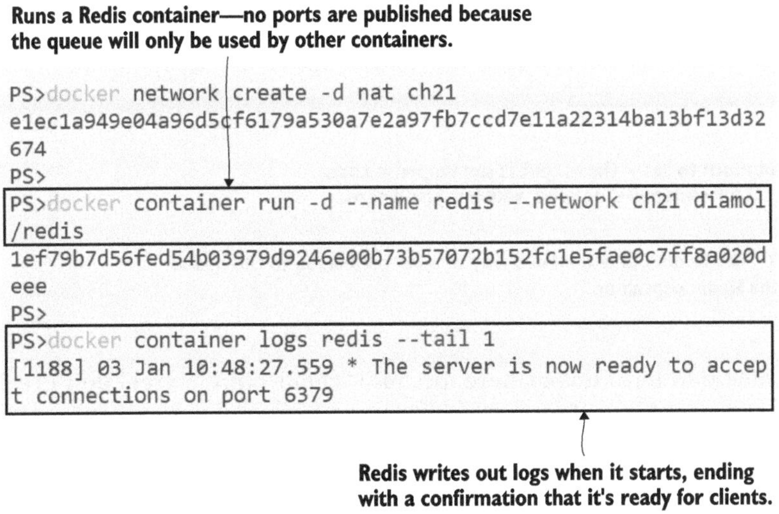

**Runs a Redis container—no ports are published because the queue will only be used by other containers.**

```
PS>docker network create -d nat ch21
e1ec1a949e04a96d5cf6179a530a7e2a97fb7ccd7e11a22314ba13bf13d32
674
PS>
PS>docker container run -d --name redis --network ch21 diamol
/redis
1ef79b7d56fed54b03979d9246e00b73b57072b152fc1e5fae0c7ff8a020d
eee
PS>
PS>docker container logs redis --tail 1
[1188] 03 Jan 10:48:27.559 * The server is now ready to accep
t connections on port 6379
```

**Redis writes out logs when it starts, ending with a confirmation that it's ready for clients.**

Figure 21.2 A message queue is just like any other background container, waiting for connections.

request and waits for an acknowledgement that it has been received. Queues don't do any complex processing on the message, so they should easily handle thousands of messages per second.

> **TRY IT NOW**   We won't send thousands of requests, but we'll use the Redis CLI to send a few messages. The command syntax is a bit involved, but this is going to publish the message "ping" on the channel called channel21, and it will repeat that message 50 times with a 5 second interval in between:

```
# run the Redis client in the background to publish messages:
docker run -d --name publisher --network ch21 diamol/redis-cli -r 50 -
    i 5 PUBLISH channel21 ping

# check the logs to see messages are being sent:
docker logs publisher
```

This Redis client container will sit in the background and send a message every five seconds. The log output just shows the response code from each message send, so if everything is working, you'll see lots of zeros, which is the "OK" response. You can see mine in figure 21.3.

**The Redis CLI uses the Redis messaging protocol. This container runs a command that sends 50 messages with a 5 second wait after each one.**

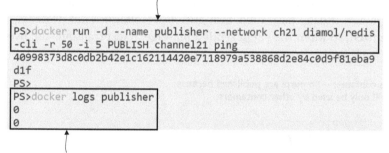

**There's not much to see—the output is the response code from the CLI for each message send, which is just a zero.**

**Figure 21.3   The Redis CLI is a simple way to send messages to the queue running in the Redis container.**

There's some new terminology here, because "client" and "server" don't really make sense in messaging terms. Every component is a client of the message queue; they just use it in different ways. The component sending messages is the *publisher*, and the component receiving messages is the *subscriber*. There could be lots of different systems using the queue, so Redis uses *channels* to keep messages separate. In this case, the publisher is sending messages on the channel called channel21, so for a component to read those messages, it needs to subscribe to the same channel.

**TRY IT NOW**   Run another container with the Redis CLI, this time subscribing to the channel where the other container is publishing messages:

```
# run an interactive subscriber and you'll see messages received every
# five seconds:
docker run -it --network ch21 --name subscriber diamol/redis-cli
    SUBSCRIBE channel21
```

We're using the Redis CLI, which is a simple client that talks using the Redis messaging protocol—there are Redis SDKs for all the major application platforms, so you can integrate it with your own apps too. The CLI prints output across multiple lines, so you'll first see the output from subscribing to the queue. The publishing container is still running in the background, and every time it publishes a message, Redis sends a copy to the subscriber container—then you'll see the message detail in the logs. Mine is in figure 21.4.

**This is an interactive container running a** subscribe **command in the Redis CLI. The initial output confirms the subscription to the channel.**

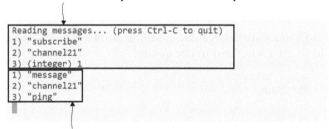

**Every time the publishing container sends a message to Redis, it gets delivered to this container because it's subscribing to messages on the same channel. The output shows a message has been received on channel 21 with the content "ping".**

Figure 21.4   A subscriber to the queue receives a copy of every message published on the channel.

You can exit from the container with Ctrl-C, or kill the container with `docker container rm -f subscriber`. Until then, it will keep listening for messages. You can see that this is asynchronous communication: the publisher was sending messages before there were any subscribers listening, and the subscriber will keep listening for messages even when there are no publishers. Each component works with the message queue, and it doesn't know about other components that are sending or receiving messages.

This simple principle of decoupling senders and receivers with a queue helps you make your apps performant and scalable, and you'll see that next with a new version of the to-do list app.

## 21.2 *Using a cloud-native message queue*

The to-do application has a web frontend and a SQL database for storage. In the original implementation, all the communication between components was synchronous—when the web app sends a query or inserts data, it opens a connection to the database and keeps it open until the request is finished. That architecture doesn't scale well. We could run hundreds of web containers to support high user load, but eventually we'd hit a limit where we're using all the available database connections and the app would start to fail.

This is where a message queue helps with performance and scale. The new version of the to-do app uses asynchronous messaging for the save workflow—when users add a new to-do item, the web app publishes a message on a queue. The queue can handle many more connections than the database, and connections have a much shorter lifespan, so the queue won't get maxed out even under very high user load. We'll be using a different queue technology for this exercise: NATS, which is a Cloud Native Computing Foundation (CNCF) project that's mature and widely used. It stores messages in memory, so it's very fast and perfect for communication between containers.

> **TRY IT NOW**    Run NATS in a container. It has a simple admin API you can use to see how many clients are connected to the queue:

```
# switch to the exercise folder:
cd ch21/exercises/todo-list

# start the message queue:
docker-compose up -d message-queue

# check the logs:
docker container logs todo-list_message-queue_1

# and check active connections:
curl http://localhost:8222/connz
```

The connections API call returns JSON details about the number of active connections. There could be many thousands, so the response is paged, but in this case there's only one page of data because there are zero connections. You can see my output in figure 21.5.

There's development work involved when you move to async messaging, and for the to-do app that meant some changes to the web application. Now when users add a to-do item, the web app publishes a message to NATS, rather than inserting data in the database. The changes are actually pretty small. Even if you're not familiar with .NET Core, you can see in listing 21.1 that there isn't much work involved in publishing a message.

The Compose file defines the whole to-do list app. This command just runs the NATS message queue.

NATS listens on different ports for clients and for the admin API. The Compose file publishes API port 8222.

```
PS>cd ch21/exercises/todo-list
PS>
PS>docker-compose up -d message-queue
Creating todo-list_message-queue_1 ... done
PS>
PS>docker container logs todo-list_message-queue_1
[1376] 2020/01/03 12:08:32.274131 [INF] Starting nats-server
version 2.1.2
[1376] 2020/01/03 12:08:32.275130 [INF] Git commit [679beda]
[1376] 2020/01/03 12:08:32.277128 [INF] Starting http monitor
 on 0.0.0.0:8222
[1376] 2020/01/03 12:08:32.278128 [INF] Listening for client
connections on 0.0.0.0:4222
[1376] 2020/01/03 12:08:32.278128 [INF] Server id is NAFKYQSP
XKLDI3RZV4OUW6EFVYAG67PH4OJQMS6RYX7V3ZYW626FCF3X
[1376] 2020/01/03 12:08:32.278128 [INF] Server is ready
[1376] 2020/01/03 12:08:32.290144 [INF] Listening for route c
onnections on 0.0.0.0:6222
PS>
PS>curl http://localhost:8222/connz
{
  "server_id": "NAFKYQSPXKLDI3RZV4OUW6EFVYAG67PH4OJQMS6RYX7V3
ZYW626FCF3X",
  "now": "2020-01-03T12:09:10.2655257Z",
  "num_connections": 0,
  "total": 0,
  "offset": 0,
  "limit": 1024,
  "connections": []
}
```

The admin API includes a connection count, showing how many clients are connected to the queue—right now there are none.

Figure 21.5  NATS is an alternative message queue; it's very lightweight and has an admin API.

Listing 21.1  Publishing a message instead of writing data to the database

```
public void AddToDo(ToDo todo)
        {
            MessageQueue.Publish(new NewItemEvent(todo));
            _NewTasksCounter.Inc();
        }
```

NATS doesn't use the same channel concept as Redis. Instead, every message has a *subject*, which is a string used to identify the type of the message. You can choose your own naming scheme for message subjects. The subject for this one is events.todo .newitem, which says it's a new-item event in the to-do application. Subscribers will be able to listen for messages with that subject if they're interested in new-item events, but even if there are no subscribers, the app will still publish messages.

> **TRY IT NOW**   Run the new version of the to-do web application and the database. You'll see that the app loads and you can use it without any errors, but it doesn't quite work correctly:

```
# start the web and database containers:
docker-compose up -d todo-web todo-db

# browse to http://localhost:8080 and add some items
```

You'll find that the app gladly lets you add new items, but when you browse to the list, there are none. That's because the list page fetches data from the database, but the new-item page doesn't insert data into the database any more. New-item event messages are being published to the NATS message queue, but nothing is listening to them. You can see my empty to-do list (which is not representative of real life at all) in figure 21.6.

**Runs the web app and database containers from the app's Compose file**

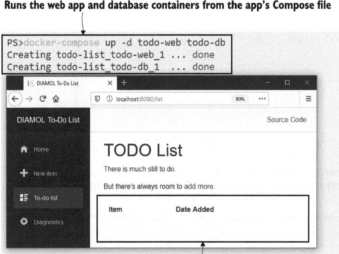

**I've added items to the list, but they don't appear—messages are being published to the queue, but there are no subscribers to act on them.**

Figure 21.6   The to-do app with messaging publishing; without any subscribers, there are missing features.

There are lots of message queue technologies with different approaches for dealing with this situation—where a message is published but there are no subscribers. Some queues move them to *dead-letter queues* for admins to manage, others store the messages so they can deliver them when a client connects and subscribes. Redis and NATS effectively swallow those messages—they acknowledge receipt to the client, but there's nowhere to send them, so they get dropped. New subscribers to Redis or NATS queues only receive messages that get published after they start listening.

**TRY IT NOW** There's a simple NATS subscriber tool from the project's examples on GitHub. You can use it to listen for messages with a particular subject, so we can check that the to-do events are actually being published:

```
# run a subscriber listening for "events.todo.newitem" messages
docker container run -d --name todo-sub --network todo-list_app-net
    diamol/nats-sub events.todo.newitem

# check the subscriber logs:
docker container logs todo-sub

# browse to http://localhost:8080 and add some new items

# check that the new item events are published:
docker container logs todo-sub
```

The user experience is exactly the same—the web app still doesn't work. It publishes messages and doesn't know what happens to them, but now there is a subscriber that receives a copy of each message. If you enter some to-do items in the website, you'll see them listed in the logs for the subscriber—mine are shown in figure 21.7.

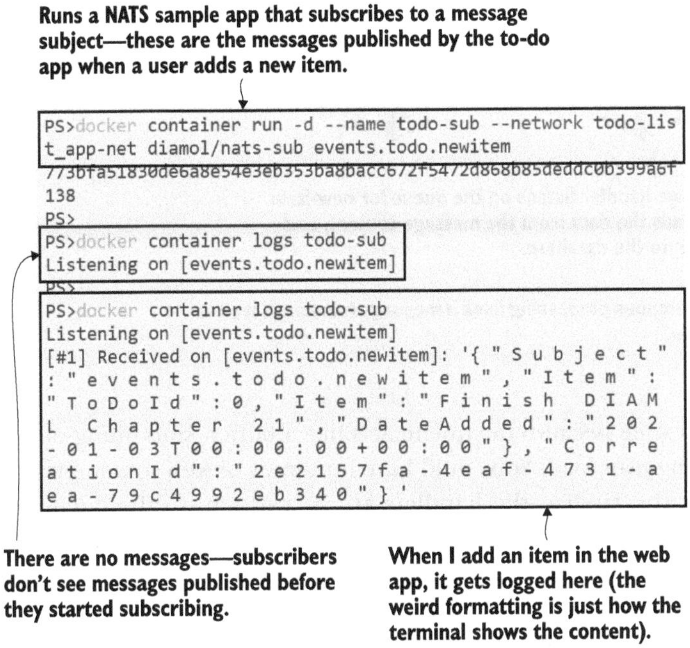

**Runs a NATS sample app that subscribes to a message subject—these are the messages published by the to-do app when a user adds a new item.**

**There are no messages—subscribers don't see messages published before they started subscribing.**

**When I add an item in the web app, it gets logged here (the weird formatting is just how the terminal shows the content).**

**Figure 21.7** A simple subscriber that logs messages is a good to way to check that they're being published.

You'll have realized by now that the to-do app is lacking a component that acts on the messages being published. There are three pieces of work you need to do to move to asynchronous messaging: run a message queue, publish messages when interesting events happen, and subscribe to those messages so you can do some work when the events happen. The to-do app is missing the final part, which we'll add next.

## 21.3   *Consuming and handling messages*

The component that subscribes to the queue is called a message handler, and typically you'll have one handler for each type of message (each channel in Redis or subject in NATS). The to-do app needs a message handler that listens for new-item events and inserts the data in the database. Figure 21.8 shows the completed architecture.

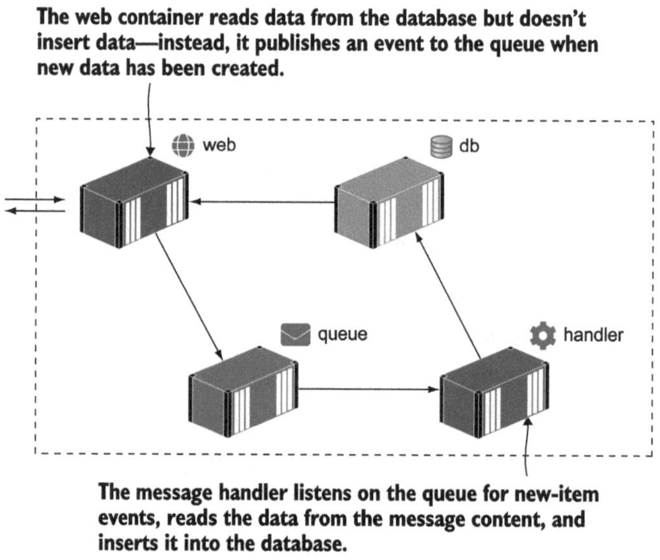

**The web container reads data from the database but doesn't insert data—instead, it publishes an event to the queue when new data has been created.**

**The message handler listens on the queue for new-item events, reads the data from the message content, and inserts it into the database.**

Figure 21.8   Asynchronous processing uses a message handler as well as an event publisher.

This design does scale because the queue acts like a buffer, smoothing out any peaks from the incoming user load. You could have hundreds of web containers but only 10 message-handler containers—the handlers are in a group, so the queue shares the messages around, and each message is handled by a single container. Containers handle messages one at a time, so that would limit the maximum number of SQL connections used for inserting data to 10, no matter how many thousands of users there are, wildly clicking buttons. If there's more load coming in than those 10 handlers can deal with, the messages get saved in the queue until the handlers are ready to process more. The app keeps working, and the data gets saved eventually.

**TRY IT NOW** The message handler for the to-do app is already built and published to Docker Hub, so it's ready to go. Run it now and see how the app
works with async messaging:

```
# start the message handler:
docker-compose up -d save-handler

# check the connection from the container logs:
docker logs todo-list_save-handler_1

# browse to http://localhost:8080 and add some new items

# check that the events have been handled:
docker logs todo-list_save-handler_1
```

The app is working again! Almost. You'll find that you can add new items, and they
appear in the list page, but not immediately. When you save an item, the web app redirects to the list page, which loads while the message is still working its way through the
queue and the handler. The new item hasn't been saved by the time the query runs on
the database, so the new data isn't shown. You can see my output in figure 21.9—at
this point my web page showed no items, even though a new one had been saved.

**Runs the missing component—a message handler
that subscribes to the queue and saves new to-do
items to the database when it receives messages**

**The app logs that
it has subscribed
to the queue**

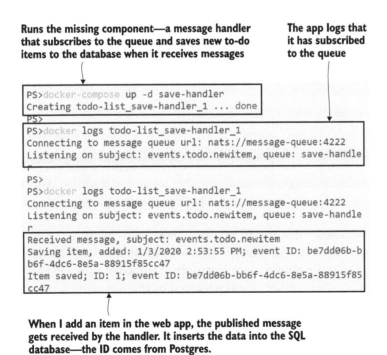

```
PS>docker-compose up -d save-handler
Creating todo-list_save-handler_1 ... done
PS>
PS>docker logs todo-list_save-handler_1
Connecting to message queue url: nats://message-queue:4222
Listening on subject: events.todo.newitem, queue: save-handle
r
PS>
PS>docker logs todo-list_save-handler_1
Connecting to message queue url: nats://message-queue:4222
Listening on subject: events.todo.newitem, queue: save-handle
r
Received message, subject: events.todo.newitem
Saving item, added: 1/3/2020 2:53:55 PM; event ID: be7dd06b-b
b6f-4dc6-8e5a-88915f85cc47
Item saved; ID: 1; event ID: be7dd06b-bb6f-4dc6-8e5a-88915f85
cc47
```

**When I add an item in the web app, the published message
gets received by the handler. It inserts the data into the SQL
database—the ID comes from Postgres.**

**Figure 21.9  Message handlers subscribe to the queue, receive a copy of
every message, and act on it.**

This is a side effect of async messaging called *eventual consistency*—the state of your application data will be correct when all messages have been processed, but until then you may get inconsistent results. There are ways to fix this that work toward making the whole UI async, so the to-do web app would listen for an event stating that the list has changed and then refresh itself. That push model can be a lot more efficient than polling queries, but it's too much for this book. We can just hit refresh for now.

It's a fairly big architectural change to move to asynchronous messaging, but it opens a lot of opportunities, so it's definitely worth knowing how this works. Message handlers are small, focused components that can be updated or scaled independently of the main application or each other. In this exercise we've used the queue to solve a scale-out problem, and now we can run multiple instances of the save message handler to work through the incoming load, while effectively rate-limiting the number of SQL connections we use.

> **TRY IT NOW**   Message handlers are internal components; they don't listen on any ports, so you can run them at scale with multiple containers on a single machine. NATS supports load balancing to share messages if there are several instances of the same handler running:

```
# scale up the handlers:
docker-compose up -d --scale save-handler=3

# check that one of the new handlers has connected:
docker logs todo-list_save-handler_2

# browse to http://localhost:8080 and add some new items

# see which handlers have processed the messages:
docker-compose logs --tail=1 save-handler
```

You'll see that messages are sent to different containers. NATS uses round-robin load balancing to share the load between connected subscribers, and you'll find that the more load you put through, the more evenly distributed it will be. My output in figure 21.10 shows that containers 1 and 2 have processed messages, but not container 3.

It's important to realize that I didn't change anything to get three times as much processing power for my new-item feature—the web site and message handler code is exactly the same. I'm just running more instances of the same message-handler container. If you have another feature that is triggered by the same event, you can run a different message handler that subscribes to the same message subject. That opens up the interesting option of being able to deploy new features to your app without changing existing code.

Async processing can be scaled just by adding more
containers—the NATS queue distributes the messages
across all connected message handlers.

```
PS>docker-compose up -d --scale save-handler=3
todo-list_message-queue_1 is up-to-date
Starting todo-list_save-handler_1 ...
todo-list_todo-db_1 is up-to-datee
Starting todo-list_save-handler_1 ... done
Creating todo-list_save-handler_2 ... done
Creating todo-list_save-handler_3 ... done
PS>
PS>docker logs todo-list_save-handler_2
Connecting to message queue url: nats://message-queue:4222
Listening on subject: events.todo.newitem, queue: save-handle
r
PS>
PS>docker-compose logs --tail=1 save-handler
Attaching to todo-list_save-handler_3, todo-list_save-handler
_2, todo-list_save-handler_1
save-handler_1   | Item saved; ID: 6; event ID: 84416d3e-a52c
-443b-b026-933805e4f4dc
save-handler_2   | Item saved; ID: 5; event ID: d89e3b12-925a
-477f-b892-dbcfbdebd8a6
save-handler_3   | Listening on subject: events.todo.newitem,
 queue: save-handler
```

After adding some more items in the web UI—they all get
published as events to the queue, but different handlers
pick them up and process them.

Figure 21.10  Multiple message handlers share the workload so you can
scale to meet demand.

## 21.4  *Adding new features with message handlers*

We've moved the to-do app towards an *event-driven architecture*, which is a design where
the application publishes events to say that things have happened, rather than processing everything as soon as it happens. It's a nice way of building a loosely coupled
application, because you can change what happens in response to events without
changing the logic that publishes the event. We're just using it for a single type of
event in this application, but that still brings the flexibility to add new features without
changing the existing app.

The simplest way to do that is to add a new message handler in a new group that
gets a copy of every event but does something different in response. The existing message handler saves the data in a SQL database; a new message handler could save the
data in Elasticsearch to make it easy for users to query in Kibana, or it could add the item
as a reminder in a Google Calendar. We have a much simpler example for the next
exercise—a handler that works like an audit trail, writing log entries for every new to-
do item.

**TRY IT NOW**    The new message handler is in a Compose override file. When you deploy it, you'll see that this is an additive deployment. Compose creates one new container, but none of the other containers change:

```
# run the audit message handler, keeping same scale for the save
# handler:
docker-compose -f docker-compose.yml -f docker-compose-audit.yml up -d
    --scale save-handler=3

# check that the audit handler is listening:
docker logs todo-list_audit-handler_1

# browse to http://localhost:8080 and add some new items

# check the audit trail:
docker logs todo-list_audit-handler_1
```

This is a zero-downtime deployment; the original app containers are unchanged, and the new feature gets implemented in a new container. The audit handler subscribes to the same message subject as the save handler, so it gets a copy of every message, while another copy of the message is sent to one of the save handler containers. You can see my output in figure 21.11, where the audit handler writes out the to-do item date and text.

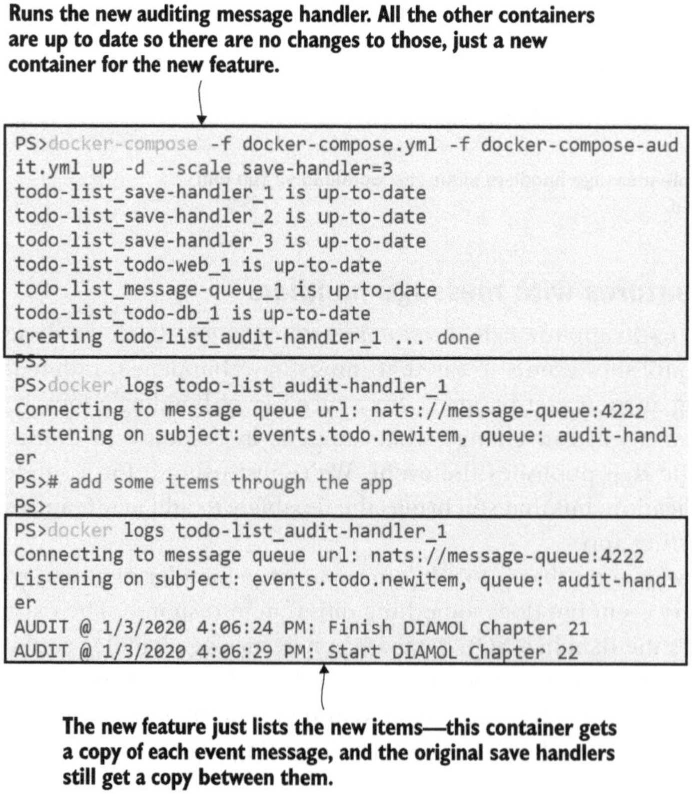

Runs the new auditing message handler. All the other containers
are up to date so there are no changes to those, just a new
container for the new feature.

```
PS>docker-compose -f docker-compose.yml -f docker-compose-aud
it.yml up -d --scale save-handler=3
todo-list_save-handler_1 is up-to-date
todo-list_save-handler_2 is up-to-date
todo-list_save-handler_3 is up-to-date
todo-list_todo-web_1 is up-to-date
todo-list_message-queue_1 is up-to-date
todo-list_todo-db_1 is up-to-date
Creating todo-list_audit-handler_1 ... done
PS>
PS>docker logs todo-list_audit-handler_1
Connecting to message queue url: nats://message-queue:4222
Listening on subject: events.todo.newitem, queue: audit-handl
er
PS># add some items through the app
PS>
PS>docker logs todo-list_audit-handler_1
Connecting to message queue url: nats://message-queue:4222
Listening on subject: events.todo.newitem, queue: audit-handl
er
AUDIT @ 1/3/2020 4:06:24 PM: Finish DIAMOL Chapter 21
AUDIT @ 1/3/2020 4:06:29 PM: Start DIAMOL Chapter 22
```

The new feature just lists the new items—this container gets
a copy of each event message, and the original save handlers
still get a copy between them.

Figure 21.11  Publishing events decouples the components of your app and lets you add new features.

Now two processes are triggered in response to the user creating a to-do item, and they both get actioned in separate components running in separate containers. Those processes could take any length of time and it wouldn't impact the user experience, because the web UI doesn't wait for them (or even know about them)—it just publishes the event to the queue, and that behavior has the same latency no matter how many subscribers are listening for it.

You should get some idea of how powerful this architecture is, even from this simple example. Once your app is publishing key events as messages to the queue, you can build whole new features without touching existing components. The new feature can be independently built and tested, and it can be deployed with no impact to the running application. If there's an issue with the feature, you can just undeploy it by stopping the message handlers.

We'll look at one last exercise for this chapter to help convince you that async messaging is a pattern you should consider for your apps. We can have multiple subscribers for a certain type of event, but we can also have multiple publishers. The new-item event is a fixed structure in code, so any component can publish that event, which gives us new options for creating to-do items. We'll use that to deploy a REST API for the app without changing any existing parts.

**TRY IT NOW**  The to-do list API is already written and ready to deploy. It listens on port 8081 and publishes a new-item event when users make HTTP POST requests:

```
# start the API container, defined in the override file:
docker-compose -f docker-compose.yml -f docker-compose-audit.yml -f
    docker-compose-api.yml up -d todo-api

# add a new item through the API:
curl http://localhost:8081/todo -d '{"item":"Record promo video"}' -H
    'Content-Type: application/json'

# check the audit log:
docker logs todo-list_audit-handler_1
```

The new API is a simple HTTP server, and the only real logic in there is to publish an event to the queue using the same message-queue method from listing 21.1. You'll see that new items entered through the API get processed by the audit handler and the save handler, so there are audit entries, and when you refresh the web app you'll see the new items are in the database. My output is in figure 21.12.

This is powerful stuff, and it's all from a single event being published in the app. Async messaging enables you to build more flexible applications, which are easier to scale and update, and you can add all this goodness to your existing apps too, starting with just a few key events and building from there.

Before you head off to the whiteboard, we'll finish the chapter with a closer look at messaging patterns so you're aware of what you might be heading into.

The REST API is a simple component that just publishes
a new-item event, and that triggers all the existing logic
in the message handlers.

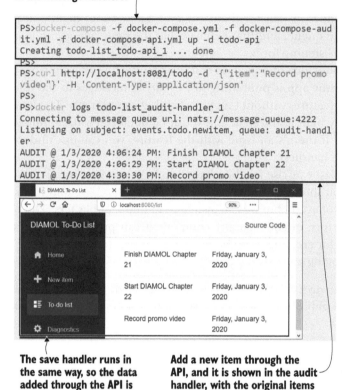

The save handler runs in
the same way, so the data
added through the API is
shown in the web app.

Add a new item through the
API, and it is shown in the audit
handler, with the original items
added through the web app.

Figure 21.12   Events can
have many subscribers and
many publishers, which
makes for loose coupling.

## 21.5   *Understanding async messaging patterns*

Asynchronous messaging is an advanced topic, but Docker really lowers the entry bar
because it's so easy to run a queue in a container, and you can quickly prototype how
your app might work with event publishing. There are different ways to send and
receive messages on a queue, and it's worth understanding a couple of alternatives.

The pattern we've used in this chapter is called *publish-subscribe* (or "pub-sub"), and
it allows zero or more subscribers to receive published messages, as in figure 21.13.

This pattern doesn't fit every scenario, because the message publisher has no
knowledge of who consumes the message, what they do with it, or when they've finished. An alternative is *request-response* messaging, where the client sends a message to
the queue and waits for a response. The handler processes the request message and
then sends a response message that the queue routes back to the client. This can be
used to replace standard synchronous service calls, with the advantage that handlers
won't get overloaded and clients can be doing other work while they wait for a
response. Figure 21.14 shows this pattern.

The web app is the publisher, sending messages to the queue, which could be events, commands, or queries. The publisher only sees the message queue; it has no idea of the handlers listening for messages.

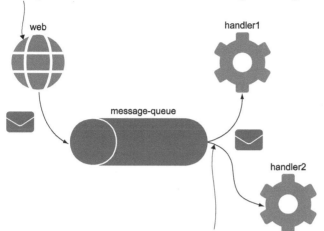

The handlers are subscribers, listening for certain types of messages. When there are multiple subscribers for a message type, they all get copies of the message. If there are no subscribers, the message might be dropped or archived.

Figure 21.13 Pub-sub messaging lets many processes act on the same message being published.

The web app sends a request message to the queue. The message contains the address on the queue where the web app is listening for a response.

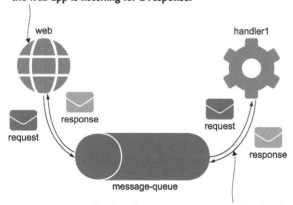

The handler receives the request and actions it, sending the response as a message on the queue, addressed to the client who sent the request message.

Figure 21.14 Request-response messaging is client-service communication without a direct connection.

Pretty much all queue technologies support these patterns, as well as variations like *fire-and-forget* (where the client sends a command request in a message rather than publishing an event, but doesn't care about the response) and *scatter-gather* (where the client publishes a message that several subscribers act on, and then collates all the responses). We've looked at Redis and NATS in this chapter, but there's one more technology you should also consider: RabbitMQ. RabbitMQ is a more advanced queue that supports complex routing and persistent messaging, so messages are saved to disk and the queue contents survive a container restart. All these queue technologies are available as official images on Docker Hub.

Message queue technology can liberate your application design. You can build in an event-driven architecture from the start, or gradually evolve toward one, or just use messages for key events. When you start deploying new features with no downtime, or scaling down handlers to protect a starved database without crashing your app, you'll realize the power of the patterns and you'll be glad you made it to the end of this chapter.

## 21.6  *Lab*

It's the final lab of the book, and this one's a little bit sneaky. The goal is to add another message handler for the to-do app—one that changes the text for items after they've been saved. That handler already exists, so this is mostly about wiring the new service into the Compose file, but there are some configuration settings you'll need to dig around for too.

Your solution needs to run a new handler using the image `diamol/ch21-mutating-handler` from Docker Hub, and when you have that working there are a couple of things to investigate:

- The new component listens for events called `events.todo.itemsaved`, but nothing publishes those events yet. You'll need to search for a config setting you can apply to one of the existing components to make it publish those events.
- The new component has a bad set of default configuration, so it's not using the right address for the message queue. You'll need to search for the setting and fix that too.

This is not as nasty as it seems; the answers you need are all in the Dockerfiles, and you're just going to set values in your Compose file—no need to change source code or rebuild images. It's a useful exercise, because you'll certainly spend some time trying to figure out config settings when you use Docker for real, and the final message handler adds a useful feature to the to-do app.

My solution is up on GitHub as always, with a screenshot to prove it works: https://github.com/sixeyed/diamol/blob/master/ch21/lab/README.md.

# Never the end

Docker is a really exciting technology to learn because it has so many uses—everything from running your own Git server to migrating legacy apps to the cloud to building and running all-new cloud-native apps. I hope the journey we've been on in this book has helped you gain confidence with containers, and now you know where you can put them to use in your current or your next project. This final chapter gives you some hints on how you can make that happen successfully, and it ends with an introduction to the Docker community.

## 22.1 Run your own proof-of-concept

The more you use Docker, the more comfortable you'll become with containers and the more you'll get out of the technology. Pretty much any app can be containerized, so running a proof of concept (PoC) to migrate one of your own applications to Docker is a great start. It will give you a chance to bring the practical skills from this book into your own work, and the end result will be something you can demonstrate to the rest of your team.

There's more to a successful PoC than just `docker image build` and `docker container run`. If you really want to show people the power of containers, your PoC should have a bit more in scope:

- Aim to Dockerize more than one component, so you can show the power of Docker Compose to run different configurations of the app (see chapter 10).
- Start with best practices from the beginning, and show how the move to Docker improves the whole delivery life cycle—use multi-stage Dockerfiles and optimize them, including your own golden images (chapter 17).

- Include observability with centralized logging (chapter 19) and metrics (chapter 9). A meaningful Grafana dashboard and the ability to search logs with Kibana takes your PoC beyond the basics.
- Build a CI/CD pipeline, even if it's a very simple one using Jenkins in a container (chapter 11) to show how everything can be automated with Docker.

The PoC doesn't need to involve a huge effort. Even with an expanded scope like this, I think you could comfortably limit the exercise to five days if you start with a fairly straightforward app. You don't need the whole team involved; it can just be a side project at this stage.

But if you can't get the go-ahead to use Docker at work, that doesn't mean you need to stop—plenty of Docker power users started at home. You can run some pretty impressive software in containers on a Raspberry Pi, and that will get you using Docker regularly.

## 22.2  *Make a case for Docker in your organization*

Docker is a huge change for most organizations because it impacts pretty much every aspect of IT, and not every team is ready to embrace a new way of working. There should be enough in this book to help you show other technology groups the advantage of moving to Docker, but here are the key topics that I find appeal to different stakeholders:

- *Developers* can run whole application stacks on their machines with the exact same technology used in production. There's no more wasted time tracking down missing dependencies or juggling multiple versions of software. The dev team use the same tooling as the operations team, so there's common ownership of components.
- *Operators and admins* get to use standard tools and processes for every application, and every containerized component has a standard API for logging, metrics, and configuration. Deployments and rollbacks become fully automated, failures should become rare, and releases can happen more frequently.
- *Database administrators* won't want to run database containers in production, but containers are a great way to give developers and test teams self-service, so they don't need DBAs to create databases for them. Database schemas can move to source control and be packaged in Docker images, bringing CI/CD to database development too.
- *Security teams* will be concerned about container compromise at runtime, but Docker lets you adopt security in depth all through the life cycle. Golden images, security scanning, and image signing all provide a secure software supply chain that gives you greater confidence in the software you deploy. Runtime tools like Aqua and Twistlock can automatically monitor container behavior and shut down attacks.
- *Business stakeholders and product owners* understand the language of releases—they know historical problems with releases led to more and more quality gates, which

led to fewer and fewer releases. Self-healing applications, health dashboards, and continuous deployment should all encourage users that the move to containers means better quality software with less time to wait for new features.

- *Senior management*'s interests will align with the business (hopefully), but they'll also have a close eye on the IT budget. Moving applications from VMs to containers can save very large sums because you can consolidate hardware when you run more apps run on fewer servers in containers. That also reduces operating system licenses.
- *IT management* should be aware that the container trend isn't going away. Docker has been a successful product since 2014, and all the major clouds offer managed container platforms. Bringing Docker into your roadmap will make your technology stack current and keep the teams happy.

## 22.3 *Plan the path to production*

It's important to understand where you're going with Docker if you want your organization to come with you. At the start of this book I walked you through five types of projects that are empowered by Docker—from modernizing legacy apps to running serverless functions. Whether your PoC fits in one of those definitions or you're doing something more exotic, you'll want to understand the end goal so you can plan your roadmap and track progress.

The major decision you'll need to make is between Docker Swarm and Kubernetes. You've used Swarm in this book, and it's a great way to get started, but if you're looking to the cloud, Kubernetes is a better option. You can use all your Docker images in Kubernetes, but the application definition format is different from Docker Compose, and there's a pretty steep learning curve you'll need to factor in; *Learn Kubernetes in a Month of Lunches* will help you through it. If you're planning to run a container platform in the datacenter, my advice is to start with Docker Swarm, which is operationally easy to manage. Kubernetes is a complex system that will need a dedicated admin team, and a commercial offering might be a better option.

## 22.4 *Meet the Docker community*

I'll end by making sure you know that you're not alone. The Docker community is huge, there's a very active online space, and there are in-person meetups worldwide. You're sure to find people who are happy to share their knowledge and experience, and the Docker community is just about the friendliest one out there. Here's where to join:

- The Docker Community Slack group—https://dockr.ly/slack.
- Find an in-person or virtual meetup—https://events.docker.com.
- Follow the Docker Captains; these are community members recognized by Docker for their expertise and sharing—www.docker.com/community/captains.
- DockerCon, the container conference—https://dockercon.com.

I'm part of that community too—you'll find me on the Community Slack @elton-stoneman and on Twitter @EltonStoneman; feel free to reach out to me anytime. Other places you'll find me are GitHub (@sixeyed) and my blog, https://blog.sixeyed .com. Thanks for reading. I hope you found the book useful, and I hope Docker takes you places.

# index

## RELATED MANNING TITLES

*Kubernetes in Action,* Second Edition
by Marko Lukša

ISBN 9781617297618
775 pages, $59.99
July 2020

*Docker in Action,* Second Edition
by Jeff Nickoloff and Stephen Kuenzli

ISBN 9781617294761
336 pages, $49.99
October 2019

*Docker in Practice,* Second Edition
by Ian Miell and Aidan Hobson Sayers

ISBN 9781617294808
384 pages, $49.99
February 2019

*Cloud Native Patterns:*
*Designing change-tolerant software*
by Cornelia Davis

ISBN 9781617294297
400 pages, $49.99
May 2019

*For ordering information go to www.manning.com*